T0208142

THE NORTH THE SOUTH

AND THE ENVIRONMENT

THE NORTH THE SOUTH

AND THE ENVIRONMENT

ECOLOGICAL CONSTRAINTS AND THE GLOBAL ECONOMY

EDITED BY
V BHASKAR AND ANDREW GLYN

United Nations
University Press

TOKYO • NEW YORK • PARIS

from Routledge

First published by Earthscan in the UK and USA in 1995

This edition published 2013 by Earthscan

For a full list of publications please contact:

Earthscan
2 Park Square, Milton Park, Abingdon, Oxon OX14 4RN
Simultaneously published in the USA and Canada by Earthscan
711 Third Avenue, New York, NY 10017

*Earthscan is an imprint of the Taylor & Francis Group,
an informa business*

Copyright © United Nations University, 1995

The United Nations University Press has exclusive rights to distribute this book in Japan and South-East Asia.

Earthscan Publications Limited has exclusive rights to distribute this book throughout the rest of the world

All rights reserved. No part of this book may be reprinted or reproduced or utilised in any form or by any electronic, mechanical, or other means, now known or hereafter invented, including photocopying and recording, or in any information storage or retrieval system, without permission in writing from the publishers.

A catalogue record for this book is available from the British Library

ISBN: 978-1-85383-215-4 (pbk)

Typesetting and figures by PCS Mapping & DTP, Newcastle upon Tyne

United Nations University Press is the publishing division of the United Nations University.

CONTENTS

List of illustrations

FIGURES

TABLES

Glossary

BCSD	British Council for Sustainable Development
CA	Communal Area
CAP	Common Agricultural Policy
CFC	chlorofluorocarbons
CITES	Convention of Trade in Endangered Species
CVM	Contingent Valuation Methodology
ECU	European currency unit
EIC	environmental impact coefficient
FAO	Food and Agriculture Organisation
GATT	General Agreement on Tariffs and Trade
GDP	Gross Domestic Product
GG/GHG	greenhouse gases
IPCC	Intergovernmental Panel on Climate Change
MMPA	Marine Mammals Protection Act
MOHPPE	Dutch Environmental Policy Plan
NAFTA	North American Free Trade Agreement
NEPP	Netherlands National Environmental Policy Plan
NIC	Newly Industralized Countries
NR	Natural Regions
OECD	Organization for Economic Cooperation and Development
PNPL	Public Nuisance Prevention Law
R/P ratio	reserves/annual production ratio
SPM	suspended particle matter
TFP	total factor productivity
UNCED	UN Conference on Environment and Development
UNCTAD	UN Conference on Trade and Development
UNDP	United Nations Development Programme
UNEP	United Nations Environment Programme
WHO	World Health Organization
WRI	World Resources Institute
WIDER	World Institute for Development Economics Research

The Contributors

Franck Amalric   Department of Economics, Harvard University, Cambridge MA 02138, USA

V Bhaskar   Delhi School of Economics, Delhi University, Delhi 110007, India

Will Cavendish   Centre for the Study of African Economics, University of Oxford and St John's College, Oxford, UK

Paul Ekins   Department of Economics, Birkbeck College, University of London, Gresse St, London W1P 1PA, UK

Andrew Glyn   Corpus Christi College, Oxford OX1 4JF, UK

Michael Jacobs   Centre for the Study of Environmental Change, Lancaster University, Lancaster LA1 4YF, UK

Alain Lipietz   CEPREMAP, 142 rue due Chevalent, 25013, Paris, France

Juliet B Schor   Women's Studies, Harvard University, 34 Kirkland St, Cambridge, MA 02138, USA

Partha Sen   Delhi School of Economics, Delhi University, Delhi 110007, India

Gita Sen   Indian Institute of Management, Bannarghata Road, Bangalore 560076, India

Bob Sutcliffe   HEGOA, Facultad de Ciencias Economicas, Leherdakari Aguire 83, 48015 Bilboa, Spain

Jong-II You   Faculty of Economics, Ritsumelkan University 56-1 TOJI-IN Kita-machi Kita-Ku Tokyo 603-77, Japan

Acknowledgements

This book was written as part of the World Institute for Development Economics Research's Macroeconomics Research Project. All involved would like to express their thanks to Stephen Marglin, director of the project, for his enormous contribution, organizational as well as intellectual. Several contributors to this volume have been associated with the project for a number of years and, thanks to his efforts, it has formed an ideal context for collaborative work.

Drafts of most of the chapters were discussed at a meeting at Corpus Christi College, Oxford in June 1993 and the value of these discussions was much enhanced by the work of Alvin Birdi as rapporteur.

Thanks are also due, for comments or other assistance with particular chapters, to Wendy Carlin and Bob Rowthorn (chapter 3), Jeff Chou, Heidi Ho and Tracy Terfertiller (chapter 4), Herman Cesar, Gerry Cohen and Bishnupriya Gupta (chapter 6), Mamta Mittal, Manoj Panda and Jyotsna Puri (chapter 8) and Jung Wk Kim (chapter 9).

Foreword

International environmental policies must respond to the great array of specific problems regarding the future of the ecosystem. The ecosystem is the 'media' in which human development takes place; sustained within its narrow bio-geo-chemical parameters, it is widespread, complex and diverse. Environmental policies cannot be dealt with in isolation from global socio-economic and techno-economic development.

Since the 1960s, issues connected with the adverse changes in the ecosystem have become centrally important to the agendas of the academic community, governments, and increasingly to intergovernmental agencies and programmes as well. This process has been due to a few important factors:

- There was a noticeably accelerating degradation of the ecosystem, which was seen to endanger the life-sustaining capacity of the earth; moreover, the consequences of its effects on the biosphere were seen as becoming irreversible in some areas.
- Major environmental catastrophes took place in different parts of the world, such as Bhopal (India), Japan and the Soviet Union, which signalled increasing dangers.
- Interdependence between political, economic, social and environmental issues increased and became more complex with the growth of the global population and the spreading and intensifying of sources of pollution.
- The conflicts of interest in environmental issues between the main actors of international life became clearer, better articulated and more difficult to harmonize.
- There has been a relatively rapid spread of knowledge about environmental problems and their dangers. A new multi-disciplinary area has emerged called 'environmental studies', which has involved a great number of academics from diverse disciplines, who have studied the interactions between complex environmental systems, national and international policies, and behaviours of human beings and their effects on the ecosystem.
- Ecological problems coupled with this spread of knowledge have increased public concern and mobilized millions of people at the grassroots level in many countries. At the 'Earth Summit' held in Rio in June 1992 there were more than 1200 NGOs participating in the special forum.

Of all the major global policy issues, cooperation in the field of environment has received the strongest support so far during the past decade. This is due to its growing importance and to the level and the spread of the dangers. Among the non-military factors that endanger global security, 'environmental' issues have been of key importance in recent years. In its research programmes, UNU/WIDER has considered environmental risks (including stratospheric ozone depletion; global warming; desertification; deforestation; soil erosion; and pollution) and their socio-economic implications as vitally important issues on the agenda of national policies and international cooperation.

This book reflects the main issues and problems national and global environmental policies have to face, and is an important background to the outcome and follow-up of the Rio Conference. The chapters also reflect the concern that, in spite of the basically positive approach to environmental issues by governments and the fact that a broad coalition of non-governmental actors supports common international action, real progress towards a globally or even regionally implemented environmental policy is still very slow. This is obviously due to the different and sometimes diverging interests of actors concerning priorities and specific measures for undertaking joint environmental policies.

This divisiveness over priorities predominantly occurs between the North and the South. As the developed industrial countries generate about 80 per cent of total global pollution, developing countries often remark that they do not want to sacrifice their development – thus mitigating some environmental damage – in order to manage the problems caused by the industrialized countries. Some of the more radical experts or political figures of the South even accuse the North of environmental imperialism and insist that environmental issues cannot be dealt with in isolation from general global socio-economic inequalities. There are, however, important differences between the developing countries in resource management, in natural resource pricing, and in the commercial utilization of such resources as forests. Some developing countries, in order to promote industrial development, subsidize energy prices and are less focused on inefficient use.

The North is also quite heterogeneous considering its area, scope and character, and also in its willingness to assume the responsibility or costs for environmental safeguards in such areas as CO_2 emissions. There are also strong and diverging interests connected with the traditional sources of energy. The uncertain character of information, difficulties in monitoring compliance, and a reluctance to commit to unilateral measures and costs (because such costs would increase production costs and/or divert funds from other investments), are some of the stumbling blocks to achieving cooperation and implementing common policies. For the developed industrial countries, the costs of environmental measures and their influence on competitiveness have been an important source of disagreement. The diversity of interests is aggravated by systemic factors, as the great variety of national economic models makes even the very enacting of multinational measures difficult.

Many of the agreements were unable to find their way into national legislatures and governmental structures – that is, into those institutions which determine national norms and policies. It has nevertheless been observed that because of the influence of different pressure groups in some industrial countries, even in the face of scientific uncertainty on several issues, major changes have been initiated by governments, business groups and the population alike.

Environmental policies influence important economic interests because the problems they seek to solve are rooted in traditional patterns of production and consumption. Because economic interests are strong, national environmental policies and actions, through which international policies are in turn enacted, must also be strong and have effective machinery. The Rio Conference, unfortunately, left most of these issues unresolved.

This book provides important intellectual support to the ideas of sustainable economic development, which could introduce greater rationality into national and global economies and enhance cooperation in many related areas, thereby influencing national policies and the functioning of global markets.

Professor Mihály Simai
Director, UNU/WIDER
Helsinki, January 1995

Chapter One

Introduction

V Bhaskar and Andrew Glyn

The Rio Meeting of the UN Commission on the Environment and Development (UNCED) in 1992 showed that environmental issues have moved to the centre-stage of political and economic debate. Green concerns, which were once limited to a vocal fringe of society, have become a preoccupation of our age. It is now clear that a finite earth cannot bear an infinite burden, and untrammelled economic growth is unviable. This is exemplified most starkly by global problems such as global warming, acid rain, deforestation and loss of biodiversity, as well as more local ones such as urban pollution and contamination of water resources.

This book is concerned with the impact of environmental constraints on the pattern of development within the North and within the South and the relations between the two. While few contributors to the environmental debate question the importance of environmental issues and the necessity for effective policies to meet them, there is much less unanimity on how they will impinge on the trajectory of the world economy. At one end of the spectrum is the 'Limits to Growth' School, which has done much to dramatise the issue of environmental constraints by projections of drastic slowdown and even collapse. At the other are the technological optimists, exemplified perhaps by parts of the World Bank's *World Development Report*, who argue that resource constraints can be overcome at relatively little cost provided the correct (usually market-oriented) policies are put in place.

The fundamental idea of Limits to Growth is extremely simple and very much in the tradition of the classical economists, especially Ricardo and Malthus. The world economy, it claims, faces a series of environmental resource constraints – increased extraction costs of raw materials and energy as the best sources are exhausted, increased costs of food production as the intensity of cultivation rises with population growth, and increased costs of pollution control/clear-up as production expands. These constraints imply that a given gross ouput requires more fixed capital (deeper and deeper mines to get minerals, extra pollution control equipment) or more intermediate inputs (more fertiliser to compensate for inferior soil). Either

1

way the ratio of net output to capital employed declines, tending to pull down the long-run growth of output and consumption.

The resonance for these ideas came from the commodity and energy price increases of the 1970s, which seemed to proclaim the arrival of just such scarcities. By the early 1990s, however, the prices of many commodities had fallen back to, or below, their real level in the 1960s, apparently banishing fears of real resource limits to expansion. However, there is an important qualification to such optimism. The industrialization and high levels of consumption in the North has depended on access to the whole world's resources. But if the majority of the rest of the world industrializes this shrinks the hinterland whose resources can be exploited for benefit elsewhere. Ratios of reserves to production look much less comforting if Northern levels of consumption were to be generalized to a world population expected to double by the middle of the next century. Conversely, potential scarcities held at bay by an unchanging and grossly unequal world distribution of consumption represent a distinctly less than comforting prospect.

However it is pollution, in its many guises, rather than resource limits, that has dominated the discussion in recent years, with the costs of containing global warming seeming to pose the greatest new threat to continued expansion of the world economy. While some argue that the scientific case for significant global warming is not yet strong enough, and the economic costs of its occurrence not yet clear enough, there seems rather widespread support, in principle at least, for taking decisive action. Given the possibility, however small, of catastrophe resulting from inaction, the case has been pithily summarized as 'If we live as if it matters and it doesn't matter, it doesn't matter. If we live as if it doesn't matter, and it matters, then it matters' (as quoted by Norman Myers).

Costs of taking action do matter, of course, if for no other reason than they may actually determine whether the necessary policies are implemented. So how costly will such action be? Just as with incipient resource scarcities, the optimists believe that it will be relatively cheap to develop the technologies required to cut greenhouse emissions very significantly. They argue that there are many 'win–win' situations where policies to reduce greenhouse emissions will actually enhance growth by eliminating inefficiencies (a well-known example being ending the subsidies to energy use which leads to a squandering of energy resources). Over this range there are no trade-offs between environmental improvement and consumption levels; indeed in principle nobody has to pay, since compensation can be found from the higher output for any groups whose consumption levels are especially hit by policies to correct environmental problems (such as those particularly affected by elimin-ation of energy subsidies). It would, however, be a super-optimist who would assert that trade-offs between environmental concerns and conventional consumption levels never occur. The mainstream position, exemplified by Nordhaus, concludes that the 'drag from resources' (higher costs of energy and minerals, plus costs of limiting pollution) might reduce Northern growth by a similar amount over coming decades as it has over the past 20 years. Given the severity of problems such as employment it might seem that the impact of environmental pressures on the world economy is hardly a matter to get too excited about.

Yet as soon as we admit that dealing with environmental problems may entail cuts in standards of living the question of who will pay becomes central; the more significant the costs the greater the potential distributional conflicts. Such conflicts constitute a major theme of this book.

The predominant paradigm in the economic literature dealing with the environment is the theory of externalities and public goods. Environmental bads are externalities inflicted by consumers and firms upon other agents in the economy, and the lack of a market in environmental goods creates an inefficiency since these effects cannot be reflected in market transactions. Environmental quality is similarly a public good; my enjoyment of the beauty of a tropical forest does not reduce your pleasure. Externalities and public goods give rise to market failures, which lead to inefficiency in the sense that potentially beneficial transactions do not take place: that is they are *Pareto inefficient*, because potential gains all round remain unexploited. Hence the need for action, either by the state or by collectivities of agents, to rectify these inefficiencies and move to a situation where all are better off. This paradigm and the consequent prescription for corrective taxes is no doubt useful. It identifies a major reason for the occurrence of win–win situations in the environmental context. But an exclusive preoccupation with this paradigm prevents engagement with other questions which are no less important. Chief among these is the issue of distribution.

Economists have been notoriously disinclined to address distributive questions, and have preferred the 'neutral' preoccupation with Pareto-efficiency. Indeed, the main economic critique of tax solutions in the sphere of externalities, due to Coase, proclaims its indifference to the question of distribution. The Coase conjecture is that any clear demarcation of property rights ensures efficiency. Provided either the polluted or polluter has a clear entitlement (to clean air or to deposit whatever he or she likes in the atmosphere respectively) then some form of bargaining can ensure an efficient outcome. A major reason for a failure of the conjecture is of course that property rights are themselves the focus of distributive struggle, and the state may be unable to define them clearly.

Distributional issues enter perforce when economists engage with more long-range environmental issues such as resource depletion or global warming. In these examples, current actions do not affect current generations, but affect those as yet unborn. Since unborn generations have no rights, except those granted at the pleasure of the living, it becomes meaningless to rely exclusively on efficiency criteria. There would be nothing inefficient in society choosing to put no weight on the interests of the unborn. The issue of inter-generational equity must therefore be addressed in this context and there is now a voluminous literature on this topic. However, there is a marked reluctance to widen this to include consideration of all aspects of equity, particularly intra-generational equity. There is a schizophrenia; while Pareto is the guru when discussing the disposal of hazardous wastes, Bentham and Rawls take over in the context of global warming.

The papers in this volume agree on the need to integrate concerns for equity and for the environment. Environmental externalities are not simply inflicted by identical agents upon each other: they are often what the rich and powerful do to the weak and hungry. They are what Union Carbide did to the people of Bhopal, what the Soviet State did to the people around Chernobyl, and what greenhouse gas emissions in the US will do to the people of Bangladesh. The victims often do not know about the potential hazards until it is too late, and therefore there is simply no possibility of bargaining *à la* Coase. And to discuss these problems purely in terms of efficiency criteria would be evasion on a monumental scale.

Environmental issues fall naturally into two main categories: global and local. Traditionally, attention has focused on local environmental issues, discussion of which can be confined to national boundaries, and on which local communities or nation states are agents for remedial action. Air and water pollution and soil erosion are examples which fit naturally into this category. While these issues retain their importance, it is the rise of global environmental issues which differentiates the present period. These are potential environmental catastrophes, the impact of which or the causes of which span international borders, if not the entire globe. The destruction of the ozone layer is the consequence of the use of CFCs by individuals the world over, and the impact in turn affects (differentially) people the world over. The ongoing large-scale extinction of species is perhaps immediately due to localized causes, being mainly in tropical forests, but the consequent loss of a diversified gene pool is to all humanity. Global warming arises due to greenhouse gas emissions the world over. The global nature of these problems has meant that there must be a global response – individual nations are too small to have any unilateral impact upon the problem, and their incentives for doing so are also inadequate given the global nature of the public good. A major theme in this volume is these global problems. How serious are they? What is the differential impact of the catastrophes across countries, particularly between the North and the South? What is the responsibility of individual nations to take remedial action?

The global concern has certainly focused attention upon the environment the world over. Even countries caught up in growth mania, with little time for niceties of environmental protection, have had their attention drawn to green concerns. Somewhat paradoxically, the North's monopoly over the international media and its ability to set the international agenda has played a positive role in this context. Now is the chance for developing countries to address the local environmental problems which have hitherto been brushed under the carpet. Indeed, given the neglect, these local problems are often much more pressing than the global ones, and the costs of remedial action are often quite small.

GLOBAL PROBLEMS AND RESPONSES

The chapter by Paul Ekins and Mike Jacobs begins with a summary of the main symptoms of environmental unsustainability – pollution and resource depletion. The archetypal global problem, which many subsequent chapters take up for discussion, is that of global warming due to emissions of carbon dioxide and other greenhouse gases. Ekins and Jacobs discuss the evidence on global warming and on the extent of cuts in emissions which are dictated by prudence. Developed countries account for a predominant share of greenhouse gas emissions, and per capita emissions are many times higher in the North as compared to the South. Developing countries, however, have a higher ratio of emissions to GDP (at least on conventional measures), and the fear is that with Southern industrial-ization, total emissions would skyrocket. Global warming is an important example of the necessity for a major reduction of what Ekins and Jacobs term the 'environmental impact' of economic activity. Southern develop-ment requires space in the global environment, which the North must vacate. This can be done either by reducing the environmental impact per unit of GDP or by reducing GDP itself. Both optimists and pessimists, while differing as to the costs of this project, agree on its necessity.

This raises the question of the feasibility, economic as well as political, of reducing the burden imposed by the North, and this is discussed in the chapters by Andrew Glyn and Juliet Schor. Glyn first shows how the impact of Northern growth on the environment has diminished substantially since 1973. His analysis of expected growth trends in the North leads to a rather surprising conclusion: that GDP growth in the North is likely to fall very substantially further. This is dictated primarily by the reduction in growth of the working population of working age, and is aggravated by the prospect of continuing poor productivity growth of the increasingly important services sector. This conclusion has contradictory implications for the global environment: on the one hand, less GDP implies less demands on the environment, whereas increased stringency allows less leeway for spending on environmental protection. This chapter then analyses existing estimates of the output cost of reducing greenhouse gas emissions. It notes in particular that if there was to be really substantial 'catch-up' of the South to the North the impact of restraints on carbon emissions would have to be more severe than currently contemplated. Only the development of cheap substitutes for carbon-based fuel, or a very inegalitarian distribution of rights to emission in favour of the North, would prevent costs to the North being rather severe.

The North could react to environmental constraints in a number of different ways: by halting the upward trend in total consumption and increasing leisure or by changing the composition of consumption expenditure away from resource intensive goods towards more environmentally-friendly welfare services, for example. Juliet Schor focuses on the first possibility and argues that the consumer society represents a socially irrational preoccupation with consumption, trapping individuals on a treadmill of 'work and spend'. She takes on the neo-classical counterargument, that competitive labour markets imply that workers get the leisure-consumption package that they prefer, by bringing in the role of consumption as a status good, and habit formation. She suggests that attitudinal surveys show signs of a shift towards post-materialism and away from consumer society, but emphasizes that the task of building on and extending this trend will face opposition from those with strong vested interests in continued economic growth.

The papers by Franck Amalric, V Bhaskar and Alain Lipietz focus directly upon the North–South distributional issue. Amalric analyses one of the most controversial matters, the role of population growth, particularly in the South, in generating global environmental problems. He focuses on the 'Ehrlich equation' which has been used to analyse quantitatively the contribution of population growth to global carbon dioxide emissions. Such analyses always generate a range of answers depending on precise assumptions. But Amalric shows that this work frequently makes a very simple analytical mistake, in its failure to take account of the much smaller consumption levels of the Southern population and particularly the Southern poor. This leads to gross exaggeration of the contribution of Southern population increases to global consumption and hence on the global environment. He argues, further, that focus on population derives from unwillingness to confront what is the ultimate problem, the failure of the institutional structures, at national and global level, to control the environmental impact of high and growing consumption levels especially in the North.

The control of global warming requires a reduction in global carbon emissions, and various criteria have been suggested for distributing emission entitlements. Bhaskar examines the ethical basis on which we can distribute claims to this global common property resource. Two different types of ethical theories are examined – welfarist theories, such as utilitarianism or Rawl's difference principle, and rights-based theories such as those of Locke and Nozick. Bhaskar argues that both of these imply that the North should bear most of the burden of emissions limitation, albeit for quite different reasons. Welfare-based theories suggest that the North should pay, since the welfare cost of a reduction in consumption is lower in the North. Rights-based theories support a distribution of emissions on a per capita base. In addition, these theories suggest that the North should compensate for its excessive pollution in the past, which is responsible for the current stock of carbon dioxide in the atmosphere.

Alain Lipietz discusses the political economy of international negotiations over three global issues: the ozone layer, biodiversity and global warming. The South persistently sees itself as being denied the path to modernization already trodden by the North, whether in the form of cheap refrigeration (involving CFCs), standardized agriculture (reducing biodiversity) or carbon-based energy (global warming). But Lipietz also shows that there can be differences of interest within both North and South: thus in the global warming negotiations, the 'virtuous' countries of Northern Europe, with relatively low carbon intensity, are prepared to implement cuts in emission for precautionary reasons, while the carbon-guzzling US is not prepared to negotiate away 'our way of life'. Southern countries with most to lose from global warming may (with financial help) support the precaution principle, while carbon-profligate Russia and the carbon-rich oil producers have little immediate interest in progress in the negotiations. Around all these discussions statistics fly back and forth in the cause of allocating 'responsibility' for the emissions and thus obligation to pay for their reduction. Lipietz concludes that some progress on these issues was made at Rio and that there are hopeful signs in Europe of a move to combine employment and environmental concerns in a shift in taxation from labour to energy.

With the growth of environmental concerns in the North pollution is now incorporated into trade theory as a factor of production. This was dramatized when a leaked memorandum by the chief economist at the World Bank advocated the transfer of dirty industries to the South. Partha Sen's chapter discusses the implications for international trade and investment of such a development. He distinguishes between industries where polluting effects are localized, such as those producing toxic wastes, and industries with global effects through emission of CFCs and CO_2. He argues that the North will be relatively unconcerned about the movement of the former to the South. However the movement of globally polluting industries, such as would occur if carbon taxes were imposed only in the North, would be resisted, particularly since emissions are likely to be higher in the South. Sen investigates the extent to which international trade fora such as GATT could be used to pressurize the South into complying with Northern standards and examines the likely role of regional trading blocks, such as NAFTA, in this context.

LOCAL ISSUES

The papers by Jong-Il You, Gita Sen and Will Cavendish turn to the second major theme of the book, ie the neglect of local environmental concerns and local aspirations in the process of development. You examines the onward march of the Korean model and documents the relentless destruction of the environment it entailed, in terms of air and water pollution, acid rain and the dumping of industrial wastes. He argues that the success of the Korean model was predicated upon the single-minded pursuit of growth maximization. This was made possible by a politically authoritarian regime which saw the articulation of any reservations about this model of development as subversive. There were examples of very successful mobilizations by the state in the cause of environmental improvement (notably reforestation). But overall the environment suffered needlessly. The authoritarianism of the regime, which allowed the state to maximize growth by riding roughshod over the interests of individual businesses, also facilitated neglect of the environmental conditions of the mass of Korean people – a facet of the Korean model which has not been widely remarked on. You emphasizes the limitations of Korea as a 'model' for development, arguing that welfare rather than growth maximization would imply growth with environmental care rather than degradation.

The paper by Gita Sen takes up the case of the Narmada valley dams in India – perhaps the most controversial of large scale irrigation projects. The paper argues that in this instance, powerful groups who stood to gain are able to project their own interests as those of national development, while simultaneously portraying those adversely affected to the extent of loss of livelihood as obstructive and 'anti-national'. Not only would the dams imply the loss of land and destruction of livelihood, but government plans for the resettlement of those ousted were woefully insufficient. Sen also points out that the ecological damage occasioned by the project, particularly due the loss of biodiversity, would be severe. However, she argues that such environmental costs are probably secondary to destruction of the livelihoods of an already marginalized tribal community; indeed, human activity should be viewed as part of the ecosystem rather than as an external force. She concludes that assessments of such projects must incorporate in central ways considerations of distribution, weighting more highly the concerns about livelihoods and survival of those who are socially or economically without privilege and ensuring that their voices have special weight in the formulation of such projects.

Environmental questions have traditionally been the preserve of environmental economists and greens. Will Cavendish argues for an integration of ecological considerations into a study of peasant economies, taking as a case in point the communal areas of Zimbabwe. He shows that the peasants under consideration have a remarkably low level of conventional income. However, their reliance upon environmental resources and forest produce shows the importance of these resources for peasant subsistence. Cavendish argues that the peasants have a sophisticated understanding of environmental constraints and the need for preventing the degradation of their environment. Government policy towards the environment has, in a simple-minded way, assumed that the peasants are facing 'the tragedy of commons'. Policy has been framed without taking into account the local information at the disposal of peasants, and has hence been a failure. This sustains the case for democratizing the formulation of policy in order to take into account both the aspirations and the informational resources of marginalized groups.

Finally, Bob Sutcliffe's chapter reviews the post-1945 history of thinking about development in the light of the environmental critique. He points out that the great debates about development in the 1950s and 1960s, concerning the role of state and market, capitalism and socialism, all agreed that development meant the situation in the most developed countries. The 1970s saw increasingly important critiques of the accepted notion that pursuit or attainment of development would necessarily increase the welfare of the people, stressing the material and cultural deprivation of much of the population. In this context environmental critiques of development, stressing both local degradation, and global problems, have recently been gaining prominence. While the welfare and environmental critiques of development are distinct and policies motivated by them can be contradictory, Sutcliffe argues for a fusion with the objective being sustainable human development. The conclusion is that the fundamental task is to secure the political support for serious measures of redistribution, from the wealthy in the North towards the poor in the South, and to future generations who may be adversely affected by the environmental implications of current consumption levels in the North.

Chapter Two

Environmental Sustainability and the Growth of GDP: Conditions for Compatibility

Paul Ekins and Michael Jacobs

ENVIRONMENTAL UNSUSTAINABILITY

Unsustainability: a Consensus

In the 20 years 1972–92, between the UN Conference on the Environment in Stockholm and that on Environment and Development (UNCED) in Rio de Janeiro, the scientific consensus has gradually hardened that the damage being inflicted by human activities on the natural environment render those activities unsustainable. It has become clear that the activities cannot be projected to continue into the future either because they will have destroyed the environmental conditions necessary for that continuation, or because their environmental effects will cause massive, unacceptable damage to human health and disruption of human ways of life.

This is not the place for a detailed review of the evidence that has led to the scientific consensus, but the now perceived seriousness of the problem can be illustrated by a number of quotations of the conclusions of reputable bodies which have conducted such a review. Thus the Business Council for Sustainable Development (BCSD) stated bluntly in its report to UNCED: 'We cannot continue in our present methods of using energy, managing forests, farming, protecting plant and animal species, managing urban growth and producing industrial goods.' (Schmidheiny 1992:5) The Brundtland Report, which initiated the process which led to UNCED, had formulated its perception of unsustainability in terms of a threat to survival: 'There are thresholds which cannot be crossed without endangering the basic integrity of the system. Today we are close to many of these thresholds; we must be ever mindful of the risk of endangering the survival of life on earth.' (WCED 1987:32–3)

The World Resources Institute (WRI), in collaboration with both the Development and Environment Programmes of the United Nations (UNDP and UNEP), concludes on the basis of one of the world's most extensive environmental databases that 'The world is not now headed toward a sustainable future, but rather toward a variety of potential human and environmental disasters' (WRI 1992:2). The World Bank, envisaging a 3.5 times increase in world economic output by 2030, acknowledged that 'If environmental pollution and degradation were to rise in step with such a rise in output, the result would be appalling environmental pollution and damage.' (World Bank 1992:9). The Fifth Action Programme of the European Community acknowledges that 'many current forms of activity and development are not environmentally sustainable' (CEC 1992a:4), as indicated by 'a slow but relentless deterioration of the environment of the Community, notwithstanding the measures taken over the last two decades' (CEC 1992b:3).

In its annual *State of the World* reports, the Worldwatch Institute has documented current environmental damage, concluding in 1993:

> *The environmentally destructive activities of recent decades are now showing up in reduced productivity of croplands, forests, grasslands and fisheries; in the mounting cleanup costs of toxic waste sites; in rising health care costs for cancer, birth defects, allergies, emphysema, asthma and other respiratory diseases; and in the spread of hunger.*

> Brown et al 1993:4–5.

These trends mean: 'If we fail to convert our self-destructing economy into one that is environmentally sustainable, future generations will be overwhelmed by environmental degradation and social disintegration.' (ibid:21)

Little wonder, therefore, that in 1992 two of the world's most prestigious scientific institutions saw fit to issue a joint statement of warning:

> *Unrestrained resource consumption for energy production and other uses... could lead to catastrophic outcomes for the global environment. Some of the environmental changes may produce irreversible damage to the earth's capacity to sustain life.... The future of our planet is in the balance.*

> RS and NAS 1992:2,4

Unsustainability: the Symptoms

The concept of sustainability will be discussed and amplified further later in this chapter. For the present, an environmentally unsustainable activity is simply to be taken to be one which cannot be projected to continue into the future, because of its negative effect either on the environment or on the human condition of which it is a part. The main symptoms of unsustainability, with their principal causative agents and the geographical level to which they mainly apply, can be simply grouped as in Table 2.1.

Two immediate observations can be made about the symptoms of

Table 2.1 Symptoms of environmental unsustainability

Problem	Principal agents
Pollution	
Greenhouse effect/	Emissions of CO_2, N_2O, CH_4
climate change	CFCs (and HFCs)
(global)	O_3 (low level)
	Deforestation
Ozone depletion (global)	Emissions of CFCs
Acidification (continental)	Emissions of SO_2, NO_x, NH_3
	O_3 (low level)
Toxic pollution (continental)	SO_2, NO_x, O_3, particulates
	Heavy metals
	Hydrocarbons, carbon monoxide
	Agrochemicals, organochlorides
	Eutrophiers
	Radiation
	Noise
Renewable Resource Depletion	
Species extinction (global)	Land-use changes
	(eg development, deforestation)
	Population pressure
	Unsustainable harvest (eg over-
	grazing, poaching)
	Climate change (possible ozone
	depletion in future)
Deforestation (global, regional)	Land use changes
	Population pressure
	Unsustainable harvest (eg hardwoods)
	Climate change (possible in future)
Land degradation/	Population pressure
loss of soil fertility	Deforestation, overgrazing
((bio)regional, national)	Unsustainable agriculture
	Urbanization, 'development'
	Climate change (possible in future)
Water depletion ((bio) regional,	Unsustainable use
national)	Climate change (possible in future)
Fisheries depletion (national, local)	Over-fishing, pollution
	Habitat destruction
Non-renewable resource depletion	
Depletion of various	High levels of consumption
resources, eg fossil fuels, minerals	
(global, national)	
Other environmental problems	
Congestion (national)	Waste disposal
	Traffic

unsustainability. The first is the extent to which the problems are interlinked. The second is the fact that the most important problems are those of pollution and depletion of renewable resources.

Unsustainability: the Evidence

Any survey of the evidence for environmental unsustainability which is serving only as an introduction to a paper is bound to be partial and simplified. At best, it can give a quantitative indication of the most important trends and processes and act as a preliminary overview, from which a more detailed exploration of the literature can be undertaken if desired. This survey draws heavily on two compendia of information: the biannual *World Resources*, produced by the World Resources Institute in collaboration with UNDP and UNEP, and the annual *State of the World* reports published by the Worldwatch Institute, which are in turn compiled from a wide range of primary datasets and research reports. It should be emphasized that uncertainty is a characteristic of much of the data, especially with reference to processes of global environmental change, which means that the effects of environmental unsustainability could be more or less serious than is currently believed likely to be the case.

Global Warming

Table 2.2 gives some best estimates of the contributions to global warming of the various greenhouse gases (GGs) and the reductions in GG emissions that are thought necessary to stabilize their atmospheric concentrations. Figure 2.1 shows the growth of emissions of carbon dioxide from fossil fuel burning since 1950.

The effects of failing to halt global warming are still highly uncertain. Possible negative effects include the extinction of species that fail either to

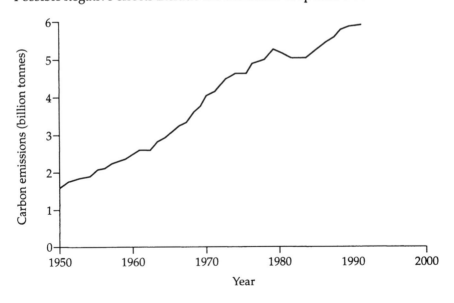

Source: Brown et al, 1992a: 61

Figure 2.1 *World carbon emissions from fossil fuel burning, 1950–1991*

Table 2.2 Greenhouse gases and the greenhouse effect

Greenhouse gas	*Main anthropogenic sources*
Carbon dioxide (CO_2)	Fossil fuel burning (77 per cent)
	Deforestation (23 per cent)
Chlorofluorocarbons (CFCs)	Various industrial uses
Related gases (HFCs, HCFCs)	(eg refrigerators)
Methane (CH_4)	Rice paddies, livestock digestion, gas
	leakage
Nitrous oxide (N_2O)	Biomass and fossil fuel burning,
	fertilizer use, land use changes
Other[b]	Fossil fuel burning

	Warming potential ($CO_2=1$)c	*% contribution to greenhouse effect[d] 1980-1990 1990+*		*Rate of growth, 1992 %[e]*	*IPCC rec. reduction, %[f]*
CO_2	1	55	61	0.5	>60
CFCs etc	7,300[g]	24	11.5	4	75–85[g]
CH_4	21	15	15	0.9	15-20
N_2O	290	6	4	0.25	70-80
Other[b]	40[h]	–	8.5	na	–

a Source: Leggett 1990:17
b Principally tropospheric ozone, O_3, formed by NO_x and CO emissions
c Source: Houghton et al 1990:60, 100 year integration time
d Source: Houghton et al 1990:xx,xxi. The 1990+ column is the GG's relative contribution over 100 years from 1990
e Source: WRI 1992:205
f Source: Houghton et al 1990:xviii
g For CFC-12, the major CFC contributor to global warming
h For tropospheric ozone

migrate or adapt to changed climatic conditions; loss of agricultural productivity where weather patterns become hotter, drier or more erratic than is agriculturally desirable; sea-level rise with inundation of coastal zones; a greater frequency of extreme weather conditions; and an increase in vector-borne diseases. The only possible benefits of global warming are enhanced agricultural productivity in some mid- and high-latitude areas, but there is no likelihood that this will significantly exceed agricultural losses elsewhere; and greater comfort in presently colder areas, which might be offset by the somewhat greater discomfort of higher temperatures in presently hotter areas.

A sea-level rise of one metre, at the top of the IPCC (Intergovernmental Panel on Climate Change) range of uncertainty for the next century, would, according to the IPCC Impacts Working Group, 'displace populations, destroy low-lying urban infrastructure, inundate arable lands, contaminate freshwater supplies, and alter coastlines' (quoted in Woodwell 1990:128). The flooding of the deltas of Egypt and Bangladesh would deprive the former of 15 per cent of its arable land and the latter of

14 per cent of its net cropped area (Woodwell 1990:128). Worldwide, hundreds of millions of people could be displaced.

The IPCC's estimate of global warming was 3±1.5°C increase in average global temperatures over preindustrial levels for a doubling of atmospheric concentration of carbon dioxide equivalents. On current trends this doubling will be achieved by 2025. Cline (1991) has criticized such a short time horizon and projected that these trends imply a mean global warming of about 10°C over 250–300 years. Such an increase could multiply by several times IPCC estimates of damage, eg a sea-level rise of 4 metres would seem likely (Cline 1991:915).

Apart from CFCs, GG emissions derive from the burning of fossil fuels, deforestation and various agricultural practices. While a majority of the world's climate scientists as represented by the IPCC regard global warming as a serious present phenomenon, considerable uncertainties remain over the basic science, the extent of the likely damage and the costs of abating greenhouse gases. Beckerman (1991) and Solow (1991) have between them marshalled the doubts over both the science and the probable damage. Beckerman's reassuring conclusion is that the actual existence of the effect is far from certain, its probable damage is small and distant in time, therefore there is no urgency, and immediate action should concentrate on improving the knowledge base on the issue. This conclusion is broadly the same as that stemming from Nordhaus' benefit–cost analysis of the issue (Nordhaus 1991), which indicates, after phasing out CFCs, an optimal reduction of CO_2 emissions (from baseline projections) of only 2 per cent.

Cline's 1992 benefit–cost analysis comes to a fundamentally different conclusion. Although his estimates of damage from global warming in the 21st century are similar to those of Nordhaus, they rise substantially thereafter, in the absence of abatement. He also factors in 20 per cent costless abatement to reflect currently unexploited no-cost energy–efficiency opportunities, and allows for risk aversion, to reflect the fact that, as Broome (1992:16) observes: 'Human-induced global warming, then, could possibly start a chain of events that could lead to the extinction of civilization or even of humanity. This is a remote possibility, but it exists.' These factors together cause him to arrive at a conclusion that: 'Using the central assumptions of this study, if there is weighting of outcomes to take account of risk aversion, the benefit-cost analysis finds that aggressive abatement action is warranted.' (Cline 1992:300) The 'aggressive abatement action' involves cutting CO_2 emissions by 82 per cent from the baseline projection by 2100 to four gigatons of carbon annually, which is only about 60 per cent of emissions in 1990.

The global warming issue in its scope and uncertainties exemplifies many of the common characteristics of the modern environmental problematique and will be further discussed both later in this chapter and elsewhere in this book.

Ozone depletion

Production of CFCs peaked in 1988 and has since fallen by 46 per cent (Brown et al 1992a:62). Under the terms of the Montreal Protocol, most recently revised in November 1992, CFCs must be phased out in industrial countries by 1996 and in developing countries ten years later. However, it will be the year 2005 before stratospheric levels of chlorine, which is what damages the ozone layer, start to decline. Until then they will continue to increase, both because of the quantities of CFCs already produced that are not yet in the lower atmosphere and, once there, the length of time (10–15 years) it takes for them to reach the upper atmosphere (Meadows et al 1992:148). It will take a further 100 years for the chlorine to be cleansed from the stratosphere (ibid:160).

The 3 per cent loss of ozone noted in 1991 over the US and other temperate countries could cause as many as 12 million extra skin cancers in the US alone (WRI 1992:200). Another 3 per cent depletion, expected by the year 2000 (ibid:200), could cause a further 9–18 per cent increase in such cancers (Meadows et al 1992:). Measurements over Antarctica in September 1991 indicated a 50–60 per cent ozone loss (WRI 1992:200).

It seems from a recent study that ozone depletion in the upper atmosphere may cause global cooling, thus offsetting some of the greenhouse effect. It may be that this is a reason why observed global warming is less than that predicted by global climate models (ibid:200).

Acid deposition

The principal effects of the deposition of acid atmospheric pollutants are the acidification of soils and water, and damage to forests, crops and buildings, and to human health (this is discussed below under toxic pollution). Water acidification results in a decline of fish and other aquatic life, which is now pronounced in several countries: more than 20 per cent of Sweden's 85,000 medium and large lakes are now acidified, with 4000 having suffered major biological damage; in Norway's four southernmost counties, fish stocks have been halved since 1940. The number of highly acidified lakes in New York's Adirondack mountains grew from 4 to 51 per cent between the 1930s and 1970s. Ninety per cent of the affected lakes had lost all their fish (McCormick 1989:37).

Symptoms of forest decline grew fast during the 1980s: by 1986 87 per cent of West Germany's firs were damaged, two thirds of them seriously (McCormick 1989:30). A study in 1990 concluded that 75 per cent of Europe's forests suffer damaging levels of sulphur deposition, and 60 per cent of them endure nitrogen deposition above their critical loads (WRI 1992:198). While there is considerable uncertainty over the actual figures, damage to crops and buildings is thought to be economically substantial: for example, $31 billion in 1983 to US wheat, corn, soybeans and peanuts; $500 million in eleven European countries in 1981 (McCormick 1989:40–41). The cost to Europe of corrosion of buildings has been estimated by the UN Economic Commission of Europe as $1.3–$6.5 billion pa.

Trends for global emissions of the principal acid gases, sulphur dioxide and nitrogen oxide, are difficult to assess. In OECD countries sulphur dioxide emissions fell by 25 per cent over the 1980s and by 38 per cent between 1970 and the late 1980s, even while GDP grew by 30 per cent over the 1980s, and 77 per cent from 1970. However, nitrogen oxide emissions grew by 12 per cent from 1970–87, largely because road traffic grew by 93 per cent, faster than GDP (OECD 1991b:21,23,53,61). The USSR and countries of Eastern Europe all had higher per capita sulphur emissions in 1989 than in Western Europe and North America (WRI 1992:64), though the restructuring of and, in some cases, reduction in economic activity since then may have reduced them. Nitrogen dioxide emissions, on the other hand, are more equal between the West and former Communist countries, reflecting the former's far higher rate of car ownership and use. While lack of data prevent any clear quantitative assessment of Third World trends in this area, it is clear that air pollution in rapidly industrializing countries is increasingly damaging both the environment and human health. In gross (as opposed to per capita) terms, China is already the third largest emitter of SO_2 worldwide.

Toxic pollution

There are many pollutants which are injurious to health and only the briefest account of their scope and effects can be given here. The great majority of these pollutants are the products of industrial development, but two significant exceptions are pollution by sewage and from indoor fires. Indoor pollution, from cooking or heating by burning wood, straw or dung, adversely affects 400–700 million people and contributes to acute respiratory infections that kill up to four million children annually, permanently damaging the health of many more, children and adults (World Bank 1992:52). Sewage is the major cause of water contamination worldwide, with 1.7 billion people still not having access to adequate sanitation, a number that grew by 70 million during the 1980s. Sewage treatment is rarer still: in developing countries over 95 per cent is untreated before being discharged into surface waters (WRI 1992:167). Universal access to clean water and adequate sanitation would cut the incidence of Third World country disease dramatically: per year, two million fewer child deaths from diarrhoea, and 200 million fewer episodes of the illness; 300 million fewer people with roundworm; 150 million fewer with schistosomiasis (World Bank 1992:49). Needless to say, growing water scarcity (see below) and pollution from other sources are making access to clean water and adequate sanitation more difficult to provide.

Pollutants from industrialization are seriously degrading the quality of air, water and soils. Outdoor air pollution has three principal man-made sources – domestic energy use, vehicular emissions and industrial production – all of which increase with economic growth unless they are abated. The World Bank notes:

> *If the projected growth in demand for vehicular transport and electricity were to be met with the technologies currently in use, emissions of the main pollutants deriving from these sources would increase fivefold and elevenfold, respectively, by about 2030. Yet in the mid-1980s more than 1.3 billion people, mainly in the Third World, already lived in cities with air which did not meet WHO standards for SPM (suspended particulate matter), causing an estimate 300,000–700,000 premature deaths.*

> World Bank 1992:52

Lead is the other major pollutant in Third World cities, principally from car exhausts. Over half the newborns in Mexico City have blood lead levels high enough to impair their development (WRI 1992:51), while in Bangkok children have lost an average of four IQ points or more by age 7 because of lead pollution (World Bank 1992:53). How bad such situations can become is illustrated by Katowice in Poland, where lead levels in the soil reach about 50 times the permitted level. One study showed the difference in IQ between children with high and low blood lead levels to be 13 points, and indicated other profound health differences (WRI 1992:62).

Central and Eastern Europe provide many examples of the appalling damage uncontrolled industrializm can cause. Among 'serious environmental health hazards', WRI lists

> *high levels of sulphur dioxide, oxides of nitrogen, lead and other*
> *hazardous chemicals in the ambient air ...; contamination of*
> *groundwater and soil by nitrogenous fertilizers, pesticides and*
> *toxic metals; contamination of rivers by sewage and industrial*
> *waste; and a variety of chemical, physical, biological and*
> *psychosocial health hazards in the workplace.*

> WRI 1992:62

In assessing the results of such a situation in Russia, the head of the Russian Academy of Medical Sciences shocked the world with his frankness: 'We have already doomed ourselves for the next 25 years.' Eleven per cent of Russian infants suffer from birth defects. 'With half of the drinking water and a tenth of the food supply contaminated, 55 per cent of school age children suffer health problems.' (Brown et al 1993:10).

Although in OECD countries the health impacts of pollution are much less severe, 'On a per capita basis, the OECD countries are overwhelmingly the world's major polluters, both within their own borders and in their contribution to global environmental degradation.' (WRI 1992:18) Their 16 per cent of the world's population consumed 43 per cent of 1989's global production of fossil fuels, most of its production of metals and well over a proportionate share of industrial materials and forest products. Per capita consumption of resources in OECD countries is often several times the global average. For example, OECD countries account for 78 per cent of all road vehicles (OECD 1991a:13). Because current technologies turn resources inexorably into wastes, the pollution emanating from these countries should come as no surprise: 40 per cent of global sulphur dioxide and 54 per cent of nitrogen oxides emissions; 68 per cent of industrial wastes by weight; 38 per cent of global potential warming impact from emissions of greenhouse gases (WRI 1992:17) OECD pollution may be killing fewer people than that from other regions, but its 'industrial residues – acidic materials, heavy metals, and toxic chemicals – degrade soils, damage plants, and endanger food supplies' (WRI 1992:18) just as unsustainably.

Species extinction

'When we consider just the numbers involved,' wrote Norman Myers in 1986, 'let alone the compressed time-frame of the episode,... we may suppose we are on the verge of one of the greatest extinction episodes to occur during the four billion years since the start of evolution.... The extinction spasm pending may well rank as the greatest impoverishment of Earth's species since the first flickerings of life.' (Myers 1986:4) Yet, as the World Bank notes, 'The complex web of interactions that sustains the vitality of ecosystems can unravel even if only a small number of key species disappear.' (World Bank 1992:59) On no issue of unsustainability is human ignorance so profound as in its understanding of biodiversity. Identified species are fewer than 1.5 million, but over 30 million, of which over 90 per cent are insects, are thought to exist (ibid:60). At such levels of ignorance, figures of extinction rates are little more than informed speculation. Harvard biologist Edward O Wilson puts the minimum loss of invertebrate species at 50,000 per year (Brown et al 1992b:9). More certain is that the tropical forests, covering 6–7 per cent of the Earth's land surface, contain 50-90 per cent of all species. Myers places nearly 40 per cent of all species in the forests of Latin America outside Amazonia and those of Africa outside the Zaire basin (Myers 1986:12), most of which look likely to disappear by the early years of the next century. Myers writes: 'We are unconsciously conducting a superscale experiment with Earth's biotas.' (ibid:2) Unfortunately it is an experiment conducted in almost total ignorance, and which can never be repeated. This is a strange way for an age which prides itself on rationality and scientific prowess to be proceeding.

Deforestation

It is estimated that the Earth's forest cover is now only two thirds of what it was in pre-agricultural times, but the amount of undisturbed, primary forest is only a quarter of that amount. Europe has practically no original forests; the US outside Alaska has only 5 per cent (Brown et al 1991:74). The large expanses of remaining primary temperate forests in Canada and the former Soviet Union, saved so far by their remoteness, are now also being felled, with Canada losing 200,000 hectares (ha) pa (Brown et al 1993:6).

In tropical countries only half the original area of forests remains, and over half of this has already been logged or degraded in some way (Brown et al 1991:74). Moreover, the rate of tropical deforestation accelerated markedly during the 1980s, reaching 17 million ha pa in 1991, compared to 11.3 million in the early 1980s, an increase of 50 per cent (WRI 1992:118). Some countries' deforestation has proceeded even faster than this. Thus Indonesia's rate has quadrupled since 1970, now destroying 1 million ha annually. Thailand's forest cover between 1961 and 1988 shrank from 55 per cent to 28 per cent (WRI 1992:47).

Land degradation

In the past 45 years 'about 11 per cent of the Earth's vegetated soils have become degraded to the point that their original biotic functions are damaged and reclamation may be costly or, in some cases, impossible' (WRI 1992:111). Since 1972, farmers have lost nearly 500 billion tons of topsoil (Brown et al 1993:4), a process that continues at a rate of 24 billion tons a year (ibid:12). Table 2.3 shows how 'moderate, severe and extreme' land degradation affects different regions.

Table 2.3 Land degradation by region

	Degraded area (DA) (million hectares)	DA as % of vegetated land
World	1215.4	10.5
Europe	158.3	16.7
Africa	320.6	14.4
Asia	452.5	12.0
Oceania	6.2	0.8
North America	78.7	0.4
Central America and Mexico	60.9	24.1
South America	138.5	8.0

Source: WRI 1992:112

Land degradation is caused by wind and water erosion and by chemical or physical factors, the former including salinization, acidification and pollution, the latter including compaction and waterlogging. The activities principally leading to land degradation are deforestation, overgrazing and agriculture.

Water depletion

The most obvious reason for water scarcity, of course, is drought: about 80 arid and semi-arid countries with some 40 per cent of the world's population experience periodic droughts (WRI 1992:160). Increasingly, however, burgeoning levels of water use are threatening water scarcity: global water use has risen by a factor of three, or by 50 per cent per capita, since 1950 (Brown et al 1993:22). Sixty-nine per cent of this is used for agriculture, 23 per cent for industry and 8 per cent for domestic uses. By the year 2000 water withdrawals for irrigation are expected to increase by 17 per cent and for industry by 61 per cent. Domestic use is also projected to rise sharply (WRI 1992:161). Such increases can only serve to exacerbate already severe trends in some places of falling water tables, depleted groundwater resources and inadequate supplies.

Thus in Beijing water tables have been falling 1–2 metres per year and a third of the wells have run dry, yet its total water demand in the year 2000 is projected to outstrip its current supply by 70 per cent (Brown et al 1993:26). The countries of the Middle East and North Africa face a situation of particular difficulty. Nearly all available supplies are being used, yet populations in some of the countries are projected to double over the next 25 years. The potential conflict in the situation is obvious, especially where water resources are shared. For example, 86 per cent of Egypt's water comes from the Nile, most of the waters of which originate in eight countries upstream.

Water withdrawn for industrial and domestic uses is largely returned to surface water systems after use, but often in a polluted condition, where it can degrade the water resource for other users or damage the environment.

Fish depletion

In 1990 the total global fish catch declined for the first time in thirteen years. The following year the UN Food and Agriculture Organisation (FAO) reported that most traditional marine fish stocks have reached full exploitation. Although there was a record harvest in 1989, intensified fishing effort would only increase the catch by depleting fish populations. The FAO considers that four of its 17 major marine fishing areas are already overfished. Further evidence of a fish catch limit having been reached came from a 1990 US study, which showed that 18 per cent of US fish stocks are overexploited and 30 per cent of US fish stocks have declined since 1977 (WRI 1992:179). In July 1992 Canada reacted to dwindling catches off Nova Scotia and Labrador by banning all cod and haddock fishing in the area for two years, at a cost of $400 million in unemployment compensation and retraining (Brown 1993:8).

Perhaps even more threatening to fish stocks in the long term than overfishing is the ongoing pollution and destruction of coastal habitats where 90 per cent by weight of the world marine catch reproduces. Wetlands, mangroves and salt marshes are being rapidly cleared for urban, industrial and recreational uses: tropical countries have lost over 50 per cent of their mangroves and the US 50 per cent of its wetlands (WRI 1992:177) Most of the world's sewage still flows untreated into coastal waters (ibid:176), its pollution augmented by a variety of toxic chemicals, and further pollution from rivers. Thus a 1991 survey of 85 coastal watersheds in the US found that upstream sources, including agricultural and urban run-off, accounted for about 70 per cent of the nitrogen and 60 per cent of the phosphorus in the estuaries studied (WRI 1992:182). Such pollution can cause algal blooms, which have been reported from coastal areas around the world, and which can lead to mass kills of fish; or it can cut harvests, as in the US's Chesapeake Bay, which produced only one eighth the oyster catch of a century ago (Brown et al 1993:8); or it can render fish unfit for human consumption. These trends augur very badly for the future of tropical developing countries, many with fast-growing populations, 60 per cent of whom currently rely on fish for 40 per cent or more of their protein.

Non-renewable resource depletion

The depletion of non-renewable resources (eg minerals, fossil fuels) which caused much of the anxiety about unsustainability in the 1970s (see for example Meadows et al 1972), and which appears to be an unsustainable activity by definition, has declined dramatically in perceived importance. New discoveries and more efficient use of, and substitution away from, non-renewable resources has tended to keep constant, or even lengthen, their life-expectancies (defined as the known reserves/annual production, or R/P, ratio). As an example, the R/P ratio of oil and natural gas increased from 31 and 38 to 41 and 68 years respectively from 1970 to 1989 (Meadows et al 1992:68). Similarly Table 2.4 shows the R/P ratio for seven minerals in 1970, 1988 and 1990, using three different sources of data.

Table 2.4 World production, reserves and R/P ratios for various minerals at various dates

Minerals	World production (million metric tons)		R/P ratios years[a]			Reserves ratio[b]
	1970[c]	1990[d]	1970[c]	1988[e]	1990[d]	
Copper	8.56	8.81	36	32	36	1.04
Aluminium	75.00[f]	109.00	100	1000	200	3.73[g]
Lead	3.5	3.37	26	12	21	0.77
Mercury	8.7[f]	5.8	13	–	22	–
Nickel	0.81[f]	0.94	150	59	52	0.72[g]
Tin	0.25	0.22	17	27	27	1.38
Zinc	5.35	7.33	23	500	20	1.17

a   R/P ratios can be interpreted as life expectancies at a constant rate of production with no new discoveries
b   This Reserves ratio has been calculated by dividing 1990 by 1970 world reserves, as given in sources c and d below (– indicates that the ratio could not be calculated from the data in these sources)
c   Source: Meadows et al 1972:56–9
d   Source: WRI 1992:320–1
e   Source: World Bank 1992:37
f   This figure came from source d for the year 1975
g   This figure came from source e, and is the reserves ratio for 1988 with respect to 1970

Although several of the 1990 R/P figures seem quite short periods of time, they are little changed from the 1970 figures. Some, indeed, have increased. Only lead and nickel appear to have become substantially more scarce, but the 1970 R/P ratio for nickel must be suspect, as it indicates a reserve level of the resource which must have been revised substantially downwards given the 1990 R/P ratio and interim production. The World Bank 500 year R/P ratio must be accounted doubtful in view of the other sources' estimates.

In one sense, any level of use of non-renewable resources is unsustainable, and, of course, new discoveries and the emergence of substitutes cannot be guaranteed. But the timescales involved in this depletion now seem much less pressing than for pollution and the depletion of renewable resources.

Interlinkages

One of the most striking observations about the symptoms of unsustain-ability is the number of interlinkages between them, unfortunately usually tending to reinforce their negative effects. Some of these are specifically noted in Table 2.1 or in the evidence given above, but there are many others. Thus deforestation is a major cause of land degradation and increases in sedimentation and downstream nutrient enrichment of rivers and lakes worldwide (WRI 1992:169), as well as of species extinction and global warming. Acid deposition kills forests and pollutes water sources. Two of the most promising non-ozone–depleting potential substitutes for CFCs,

HFCs and HCFCs, are potent greenhouse gases. The extra UV-B radiation reaching the Earth due to ozone depletion may damage fish larvae and juveniles and the phytoplankton at the base of the food web (WRI 1992:196), as well as cause damage to crops. Toxic pollution of freshwater increases its effective scarcity for human purposes. And, of course, practically all the problems are worsened, and the achievement of solutions to them rendered more difficult, by continuing population growth which adds over 90 million to human numbers each year.

This is the complex context within which environmental economic policy must be formulated. For some analysts, the evidence of environmental damage cited above is either not conclusive enough to warrant action, or they believe that the economy will react appropriately to emerging environmental scarcity without policy intervention (see for example Bernstam 1991). Others believe that active intervention is justified in order to achieve a 'sustainable development' that is compatible with continuing economic growth (see for example World Bank 1991). Others still believe that the environmental problems are evidence of limits to that growth (see for example Meadows et al 1992). The next section reviews these positions and focuses especially on the emerging concept of environmental sustainability.

GROWTH AND SUSTAINABILITY

This paper seeks to answer the question: does the achievement of environmental sustainability necessarily mean a reduction in rates of economic growth? If not, under what conditions can the two objectives be met simultaneously?

Definitions

Growth

It is important in this debate to clarify and distinguish between three difference kinds of 'growth':

1. Growth of the economy's biophysical throughput.
2. Growth of production (or income), as measured by GDP.
3. Growth of human welfare.

These three kinds of growth have a complex and by no means fixed relationship to each other. This paper is concerned with the relationship between biophysical throughput and GDP. Based on the evidence given earlier, it is assumed that sustainability requires the overall rate of biophysical throughput to contract. The question is then whether this requires a contraction – or at least a slowing down – of income growth. Since GDP is the variable of most concern to macroeconomists and politicians, and the fear of negative impacts on growth is probably the principal source of resistance to environmental policy, this is an important question.

It is not the same, however, as asking whether environmental sustainability would reduce welfare. There is no agreed definition or measurement of welfare, and its relationship to GDP growth is a matter of dispute. The conventional economic view, defended for example by Beckerman (1974), is that GDP and welfare are closely correlated; and therefore that any reduction in GDP almost certainly implies a reduction in welfare. By contrast Mishan (1967, 1977) argues that, at a certain stage of development, the costs of GDP growth come to exceed its benefits, so that the growth paths of welfare and GDP diverge.

Both Mishan and Beckerman call GDP growth 'economic growth', a terminology that is hotly disputed by Hueting (1986:244), who contends that the objective of economics is to increase human welfare, not production, and that welfare has several contributing components apart from production. Hueting actually identifies the components of welfare as production (GDP), environment, employment, leisure, working conditions, income distribution, and safety of the future.

Assuming that GDP and environmental quality are both important components of welfare, it is important to know what is the nature of the trade-offs which can be made. Even if it were the case that protecting the environment requires a major reduction in GDP growth, this could increase rather than reduce welfare, depending on the relative weight given to the components' production, environment and 'safety of the future'. These issues are discussed further in Ekins 1993, but are not further addressed here.

In fact GDP is a poor measure, not simply of welfare, but of production itself. This is not just because GDP does not include the great majority of non-monetary economic production and therefore understates production by the huge amount of unpaid and household voluntary work undertaken in the economy; GDP is not even an accurate indicator of monetized production, because of its treatment of environmental inputs, and of the defensive expenditures in environmental and other areas associated with some of its outputs (defensive expenditures are discussed in Leipert 1989; taking environmental issues into GDP accounting methods is discussed in Ahmad et al 1989, Lutz 1993; literature on national accounting and the environment is reviewed in Ekins 1994a, forthcoming).

Sustainability

Sustainability literally means the capacity for some state or condition to be continued more or less indefinitely. For economic development to be termed sustainable, it is normally considered that it is the level of economic welfare that must be sustained. As discussed above, economic welfare derives from, *inter alia*, income and from the environment, which performs various functions, some of which contribute to welfare directly. Income is generated by stocks of capital, including manufactured, human and natural capital. Natural capital also performs the welfare-creating environmental functions. Non-declining economic welfare requires, *ceteris paribus*, that the stock of capital be maintained (Pezzey 1992:14).

There is then the issue as to whether it is the total stock of capital that must be maintained, with substitution allowed between various parts of it, or whether certain components of capital, particularly natural capital, are non-substitutable, ie they contribute to welfare in a unique way that cannot be replicated by another capital component. 'Weak' environmental sustainability conditions derive from a perception that welfare is not normally dependent on a specific form of capital and can be maintained by substituting manufactured for natural capital. 'Strong' sustainability conditions derive from a different perception that substitutability of manufactured for natural capital is seriously limited by such environmental characteristics as irreversibility, uncertainty and the existence of 'critical' components of natural capital, which make a unique contribution to welfare. (Pearce and Atkinson 1992, Turner 1992). An even greater importance is placed on natural capital by those who regard it in many instances as a complement to man-made capital (Daly 1992).

The difference between weak and strong sustainability is important to the argument about the compatibility of sustainability and GDP growth. In general, it may be said that value added (GDP) is generated by transforming energy and materials from the natural environment into human-made goods and services. Ferwer environmental goods can be permanently transformed into human-made capital under strong sustainability than under the weak version. All other things being equal, strong sustainability conditions could therefore be expected to make the generation of GDP more difficult. This paper discusses the general conditions for compatibility of GDP growth and environmental sustainability, making no distinction between weak and strong versions of sustainability. But it should be noted that the fewer the substitution possibilities allowed, the more stringent the conditions in practice become.

Base case GDP growth

In discussing whether the achievement of sustainability would reduce GDP growth it is important to distinguish between absolute reductions in GDP – ie negative growth – and reductions in the rate of growth in comparison with a 'base case' in which policy measures for sustainability are not taken. The question at issue might be simply; can sustainability be compatible and GDP growth, at any positive level? Or it could be: would policies for sustainability reduce growth below the rate which it would otherwise be?

The discussion below principally concerns the first question, that of general compatibility of sustainability and positive rates of growth. Since neither the exact rates of growth achievable under sustainability constraints, nor the precise rate level of growth in the 'base case' (particularly in the long term) are known, the second question cannot be answered definitively, although as will be seen later, there is little evidence that environmental policy to date has acted as a serious constraint on growth. However it should be pointed out that if policies for sustainability could generate positive rates of growth which are within, say, 0.25 per cent pa of the expected base case, this would at least calm macroeconomic and political fears of a 'collapse in living standards' associated with moves towards sustainability.

A further point may be made. Most of the literature in the field (for example, on reduction of carbon dioxide emissions) assumes a base case in which growth continues at historical trend rates, and then compares the growth rate which would result from environmental policies. However it is not clear that historical trends will continue – for environmental reasons. Firstly, growth rates may decline for reasons quite unconnected with environmental problems. Secondly, in the absence of more stringent environmental policies GDP growth might eventually slow down because of environmental constraints.

There are a number of reasons to suppose that the environment may eventually act as a constraint on GDP growth:

- the capital costs of obtaining raw materials and energy may rise as depletion occurs (for example, deeper oil wells must be drilled, more inaccessible timber must be forested);
- the inputs required to produce each unit of output from the same capital may rise (for example, more fertilizer and pesticides are required in agriculture);
- the demand for human quality of life (reproduction of the labour force) may require higher costs of pollution prevention and clean-up. This may be registered as higher input costs (if pollution control is carried out by firms, whether end-of-pipe or integral to the production process) or higher government or household expenditures.

All these trends will tend to increase the intermediate input costs of each unit of real output, ie reduce the value added. (Though note that if pollution control is carried out by government or households it will not be counted as an intermediate input in GDP, and will therefore – illogically – register as final production.) Put another way, a higher proportion of final output will have to be devoted to maintaining output, and less will be available for increasing it. Unchecked, these trends would retard growth. This is the familiar classical formulation of a rising capital–output ratio.

It is not clear to what extent these trends will occur, or will be offset by 'autonomous' technological change (ie not induced by environmental policy). But if they do, then the base case is of lower growth than generally anticipated. In turn this may cast a more favourable light on the growth rates achievable with sustainability policies.

The Environmental Impacts of Growth

There is no dispute that the negative environmental effects of production are associated with the economy's biophysical throughput: its conversion of energy and material resources into wastes. However, this process is not part of production's desired objective, which is to add value to its resource and energy inputs. When aggregated this added value becomes Gross Domestic Product. The key consideration as to whether GDP growth is or can be environmentally sustainable is the extent to which production processes can add value without increasing associated environmentally negative biophysical throughputs.

All economic activity requires three functions from the environment:

1. raw materials and energy as factor inputs;
2. the assimilation of wastes;
3. the maintenance of life support systems (such as climate regulation and maintenance of genetic diversity).

Ceteris paribus, it can be observed that as production increases, increasing stress will be placed on these three functions, leading to environmental degradation.

In order to examine how this trend might be reversed, use can be made of the concept of the *environmental impact coefficient (EIC)* of output (Jacobs 1991): that is, its average unit impact on the environment through the consumption of resources and production of wastes. The three systematic changes in production processes which can theoretically reduce the EIC and thus enable value-added to increase while reducing environmental impacts are, as identified by Lecomber (1975):

1. changing the composition of output towards less damaging products (for example, goods to services);
2. substituting less damaging factor inputs for more damaging ones (for example, fossil fuels to renewables);
3. increasing the efficiency of resource use through technical progress (for example, energy conversion efficiency).

The same idea is expressed thus by the World Bank: 'Whether (environmental) limitations will place bounds on the growth of human activity will depend on the scope for substitution, technical progress and structural change.' (World Bank 1992:9)

By reducing the EIC, each of these changes counteracts the rising capital–output ratio, and can therefore put off the moment when growth runs up against environmental limits. In principle, so long as EIC rises faster than growth, the environmental limits can be postponed indefinitely.

Environmentally sustainable GDP growth thus depends on the achievement of substitution and technical and structural change in order to keep environmental impacts within conditions of environmental sustainability. However, this is not sufficient, since first a state of environmental sustainability must be achieved, and, as shown previously, the global economy is far from such a state. Remedying the environmental impacts caused by past economic activities is likely to reduce growth. In addition, because of the environmental unsustainability of current activity, substitution and change must reduce the environmental impact of current output *as well as* of further growth in that output, if environmental sustainability is to be attained. Where environmental damage is irreversible, of course, improving EIC will not be effective.

The 'all-important equation' (Ehrlich and Ehrlich 1990:228) expressing the relationship between environmental impact and human activity was written (Holdren and Ehrlich 1974:288) as

$$I = P\,C\,T$$

where I is environmental impact, P is population, C is consumption per head, and T is impact per unit of consumption, earlier called the environmental impact coefficient (EIC). T can be thought of as indicating the technology of consumption (and production). In some cases it will mainly reflect the inputs of production, the processes of transformation of production and consumption, and the disposal of wastes; in other cases it may be influenced by social arrangements such as property rights and the effectiveness of legal systems.

I (and therefore the numerator of T) could be one of a large number of environmental impacts with no common unit of measurement. To express multiple impacts, the equation should, strictly, be written in vector form

$$I = P\,C'\,T$$

where, T are column vectors of individual impacts, C is a vector of consumption quantities relating to those impacts and P is a scalar.

Holdren and Ehrlich recognise that P, C and T are not independent; for example, T may vary with consumption per head. It is even possible that falls in consumption could increase environmental damage, as expressed, for example, in the South Commission report's statement that 'poverty is also a great degrader of the environment' (South Commission 1990:279). Such interdependencies raise serious problems for attempts to use the equation to identify the separate contributions of individual factors to past environmental degration (as discussed in Amalric's chapter in this volume) but do not prevent the equation being a useful device to illustrate the improvements in environmental efficiency reductions in T) required to achieve environmental sustainability under alternative scenarios.

In accordance with the reports already cited, and the widespread agreement at UNCED, it is assumed that current levels of I are unsustainable. As we saw earlier with regard to global warming, the IPCC calculates that carbon dioxide emissions will quickly have to fall by a minimum of 60 per cent to stabilize atmospheric concentrations of CO_2, and three other greenhouse gases – N_2O, CFC-11, CFC-12 – need cuts of more than 70 per cent. With regard to other environmental problems, the Dutch National Environmental Policy Plan (MOHPPE 1988) argues for cuts in emissions of 80–90 per cent for SO_2, NO_x, NH_3 and waste-dumping, 80 per cent for hydrocarbons and 100 per cent for CFCs. Thus with regard to I overall, it seems conservative to suggest that sustainability demands that it should fall by at least 50 per cent. With regard to consumption, what is considered a moderate economic growth rate of 2–3 per cent results in a quadrupling of output over 50 years. With regard to population the UN's recent projections indicate a global figure of 10 billion by about 2050 (Sadik 1991:3), about twice today's level, with 95 per cent of population growth in the Third World. Using this assumption and classifications and data from World Bank 1992, the necessary reductions in T (T_R) in order to reduce environmental impacts to 50 per cent of the current value by 2050 would be as follows (see Appendix for detailed calculation):

1. No growth in P or C : $T_{R1} = 50\%$
2. Growth in P, no growth in C : $T_{R2} = 65\%$
3. Growth in P, growth in C in South : $T_{R3} = 81\%$
4. Growth in P, growth in C in North : $T_{R4} = 89\%$
5. Growth in P and C in North and South : $T_{R5} = 91\%$

These figures clearly illustrate some important aspects of the technology/sustainability relation. Comparing T_{R1} and T_{R2}, expected population growth at existing consumption levels increases the required cut in T from one half to two thirds. Although 95 per cent of the population growth takes place in the South, the detailed calculation shows that the far higher level of consumption in the North means that the growth of population in the North (5 per cent of total population growth) accounts for well over one half of the increase in environmental impact due to population growth as a whole and thus over one half of the extra required reduction in T due to that growth.

Comparing T_{R4} with T_{R2} (89 per cent to 65 per cent) shows the extent to which growth in the North makes the achievement of environmental sustainability more technologically demanding. Comparison of T_{R4} with T_{R3} shows that the sustainable quadrupling of just the North's consumption per head, from a high base, demands considerably greater technical change than sustainably quadrupling the South's consumption per head for more than double its present population (89 per cent as opposed to 81 per cent reduction in T). In the latter case the calculation shows that even after quadrupling the South's per capita consumption, this is still only about one sixth of current levels in the North. It is also clear that the required technological improvement in the North, even without Northern growth, is substantial if the South is to have 'ecological space' for environmentally sustainable growth (Goodland and Daly 1992:130, also make this point).

Finally, the size of the necessary improvement in T (91 per cent) given growth in both North and South, which remains the principal, practically unchallenged global aspiration, must be noted. The remainder of this paper examines the feasibility and implications of changes on this scale.

THE COSTS OF ACHIEVING ENVIRONMENTAL SUSTAINABILITY

Theoretical Discussion

Reducing the EIC provides the basic *physical* condition for the compatibility of sustainability and growth. But there is also an economic condition. Reducing the EIC is likely to require resources in new capital and often in more expensive inputs. If the cost of reducing EIC rises faster than output growth, postponement of the environmental limits will have been bought only at the expense of higher intermediate costs, which will have the same effect of retarding growth as a rising capital–output ratio. Therefore for sustainability not to constrain GDP growth, the net costs of reducing EIC must be neutral or negative.

There are two broad ways in which improving the environmental efficiency of production might also involve raising general productivity (ie where policy for environmental sustainability will also promote GNP growth):

1. Situations in which governments change policies which are economically inefficient as well as environmentally damaging.
2. Situations in which public or private sector businesses introduce changes in methods, processes or products, including systems of resource and waste management, which both improve environmental quality *and* turn out to be cost-saving or product-improving.

The first kind of situation may be considered an example of double government failure (policies that are economically and environmentally flawed), and the second exhibits a kind of double market failure (environmental externality and economic inefficiency). There is substantial evidence, some of which will be reviewed in the next section, that both these kinds of failure are surprisingly widespread.

It is important to recognize that the cost reductions need not accrue to the economic agent undertaking the environmental measure as when a requirement for a manufacturing firm to cut water emissions reduces the cost of water treatment undertaken by the water utility.

If some environmental improvement measures may in themselves be net cost-reducing, while others are net cost-increasing, this gives us three broad scenarios:

1. EIC is reduced to counteract environmental impacts and this raises general productivity – growth increases and environmental quality improves ('win–win'). This effect could occur as a result of correcting either government or market failures as part of implementing environmental policies.
2. EIC is reduced to counteract environmental impacts but this raises intermediate costs – growth declines, but some aspects of environmental quality improve, or decline less slowly ('win–lose').
3 Nothing is done to counteract rising 'environmental' intermediate costs – environmental quality declines and, if it falls far enough, so does growth (the 'lose–lose' scenario).

The financial implications of scenarios 1 and 2 are shown in sectors A, B and C of Figure 2.2, in which the total benefits can be regarded as the 'demand curve' for environmental quality, and the costs incurred as the 'supply curve'. Either the policies cost nothing and result in both financial and environmental gains, because they represent the correction of government policy that was economically inefficient as well as environmentally damaging (sector A); or the policies have a financial cost

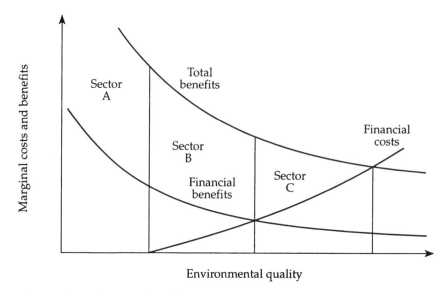

Source: adapted from World Bank, 1992: 66

Figure 2.2 *Benefits and costs of environmental policies*

which is outweighed by the financial gain, in addition to the environmental gain (sector B); or the policies have a net financial cost which is outweighed by the environmental gain (sector C). The first two cases may be characterized as 'win–win changes' corresponding to scenario 1, and the third as 'trade-off situations' corresponding to scenario 2.

Essentially, the question of whether sustainability and GDP growth are compatible then becomes one concerning the relative sizes of Sectors A, B and C.

The empirical evidence on this will be reviewed in the next section. First, however, it may be helpful to summarize the theoretical position. There are two requirements for growth not to run up against environmental limits:

1. The average environmental impact coefficient must be reduced.
2. This must be cost-neutral or must positively increase general productivity.

Three further conditions must be met:

1. The improvements in EIC and productivity gains must be continuous (and exponential); if not, continuing growth will soon overcome the gains made. It should be noted that if an improvement in EIC relaxes a constraint, this will itself encourage growth, thereby wiping out at least part of the gain.
2. The improvements in EIC and productivity must occur across all environmental impacts relevant to the environmental sustainability of

GDP growth. If recycling of materials requires more energy consumption, for example, the environmental constraint will simply be relocated, not removed.
3. The growth-retarding effects of any environmental impacts caused by past actions must be cleared up along with current impacts; for example, hazardous waste treatment, ozone depletion, desertification and so on.

There is no question in principle, both that each of the three methods for reducing EIC is possible, and that some methods of reducing EIC will also lead to general productivity improvements. But the theoretical possibility of 'delinking' biophysical throughput from GDP growth does not guarantee its practical achievability. As Lecomber has put it, this

> *establishes the logical conceivability, not the certainty, probability or even the possibility in practice, of growth continuing indefinitely. Everything hinges on the rate of technical progress and possibilities of substitution. This is perhaps the main issue that separates resource optimists and resource pessimists. The optimist believes in the power of human inventiveness to solve whatever problems are thrown in its way, as apparently it has done in the past. The pessimist questions the success of these past technological solutions and fears that future problems may be more intractable.*
>
> Lecomber 1975:42

Ultimately it is an empirical matter whether the two requirements for reconciling sustainability and GDP growth, under the four given conditions, can be achieved in practice.

Empirical Evidence

In a Background Paper for the World Bank's *World Development Report 1992*, Anderson (1992) provides impressive evidence that the potential exists, or soon will exist, to reduce EICs on the scale required by the Ehrlich equation in each of the major fields of global environmental impact: water, food production, pollution from energy, global warming and pollution from industry (Table 2.5). (The analysis focuses on substitution between factor inputs and raising technical efficiency; only in energy production is changing the composition of output considered). He further argues that many of these methods themselves raise productivity. On the basis of this analysis Anderson concludes that – so long as the correct policies are put in place – growth over the next thirty to forty years need not be constrained, and indeed can be enhanced, by protection and improvement of the environment. (He acknowledges that time lags in investment will mean that environmental problems, particularly in the South, will get considerably worse before they get better.)

Table 2.5 Polluting and low-polluting practices

Source	Basis of index of damage	Polluting	Non-polluting	Nature of alternatives
Particulate matter	⎫	100	<0.1	⎫ Natural gas; clean
CO	⎟	100	<0.1	⎟ coal technologies;
SO_2	⎟	100	0 to <5	⎬ scrubbers; low
NO_x	⎬ Emissions	100	5 to <10	⎭ sulphur fuels
CO_2	⎟	100	0	⎫ Renewables
Pb	⎟	100	<0.1	⎟ New octane
	⎟			⎬ enhancers;
VOCs	⎭	100	<2	⎭ catalytic converters
Marine pollution (oil)	Spills and wastes	100	<10	
Surface water pollution	Volume of wastes	100	negligible	Sewerage works; effluent control technologies
Soil erosion	Soil loss	100	negligible	Agro-forestry; soil erosion prevention practices
Forestry	Areas cleared in damaging ways	100	negligible	'Sustainable' practices
Industrial effluents and wastes	Emissions and wastes (by weight and volume)	100	small	Effluent control technologies; waste reduction or 'prevention'

Source: Anderson 1992:6

Anderson does not attempt to integrate the results in the different fields, so it is not clear whether (for example) the additional commercial energy and industrial inputs required to improve agricultural productivity can be accommodated within the win–win energy and industrial pollution scenarios. Nor is it clear whether the gains in general productivity made in some sectors outweigh overall the losses acknowledged in others. (In effect the losses are regarded as so small in relation to total output that they are deemed not to be sufficiently serious to inhibit growth.)

The potential of new technologies to enable production to be considerably less damaging environmentally would seem indubitable. Whether such potential is realized in practice depends on whether government and market failures can be successfully addressed.

Government failure

The notion that government is in some sense a natural protector of the environment was dealt a probably terminal blow by the revelations of environmental damage in Central and Eastern Europe and the former Soviet Union (see WRI 1992, Chapter 5 for a survey). It is clear that there are many other governmental contributions to environmental destruction that are also economically inefficient.

One of the largest examples of such governmental lose–lose policies is the Common Agricultural Policy (CAP) of the European Community. The basic mechanism of the CAP is price support of marketed farm products, which, because of intensification of production involving greater specialization and greater use of chemicals and machinery, has led to a number of adverse environmental effects including soil degradation, water pollution and the loss of amenity and diversity (OECD 1991a:184). In aggregate the energy intensity of OECD agriculture increased by 39 per cent over the period 1970–88 (OECD 1991a:173).

In 1984 the net economic costs of the CAP, including losses to taxpayers and consumers, were nearly 14 billion Ecu, leading a study in 1990 to conclude: 'What is certain, therefore, is that... on narrow economic grounds a fundamental reform of current policy would be beneficial, even before the environmental benefits of reform are taken into account.' (Jenkins 1990:47) In terms of Figure 2.2, such a policy reform is in sector A, where both economic and environmental benefits can be obtained at zero cost.

Just as price supports for output can inefficiently increase both output and associated environmental damage, so can subsidies for inputs. As the World Bank notes, 'both economic and environmental benefits will be achieved by removing subsidies that encourage the use of coal, electricity, pesticides and irrigation and promote expansion of grazing and timber extraction on public lands.' Such subsidies are common. In China, Poland and Mexico users pay less than 40 per cent of the production cost of electric power; the figure for coal in the former USSR is 10 per cent and for Sri Lanka for nitrogen fertilizer is about 60 per cent; in India and Bangladesh irrigation water is practically free (World Bank 1992:68–9). A string of publications from the World Resources Institute (Kosmo 1987, Repetto 1985, 1986, 1988) gives many other examples of inefficient, environmentally-damaging policies in energy, agriculture and forestry. Policies to rectify these economic and environmental inefficiencies also fall with sector A of Figure 2.2.

Of major importance to both environmental conservation and poverty alleviation in developing countries is the regeneration of degraded land, which alone covers some 69 million hectares. Chambers (1992:222–3) has written:

> *Paradoxically, degradation often protects potential for the poor. Because land is degraded – deforested, eroded, waterlogged, saline, bare from overgrazing, flooded or unsustainably cropped – it has low value, especially where current management practices seem likely to persist. But again and again, when management priorities are changed, remarkable bioeconomic potential is revealed.*

Conventional 'development' practice has to date been more concerned with harvesting biomass, or even destroying it through industrial projects, than with regenerating it, so a focus on such regeneration would mark a significant change of development direction and approach, with two essential ingredients. The first is a high level of motivation and commitment of both individuals and communities, both to carry out the environmental reparations on a long-term basis. Such commitment will only be forthcoming if the people involved are assured of rights of use of the biomass they have produced. Inalienable rights of tenure, usufruct and control over the regenerated land is an essential condition for the regeneration to take place.

This is a fundamental policy issue for countries with skewed land distribution and a history of concentrated ownership, unsustainable use of land and biomass, and exclusion of peasant farmers from land or their insecure title to it. The World Bank identified the clarification and enforcement of property rights as a key zero cost (sector A, Figure 2.2) policy geared to both development and environmental conservation (World Bank 1992:66, 68–70).

Secondly, the regeneration of biomass often demands low rather than high levels of financial investment, offering the prospect of sector B gains, in terms of Figure 2.2. However, development 'projects' based on biomass regeneration will only succeed if they are rooted in communities' skills, technologies and own perceived priorities. Participation, of course, has been a buzzword in development parlance for some years, but it rarely extends to 'beneficiary' communities both setting the agenda for their development and playing the principal decision-making role in achieving it. Biomass regeneration demands both.

Where these ingredients are present, there is not the slightest doubt, on the basis of successful examples from different countries, that biomass generation is both feasible and yields large, sustainable benefits to the populations concerned. Conroy and Litvinoff (1988) report successful experiences of this kind from north India, Nepal, Honduras, Niger, Burkina Faso and Haiti. Harrison (1987) gives many examples from Africa. Pangare and Pangare (1992) give an in-depth account of regenerative success in Maharashtra, central India.

A relevant question for this chapter is whether, if biomass regeneration were to be achieved on a large scale by participatory processes under the control of the rural poor, this would result in GDP growth. To the extent that the new biomass found its way onto the market it obviously would, but it is likely that a considerable portion of the output would be consumed for the producer's own subsistence and so would not be thus recorded. It is essential, therefore, that measures of the effectiveness of such processes take account of subsistence production if they are not seriously to understate the results achieved.

Market failure and business successes

With regard to market failures, a number of case studies now attest to corporate improvements in environmental performance which have also yielded economic benefits. Thus the Business Council for Sustainable Development states: 'Many of the waste reduction and environmentally positive programs in business are economically viable and are providing positive rates of return in relatively short time periods.' (Schmidheiny 1992:96) Sometimes the benefit comes in the form of straight cost reductions, a well-known example of which is the Pollution Prevention Pays (3P) programme of the 3M Corporation, which from 1975–1990 cut air pollutants by 122,000 tons, water pollutants by 16,000 tons, solid waste by 400,000 tons and waste water by 1.6 billion gallons – and saved $482 million (Business International 1990:188). Similarly, Northern Telecom, in phasing out its use of ozone-depleting CFC-113 between 1988 and 1991, spent $1 million putting a substitute in place, but saved $4 million on purchasing the CFC, associated taxes and waste disposal (Schmidheiny 1992:230). In India Harihar Polyfibres implemented 200 projects at its pulp mill between 1983 and 1989, aimed at resource efficiency. Although its production increased by 20 per cent in this period, energy consumption fell by 60 per cent, chemical consumption by 55 per cent and the effluent load by 55 per cent. $69.5 million was invested in the projects, but the payback period was less than two years (ibid:272–3). In California several companies have found that investment in industrial water conservation can result in substantial savings of water with a payback period of a year or less. For example, the California Paper-Board Corporation cut its water consumption by 72 per cent from 2.5 to 0.7 million cubic metres per year with a payback period on investment of only 2.4 months (Brown et al 1993:34). In another example, Ayres and Walter (1991:251) report that the average return on investment for 167 energy saving projects undertaken by the Louisiana Division of Dow Chemical Co over the years 1982–88, as part of an 'energy-contest' initiative, was 198 per cent.

All these examples fall within sector B of Figure 2.2. Some investment is required (which could be public as well as private), but it yields net financial as well as environmental gains, and so can be justified in terms of financial return irrespective of environmental considerations. In a competitive market it is surprising that there are so many opportunities for profitable investment that appear to have been overlooked. It appears that business managers have been widely unaware of the *economic*, let alone the environmental, costs of resource use and waste disposal, and needed the pressure of public opinion drawing attention to the latter before they gave serious consideration to the former. As it happens, Harihar Polyfibres' environmental improvements failed to keep up with public opinion, and it was taken to court in 1988 – it has now installed a comprehensive waste water treatment plant (Schmidheiny 1992:273).

Environmental pressure can also achieve economic benefits by stimulating creativity and innovation which results in new products or new business opportunities. Thus the Costa Rican firm RICALIT developed a fibre cement in 1981–2 to replace its asbestos cement which was subject to increasing concern over safety. The substitute proved both less expensive and more manageable than asbestos cement, and was highly profitable, with sales more than doubling to over $6 million in 1991 (ibid:215–6). An example of a new business opportunity is that presented by energy conservation to traditional energy supply companies. The New England Electric (NEE) company realized as long ago as 1979 that energy conservation made more economic sense than providing new supply, but it was not until 1989 that the utilities' regulatory system permitted the company to make a financial return on investments in conservation. In 1990 NEE spent $71 million on energy conservation projects, saving

194,300 MW-hours of electricity and $161 million. NEE retained $8.4 million (9 per cent) of this $91 million net saving, the rest being passed on as benefits to customers. NEE projects that it could spend $100 million a year to the year 2000 on economically viable conservation projects in its service area (ibid:187–8).

It should be noted that all the examples given so far represent unequivocal increases in production – cost-saving investments that either increase production themselves or free up resources for use elsewhere in the economy, as well as improving the environment. They are a special (and perhaps exceptional) subset of the environmental protection industry, which is worth $70–100 billion in OECD countries and probably half as much again worldwide (OECD 1991a:198, Business International 1990:157). While this sector undoubtedly offers many business opportunities to individual companies, at the same macro level much of it (but not the examples above) represents a cost to society, increasing the price of goods or services, or using investment, in order to restore or maintain environmental quality. This point will be discussed further below.

Trade-off situations

In contrast to sectors A and B in Figure 2.2, sector C involves real trade-offs between the production of goods and services for the market and the production, or conservation, of non-market environmental goods and services. Economic resources are allocated for the production of the latter rather than the former which must, therefore, have a negative effect on GDP growth. It is important to recognize that, because the environmental and other benefits from such an allocation are greater than the costs, it still represents an increase in economic efficiency, being a correction of an externality or some other resource misallocation; but it still reduces GDP growth. As Lecomber says:

> It is misleading to regard environmental policies of this sort as alternatives to reducing economic growth, since this would be their incidental effect. Benefits which are not included in GNP would be traded for other (smaller) benefits which are. GNP would fall and, during the period of transition to such policies, growth would fall, probably substantially.
>
> Lecomber 1975:59

Two points follow. The first is that, if the methodology for calculating GDP were to be changed to take into account environmental costs and benefits, then GDP would increase as a result of these environmental policies. One such change in methodology is proposed in Hueting et al 1991. This involves the setting of sustainability standards of environmental quality; the calculation of the costs that would be incurred in reaching those standards; and the subtraction of these costs from the GDP figure. As the application of policies causes the sustainability standards to be approached, this shows up as an increased (adjusted) GDP, because the subtractions become less.

The second point is that, although the cost curve in Figure 2.2 can normally be calculated with a fair degree of reliability, the same is not true of the total benefits curve. In fact, for the most pervasive environmental effects (global warming, ozone depletion, species extinction), it is difficult to put any meaningful figure on the benefits of conservation (stable climate, undepleted ozone layer, biodiversity). (See Ekins 1994b, forthcoming, for a discussion of this issue.) This introduces a level of uncertainty into the practical situation which belies the theoretical simplicity of Figure 2.2 and which is certain also to result in controversy where substantial values are at stake. Because some of the costs and benefits are likely to arise in the future, the benefits curve will also be dependent on the discount rate chosen to convert these into present values. This is certain to be the cause of further controversy.

Optimists and Pessimists

Whether the achievement of environmental sustainability is theoretically compatible with GDP growth depends, therefore, on the manner of calculation of GDP and on the relative size of Figure 2.2's sector C expenditures which do or can restrain GDP growth) to sectors A and B (which represent policies or expenditures which do not). Whether it is practically compatible depends on it being politically possible to address government and market failures.

The question of the relative sizes of sectors A, B and C is still open to conjecture, and is at the heart of the debate about sustainability and growth. This has been characterized by often heated conflict between pessimists – such as Meadows et al, authors of *Limits to Growth* (1972) and *Beyond the Limits* (1992) – and optimists, epitomized by Anderson (1992) and the World Bank itself (1992).

The viewpoint of the former is well expressed by Tinbergen and Hueting:

> *Saving the environment without causing a rise in prices and*
> *subsequent check of production growth is only possible if a*
> *technology is invented that is sufficiently clean, reduces the use of*
> *space sufficiently, leaves the soil intact, does not deplete energy*
> *and resources... and is cheaper (or at least not more expensive)*
> *than current technology. This is barely imaginable for our whole*
> *range of current activities.... From the above it follows that saving*
> *the environment will certainly check production growth and*
> *probably lead to lower levels of national income.*

Tinbergen and Hueting 1993:55–6

Tinbergen and Hueting clearly believe sector C to be the one most often relevant to environmental policy. The World Bank, though not unambiguously, believes that sectors A and B have more to offer. Thus: 'The evidence indicates that the gains from protecting the environment are often high, and that the costs in foregone income are often modest if appropriate policies are adopted.' (World Bank 1992:1) The gains from 'win–win' opportunities on the one hand, and only modest costs on the other, could on this analysis result in both a 3.5 times rise in world output and 'better environmental protection, cleaner air and water, and the virtual elimination of acute poverty.' (ibid:2) Such quotes illustrate a clear perception of the dominance of sector A and B opportunities, but the World Bank's report ends its overview with a classic statement envisaging sector C type costs: 'Accepting the challenge to accelerate development in an environmentally-responsible manner will involve substantial shifts in policies and priorities and will be costly. Failing to accept it will be more costly still. '(ibid:24)

The evidence to date would seem to bear out the World Bank's predominantly optimistic position. Pearce (1993) reviews a number of studies and projections which show relatively little impact on growth from environmental policy. An OECD study from 1985 reports:

> *The main conclusion which emerges from these results is that the macroeconomic effect of environmental policies is relatively small.... Furthermore, it is important to recall that these small effects were registered during a period (the 1970s) of peak pollution control activity, when efforts were directed not only at limiting ongoing pollution, but also at cleaning up the backlog caused by the neglect of the environment during the 1950s and 1960s.*
>
> OECD 1985, quoted in Pearce 1993:103

However, environmental policy in the future is going to have to be far more stringent than that in the past, which by no means succeeded in curbing environmental degradation, and given that the past legacy of environmental damage has by no means been adequately addressed. Brown et al (1993) identifies the US as facing clean-up costs of $750 billion for hazardous waste sites and $200 billion for nuclear weapons manufacturing facilities (Brown et al 1993:10) Such clean-up problems face all industrial countries to some extent; the costs involved are almost certainly sector C (constraining growth) rather than sector B costs.

Jorgenson and Wilcoxen (1990) found that environmental regulation reduced the US GDP growth rate by an average of 0.19 per cent pa between 1973 and 1985. Jorgenson also finds that the increase in energy prices in the 1970s was a major cause of the reduction in US GDP growth in the 1970s and 1980s (Jorgenson 1990:85). A similar decline in GDP growth, projected into the future, emerges from several models of the effects of introducing a carbon tax (reviewed in Boero et al 1991). In the nine studies surveyed, GDP losses ranged from 1 per cent by 2050 to 7.5 per cent by 2075.

Not all carbon tax simulations show a negative effect on GDP of applying such a tax, however, Barker et al's (1993) modelling of both and EC- and OECD-wide tax shows a small GDP increase in both cases. Ingham and Ulph (1991) similarly find that imposing a carbon tax leads to an increase in economic activity. The Barker et al result is due to the way the revenues from the tax are recycled back through the economy by offsetting reductions in VAT or income tax. Pearce (1991:940) has written of the possibility of achieving a 'double dividend' by replacing distortionary taxes (eg on labour or capital) with a carbon tax which is itself correcting the distortion from an environmental externality. In the Ingham and Ulph result 'in the short run output falls, and this induces considerable scrapping of equipment which leads to lower costs and prices, and output being higher in the longer term than in the case where demand is determined exogenously. In the extreme case, output growth rises from 2 to 4.4 per cent.' (Ingham and Ulph 1991:198–9)

Several modelling projections have also found negligible negative effects on GDP from future environmental policies. Thus Barker and Lewney (1991) have combined a carbon tax designed to reduce UK CO_2 emissions back to 1990 levels by 2005, a fourfold rise in industrial pollution abatement expenditures by 2000, and an intensified water clean-up policy. This reduces GDP in 2010 by less than 1 per cent. Similarly the Netherlands National Environmental Policy Plan (NEPP) projected the decrease of a number of emissions and waste discharges by between 70 and 100 per cent, and a doubling of environmental expenditures: by 2010 GDP had grown to 95 per cent above its 1985 level, in contrast to a 98 per cent growth with a base case of unchanged policy. These effects are very small compared to the environmental benefits achieved.

It is not easy to judge between these different projections of different macroeconomic impacts from environmental policies. First there is the validity of the models themselves. Far-reaching environmental policies of the kind envisaged in NEPP are likely to make structural changes to the economy, perhaps invalidating the econometric relationships from which the projections are derived.

Second, with regard to the carbon tax, it is possible that complementary government initiatives to encourage energy conservation and efficiency, and investment in clean energy technologies, would cost relatively little and significantly increase the energy elasticities on the basis of which the costs of a carbon tax are calculated, thereby reducing the cost of achieving any given CO_2 reduction target. Jackson (1991) provides evidence that the energy market is far from perfect. He finds that out of 17 technological possibilities for the reduction of CO_2 emissions, eight could be implemented at negative cost on the basis of current prices, saving a total of 165 million tonnes of CO_2 per year by 2005, or 24 per cent of UK 1991 emissions. On this analysis the UK could exceed the Toronto target for CO_2 emissions (20 per cent reduction from 1988 levels by 2005) *and* save money.

Whatever the balance of empirical evidence, both optimists and pessimists accept the foregoing analysis about the environmental effects of continuing present patterns of economic growth. Both acknowledge that reducing the material intensity or environmental impact of economic activity is possible. In this they both differ from certain fundamentalist Greens, eg Irvine 1990. Moreover, both argue that this will only happen if proactive governmental policies are put in place, an opinion which differs from that of free market economists such as Simon (1981), Simon and Khan (1984) and Bernstam (1991).

The major difference between the two views is that Anderson and the World Bank project win–win scenarios up to about 2030, in which strong environmental policy protects the environment, but helps growth as much as it hinders it, so that growth proceeds largely unconstrained. Meadows et al agree that growth may be able to continue until 2030, but only at the cost of great environmental degradation, which precipitates catastrophe soon after. They perceive that effective environmental policy will constrain growth.

Both sides, however, agree that without effective environmental policy, growth will cause appalling environmental damage before 2030. It would seem sensible therefore to concentrate on this consensus in order to get such policy implemented whether one is optimistic or pessimistic about the impacts on growth or the longer term forecast. There is little sign of such implementation at present. The continuing existence of, for example, financial subsidies that are grossly economically inefficient as well as environmentally damaging, highlights the great danger that it will prove politically impossible to realize in practice the opportunities for environmentally sustainable growth, so that environmental degradation will proceed until such growth becomes impossible.

CONCLUSIONS

It is clearly theoretically possible for GDP growth and environmental sustainability to be compatible. Environmental sustainability is affected by the economy's throughput of energy and materials; on a finite planet there is obviously a limit to this throughput. GDP measures value-added. The relationship between value-added and material throughput is variable and can be altered by structural economic change, substitution between factor inputs, and more efficient use of the same input. These changes are obviously crucially dependent on technological developments.

Once environmental sustainability has been achieved, its maintenance requires a rate of diminution in environmental impact per unit of value-added (environmental impact coefficient or environmental intensity) that is the same as the rate of growth of that value-added. Achieving environmental sustainability in the first place, especially with projected rates of population growth, calls for a substantial one-off improvement in environmental intensity. Putting the two together suggests that, if world GDP growth is to be maintained at modest levels over the next 50 years, the environmental sustainability is to be achieved in the same period, technology must reduce environmental intensity overall by nine tenths.

This is a formidable challenge. Those who believe it to be a practical possibility are united with those who do not in arguing that it can only be approached by determined government policy. The market has an important role, but it will need to be informed, stimulated and guided by market-based and regulatory instruments emanating from government. While the introduction of these instruments will be in the interest of greater social welfare in the long term, they will run counter to currently powerful vested interests. Their introduction will depend on the existence of democratic political institutions sufficiently robust to legislate for the wider good.

Where these instruments involve changes to government policies that are economically inefficient as well as environmentally damaging, they can promote GDP growth as well as environmental sustainability at zero cost. Where they require investments for environmental sustainability, sometimes these investments will also yield a net financial return; sometimes the environmental gain will only be achievable at net financial cost. Whether GDP growth (as currently calculated) as well as environmental sustainability will emerge from the application of these instruments depends on the relative availability of 'win–win' to 'trade-off' opportunities.

The empirical evidence to date is not decisive on this point. Past environmental policies do not seem to have had undue negative impact on GDP growth, but they are an unreliable guide to the more stringent policies needed in the future. Past policies have tended to be based on regulatory instruments, which are theoretically less efficient than market-based mechanisms, but it remains to be seen whether such mechanisms can either be introduced at the required level or will work as efficiently as predicted. There are many examples at the micro-level of 'win–win' possibilities for individual companies or across whole policy areas (eg energy efficiency/conservation, rural development), but again, it remains to be seen whether they can be realized economy-wide in practice.

The compatibility or otherwise of GDP growth and sustainability has the following implications for welfare. If they prove compatible, and both growth and environmental quality are higher than in the base case, then welfare unequivocally rises (assuming no negative impacts on welfare's other components). If moves towards sustainability decrease the rate of growth but this remains positive, then welfare again unequivocally rises, but may fall relative to the unconstrained base case, depending on the relative weights in welfare of the environmental gains and the production foregone. If moves towards sustainability decrease the level of GDP, then welfare may rise or fall, again depending on the relative weights in welfare of the environmental gains and the production foregone. If inadequate environmental policy means that environmental degradation continues, and this causes the GDP level to decline, then welfare unequivocally declines. This, of course, is the condition of unsustainability.

To summarize, it is clear that as far as environmentally sustainable GDP growth is concerned, there is everything to play for but the going will be exceptionally tough. In the short term it is likely that it will be easier to achieve GDP growth than to start moving systematically towards environmental sustainability. Giving such a move top short-term priority is probably, therefore, a necessary condition to achieving environmentally sustainable GDP growth in the future. It is certain that the currently dominant business-as-usual approach, going for GDP growth with a few environmental add-ons, will not address the gathering environmental crisis, some evidence for which was presented at the beginning of this paper. The most open question of all is whether the political will can be found to go beyond this minimalist approach before the scale of environmental disruption makes rational response increasingly difficult.

APPENDIX

Calculations of required reductions in environmental intensity to achieve sustainability, using the Ehrlich equation, $I = PCT$.

Where subscript 1 indicates the quantity now, subscript 2 indicates the quantity in 50 years' time; superscript 1 indicates high income countries, superscript 2 low and middle income countries (the 'Third World'), according to the World Bank's classification and using data from World Bank 1992, and superscript T indicates the whole world. Using the assumptions for population growth and sustainability, we have:

$I_1 = 2 \times I_2$ for sustainability

$P_1^T = P_1^1 + P_1^2$

$P_2^T = P_2^1 = P_2^2 = 2 \times P_1^T$;   population growth $= P_1^T$

$P_2^1 = P_1^1 + 0.05 \times P_1^T$; $P_2^2 = P_1^2 + 0.95 \times P_1^T$

$P_1^1 = 816.4$ million; $P_1^2 = 4146$ million; $P_1^T = 4962$ million (exc former USSR)

$P_2^1 = 1064$ million; $P_2^2 = 8860$ million; $P_2^T = 9924$ million

$C_1^1 = \$19,590$; $C_1^2 = \$840$

$P_1^1 C_1^1 = \$15.99 \times 10^{12}$; $P_1^2 C_1^2 = \$3.48 \times 10^{12}$; $(P_1 C_1)^T = \$19.47 . 10^{12}$

$I = (PC)^T . T$

Where $(PC)^T = P^1 C^1 + P^2 C^2 = $ Total global consumption.

Using this formulation and the earlier assumptions about population and sustainable environmental impact, the environmental implications of five different development paths can be analysed.

1. No growth in population or consumption:
T must be reduced by 50%

Growth in population, and, with regard to consumption:

2. No growth in consumption: $C_2^1 = C_1^1, C_2^2 = C_1^2$

$P_2^1 C_2^1 = 1064 \times 19590 \times 10^6 = \$20.8 \times 10^{12}$

$P_2^2 C_2^2 = 8860 \times 840 \times 10^6 = \$7.44 \times 10^{12}$

$(P_2 C_2)^T = P_2^1 C_2^1 + P_2^2 C_2^2 = \$28.2 \times 10^{12}$

$T_2 = 1/2 \times (P_1 C_1)^T / (P_2 C_2)^T \times T_1 = 1/2 \times (19.47)/(28.2) \times T_1 = 0.35 \times T_1$

So T must be reduced by 65%.

3 Growth only in the South: $C_2^1 = C_1^1, C_2^2 = 4 \times C_1^2$

$C_2^2 = \$3360$

$P_2^1 C_2^1 = 1064 \times 19590 \times 10^6 = \$20.8 \times 10^{12}$

$P_2^2 C_2^2 = 8860 \times 3360 \times 10^6 = \$29.8 \times 10^{12}$

$(P_2 C_2)T = P_2^1 C_2^1 + P_2^2 C_2^2 = \$50.7 \times 10^{12}$

$T_2 = 1/2 \times (P_1 C_1)^T / (P_2 C_2)^T \times T_1 = 1/2 \ (19.47)/(50.7) \times T_1 + 0.19 \times T_1$

So T must be reduced by 81%

4. Growth only in the North: $C_2^1 = 4 \times C_1^1$, $C_2^2 = C_1^2$
$C_2^1 = \$78360$
$P_2^1 C_2^1 = 1064 \times 78360 \times 10^6 = \$83.4 \times 10^{12}$
$P_2^2 C_2^2 = 8860 \times 840 \times 10^6 = \$7.44 \times 10^{12}$
$(P_2^2 C_2^2)^T =- P_2^1 C_2^1 = P_2^2 C_2^2 = \$90.84 \times 10^{12}$
$T_2 = 1/2 \times (P_1 C_1)^T/(P_2 C_2)^T \times T_1 = 1/2 \times (19.47)/(90.84) \times T_1 = 0.11 \times T_1$

So T must be reduced by 89%

5. Growth in the North and South: $C_2^1 = 4 \times C_1^1$, $C_2^2 = 4 \times C_1^2$
$C_2^1 = \$78360$
$C_2^2 = \$3360$
$P_2^1 C_2^1 = 1064 \times 78360 \times 10^6 = \$83.4 \times 10^{12}$
$P_2^2 C_2^2 = 8860 \times 3360 \times 10^6 = \$29.8 \times 10^{12}$
$(P_2 C_2)T = P_2^1 C_2^1 + P_2^2 C_2^2 = \$113 \times 10^{12}$
$T_2 = 1/2 \times (P_1 C_1)^T/(P_2 C_2)^T \times T_1 = 1/2 \times (19.47)/(113) \times T_1 = 0.09 \times T_1$

So T must be reduced by 91%

REFERENCES

Ahmad, Y, El Serafy, S & Lutz, E (1989) *Environmental Accounting for Sustainable Development* World Bank, Washington DC

Anderson, D (1992) 'Economic Growth and the Environment' Background Paper for the *World Development Report 1992*, World Bank, Washington DC

Ayres, R & Walter, J (1991) 'The Greenhouse Effect: Damages, Costs and Abatement' *Environmental and Resource Economics* vol 1, pp 237–70

Barker, T & Lewney, R (1991) 'A Green Scenario for the UK Economy' in T Barker (ed) (1991) *Green Futures for Economic Growth: Britain in 2010* Cambridge Econometrics, Cambridge

Barker, T, Baylis, S & Madsen, P (1993) 'A UK Carbon-Energy Tax: the Macroeconomic Effects' *Energy Policy* vol 21, no 3 (March), pp 296–308

Beckerman, W (1974) *In Defence of Economic Growth* Jonathan Cape, London

Beckerman, W (1991) 'Global Warming: a Sceptical Economic Assessment' in D Helm (ed) (1991) *Economic Policy Towards the Environment* Blackwell, Oxford, pp 52–85

Bernstam, M (1991) *The Wealth of Nations and the Environment* Institute for Economic Affairs, London

Boero, G, Clarke, R & Winters, L (1991) *The Macroeconomic Consequences of Controlling Greenhouse Gases: a Survey* HMSO, London

Broome, J (1992) *Counting the Cost of Global Warming* White Horse Press, Cambridge

Brown, L et al (1991) *State of the World 1991* Earthscan, London

Brown, L, Flavin, C & Kane, H (1992a) *Vital Signs* W W Norton, New York/London

Brown, L et al (1992b) *State of the World 1992* Earthscan, London

Brown, L et al (1993) *State of the World 1993* Earthscan, London

Business International (1990) *Managing the Environment: the Greening of European Business* Business International, London

CEC (Commission of the European Communities), 1992a Proposal for a Resolution of the Council of the European Communities, *Towards Sustainability: a European Community Programme of Policy and Action in Relation to the Environment and Sustainable Development*, vol 1, Commission of the European Communities, Brussels

CEC (Commission of the European Communities), 1992b Executive Summary, *Towards Sustainability: a European Community Programme of Policy and Action in Relation to the Environment and Sustainable Development*, vol 2, Commission of the European Communities, Brussels

Chambers, R (1992) 'Sustainable livelihoods: the poors' reconciliation of environment and development' in P Ekins & M Max-Neef (eds) (1992) *Real-Life Economics: Understanding Wealth Creation* Routledge, London, pp 214–29

Cline, W (1991) 'Scientific Basis for the Greenhouse Effect' *Economic Journal* 101 (July 1991), 904–19

Cline, W (1992) *The Economics of Global Warming* Institute for International Economics, Washington DC

Conroy, C & Litvinoff, M (eds) (1988) *The Greening of Aid* Earthscan, London

Daly, H (1992) 'From Empty World to Full World Economics' in R Goodland, H Daly & S El Serafy (1992) *Population, Technology and Lifestyle: the Transition to Sustainability*, Island Press, Washington DC

Ehrlich, P & Ehrlich, A (1990) *The Population Explosion* Hutchinson, London

Ekins, P (1993) '"Limits to Growth"' and "Sustainable Development": Grappling with Ecological Realities' *Ecological Economics*, vol 8, pp 269–88

Ekins, P (1994a, forthcoming) 'The Rationale for Adjusting the National Accounts for the Environment' in W Van Dieren (ed) *Towards a Sustainable National Income*, a Report to the Club of Rome

Ekins, P (1994b, forthcoming) 'The environmental sustainability of economic processes: a framework for analysis' in J van den Bergh & J van der Straaten (eds) *Concepts, Methods and Policy for Sustainable Development: Critiques and New Approaches* Island Press, Washington DC

Goodland, R & Daly, H (1992) 'Ten Reasons Why Northern Income Growth is not the Solution to Southern Poverty' in R Goodland, H Daly & S El Serafy (1992) *Population, Technology and Lifestyle: the Transition to Sustainability* Island Press, Washington DC

Harrison, P (1987) *The Greening of Africa* Paladin, London

Holdren, J & Ehrlich, P (1974) 'Human Population and the Global Environment' *American Scientist* vol 62 (May-June), pp 282–92

Houghton, J, Jenkins, G & Ephraums, J (eds) (1990) *Climate Change: the IPCC Scientific Assessment* Oxford University Press, Oxford

Hueting, R (1986) 'An Economic Scenario for a Conserver Economy' in P Ekins (ed) (1986) *The Living Economy: a New Economics in the Making* Routledge & Kegan Paul, London, pp 242–56

Hueting, R Bosch, P & de Boer, B (1991) *Methodology for Calculating Sustainable National Income* Netherlands Central Bureau of Statistics, Voorburg

Ingham, A & Ulph, A (1991) 'Carbon Taxes and the UK Manufacturing Sector' in F Dietz, F Van der Ploeg & Van der Straaten (eds) (1991) *Environmental Policy and the Economy* Elsevier, Amsterdam, pp 127–239

Irvine, S (1990) 'No Growth in a Finite World' *New Statesman and Society*, 23 November

Jackson, T (1991) 'Least-Cost Greenhouse Planning' *Energy Policy*, January/ February, pp 35–46

Jacobs, M (1991) *The Green Economy* Pluto Press, London

Jenkins, T (1990) *Future Harvests* Council for the Protection of Rural England, London and World Wide Fund for Nature, Godalming, Surrey

Jorgenson, D (1990) *Productivity and Economic Growth* Harvard Institute of
 Economic Research, Harvard University, Cambridge MA
Jorgenson, D & Wilcoxen, P (1990) 'Environmental Regulation & US Economic
 Growth' *RAND Journal of Economics*, vol 21, no 2, Summer
Kosmo, M (1987) *Money to Burn? the High Cost of Energy Subsidies* World
 Resources Institute, Washington DC
Lecomber, R (1975) *Economic Growth versus the Environment*, Macmillan, London
Leggett, J (ed) (1990) *Global Warming: the Greenhouse Report* Oxford University
 Press, Oxford/New York
Leipert, C (1989) 'Social Costs of the Economic Process and National Accounts:
 the Example of Defensive Expenditures' *The Journal of Interdisciplinary
 Economics*, vol 3, no 1, pp 27–46
Lutz, E (ed) (1993) *Toward Improved Accounting for the Environment* World Bank,
 Washington DC
McCormick, J (1989) *Acid Earth* Earthscan, London
Meadows, D Meadows, D, Randers, J & Behrens, W (1972) *The Limits to Growth*
 Universe Books, New York
Meadows, D Meadows, D Randers J (1992) *Beyond the Limits* Earthscan, London
Mishan, E (1967) *The Costs of Economic Growth* Staples Press, London
Mishan, E (1977) *The Economic Growth Debate: an Assessment* George Allen &
 Unwin, London
MOHPPE (Ministry of Housing, Physical Planning and Environment) (1988) *To
 Choose or to Lose: National Environmental Policy Plan* MOHPPE, The Hague
Myers, N (1986) 'Tackling Mass Extinction of Species: a Great Creative Challenge'
 XXVIth Horace M Albright Lecture in Conservation, University of California,
 Berkeley
Nordhaus, W (1991) 'To slow or not to slow: the economics of the greenhouse
 effect' *Economic Journal*, 101 (July 1991), pp 920–37
OECD (Organisation for Economic Cooperation and Development) (1985) *The
 Macroeconomic Impact of Environmental Expenditure*, OECD, Paris
OECD (Organisation for Economic Cooperation and Development) (1991a) *The
 State of the Environment* OECD, Paris
OECD (Organisation for Economic Cooperation and Development) (1991b)
 Environmental Indicators OECD, Paris
Pangare, G & Pangare, V (1992) *From Poverty to Plenty: the Story of Rahegan Siddhi*
 Indian National Trust for Art and Cultural Heritage, New Delhi
Pearce, D (1991) 'The Role of Carbon Taxes in Adjusting to Global Warming'
 Economic Journal vol 101, pp 938–48
Pearce, D (1993) *Economic Values and the Natural World* Earthscan, London,
 pp 95–104 (Appendix 1: 'Environmental Policy as a Constraint on Economic
 Growth)
Pearce, D & Atkinson G (1992) 'Are National Economies Sustainable?: Measuring
 Sustainable Development' CSERGE Discussion Paper GEC 92-11, University
 College London
Pezzey, J (1992) *Sustainable Development Concepts: an Economic Analysis* World
 Bank Environment Paper no 2, World Bank, Washington DC
Repetto, R (1985) *Paying the Price: Pesticide Subsidies in Developing Countries* World
 Resources Institute Wasington DC
Repetto, R (19865) *Skimming the Water: Rent-Seeking and the Performance of Public
 Irrigation Systems* World Resources Institute, Washington DC
Repetto, R (1988) *The Forest for the Trees? Government Policies and the Misuse of
 Forest Resources* World Resources Institute, Washington DC
RS & NAS (Royal Society & National Academy of Sciences) (1992) *Population
 Growth, Resource Consumption and a Sustainable World* Royal Society, London

and National Academy of Sciences, New York

Sadik, N (1991) *The State of the World Population 1991* UNFPA (UN Fund for Population Activities), New York

Schmidheiny, S (with the Business Council for Sustainable Development) (1992) *Changing Course: a Global Business Perspective on Development and the Environment* MIT Press, Cambridge MA

Simon, J (1981) *The Ultimate Resource* Martin Robertson, Oxford

Simon, J & Kahn, H (1984) *The Resourceful Earth: A Response to Global 2000* Basil Blackwell, Oxford

Solow, A (1991) 'Is There a Global Warming Problem?' in R Dornbusch & J Poterba (eds) *Global Warming: Economic Policy Responses* MIT Press, Cambridge MA, pp 7 –28

South Commission (1990) *The Challenge to the South: the Report of the South Commission* Oxford University Press, Oxford/New York

Tinbergen, J & Hueting, R (1993) 'GNP and Market Prices' in R Goodland, H Daly & S El Serafy (eds) (1993) *Population, Technology and Lifestyle: the Transition to Sustainability* Island Press, Washington DC, pp 52-62

Turner, K (1992) *Speculations on Weak and Strong Sustainability* CSERGE Working Paper GEC 92-26, CSERGE, University of East Anglia, Norwich

WCED (World Commission on Environment and Development) (1987) *Our Common Future* (The Brundtland Report) Oxford University Press, Oxford/New York

Woodwell, G (1990) 'The Effects of Global Warming' in Leggett 1990, pp 116–132

World Bank (1992) *World Development Report 1992* Oxford University Press, Oxford/New York

WRI (World Resources Institute) (with UNDP and UNEP) (1990) *World Resources, 1990–91* Oxford University Press, Oxford/New York

WRI (World Resources Institute) (with UNDP and UNEP) (1992) *World Resources, 1992–93* Oxford University Press, Oxford/New York

Chapter Three

Northern Growth and Environmental Constraints

Andrew Glyn

INTRODUCTION

It is easy to understand why the early 1970s brought predictions that growth in the North would be limited by resource constraints. Over the previous decade use of both energy and steel was growing at more than 5 per cent per year in the OECD. If these growth rates had continued, resource use would have doubled by 1987 and quadrupled by 2000. Such patterns of growth in the North, which were so profligate with resources, seemed evidently unsustainable. In the event by 1990 energy consumed was only 17 per cent higher than in 1973, and steel use was down by around one quarter. Section I of this chapter outlines how the pattern and rate of growth has shifted in the North since the early 1970s so that demands on resources are no longer increasing nearly so fast. Most attempts at modelling Northern pressure on the environment, notably in the context of global warming, assume that the rate of growth will slip down somewhat further in the decades up to the middle of the next century. Examination of the likely pattern of structural and demographic change in the North later in the chapter suggests that these projections may be too optimistic and that growth rates could well decline to something close to zero. If current growth in the North is putting rather little extra pressure on resources, and if growth rates seem destined to fall substantially further, then the task of reducing environmental impact in order to ensure sustainability (see previous chapter) is less demanding, supporting estimates that the costs to Northern GDP of overcoming these pressures will be relatively small

Such a perspective leaves aside the question of growth in the South, however. The final part of this chapter notes that attempts to model global pressure on the environment typically assume very little or no 'catch-up' of Southern incomes towards Northern levels; it is taken for granted that

Table 3.1 Resource use in the OECD, 1960-89

Average annual % changes	Energy Total	Per capita	Steel Total	Per capita	Non-ferrous metals Total	Per capita
1960–73	5.1	4.0	5.3	4.2	5.9	5.0
1973–79	1.5	0.7	−1.4	−2.2	0.9	0.1
1979–89	0.7	−0.1	−2.2	−2.9	0.1	−0.6

Sources: Energy OECD *Energy Balances, 1960–79, 1980–90*; Metals Tilton, 1990–, OECD *Historical Statistics*, 1990
Notes: Non-ferrous metals refers to unweighted average of five metals. Steel and non-ferrous metals final period is 1979-87. Energy refers to Total Primary Energy Supplied.

the existing gross disparities in income levels persist in the very long term. If, however, the South made really substantial inroads into these disparities, then pressure on resources would be much increased and the costs of overcoming the resulting problems (pollution, higher costs of resource extraction and so forth) would be correspondingly greater. This scenario is then applied to the large body of work dealing with costs of overcoming global warming. It is argued that serious catch-up of the South to the North would inevitably increase the restraint required in Northern carbon emissions. Like many environmental problems this could in principle be solved without great cost by new technology – in this case the development of carbon-free substitute fuels. But if such technology proved expensive, then the generalization to the South of Northern consumption levels would mean much greater costs to the North of measures to contain global warming. Moreover slow growth in the North would be an unfavourable backdrop against which to gain acceptance that these costs should be absorbed. The conclusion suggests the importance of beginning to think now of how the North could adjust to stable or even falling levels of consumption.

NORTHERN GROWTH, STRUCTURAL CHANGE AND RESOURCE USE

This section records how the pressures on the use of resources deriving from economic growth have diminished in the North over the past two decades. For analysing scarcity and global environmental impact total use of resources is the key indicator; when examining the distribution of resources between North and South this must be supplemented with resource use per capita. Table 3.1 presents some basic series for energy and metals use in the North.

After 1973 the growth rate of energy and metals use dropped very sharply. By the 1980s per capita usage of metals was falling, and was stabilized in the case of energy, compared to increases of 4–5 per cent per year during the 1960s. Similar trends are apparent for other materials; for example per capita use of cement began to decline in the early 1970s (Goldemburg et al 1987) after steady increase earlier.

Table 3.2 OECD energy use and energy intensity, 1960–90

Average annual changes (%)	Energy use	GDP	Energy intensity
1960–73	5.1	4.8	0.3
1979–90	0.7	2.8	−2.1
changes	−4.4	−2.0	−2.4

Source: as Table 3.1

The stabilization, or even fall in input use per capita occurred while per capita incomes continued to increase (by 1.9 per cent per year since 1973). This suggests that the slowdown in growth after 1973 was only partly responsible and that changes in the pattern of that growth should be examined as well.

Resource Intensity

A conventional 'decomposition' of resource use (R) separates out the influences of GDP and resource intensity (R/GDP):

$$R = R/GDP \times GDP.$$

Applying this to changes over time, the growth in energy use can be split into the growth of output and the growth in energy intensity. Table 3.2 shows that just over half the change in the trend in energy use in the 1980s as compared to the 'Golden Age of Capitalism' (1950s and 1960s), represented the change in the trend in energy intensity. Energy intensity fell sharply after 1973; declines of around 2 per cent per year after 1973 were very common in OECD countries, including those with high (eg Belgium), middling (eg the US, UK and Germany), and low (eg Japan) energy intensity at the end of the golden age; rises in energy intensity after 1973 were exceptional (Portugal, New Zealand, Greece and Spain).

It might be expected that the improvement in the trend in energy/materials intensity was closely connected with 'deindustrial-ization' – a switch away from resource using industry towards services. Industry (together with its associated transport) is about eight times as energy intensive as services and a switch of 1 per cent of GDP from industry to services would reduce energy demand by about 1 per cent of total energy use.[1]

---

1 Industry contributes about one half as much as services to GDP (reckoned in current prices), and together with associated transport of goods they are responsible for respectively 40 per cent and 10 per cent of energy use in the North. Ignoring (relatively insignificant) agriculture a shift of 1 per cent of GDP from industry to services implies a 3.3 per cent fall in industrial output and a 1.7 per cent increase in services output. This will imply a 1.3 per cent fall in total energy demand (3.3 x 0.4) from industry and a 0.17 per cent rise from services (1.7 x 0.1). So total energy demand falls by 1.1 per cent, rounded to 1 per cent. A 1 per cent faster growth rate in services than in industry (implying that services growing 0.33 per cent faster than GDP as a whole and industry 0.67 per cent less) implies only one fifth as large a shift and would therefore reduce total energy demand by 0.2 per cent.

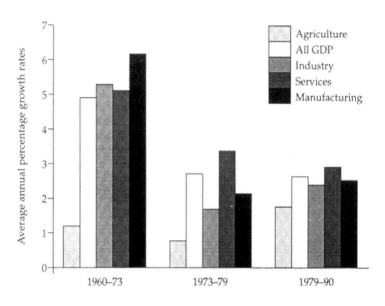

Source: OECD Historical Statistics

Figure 3.1 *Sectoral output growth, OECD, 1960–1990*

While industrial output grew very slowly between 1973 and 1979, as investment spending stagnated, since 1979 its shortfall behind GDP growth has been small and accounted for by the decreasing importance of net exports of manufactures to the rest of the world (Figure 3.1 shows sectoral growth rates for the OECD since 1973). So 'deindustrialization' is a term properly applied to the structure of employment, not output. There has indeed been a sharp fall in the share of industrial employment (from 36.4 per cent of the total in 1973 to 29.6 per cent in 1990), but this overwhelmingly reflected faster productivity growth in industry than for the economy as a whole rather than slower output growth (Baumol et al 1989).

The shift in production from industry to services is relatively slight, therefore, and could account for only around a 0.1 per cent annual fall in overall energy intensity. So if structural change was important in explaining the break in the trend of input intensities after 1973 it must have operated largely at a more disaggregated level than captured by the notion of the 'service economy' – that is a switch away from heavy (materials and energy intensive) manufacturing towards 'lighter' sectors. The World Resources Institute believes that this has been important in relation to materials:

> *the demand for a wide range of materials, both traditional and modern, is no longer increasing in physical terms [per capita]. Both traditional and modern materials are being used more*

> *efficiently – for example through the development of higher strength or more durable products....Although materials substitution and increased efficiency of materials use are clearly contributing to the shift away from basic materials, today these factors are probably not as important as the saturation of markets for bulk materials and heavy consumer goods and the shifting of consumer preferences to products characterised by a higher ratio of value added to materials content.'*

> Goldemberg et al 1987:36–7

Energy used per unit of industrial output fell by about 2.6 per cent per year after 1973; here the OECD (1992b) suggested that 'efficiency gains [within individual industries] influenced energy intensity trends more than structural changes.' The pattern of decline over time is interesting; falls of 2 per cent per year between the Oil Shocks, 3.9 per cent per year 1979–86, but back to 1.3 per cent per year (the pre-1973 rate) after the oil price fall in 1986. This illustrates the build up of price-induced substitution, superimposed on quite marked underlying technological trends tending to reduce energy intensity in industry. The latter are reflected in estimates in the global warming models that 'autonomous' energy intensity (without changes in relative prices) will decline by 0.5 per cent to 1 per cent per year for the economy as a whole over the very long term (though the weak basis for quantitative prediction is generally admitted).

While use of materials takes place overwhelmingly within industry, this is less true of energy. Residential uses and private transport (about two thirds of total transport) each consume about 20 per cent of total energy directly (see Table 3.3). Per capita energy use for residential purposes has declined by 0.8 per cent per year (and twice as fast per unit of floorspace). Energy use for transport has grown by 1.8 per cent per year since 1973, a per capita increase of 1 per cent per year; transport accounts for all the increase in OECD energy use since 1973.

Output and Productivity growth

The previous sub-section showed that the slowdown in output growth accounted for nearly half of the decline in the growth of energy use in the

Table 3.3 OECD energy uses

	Share of total 1990	*% Annual growth rate per capita, 1973–90*
Industry	33.6	–1.2
Residential	17.9	–0.8
Commercial/public	10.6	0.4
Transport	31.3	1.0
Total		–0.3

Source: as Table 3.1

1980s. Perhaps surprisingly, given the upward trend in unemployment, none of this reflected slower growth of total labour input. Total hours worked in the North actually rose faster in the 1980s than in the 1960s as employment growth was maintained and hours worked per worker fell more slowly (0.4 per cent per year after 1979 as compared to nearly 1 per cent per year previously). Thus all the slowdown in output growth (and consequent effects on resource use) reflected the productivity slowdown (nearly 2 per cent annual growth of hourly productivity for the period 1979–90 as compared to nearly 5 per cent per year for the period 1960–73).

There has been an enormous literature on, and little agreement on the causes of, the productivity slowdown (see Englander and Mittelstadt 1988). But Nordhaus' conclusion (1992) that resource depletion, including pollution reduction, played a subsidiary role (he estimates the effect at about 0.25 per cent per year) is widely accepted. To this direct effect should be added the impact of the oil and materials price increases in the early 1970s and 1980s in exacerbating profit squeezes and inflation. These in turn inhibited capital accumulation both directly and via the deflationary policies which resulted. But resource price increases were only one contributory factor to the turbulence of this period, arguably less important than the enhanced economic power of labour as a result of the long-boom (Marglin and Schor 1990). Thus the conclusion that resource costs and prices were not the dominant cause of the productivity slowdown is still plausible when indirect effects are included.

Evidence of Resource Scarcities

Even if resource scarcities have not played the major role in the growth slowdown it is important to have some perspective on their magnitude. The prices of materials and energy, relative to the implicit deflator for GDP say, provide evidence of cost trends.[2] There is general agreement in a range of studies (Barnett and Morse 1963, Barnett 1979, Slade 1982, Baumol et al 1989, Nordhaus 1992), that relative prices of resources generally trended downwards until the 1970s (timber being an exception); the early 1970s saw sharp upward movements (relative to the prices of manufactures), succeeded by large falls in the 1980s (one half for petrol, food, one third for coal and agricultural commodities and around one quarter for metals and timber). By 1991 petroleum and timber prices in real terms were still well above (double and 50 per cent higher respectively) the levels of the 1960s, whereas agricultural commodities (both food and other) were only half the level of the 1960s and metals and minerals about two thirds of the earlier level.

Such prices give information on scarcity at a world level. But what of Northern production itself? Here total factor productivity (TFP) is a simple indicator of the real costs (in terms of capital and labour inputs) of

---

2 If relative factor incomes in extraction and elsewhere did not shift, then output prices of extractive industries relative to other products would show how total factor productivity (TFP) in extraction had moved in relation to TFP overall.

resource extraction. Data for the US show rising TFP (and thus declining real input costs) in the extractive industries up to the 1960s (Barnett and Morse 1963, Barnett 1979). But the increases slowed down in the 1960s and after 1970 mining TFP declined (Kendrick and Grossman 1980), by around 5 per cent pa from 1973–83 (Englander and Mittelstadt 1988). Imports may limit productivity declines and thus the extent of increasing real costs of domestic production, as in Ricardo's discussion of the Corn Laws; but imports appear not to have been a major factor in the US up to the 1950s (Barnett and Morse 1963). Thereafter the huge increase in oil imports played an important role; labour productivity in natural gas and petroleum mining rose by about 4 per cent pa up to 1973, fell at 9 per cent pa from 1973–82 as the oil price increases stimulated domestic production and then increased by 3 per cent pa for 1982–89 (Nordhaus 1992).

The US is an interesting case because it comprises such a substantial share of Northern production and because it is thought of as a resource rich country. Data for other OECD countries (Englander and Mittelstadt) suggest that TFP declines in mining were general over the period 1973–83, with the exception of countries benefiting from North Sea Oil.

Despite this evidence of scarcity *within* the North, the slowdown of growth in the world economy and opening up of reserves in other parts of the world has held at bay or reversed the symptoms of global scarcities which characterized the early 1970s. Nordhaus' conclusion that the evidence does not indicate that the 'major appropriable resources have taken a major turn towards scarcity during the last century' (1992:28) seems justified. But the importance of imports of fuel and materials into the North must be underlined – they still represented some 1.5 per cent of OECD GDP in 1990 despite the generally low prices described above (in 1974 the figure was 3.6 per cent). If the South achieved its aspiration of industrializing to Northern levels, where would be the hinterland which would supply cheap energy and materials?

LONG-RUN GROWTH IN THE NORTH

The pattern of Northern growth since 1973 appears much less threatening to the environment than that of the golden age. Further reassurance comes from findings (Shafik and Bandyopadhyay 1992, Holtz-Eakin and Selden 1992, and Grosmann 1993) that the income elasticity of pollution generally declines with per capita GDP and even becomes negative in a number of cases where higher incomes generate financeable demands for effective pollution control policies. Nevertheless if growth could be expected to accelerate sharply back to golden age rates there would be recurring worries about resource availability, the extent of emission cutbacks necessary to contain global warming and so forth.[3]

---

3 Holtz-Eakin and Selden (1992) find a diminishing marginal propensity to emit CO_2 which they extrapolate to suggest declining emissions after per capita income reaches $35,000; but this is more than 50 per cent above the US level and they admit that ' within the sample we observe only a stabilization of emissions at best'

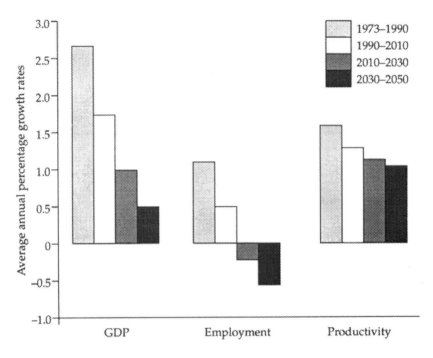

Source: see text

Figure 3.2 *OECD output projections, 1973–2050*

Far from assuming faster Northern growth some further slowdown is usually built into long-term assessments of environmental impacts such as global warming. Thus the OECD Model Comparisons project assumed that OECD growth would decline from 2.7 per cent per year 1979–90 to 1.5 per cent per year 2025–2050 (Dean and Hoeller 1992 Table A2), whereas Cline (1992 Table 7.2) assumes the decline will be to 1.2 per cent per year. These projections are typically presented without much discussion. Here we examine likely trends in the population and in the industrial structure which confirm the likelihood of a distinct slowdown in Northern growth. Firstly, population growth is expected to decline and the proportion of population of working age to fall considerably. Second, the continued shift in the employment structure towards services, where productivity grows slowly, will tend to reduce average productivity growth. In combination they actually suggest a greater slowdown than is commonly assumed.

The projections for OECD output growth shown in Figure 3.2 are based on the following assumptions about labour productivity growth within each sector, the pattern of output growth and the growth of labour input:

1. Labour productivity growth in each sector (agriculture, industry and services) continues at the rates observed over the period 1973–90 (3.8 per cent, 2.2 per cent and 0.8 per cent pa respectively);
2. Agricultural output grows in line with population while industrial

output grows slightly slower than GDP and services output slightly faster;[4]
3. Employment growth is built up from OECD projections of total population, and of the ratio of population of working age to total population, together with assumptions that the post-1979 trends continue for the ratio of employment to population of working age and average hours worked.

These assumptions generate a slowdown in GDP growth from 2.7 per cent per year during 1973–90 to 0.5 per cent per year for 2030–2050. The first two assumptions imply that the shift of employment from industry (and less importantly agriculture) continues. By 2050 the share of industry has shrunk by more than one half and provides jobs for only 14 per cent of those in work as compared to 29.7 per cent in 1990 (services' share rises from 65 per cent to 85 per cent). As in the past, the main force for the swing out of industry is its much faster labour productivity growth, with slower output growth playing a subsidiary role. The increasing share of services employment, where productivity is assumed to continue growing more slowly, pulls average productivity growth down, from 1.6 per cent per year for 1973–90 to 1.0 per cent per year for 2030–2050. Thus of the 2.2 per cent points decline in the projected growth rate of GDP, 0.6 per cent points, or around one quarter, flows from the impact of structural change on average productivity growth.

The remainder of the slowdown derives from declining growth of labour input. Indeed employment growth declines from 1.1 per cent per annum for 1973–90 to –0.6 per cent per year during 2030–50.[5] Figure 3.3 shows the components of this decline; population growth slips from 0.6 per cent per year during 1973–90 to a decline of 0.1 per cent per year for 2030–2050. The further implication of OECD's demographic assumptions is that the growth of population of working age declines much faster – from 0.9 per cent per year in 1973–1990 to –0.8 per cent per year for 2030–2050. Employment is assumed to fall a little less fast than population of working age (bringing the average employment rate to 76 per cent in 2050, still below the levels achieved in Sweden and Denmark in 1990).[6]

Thus it is the decline in population of working age which drives the decline in labour input, which in turn explains more than two thirds of the projected decline in the growth rate. Since the decline in population of working age flows mainly from the increasing 'dependency ratio' (those

---

4 It is assumed that the elasticity of demand for industrial products with respect to per capita GDP is 0.8; this gives a differential between services and industrial output growth in 1990–2000 identical to that for 1979–90 which could be interpreted as implying either a continuation of the trend away from net exports of industrial products or that the pattern of demand within the North does shift slowly towards services. Over the whole period to 2050 services output grows 0.4 per cent per year faster than industry.
5 Turkey is excluded from the projections of OECD growth since it has a much lower level of per capita income and its much higher population growth (and agricultural sector) affects the OECD total substantially.
6 Hours of work are implicitly assumed to continue to fall at the recent rate in the projection on current sectoral productivity growth (per worker).

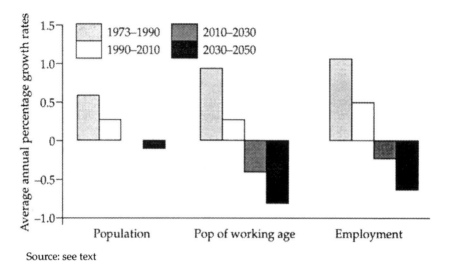

Source: see text

Figure 3.3 *OECD employment projections, 1973–2050*

under 16 and especially those over 65) rather than from slower total population growth, then the fall in per capita GDP growth is nearly as steep as for GDP as a whole (from 2.1 per cent per year in 1973–90 to 0.5 per cent per year during 2030–2050). This is important since funding expenditure on the environment may well be more difficult the slower the growth of per capita income.

The history of economics is littered with incorrect predictions that capitalist economies will converge towards zero growth. Any such projections are no more convincing than their assumptions. The growth of services productivity is a key issue because, if it *is* both low and below that in industry, then it persistently drags down average productivity growth provided demand for services grows in line with incomes. A case can be made for there being systematic underestimation of services productivity growth in the national accounts; in the US, for example, the output of significant parts of the finance sector and the general government is estimated by labour input implying zero labour productivity growth, while direct estimates suggest productivity growth in these areas of 1–1.5 per cent per annum.[7] Baily and Gordon (1988) give plausible examples for retailing of output growth being underestimated by ignoring improved quality in the form of expanded convenience and choice; but there are contrary dangers that measured increases in the productivity of activities, where personal contact forms an essential part of the service, may hide a real deterioration in quality. There seems no reason to believe that underestimation of output changes apply more to services than to industry (the evidence on US capital goods suggests persistent underestimation of quality changes and thus

---

7 See Parker (1993) and Kronemer (1993); government output is measured by labour input weighted by education and experience, but it seems unlikely an increase in labour ' quality' could explain the estimated 1 per cent pa productivity growth.

output growth of about 3 per cent per year – Gordon, 1990). So *slowdown* of average productivity growth as a result of the shift to services has not been put in question by available evidence on mismeasurement. Nor does there seem any hard evidence that the problem of underestimating quality improvements has been increasing, to judge by evidence on US capital goods (Gordon 1990). So measurement problems do not seem able to explain the productivity slowdown since 1973, nor do they undermine the idea that structural change will further reduce average productivity growth.

The possibility that technological breakthroughs will transform the prospects for services productivity growth cannot be discounted. The increasing importance of the sector will tend to generate more research effort directed to that end. Much has been expected from computerization, in particular, the results of which, however, have been notably disappointing thus far (see Englander and Mittelstadt, 1988).

While the possibility of revolutionary technologies in the services sector cannot be ruled out, there are several reasons for believing that projecting on recent productivity performance may in fact exaggerate growth prospects. Firstly the tendency for employment to gravitate towards sectors with low productivity growth applies within services, and not just between industry and services (see Baumol et al, 1989). The share of community, social and personal services in total employment in the OECD rose from 21.8 per cent to 29.3 per cent between 1970 and 1990. Although the increase slowed in the 1980s, reflecting the widespread assault on the welfare services, it was not halted. These are precisely the sectors where productivity is inherently most difficult to increase (and not just to measure). The trend towards a larger proportion of elderly people will stoke up the pressure for more spending on these services and this will tend to drag down average productivity growth within services as a whole.

Secondly the demographic changes making for slower output growth will reduce the scope for further exploiting economies of scale. This will tend to restrain productivity growth both within industry and also in those sectors of services (eg retail trade, goods transportation) closely dependent on throughput from industry (currently comprising around 20 per cent of total employment – Blades 1987). It is notable that the decline in TFP growth after 1973 in retail and wholesale trade was as great as in manufacturing (Englander and Mittelstadt 1988).

Finally there is the international dimension. If projections are made separately (according to the same assumptions) for the US, Japan and Europe, then pushing the existing growth differential on for 60 years inevitably leads to a vast relative expansion of Japan (whose GDP would quadruple, as compared to a less than a doubling in the US). Now there can be little doubt that there is still an element of catching up in Japan's growth performance; while Japan leads the world in much of the machinery sector, in other parts of the economy, particularly services and agriculture, productivity levels are quite low by international standards. Part of the higher growth of productivity in much of the Japanese economy involves a process of convergence. As this 'growth bonus' exhausts, productivity growth in Japan would tend to decline, pulling down that for the North as a whole. Acting in the contrary direction, when there are more countries at the technological frontier in a particular sector they may push it along faster.

The demographic projections that the population of working age, which was growing by 0.9 per cent per year during 1973–90 will be declining by 0.8 per cent per year during 2030–50, are very striking. They are based (Hagemann and Nicoletti, 1989) on assuming that fertility rates, most of which are currently below replacement in the North, converge to replacement levels by 2050; that average life expectancy rises by a further two years and that international migration continues at current rates. There seem no obvious reasons to regard these projections as too low.[8] Indeed if fertility did not converge back to replacement the fall off in population growth would be sharper still. The projection of current trends in employment rates and working hours again seems reasonable (though the slow rate of growth of real incomes would certainly generate pressures for more work).

In respect of productivity particularly, it seems just as likely that the projected growth rates may be over-optimistic than the reverse. Thus there seems a real possibility that the internal logic of Northern growth will pull the growth rate of conventionally measured GDP close to zero in the middle of the next century. The reasons for this demographic and structural change have played no substantial role in the growth slowdown since 1973. The social and political problems of adjusting to such trends will be very severe, as discussed in the next chapter. But the rather reassuring trends in the environmental impact of Northern growth, suggested by the examination earlier in the chapter of recent patterns of resource use, is, if anything, reinforced by analysis of this section which suggests a further slowing of the growth rate.[9]

RESTRICTING CARBON EMISSIONS – COSTS TO THE NORTH

Pointing to less resource intensive patterns of future Northern growth is no solution to global warming. The IPCC's 'accelerated policies scenario' requires that carbon emissions be halved from the present level by 2050 through 'aggressive abatement' (Cline 1992:289). What that means for the proportionate cut in emissions in 2050, as compared to what would otherwise happen ('business-as-usual'), depends on world growth between now and then. Even with the slowdown of Northern growth discussed earlier, cuts of emissions of the order of 70–80 per cent could be required in 2050. But most existing models, as reviewed by Cline (1992), Boero et al (1991), Weyant (1993) and OECD suggest that even such major reductions in carbon emissions trends have rather small costs in terms of reduced GDP. According to the OECD's survey, reductions in carbon

---

8 The World Bank's projections for total population growth are very similar to those of the OECD.

9 A continuation of the probably modest impact of resource constraints on growth since 1973 is implicit in the projecting on of the trends in productivity growth from that period.

Table 3.4 Backstop technologies in global warming models

Coal or shale-based liquid synthetic fuel	$314 per toe
Carbon-based liquid fuel	$619 per toe
Carbon-free electric option	7.5 cents per kwh
Memorandum items	
Price band of heavy fuel oil in industry (OECD 1990)	$114–$386 per toe
Price band for electricity for industry (OECD 1989)	3.2–13.3 cents per kwh

Note: the assumptions are those of the OECD's Models Comparison Project and the Energy Modelling Forum and the backstop technologies come on stream in 2010. toe means tone of oil equivalent.
Source: Hoeller et al 1992, Table 3

emissions of 70 per cent in the North in 2050 relative to trend would reduce the *level* of GDP in 2050 of 1.5-5 per cent as compared to trend (foregoing a couple of years growth out of 60, say – Hoeller et al (1992) Table 7B). Without a major macroeconomic impact the problem of restricting emissions is the complex microeconomic and political one of designing and negotiating the appropriate policies.

As the surveys make very clear there are a number of vital assumptions involved in such projections including underlying growth rates, energy prices, energy efficiency and the development of 'backstop technologies' providing carbon-free fuel, the substitutability of energy in production and of energy-intensive products in consumption. These generate the business-as-usual paths for carbon emissions (typically rising by 1–2 per cent per year over the next century). Carbon taxes (and other policy instruments) are then calculated which, by bringing into use less (or non) carbon intensive energy or by leading to substitution away from energy use, lead to given reductions in emissions. The impact on real GDP of the use of more expensive energy sources is then calculated.

Two aspects about these models seem to be of central importance in assessing their results. First it is worth considering the assumptions about backstop technologies which provide fuel with infinitely elastic supply at the assumed prices. The assumptions used by OECD are reproduced above in Table 3.4.[10] The prices assumed for carbon-free fuel, first for generating electricity and then for replacing petrol, represent increases in costs which are by no means incomparable to the oil price hikes in 1974 and 1980 (and of course the price increases implied would be more gradual).

These backstop technologies are playing a similar role to that of imported corn in Ricardo's model which eliminated the effects of diminishing returns in agriculture. Backstop technologies eliminate the effect of increasing costs in carbon energy (the increasing costs being partly due to diminishing returns in obtaining the energy but mainly due to environmental costs as reflected in carbon taxes). It is not surprising

10. The assumptions about backstop technologies in these models are surveyed in Boero et al (1991) and Cline (1992). Johansson et al (1993) provides an exhaustive, and optimistic, discussion of the technical and economic issues surrounding renewable energy.

that if you assume that replacement fuels for those dependent on carbon are eventually available at moderate additional cost then the effects on GDP of substantial reductions in carbon emissions are relatively modest.[11] Particularly significant is the fact that it makes the costs of emissions abatement essentially linear. If it costs 1 per cent of GDP to reduce carbon emissions by 30 per cent it will cost around 3 per cent to reduce them by 90 per cent.[12] Those models reported by OECD which do not assume such backstop technologies *do* show strongly increasing costs. The ERM model shows the costs in the US of 30 per cent emission cuts (relative to baseline) are about 1 per cent of GDP while the costs of 90 per cent cuts are about 9 per cent of GDP. Whalley and Wigle (1992, Table 13) find that 40 per cent cuts in emissions on average up to 2100 compared to baseline reduce overall GDP by 3.2 per cent and 80 per cent cuts reduce GDP by 15.7 per cent. These results underline the importance of the assumptions about backstops in the estimation of the cost of emission reductions. Given the real uncertainties involved in the likely costs of carbon free fuels it should be recognized that drastic reductions in carbon use could have much larger impacts on GDP than those typically estimated.

The other fundamental assumption involved in most of these projections is that the world distribution of income will remain basically unaltered. In the OECD's own GREEN model for example, the analysis is conducted on the assumption that per capita income grows at the same rate in the North and South (just under 2 per cent per year up to 2050 – see Martin et al, 1992 Table 3). There is room for some redistribution within the North (Japan's per capita income growing about 1 per cent per year faster than in the US and EC); and the same is true within the South (China, India, the 'Dynamic Asian Economies' and Brazil showing per capita growth of around 3 per cent per year whereas the rest of the South barely achieves 1 per cent per year). Thus even the more successful Southern countries are assumed to manage only a tiny amount of 'catch-up', while the rest (Africa, much of Latin America, the Middle East and so forth) fall further behind.[13] The South's share of total output grows, but only because of faster population growth (1.3 per cent per year as against 0.1 per cent per year in the North).

These assumptions are the more surprising given the fact that developing countries have showed faster per capita growth since 1970 (2.9

---

11 The share of energy in GDP of the North is around 6 per cent (Cline, 1992:145). If an alternative, non-carbon fuel was available at double the cost of existing fuels, and emissions targets required the replacement of half carbon based fuel, then the impact would be to reduce GDP by approximately 3 per cent (or rather less once substitution away from expensive energy is taken into account). Alternatively if there was no substitute for carbon-based fuels, and cutting energy use by one half resulted in proportionate falls in output (both extreme assumptions) then the impact on GDP would be 50 per cent. Such simple calculations highlight the role of backstop technologies.

12 These figures are typical of those reported for the US – see Hoeller et al 1992:24. The modellers seem reluctant to push this to its logical conclusion which is that reducing carbon emissions by 99.9 per cent would cost 3 1/3 per cent of GDP!

13 One model which assumed much faster growth in China (7 per cent per year until 2050) is criticized (Boero et al 1991 S15) for having ' increased China's weight in the world disproportionately'

per cent per year as compared to 2.4 per cent per year in the high income countries), and are expected by the World Bank to increase this differential to 1.5 per cent per year in the 1990s (World Bank 1992). This would be far from constituting a generalization to the South of Northern consumption but it would represent definite catch-up. According to the UN's data (UN 1993, based on exchange rates) the per capita income gap between North and South would be reduced from 21:1 to 9:1 by 2050 if per capita growth was 1.5 per cent faster in the South than in the North (with growth of 1.2 per cent per year as projected above). If per capita growth was 4 per cent per year the ratio would be 4.1:1 in 2050; it would take per capita growth 5 per cent per year faster in the South than in the North to bring similar income levels by 2050.[14] So rates of growth in the South that would represent very considerable degrees of catch-up are not large compared to those achieved for example in Korea and China over recent (much shorter) periods. There is really no basis whatsoever on which to make projections of the likely degree of catch-up over very long periods. However convergence of income levels is the almost universal aspiration. It is surely desirable, therefore, to evaluate its environmental consequences.

If entitlements to emissions were to be determined entirely on the egalitarian principle of a per capita allocation (see the chapter by Bhaskar), then the fact that the North had a higher or lower share in world GDP would be irrelevant to its emissions limit. If total emissions in 2050 were at the same level as in 1988, their equal distribution per capita would imply cuts of by 89 per cent in the US, 75 per cent in Europe and Japan while they could be unchanged in China and increased to three times the existing level in India (calculated from Grubler and Nakicenovic 1992). The lower baseline growth in the North the smaller would be the cuts in emissions required to reach the given emission target. Thus the costs of curbing emissions would be smaller; the impact on growth would be correspondingly less. Slow underlying growth in the North would unambiguously reduce the costs to the North of meeting any given emissions limits; only Northern emissions and thus the level of Northern GDP (not its share of world GDP) would be relevant to the size of the reduction required.

But an egalitarian allocation of emissions per capita may well not be realized. Among many other competing criteria (see UNCTAD, 1992), one alternative, much more favourable to the North, would be to allocate emissions in proportion to the share of world GDP. Production would confer 'squatter's rights' to emit. If this was the case, a lower share of world GDP would reduce the North's entitlement to emit. A

---

14 It is tempting to use the figures for income disparities calculated from Purchasing Power Parity comparisons (UN 1993 Table 52) which show the 1990 ratio in per capita incomes as 7.2:1 (ie one third of the exchange rate comparisons); 4 per cent per capita growth in the South would bring to close to Northern levels by 2050. But such comparisons are rather misleading for growth rates in the South (in constant dollars) will be slower when reckoned at PPPs than at exchange rates if there is convergence since the ' distortion' of using exchange rate comparisons diminishes as the economic structures converge. Since growth rates for countries are typically calculated and thought about using national prices it seems less confusing to use the exchange rate comparisons.

lower level of Northern GDP (than conventionally projected), if it was just counterbalanced by higher GDP in the South, would imply an equal proportionate cut in the North's share of world GDP. Allowable emissions would thus fall just in line with the North's GDP, suggesting little or no change in the percentage cost to GDP in the North of reducing its emissions as compared to the conventional estimates. If Southern catch-up more than made up for Northern slowdown then the North's share of world GDP, and thus its right to emit, would be further reduced. The cost to the North of meeting given emissions limits would be greater.

Cline (1992) suggests that a weighted average of a country's shares in world population and world GDP might be used to allocate emissions (with the weights reflecting the degree of egalitarianism). The greater the weight of population in the formula the lower the North's right to emit in 2050. It might be that the faster the South catches up, and thus the greater its weight in the world economy, the stronger its position at the bargaining table and thus the greater the weight of population in the formula. This would imply lower Northern emissions and thus greater costs.

Thus serious catch-up in the South would impose greater costs in the North if given global emissions targets were to be met and this would be true even if slower than normally contemplated growth of Northern GDP reduced its baseline emissions. The greater impact on the North would still hold even if the total costs are minimized by some system of trading these entitlements (see UNCTAD, 1992).[15]

If the costs of cutting emissions in terms of reduction of GDP were both moderate initially and linear up to very large reductions then it would not matter *very* much what proportion of the reductions took place in (or entitlements were allocated to) the North as against the South. Indeed the overall size of emission reductions remains a relatively minor issue. Arguments about the odd per cent or two of GDP are far from trivial (compare current aid flows for example), but the whole structure of economies is not at stake. If however costs were to increase rapidly with very large reductions in emissions then the overall extent of emission reduction together with its distribution, become crucial. Acceptance by the North of anything approaching an egalitarian distribution of much reduced carbon emissions on a world scale would then have important effects on the structure of its economy. Unless rapid catch-up in the South is to be precluded from the discussion (illustrating the old claim that the standard of living in the North is directly dependent on poverty in the South) then it is necessary to explore the implications of much more similar levels of per capita resource use in North and South.

It appears that only one model has attempted to estimate the effect of

---

15 GREEN shows the costs of a 70 per cent cut in emissions in 2050 would be reduced by around one third by emission trading (Dean and Hoeller, 1992 Table 7). This reduction is less in other models (cost reductions of around one tenth); the benefit of trading declines over time in GREEN as the coming into play of backstop technologies reduces cost differences (and thus trading possibilities) between countries.

an egalitarian distribution of emissions. Whalley and Wigle (1991), whose model has strong non-linearities due to their assumption of little role for substitution by non-carbon fuels, simulate the effect of a 50 per cent reduction in overall emissions as compared to baseline in 2030 with the emissions equalized on a per capita basis. Not surprisingly they find (1991, Table 7.9) large losses in GDP in the advanced countries (18.4 per cent for North America, 6.4 per cent for the EC and 2.5 per cent for Japan) but very small ones in developing countries (1.2 per cent).[16] The distribution of the costs is quite different if emissions are cut proportionately within each country. Then North America loses 1.2 per cent of GDP and the developing countries 4.5 per cent.

It may be concluded that the widely accepted estimates of moderate costs to the North of very deep cuts in carbon emissions could prove to be grave underestimates if the following combination of circumstances arose:

- rapid growth in the South required greater cuts in Northern emissions than typically assumed;
- backstop technologies to provide non-carbon based fuel proved more expensive than typically assumed.

Similar considerations apply to other potential resource limitations on growth. How far costs rise (diminishing returns, substitutes in production and consumption etc), how far demand rises (where a major uncertainty surrounds Southern growth), and how available supplies are allocated between North and South determine the potential impact on growth of energy and materials problems in general.

Some data for energy and metals presented by Slade (1991) helps to underline these points. Table 3.5 shows that the low-income countries with over half the world's population at present absorb around 1/3 as much energy and metals per capita as the middle income countries with around 5 times their per capita incomes. These in turn consume around 1/5 of the resources per capita of the high income countries with per capita incomes over ten times as great.[17]

Suppose:

1. over next 60 years resource use per capita in the high income countries stayed unchanged but is generalized throughout the rest of the world;

16 The developing countries are aggregated with the centrally planned economies (whose emissions per capita exceeded West Germany's); it may well be that excluding USSR and Eastern Europe would leave the developing countries with no loss at all. Whalley and Wigle's model is criticized as less sophisticated than many of the others. The issue here concerns not the detail of their estimates but the thrust of their assumptions.
17 Table 3.5 omits from the ' middle-income' countries the Soviet Union and Eastern Europe whose inclusion in Slade's table doubles that group's per capita consumption of resources, since they showed per capita energy consumption 50 per cent greater than western Europe and per capita steel production greater than that of the US. In the calculations in the text these countries are assumed in the future to have similar consumption rates to the rest of the middle income group. Relative income levels are based on exchange rates (see note 14).

Table 3.5 GNP, population, per capita resources 1989

	Low income group	Medium income group	High income group
GNP (US$ billions 1980)	804	1772	12648
Population (billions)	2.823	1.374	0.799
GNP per capita (high inc =100)	1.8	8.1	100
Energy per capita	6.2	18.2	100
Steel per capita	8.5	22.3	100
Non-ferrous metals per capita	3.2	15.1	100

Source: Slade 1991 Table IV
Note: Middle Income Group excludes Eastern Europe (calculated using Slade 1991 Table V)

2. population doubles outside the high income countries but is
   unchanged in them (close to the OECD's assumptions).

If the discrepancies in resource use were eliminated in this way, and the
whole population of the world was consuming resources at the current
rate in the North, then energy use would reach six times its present level,
steel use five times its present level and non-ferrous metals nine times its
present level. It is hard to envisage that increases in resource use of such
orders of magnitude would not lead to much sharper increase in costs,
and thus constraints on growth, than are conventionally predicted (as in
Nordhaus' 1992 estimate that increasing fuel costs will reduce growth by
some 0.15 per cent per year). Alternatively, an equal per capita
distribution of resources, but with only the same total use as at present,
would require per capita consumption of resources in the North to be at
quite a small fraction of present levels. Of course technical progress *could*
allow such changes to be absorbed relatively inexpensively (as in the case
of cheap carbon-free backstops) but it is surely important to contemplate
the implications of more costly outcomes.

CONCLUSIONS

Nordhaus (1992:39) reviews the limits to growth debate and concludes that
the 'estimated drag from resources' over the next 60 years which would
reduce Northern growth by about 0.3 per cent per year on average, an
effect only a little stronger than that applying over the past twenty years,
constituting 'a small but noticeable impediment to economic growth over
the next few decades in advanced industrial countries – although an
obstacle that will continue to be surmounted by technological advance'.

   This paper has concentrated on the 'downside risk' in such projections.
The impact of continuing structural change combined with demographic
developments could lead to growth in the North that was very slow,
possibly zero by the middle of the next century, even without any
tightening of environmental constraints. Such slow growth would reduce

demands on the environment. But such a favourable side benefit of slower growth in the North could be outweighed if major inroads were made into existing disparities in the world distribution of income by rapid growth in the South, the possibility of which is never even discussed in mainstream treatments (see Nordhaus 1992 for example). Unless alternative technologies are developed at relatively little cost, there is the possibility, therefore, of serious environmental pressures on living standards.

Implicit in a projection of very low growth of GDP is that the accumulation of capital in the North will drastically slow down. If there is little possibility for increasing productivity in much of the services sector, then their expansion is predominantly an extensive form of growth. It depends upon growing employment, but this is constrained by a declining labour force and diminishing possibilities for obtaining labour from industry and agriculture. Intensive growth within industry (and some dynamic service sectors – see Rowthorn, 1992), which involves rapid accumulation of capital per worker, becomes of decreasing significance as the share of employment in these activities declines. Attempting to maintain rate of accumulation would lead to a position similar to that envisaged by Marx in his Law of the Tendency of the Rate of Profit to Fall. Capital accumulated in excess of the productive possibilities leads to declining output – capital ratios, profitability and growth rates of capital and output.

The responses to this slowdown might include:

- A general push for universalizing market solutions. Activities carried out by the state offer opportunities for profitable transfer to the private sector. There would be a continued drive to capture the expanding sector of social and community services, both in terms of production (private hospitals, schools, prisons) and financing (private health insurance, school fees financing and so on).
- Declines in the total amount of labour time available to the market sector could be stemmed by attempts to further increase labour force participation (better child care facilities, increasing the retirement age, halting the reduction of the working week).
- Immigration provides an alternative and longer-lasting solution to a declining domestic labour force; it would represent the generalization to a minute proportion of the South of Northern levels of consumption, but in a fashion which allowed the sustaining in the North of higher growth rates (as in Europe in the 1960s).
- Very slow overall growth would tend to imply intensifying competition within Northern markets, but substantial growth in Southern markets would render them increasingly important in the world economy and thus for the investment plans of multinationals.
- For many of the better off in the North the only way to maintain growth of their incomes within a stagnant economy would be through deliberately increasing inequality (cuts in state provision, reduction of minimum wages) which offloads a disproportionate share of the costs of slow growth on to poorer sections of society.

With the exceptions of immigration, these possibilities are just extra-polations from the experience of the North during the slower growth of the 1980s (see Glyn, 1994). They hardly provide an auspicious backdrop for implementing policies which further constrain conventionally measured living standards in the name of environmental protection. But if living standards in the North are stagnating anyway then a quite different attitude to consumption, and in particular to matters of distribution, would be the only way to circumvent the social conflicts which seem inevitably to result at present from economic slowdown. Such new attitudes would then have the additional, very important benefit of facilitating acceptance of the measures necessary to combat environmental degradation. The next chapter discusses whether the basis currently exists in the North for such a change in attitudes.

REFERENCES

Baily, N (1988) & Gordon R 'The Productivity Slowdown: Measurement Issues, and the Explosion of Computer Power' *Brookings Papers on Economic Activity*, 2:1988

Barnett, H & (1963) Morse, C *Scarcity and Growth* Resources for the Future, Johns Hopkins, Baltimore

Barnett, H (1979) 'Scarcity and Growth Revisited' in V K Smith (ed), *Scarcity and Growth Reconsidered*, Johns Hopkins, Baltimore

Baumol, W Blackman, S & Wolff, E (1989) *Productivity and American Leadership* MIT Press, Cambridge MA

Blades, D (1987) 'Goods and Services in OECD Countries' *OECD Economic Studies* no 8

Boero, G Clarke, R & Winters, L (1991) *The Macroeconomic Consequences of Controlling Greenhouse Gases: A Survey* Dept of the Environment, London

Cline, W. (1992) *The Economics of Global Warming* Institute for International Economics, Washington

Dean, A & Hoeller, P (1992) 'The Cost of Reducing CO_2 Emissions: Evidence from Six Global Models' *OECD Economic Studies* no 19

Englander, A & Mittelstadt, A (1988) 'Total Factor Productivity:Macroeconomic and Structural Aspects of the Slowdown' *OECD Economic Studies* no 10

Glyn, A (1994) 'Stabilization, Inegalitarianism and Stagnation: the Advanced Capitalist Countries in the 1980s' in J Epstein and H Gintis (eds) *Economic Policy in the Conservative Era* Cambridge University Press

Gordon, R (1990) *The Measurement of Durable Goods Prices* University of Chicago Press, Chicago

Goldemberg, J, Jahansson, T, Reddy, A & Williams, R (1987) *Energy For a Sustainable World* World Resources Institute, Washington

Grossman, G (1993) 'Pollution and Growth: What do we know' mimeo Princeton University

Grubler, A & Nakicenovic, N (1992) 'International Burden Sharing in Greenhouse Gas Reduction' World Bank Environment Working Paper no 55

Hagemann, R & Nicoletti, G (1989) 'Population Ageing' *OECD Economic Studies*, no 12

Hoeller, P, Dean, A & Hayafuji, M (1992) 'New Issues, New Results: The OECD's Second Survey of the Macroeconomic Costs of Reducing CO_2 Emissions' OECD Economics Department Working Paper no 123

Holtz-Eakins, D & Selden, T (1992) 'Stoking the Fires' NBER Working Paper no 4248

Johansson, T, Kelly, H, Reddy, A Williams, R & Burnham, L (eds) (1993) *Renewable Energy* Earthscan, London

Kendrick, J & Grossman, E (1980) *Productivity in the United States* Johns Hopkins, Baltimore

Kronemer, A (1993) 'Productivity in Industry and Government: 1973-91' *Monthly Labour Review*, July

Marglin, S & Schor, J (1990) *The Golden Age of Capitalism* Oxford University Press

Martin, J, Burniaux, J-M, Nicoletti, G & Oliveira-Martins, J (1992) 'The Costs of International Agreements to limit CO_2: Evidence from GREEN' *OECD Economic Studies* no 19

Nordhous, W (1992) 'Lethal Model 2: The Limits to Growth Revisited' *Brookings Papers on Economic Activity*, 1992.2

OECD (1992a) *Energy Balances* Paris

OECD (1992b) *Energy and the Environment* Paris

Parker, R (1993) 'Gross Product by Industry, 1977-90' *Survey of Current Business*, May 1993

Rowthorn, R (1992) 'Productivity and American Leadership' *Review of Income and Wealth*, 38(4)

Shafiq, N, & Bandyopadhyay, S (1992) 'Economic Growth and Environmental Quality' Policy Research Working Paper, World Bank

Slade, M (1982) 'Trends in Natural Resource Commodity Prices' *Journal of Environmental Economics and Management* 9(2):122–37

Slade, M (1991) 'Environmental Costs of Natural resource Commodities:Magnitude and Incidence' World Development Report 1992 Background Paper no 2, World Bank

Tilton, J (ed) (1990) *World Metals Demand* Johns Hopkins, Baltimore

UNCTAD (1992) *Combatting global warming* Geneva.

United Nations (1993) *Human Development Report* New York

Weyant, J (1993) 'Costs of Reducing Global Carbon Emission' *Journal of Economic Perspectives*, Fall

Whalley, J & Wigle R (1991) 'International Incidence of Carbon Taxes' in R Dornbusch & J Poterba (eds) *Global Warming* MIT Press, Cambridge, Mass

Whalley, J & Wigle, R (1992) 'Report for the OECD Comparative Modelling Project' OECD Economics Department Working Paper no 121

World Resources Institute (1992) *World Resources 1992–3* Oxford University Press, New York

Chapter 4

Can The North Stop Consumption Growth? Escaping The Cycle of Work and Spend

Juliet B Schor

INTRODUCTION

In the last half century consumption has increased dramatically in the industrialized North. The most rapid increases were during the 1950s and 1960s, the so-called 'Golden Age of Capitalism.' Beginning in the 1970s, the growth of GDP and consumption per capita slowed. But even so, since 1973 the average consumer in these countries found his or her consumption rising by an average of more than 2 per cent per year. In the United States, the country with which this paper is mainly concerned, real per capita consumption expenditures rose 2 per cent per year between 1973 and 1989 (see Table 4.1), and despite the current global slowdown, the future is likely to bring further increases in income. Productivity should increase rapidly on account of further innovations in and diffusion of new technologies. And, in much of the South, income is rising even faster than in the North. In countries such as Brazil, India and China, growing middle classes will continue to emulate western standards of living. As the 21st century approaches it is difficult to avoid the conclusion that increasing numbers of people will be consuming a bundle of goods and services resembling that of northern populations.

Table 4.1 Northern consumption per capita, 1960–89

| | Annual rates of growth (%) | |
	1960–1989	*1973–89*
Europe	2.9	2.0
Japan	4.7	2.4
US	2.5	2.0

Source: OECD National Accounts, various years

Environmentalists have made the argument that current patterns of consumption are not environmentally sustainable — in fact the world faces significant threats to survival (see Ekins and Jacobs, Chapter 2). While it is impossible to construct an index of the impact of an entire lifestyle on the environment, it is clear that northern lifestyles, and particularly that of the United States, are highly environmentally damaging. Affluence is causing air and water pollution, soil degradation, ozone depletion, species extinction, greenhouse gas emissions, toxic chemcial wastes, deforestation and other environmental disasters.

One approach is to change the way we produce and what we consume. Firms can switch to environmentally more benign production technologies. Consumers can alter the pattern of goods and services they purchase and use, for example by switching to smaller automobiles (or even to public transportation or bicycles). Consumers can also avoid buying toxic products, recycle, and insulate their homes. By shifting to less damaging methods of production and patterns of consumption, the overall (negative) environmental effect of any given level of consumption can be reduced. In the terms depicted in Figure 4.1, such changes will result in an inward shift in the growth/environment tradeoff.

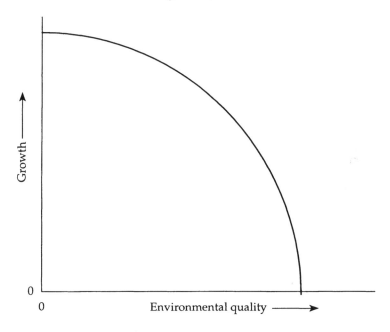

Figure 4.1 *Growth versus environmental quality*

In the short to medium term, it is not likely that these kinds of changes will produce *enough* improvement in the earth's ecology. In part this is due to linkages among components of consumption 'bundles', in particular linkages between housing and transport which represent substantial expenditures and are two major sources of environmental degradation. Consider American suburbia. Houses are large and therefore costly to build. They are energy inefficient and cannot be kept cool without air conditioning. They have large lawns, often with ecologically destructive landscaping. Because of the distances and the land-use patterns, automobile travel (extremely damaging) is almost imperative. To dramatically improve environmental impact, Americans would have to shift to smaller, differently designed houses, with new transportation systems and new conceptions of land use around households. These extraordinarily costly changes would take decades to complete. Linkages among consumption decisions as well as the fixed costs embodied in past decisions are therefore formidable barriers to rapid reduction in the 'environmental intensity' of each dollar of consumption spending.

This suggests that the road to sustainability will also include a change in the current trajectory of consumption levels. By lowering the rate of growth of consumption per capita, perhaps even to zero, the amount of 'environmental degradation' generated by each consumer will be less than it would be if consumption grew at current or historical rates. That is because it is not only *what* we consume, but *how much* we consume that matters for the ecology. That is, we need to move rightward on the growth-environment frontier. A recent poll suggests considerable awareness of these issues among the American people. Thirty-seven per cent strongly agree and 40 per cent agree somewhat that 'American over-use of resources is a major global environmental problem that needs to be changed.' (Pew 1994)

But altering the trajectory of private consumption is not an easy task. Economic growth plays a central political, economic and psycho-cultural role in western society. Since the Second World War, growth has been the foundation of political consensus and stability in the North (Marglin and Schor 1990). The postwar regime was premised on steady increases in income and consumption, in that the Keynesian alliance between business, labour and government was essentially an agreement to avoid conflict over shares by ensuring higher absolute levels for all. Similarly, redistribution among income classes was small in comparison to the impact of growth on the standard of living of lower income groups. Prosperity became key to the virtual elimination of political challenges to the system. Increasing consumption also solved the 'economic problem', that is, fear of stagnation. Productivity increases were channelled into growth in real wages and hence private consumption. Consumer credit enhanced consumer demand. The gap between what the economy was capable of producing and what people were willing to buy — the nightmare of prewar theorists — was kept to a minimum.

The centrality of growth in our political and economic culture means that moral or pragmatic environmentally-motivated appeals to reducing consumption may not be successful. But, with widespread perceptions of cultural and economic decline, the promise of a higher 'quality of life' may be. In the United States, where working hours have been rising for twenty-five years, and in Japan, where working hours are extremely high, there may be considerable receptivity to 'trading consumption for time'. I believe we now have the possibility to create a 'politics of time' which has sustainability at its core. Doing this requires extracting ourselves from what I have called the 'cycle of work and spend'. Difficult as it may be to tame northern appetites for consumer goods, there may be no other choice if the planet is to escape environmental crisis and at the same time experience significant growth in consumption per head in the South. This is the view that appears to have emerged from the Rio summit. In the pages which follow, I explore the obstacles and opportunities to a trajectory in which productivity growth in the North is channelled into shorter working hours, rather than higher income.

PATTERNS IN WORKING HOURS

Table 4.2 shows the fraction of growth in labour productivity since 1870 which has gone toward reducing hours. (These estimates are somewhat imprecise because the hours calculations, from Maddison, are rough. However, if anything, they overstate the decline in hours.) As the table clearly shows, the 'extent' of hours reduction has fallen substantially in all countries except Germany. In an absolute sense, the extent of hours reduction can be described as virtually non-existent to modest, eg a low of 4 per cent in Japan to a high of 28 per cent in the UK.

Table 4.2 Changes in hours and productivity, 1870–1984

	France	Germany	Japan	Netherlands	UK	US
1. Annual hours (% reduction)						
1870–1938	45.8	23.8	20.8	27.6	27.3	35.9
1950–84	17.1	32.1	6.3	29.5	25.3	13.4
2. Labour productivity (% change)						
1870–1938	119.0	109.0	131.0	83.0	79.0	114.0
1950–84	128.0	136.0	154.0	108.0	91.0	64.0
Hours reduction as a fraction of productivity change: row (1) divided by row (2)						
1870–1938	0.385	0.218	0.159	0.332	0.346	0.315
1950–84	0.134	0.236	0.041	0.273	0.277	0.208

Source: Angus Maddison, 'Growth and Slowdown in Advanced Capitalist Economies'
Journal of Economic Literature, vol XXV, no 2, June 1987. Tables A–5, A–9 (pp 683–686).
Notes: Annual hours are hours worked per person per year. Labour productivity is GDP per hour worked

My own estimates for the United States suggest that Maddison may have overstated the hours decline. Although there was some decline between 1950–1969, I have found that between 1969 and 1989 average hours for those who were not involuntarily working part-time or part-year have actually risen by an average of 138 hours, thereby cancelling the pre-1959 gain (Schor 1992). Similarly, in Japan, hours have most probably risen since

1973. The postwar experience therefore raises the question of why, if leisure is a 'normal' good, hours have not fallen more (or at all in some cases).

The failure of the 'market in hours'

Neoclassical economics has a straightforward explanation for situations where hours fail to fall with productivity increase: hours merely reflect the expression of consumers' preferences for income rather than leisure. The simple neoclassical model begins with individuals' preference functions. These individuals choose a level of working hours which (with a given technology) determines the level of income and free time. Employers offer job schedules which conform to individuals' preferences. This so-called 'worker sovereignty' in the labour market is ensured by competition. Should the market fail to provide the schedules people want, new employers would come along and outcompete existing firms.

This simple neoclassical story is not well supported by the evidence, at least for the United States and Japan. Most important for our purposes is the question of whether or not firms allow workers to choose hours. Studies of US workers show significant constraints on choice of hours. Altonji and Paxson's work (1988) provides evidence that workers have difficulty changing hours within jobs. Among a sample of low-income married men, Moffitt (1982) found a large discrepancy between mean desired hours (21 per week) and mean actual hours (39 per week). A second type of evidence comes from surveys. When questioned, workers report that they have little freedom to vary hours. In one study only 15 per cent of the sample were free to adjust hours up and down (Kahn and Lang 1987).[1]

One explanation for hours constraints is the structure of firms' costs. If costs do not vary by the hour, but are incurred on a per employee basis, then firms will not be indifferent to workers' schedules (this point was first made by Lewis 1969 and subsequently by Schor 1992). In the postwar period, the 'hours-invariant' component of labour costs has risen significantly in most countries of the North. The rise of hours-invariant costs has meant that employers have had a growing incentive for longer working weeks and a disincentive for reducing hours. In the US, fringe benefits (comprising mainly medical and pension payments, as well as paid time off) as a per centage of total wages and salaries rose from 17 per cent in 1955 to 39 per cent in 1992 (US Chamber of Commerce, 1993 Table 17). Employer tax contributions which are capped (such as unemployment insurance, workers' compensation etc will have a similar effect. These hours-invariant costs are probably the major reason why the current US recovery had so little job growth for so long, and why levels of factory overtime continue to be sustained at record levels.[2]

Variation in these hours-invariant costs may be useful in explaining cross-national trends in hours in the OECD. Those countries with a higher

---

1 I do not know of any studies of hours constraints in the Japanese or European cases.
2 Clearly any fixed cost per worker will have this effect, as Lewis pointed out.

share of hours-invariant welfare spending borne by employers tend to have considerably higher hours (eg United States, Japan). Countries with large public welfare states, by contrast, have lower hours (Scandinavia, West Germany). Canada and the United Kingdom are intermediate cases on both counts.

However, it is unlikely that this explanation is exhaustive, especially for adult men, whose scheduling options are most severely circumscribed. With hours-invariant costs average hours would be longer but worker sovereignty should still rule. Employers would offer short schedules and workers would pay a wage or benefit penalty to get them. One would expect far more diversity in scheduling than exists. By contrast, scheduling options have tended to be discrete: full-time positions offering full benefits and part-time positions with severe wage and benefit penalties. For example, in the US in 1985, 54 per cent of all non-farm employees had a 40 hour work schedule. By contrast, only 2.3 per cent worked 25–29 hours, 4.1 per cent worked 30-34 hours and 7.4 per cent worked 35-39 hours. Twelve per cent of workers were located in the 1–24 hours category (Smith 1986: 8). If hours-invariant costs were the only factor at work we would not expect to see clumping at 40 hours. Furthermore, it is implausible that only 2.3 per cent of workers independently prefer 25–29 hours, for example.

An alternative explanation breaks with the neoclassical model and argues that the 'market in hours' is largely absent. For the most part, employers set hours and give employees limited choices, most often 'all or nothing' (that is, work the expected hours or quit). Most workers do not have the right to refuse overtime.

Schor (1992), Seo (1993) and Schor and Seo (1994) argue that for salaried workers there is an hours externality: additional hours are free to the employer because the pay itself is hours-invariant. We find that salaried workers have significantly longer hours than hourly workers, after accounting for other determinants of hours (income, occupation, age, etc). In the United States, among male heads of households, the additional hours due to payment by salary were 140 (Seo 1993). A reasonable interpretation of these results is that employers require long hours from these employees. In addition to the fact that pay is fixed, employers may use hours as a signalling device to identify loyal or hard-working employees. As Bailyn (1993) has argued, this does not mean they are actually more productive, only that the corporate culture requires them to work long hours.

Finally, in cases where firms do not have flexibility in terms of shift work, or there is a limited supply of labour, and where capital investment is substantial, management will oppose hours reductions in order to maintain high capital utilization. This may explain why capital-intensive industries such as auto and steel have tended to have relatively high hours. The combination of hours-invariant costs, the hours externality of salaried employment and capital investment create powerful incentives for employers to schedule long hours and to oppose hours reductions.

THE WORK AND SPEND CYCLE

The failure of hours to fall in response to productivity gains is in contrast to the late 19th and early 20th centuries, when a larger fraction of productivity growth was channelled into shorter hours (see Table 4.2). In the United States and Japan, the postwar era has brought a cycle of work-and-spend, as shown in Figure 4.2. Employers set schedules and workers conform to them. When productivity rises, employers pass the gains along in the form of higher wages, rather than reduced worktime. Workers take the extra income and spend it. They become accustomed or habituated to the new level of spending and develop aversion to their previous, lower level of spending. Preferences adapt such that workers are unwilling to reduce current income in order to get more leisure. They respond to surveys saying they are satisfied with their current levels of hours and income. With respect to these surveys work and spend is observationally equivalent to neoclassical theory: in both, workers are satisfied with current hours and income. That is, the surveys cannot distinguish between workers 'getting what they want' or 'wanting what they get'.

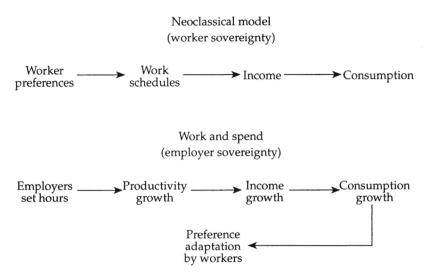

Figure 4.2 *Models of work and consumption*

The existence of a work and spend cycle has a number of implications. First, it suggests an addictive aspect to consumption. Over time, people become habituated or 'addicted' to the level of consumption which they are attaining. Goods which are originally experienced as luxuries come to be seen as necessities. Habit formation can imply the endogeneity of preferences, that is, the ability of preferences to change as consumption occurs. This seems to have occurred over time in individuals' preferred tradeoffs between hours and income (see below).

Work and spend also provides a dynamic context for status emulation, or 'keeping up with the Joneses', as described by Veblen, Duesenberry and others. In these approaches satisfaction is derived not from one's absolute level of consumption, but from one's level relative to others. In Duesenberry (1949), consumption is driven by 'demonstration' cum 'emulation' — Smiths seeing and then trying to keep up with Joneses. With rising consumption, participants in status processes mistakenly perceive their own increases in consumption as relative improvement, when they are only absolute gain. No one is made relatively better off by higher consumption, yet that is only apparent after the game has been played. If free time is *less* of a status good than commodities, and yields greater intrinsic satisfaction, then people would be better off with slower consumption growth and more free time than in the work and spend cycle (see Frank 1985 on this point).

To understand the power of work and spend, we must also recognize the extent to which consumption has come to assume a central 'psycho-cultural' role in western societies and Japan. In the United States, where this process has arguably gone farthest, society and culture are increasingly commercialized. Advertising and marketing encourage consumers to be dissatisfied with what they have and to covet more. Culturally, consumerism is remaking the landscape as the shopping mall takes over as the dominant public space, equivalent to the cathedrals of the medieval era. Consumption has also become a crucial determinant of identity: 'I shop, therefore I am.' Cutting edge advertisers, especially those whose products are symbolically intense, have begun marketing an identity concept, rather than the qualities of products. Soft drinks represent the 'new generation'. Sneaker ads have evolved into sophisticated visions of desirable lifestyles.[3] Perhaps more than any other activity, consumerism has become the lynchpin of modern economic, political, social and personal life.

Is There Public Support for Escaping Work-and-Spend?

Trading income for leisure time

Most surveys on tradeoffs between hours and income have asked about willingness to forgo current income for additional leisure time. In both the neoclassical and the work-and-spend approaches, one would not expect much inclination to reduce current income. In the former, the market reflects worker preferences. In the latter, preferences adjust to existing hours. This is the observational equivalence noted earlier. And surveys conform to this prediction: they show high levels of satisfaction with current income and little support for reducing current income.[4] For example, the 1985 Current Population Survey found that only 8 per cent of US workers wanted to work less with less pay (Shank 1986).

---

3 For a very interesting synthesis of political economy and semiotic theory, see Schuessler, 1993.
4 A 1978 survey by Fred Best also found very low preferences for that option. Earlier surveys yielded very similar results.

A 1989 international survey which included US workers found only 5.6 per cent of workers wanted the 'work less' option (Bell and Freeman, 1992, Table 3A). However, this survey has certain inconsistencies. In the same survey, 35 per cent said they would prefer to spend 'a bit' or have 'much less time at work', compared to only 16 per cent who would like to spend 'a bit' or have 'much more time' (Bell and Freeman, Table 6). There are also problems in the way the tradeoff question is typically posed:

1. It does not differentiate between involuntary underemployment and maximum hours constraints.
2. Some studies show that preferences are not linear with respect to the size of the hypothetical changes; however the questions do not specify the magnitude of the change (see Best 1980).
3. Hours tend to be inversely correlated with the intensity of work. Because the survey questions do not address intensity, they are (unwittingly) biased against shorter hours. Respondents may well be interpreting the 'work less' question as implying 'fewer hours, less pay, and harder work.'[5]

The 1977 Quality of Employment Survey in the United States found much more desire for reduced hours. For example, among dual-earner families with children under 12, 38 per cent of fathers and 53 per cent of mothers wanted shorter hours. The form of question was different, however, in its explicit mention of family time: 'Would you like to spend less time working so that you could spend more time with your (husband/wife) and (children), even if it meant less money?' (Moen and Dempster-McClain 1987; 584). A 1991 survey also found very great willingness to sacrifice current income. When asked about the desirability of taking one extra day off each week, at the cost of that day's pay, 70 per cent of respondents earning $30,000 a year or more said they would like that option, as did 48 per cent of those earning $20,000 or less. The desire for more free time showed up in all segments of the workforce, irrespective of marital status, location or educational attainment (Gunsch 1991). This change in attitudes, if it is truly indicative of a durable shift, may be explained by the fact of rising working hours and the changing gender division of labour. In the US, dual-earner and single-parent families especially are finding themselves caught between the demands of work and family, with inadequate time for either (see Hochschild 1989 and Burden and Googins 1987).

Neoclassical and work and spend approaches are not necessarily observationally equivalent with respect to future preferences. A work and spend model would predict much more willingness to trade off *future* income (ie, potential pay rises) for time than *current* income. However, work and spend would suggest that workers will not actually get the opportunity to make such a trade, and in the next period, hours will not

---

5 Researchers have failed to recognize the correlation between intensity and hours. See, for example, Bell and Freeman.

have fallen. By contrast, neoclassical theory has no a *priori* prediction about workers' preferences regarding future income, although it does contend that if workers do want to trade future income for reduced hours at time t, then at time *t+1* they should have shorter hours.

As predicted by the work and spend approach, the survey data show markedly different attitudes toward current and future income. For example, in a 1978 US survey in which few workers wanted to trade current income, 84.4 per cent said they would like to allocate at least some of a 10 per cent pay rise to more free time, with 47.3 per cent of those wanting to allocate all of the increase (Best 1980). A recent study of corporate lawyers in associate positions also found high willingness to trade future income for free time, especially if others were doing it (Landers, Rebitzer and Taylor, 1993).

European data is similar. In a 1977 survey, reducing worktime was more popular than higher incomes among West German, French and UK workers (Yankelovich 1985: 10). And a 1991 survey found that among German workers, shorter work time still holds a slight advantage over a pay increase, despite the large reductions in hours since 1977 (Bell and Freeman 1992, Table 5).

The 1978 US survey is interesting because the passage of time allows us to see whether or not preferences have been validated. They clearly have not been. While many workers have not received real pay increases (particularly male, hourly workers), salaried employees and women have experienced income gains. Yet neither group has seen their hours fall: on the contrary, hours have risen substantially since the survey was conducted, lending support to the work-and-spend rather than the neoclassical approach. Furthermore, the 1985 Current Population Study cited above which found only 8 per cent of workers wanting fewer hours also supports work-and-spend. Those who did not have their 1978 preferences for shorter hours validated apparently adjusted to their new levels of income and did not express dissatisfaction with their hours.

The work and spend approach relies on particular types of consumption behaviour. To date there has been very little empirical testing of alternative consumption theories, ie, those beyond life cycle and permanent income. Again, observational equivalence makes testing difficult. How are we to know if high dependence of present consumption on past consumption is due to habit formation or to the fact that the goods in question are merely satisfying fixed preferences? How can we tell whether correlations between income and the purchase of certain goods represents status consumption or ability-to-pay?

There is some survey data which is suggestive. In data reported by the Roper polling organization people have been asked at two different periods of time whether they consider various goods to be luxuries or necessities. The data support a habit formation approach. Only two categories (automobile and a tumble dryer) out of nine (washing machine, TV set, home air conditioning, car air conditioning, second automobile, dishwasher and second TV set) did not show a substantial increase in the fraction of people who considered them to be necessities between 1973 and 1992 (Roper 1993; 89). As habit formation theory would predict, newer goods are considered luxuries, even if they are widely owned (VCR, second phone, stereo, dishwasher).

Pollsters have also been asking, over a long period of time, about consumption expectations. Although the question does not directly address status consumption, a path of rising expectations over time is a necessary component of a dynamic Duesenberry-style model. The survey question is the following: *'In order to live in reasonable comfort around here, how much income per year do you think a family of four needs today?'* Interestingly, people always think the necessary amount is more than the median family actually has, which is consistent with a 'keeping up with the Joneses' process. Furthermore, 'needs' track income quite closely (see Table 4.3).

Table 4.3 US median income and 'reasonable comfort'

Question: In order to live in reasonable comfort around here, how much income per year do you think a family of four needs today?

	Income necessary for 'reasonable comfort' ($)	Median family income ($)
1978	19,600	17,640
1981	24,800	22,388
1983	28,400	24,673
1985	30,600	27,734
1987	32,500	30,970
1990	36,800	35,353
1992	38,000	35,939

Source: 'Reasonable comfort' series from *The American Enterprise* Washington DC: American Enterprise Institute for Public Policy Research, May/June 1993, p 86. Median family income from the *1992 Economic Report of the President.*
Note: All figures in current dollars.

Recently the gap between the two has narrowed, perhaps indicating a reduction of aspirations on account of slower income growth.[6] This data could be used to support an emulation story, which would predict that expectations track, but always exceed incomes.

The values context: the growth of 'post-materialism'

Since the Depression and the Second World War, populations in North America, Western Europe and Japan have grown progressively less concerned with material success. The research of Ronald Inglehart (1977, 1990) details these changes, using more than 200 national surveys on values. The surveys are designed to identify two basic value types —

---

6 One problem with this comparison is that the median family no longer comprises four people, and has fallen from 3.7 to 3.2 over this period. A preferable measure would be median income for families of four. The editors have also noted that people may be registering changes in prices, because median incomes have not risen much at all in this period.

Table 4.4 Distribution of materialist and post-materialist value types by age in Europe 1970–1986 (%)

Birth years of age cohort	Netherlands Mat PM	West Germany Mat PM	Great Britain Mat PM	Denmark Mat PM	Belgium Mat PM
1956–1965	20 27	22 26	22 15	24 20	30 16
1946–1955	23 23	26 19	27 14	25 19	29 16
1936–1945	26 19	34 12	29 10	32 12	34 12
1926–1935	33 13	41 9	31 9	35 9	37 10
1916–1925	35 12	42 9	35 7	38 6	42 7
1906–1915	42 8	49 6	40 6	46 4	46 5
1880–1905	43 6	53 5	45 4	49 2	51 4
N	(24,197)	(24,401)	(24,336)	(21,142)	(22,569)

Birth years of age cohort	France Mat PM	Italy Mat PM	Rep. of Ireland Mat PM	Luxemburg Mat PM
1956–1965	26 20	30 14	31 11	22 22
1946–1955	28 18	34 13	37 8	28 14
1936–1945	35 14	48 8	44 5	34 9
1926–1935	42 9	51 6	45 5	40 9
1916–1925	46 8	55 4	51 3	45 5
1906–1915	54 4	57 3	53 3	45 5
1880–1905	54 3	58 3	53 3	49 6
N	(26,192)	(26,797)	(20,947)	(6,412)

Birth years of age cohort	N. Ireland Mat PM	Greece Mat PM	Spain Mat PM	Portugal Mat PM
1956–1965	28 10	31 15	27 20	41 8
1946–1955	42 5	40 13	40 15	47 4
1936–1945	47 5	49 7	53 6	55 5
1926–1935	48 6	51 6	60 3	60 3
1916–1925	50 5	55 6	62 3	70 2
1906–1915	55 4	60 3	72 2	72 1
1880–1905	56 4	62 4	67 2	74 0
N	(6,019)	(12,216)	(2,690)	(2,728)

Source: Ronald Inglehart, *Culture Shift in Advanced Industrial Society* Princeton University Press, Princeton, 1990. Combined results from European Community surveys, 1970–1986
Note: Percentages do not add up to 100 because mixed types are omitted.

'materialist' and 'post-materialist'. In each country, beginning with those born in the late nineteenth century, each successive cohort has become less materialist and more post-materialist. By the 1986–87 surveys, there were more post-materialists than materialists among the youngest (15–24 years) age group (see Table 4.4 and Figure 4.3)

Inglehart's hypothesis is that this values shift comes from the pre-adult economic experience. He argues that cohorts which grew up in difficult

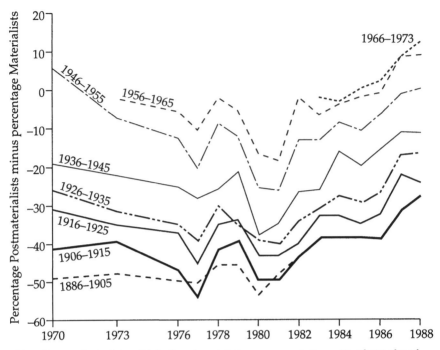

Note: Dates refer to date of birth. Based on data from representative national samples of
publics of France, Great Britain, West Germany, Italy, Belgium and The Netherlands,
interviewed in European Community surveys of 1970 and 1973 and EuroBarometer
surveys 6 through 29.
Source: Ronald Inglehart, *Culture Shift in Advanced Industrial Society* Princeton University
Press, Princeton, 1990.

Figure 4.3 *Value priorities by age in Europe, 1970–1988*

economic times and under conditions of economic deprivation are more
materialist. Those cohorts who grew up in the prosperity of the postwar
era are more post-materialist. Cross-sectionally a similar relation holds:
people from families with higher occupational status and higher income
are more likely to be post-materialist. Cohorts apparently do not become
more materialist as they age. Rather, shifts in values come about largely
through generational effects. The generational shift toward post-
materialism has had a major impact on the 'value composition' of the
public. In the European Community the ratio of materialists to post-
materialists was 4 to 1 in 1970–1; by 1988 it was 4 to 3. In the United States,
the comparable ratios were 3.5 in 1972 and 1.5 in 1987. Under conservative
assumptions, Inglehart projects that in Europe by the year 2000
materialists and post-materialists will be almost equal in the population.

One issue raised by Inglehart's analysis is the impact of business cycles
or longer term deterioration in economic performance on values. Inglehart
does find that current economic conditions have an impact. For example,
high inflation rates in the 1970s temporarily reduced the incidence of post-
materialism; similarly, current economic performance has retarded the

shift toward post-materialism. For example, the cohort born in 1966–73 is (so far) not significantly more post-materialist than its successor. This is the first cohort for which this has been the case, going back to the cohort born in 1880–1905. What does the current period of slow growth imply, then, about the future path of attitudes toward materialism? It is probably too early to say. First, current conditions, although clearly less favourable than during the 'Golden Age', are not comparable to the early 20th century or the 1930s Depression. Second, there is considerable uncertainty about future economic conditions. Third, the uneven impact of stagnation across the population might suggest growing diversity in attitudes. I would say that while it is certainly possible that younger cohorts will be less 'post-materialist' than the baby boom generation, it is by no means certain.

Finally, a caveat about public opinion data is in order. While attitudinal surveys are useful, they have certain limitations. First, the link between attitudes and behaviour is complex: respondents may be articulating what they would like to believe, rather than attitudes which inform their actual behaviour. Second, the wording and ordering of questions often affect outcomes. (However, Inglehart's results are quite robust.) Finally, in-depth interviews often reveal different sentiments than those articulated in simpler surveys. Therefore it is always wise to use survey data in a larger evidentiary context.

AN EMERGING ANTI-CONSUMERIST MOVEMENT?

Have the findings of Inglehart and others on post-materialism actually been translated into behaviour? There is some evidence on this. Inglehart has found that post-materialists are in fact 'economic under-achievers'. They earn less than materialists, once occupation and education are controlled for. Post-materialists tend to have 2.5 times the educational level of materialists, and 3 times the occupational prestige, but only 1.25 times the income. In the United States, post-materialists were less likely to have high incomes than materialists — 21 per cent of post-materialists fall into the top income quartile, as compared to 31 per cent of materialists.[7] Furthermore, these differences are showing up at the macroeconomic level. Nations with high levels of post-materialists tend to have lower levels of economic growth. The partial correlation coefficient for post-materialist values and economic growth in a regression model is minus –0.52 (significant at the 0.02 level).[8]

An extreme form of post-materialism, namely anti-consumerism, has begun to emerge at the margins of social life. In the United States it goes by the name of the 'voluntary simplicity' or 'frugality' movement. It is motivated by concern for the environment, a desire to be liberated from

---

7 Post-materialist values tend to be strongly positively correlated with parents' income and occupational status as well as respondents' own educational levels and occupational status. For comparisons of economic achievements, see Inglehart 1990, Chapter 5, Figure 5.2, p 171, and Appendix Table A.7, p. 443.
8 Inglehart, 1990, p 64 and Figure 1.10.

oppressive and meaningless work, and a traditional frugal attitude to money. Growing unemployment and consumer debt, as well as the longer-term shift to 'post-materialism', have fuelled interest in this movement. Unlike the 'back to the land' movement of the 1960s, this one does not advocate dropping out of society. It argues that a careful relationship to money can create financial independence and freedom from the 'rat race' of modern society.

My own research on anti-consumerist trends is at an early stage. However, I have some findings to report. In a 1993 survey I conducted at a Boston-area shopping mall, 72 per cent of respondents indicated that they could live a more frugal life. Twenty-two per cent said this would make them 'better off', 47 per cent said they would be 'the same' and 31 per cent said they would be 'worse'. Combining the first two categories, then, 69 per cent of respondents did not anticipate that spending less money would make them worse off. Sixty-four per cent of respondents said that they 'always' or 'often' feel Americans have or buy too much, and 31 per cent always or often feel that they personally have or buy too much. A majority (56 per cent) of respondents said they can afford everything they really need.

I have also conducted interviews with white collar workers who have lost or left their jobs and are living on reduced incomes. Most of them have gone through value changes which made them unwilling to make the personal sacrifices that had been required to succeed in demanding careers. A common theme in the interviews has been the declining importance of money, as compared to personal fulfilment, meaningful work and reasonable schedules. 'I lost my job and I've never been happier' is one refrain. Many feel that they had 'sold' their lives to someone else while they were working, and have now gained control. They are pleased to be 'doing something important and worthwhile', after 'selling computers'. They note that 'after being laid off, I got a support group of friends.' Those interviewed expressed no regrets about their decisions or even the events that they had no control over.[9]

There is also a group of people who are choosing a less dramatic reduction of consumption. These 'downshifters' have left successful and demanding careers in order to get more workplace control, time and meaningful work. Many remain in the same fields, but at lower salaries and conventional success levels. They also frequently move to smaller urban or small-town settings. Unfortunately there is very little quantitative evidence on this trend. A final and numerically far more important trend is the growth of anti-consumerist religious movements, particularly Christian evangelicals and 'New Age' spiritualists. These movements share a view that material goods are false gods and that simple lifestyles are the key to a satisfying life.

---

9 Quotes are from a workshop entitled 'Living Well on Practically Nothing', METCO Center, Needham, Mass. April 26, 1993. Interviews were conducted with participants in the workshop.

CONCLUSION

I do not intend to make too strong a case. While I believe there are significant trends moving northern countries away from current consumption patterns, the obstacles to stabilizing consumption are far greater. First, because the pattern of value shift is inter-generational, the pace of change is slow. The remaining 'stock' of strong materialist attitudes is a powerful social force.

Second, I have not talked at all about the relationship between public attitudes and the structure of social and economic power. Public opinion has only a limited impact on social, political and economic institutions. (For an excellent treatment of this issue, see Ferguson and Rogers 1986.) There are strong vested interests in continued economic growth. The ongoing integration of the world economy makes the 'economic imperative' for growth even more pressing. There is also the powerful obstacle of employer resistance to shorter hours. Only collective organization by workers and citizens can translate popular attitudes into social realities.

Third, the possibility of stagnation over the medium term means that there will be an upturn in materialist attitudes. The time series data show that temporary economic adversities lead to temporary changes in the degree of materialism. If stagnation continues over a longer period very different outcomes are possible. Aspirations may adjust, with the trajectory of falling materialism remaining unchanged. If coming years are experienced along the lines of the 1930s, new cohorts may grow up increasingly materialist.

In any case, the current mood is one of economic pessimism among all the industrialized countries. People are feeling powerless in the face of a globalizing market economy. This does not bode well for alternative economic visions. For a scenario of stable or declining consumption to be politically viable, proponents must have a credible answer to the challenge of international openness and competition. While the present moment gives us a real opportunity, capitalizing on it is a delicate and difficult task. For decades, the momentum in economic discourse has belonged to the right.

In the autumn of 1993, prompted by growing unemployment, the four day week has once again become a serious topic of discussion in Europe. The French have been debating it and Volkswagen has shifted to a four-day week with pay reductions. In the United States a four-day workweek bill has been introduced in Congress. While it is too early to know what the outcome of these discussions will be, it seems that the discourse around working time is already shifting.

REFERENCES

Altonji, J and Paxson, C (1988) 'Labour Supply Preferences, Hours Constraints and Hours-Wage Tradeoffs', *Journal of Labour Economics*, vol 6, no 2, pp 254-76
Bailyn, Lotte (1993) *Breaking the Mold* The Free Press, New York
Bell, L and Freeman, R (1992) 'Why do Americans Work More Hours Than Germans?' mimeo

Best, F (1980) 'Exchanging Earnings for Leisure: Findings of an Exploratory National Survey on Work Time Preferences', *R & D Monograph*, 79 US Department of Labour, Employment and Training Administration, pp 147–60

Burden, D and Googins, B (1987) 'Balancing Work and Homelife Study' Center on Work and Family, Boston University

Duesenberry, J (1949) *Income, Saving and the Theory of Consumer Behavior* Harvard, Cambridge

Ferguson, T and Rogers, J (1986) *Right Turn: The Decline of the Democrats and the Future of American Politics* Hill and Wang, New York

Frank, R (1985) *Choosing the Right Pond: Human Behavior and the Quest for Status* Oxford, New York

Gunsch, D (1991) 'For Your Information' *Personnel Journal*, October 1991, p 22

Hochschild, A (1989) *The Second Shift: Working Parents and the Revolution at Home* Viking Penguin, New York

Inglehart, R (1977) *The Silent Revolution* Princeton University Press, Princeton

Inglehart, R (1990) *Culture Shift in Advanced Industrial Societies* Princeton University Press, Princeton

Kahn, S and Lang, K (1987) 'Constraints on the Choice of Work Hours: Agency versus Specific-Capital' National Bureau of Economic Research, Cambridge, Massachusetts, working paper no 2238, May

Landers, R, Rebitzer, J and Taylor, L (1993) 'Rat Race; Adverse Selection in the Determination of Work Hours' unpublished mimeo, Massachusetts Institute of Technology

Lewis, H G (1969) 'Employer Interests in Employee Hours of Work' unpublished mimeo, University of Chicago

Maddison, A (1987) 'Growth and Slowdown in Advanced Capitalist Economies' *Journal of Economic Literature*, vol XXV, no 2, pp 649–98

Marglin, S and Schor, J (1990) *The Golden Age of Capitalism: Reinterpreting the Postwar Experience* Clarendon Press, Oxford

Moen, P and Dempster-McClain, D (1987) 'Employed Parents: Role Strain, Work Time, and Preferences for Working Less' *Journal of Marriage and the Family*, vol 49, pp 579–90

Moffitt, R (1982) 'The Tobit Model, Hours of Work, and Institutional Constraints' *Review of Economics and Statistics* vol 64, August, pp 510–15

Pew Global Stewardship Initiative Survey (1994) unpublished results

Roper Organization (1993) 'How We Classify Ourselves' *The American Enterprise*, pp 82–89

Schor, J (1992) *The Overworked American: The Unexpected Decline of Leisure* Basic Books, New York

Schor, J and Hilary Seo (1994) 'The Effect of Payment by Salary on Hours of Work' unpublished mimeo, Harvard University

Schuessler, A (1993) 'Presidential Campaigning and Mass Consumption' Harvard/MIT Research Training Group in Positive Political Economy, manuscript, January

Seo, H (1993) 'Hours Levels, Hours Variation, and Hours Determination' Harvard University undergraduate thesis

Shank, S (1986) 'Preferred Hours of Work and Corresponding Earnings' *Monthly Labor Review*, November

Smith, S (1986) 'The growing diversity of work schedules' *Monthly Labor Review*, November

US Chamber of Commerce (1994) *1993 Employee Benefits Report*, Washington DC

Yankelovich, D (1985) *The World of Work: An International Report on Jobs, Productivity and Human Values* Octagon Books, New York

Chapter Five

Population Growth and the Environmental Crisis: Beyond the 'Obvious'

Franck Amalric

O n many accounts, the twentieth century has witnessed an unprecedented transformation of the world. Economic growth, technological innovation, the shrinking of the world due to the emergence of modern means of transport and of communication, the globalization of the economy, sometimes of politics, two world wars and the multiplication of regional conflicts, are among the many phenomena of historical dimension that have reshaped the world during this century. And undeniably, the increase in the number of persons living on Earth is another facet of this profound transformation.

The figures are indeed impressive: at the turn of the century, world population is estimated to have been about 1.5 billion. It reached 2 billion around 1930, 2.5 billion in 1950. It is now well over 5 billion, and prospects for the year 2025 are between 7.6 and 9.4 billion, with a medium variant at 8.5 billion(UN 1991). Although such an increase necessarily raises a number of issues, in particular the capacity of adaptation of the different societies in which it takes place, it is still necessary to stress that the number of people living on earth cannot be a problem *per se*, but only the possible cause of a problem. Health, particularly of women, the environmental crisis, poverty, food security, international security, are the ultimate issues that need to be addressed. It is only in relation to them that looking at the consequences of population growth becomes relevant.

As in the rest of this volume, this chapter is mainly concerned with issues pertaining to the global level. It therefore leaves out a number of topics often associated with population growth, like the impact on the local environment or the consequences for economic development. Our focus here is population growth in the perspective of the global environmental crisis.

The contribution of population growth to the environmental crisis is a very controversial topic. In the recent literature, however, there has been several attempts to synthesize the different views within a single theoretical framework, known as the *Ehrlich equation*. This paper shows the limits of this framework, not only in its capacity to explain the process of environmental degradation, but also in its capacity to provide guidelines for policies. Two shortcomings of the equation are discussed. First, although it is presented as giving a neutral account of the issue, in practice it appears decisively biased against the population factor. Second, applying the equation can only assess the contribution of one factor in generating additional environmental degradation, leaving out those factors that created the problem in the first place. In response, I propose an alternative way to use the equation, one which yields quite different results indeed. But let us start by giving a short account of the debates around population growth.

THE CONTEXT

As one facet of the transformation of the world, population growth occupies a special place. First, although undeniably a central feature of this century, it has nevertheless been opposed to the larger historical trend, that of modernization. The world has been viewed as a world in transition towards development, and population growth as stemming from behaviours – namely high fertility rates – characterizing the non-modern or undeveloped world. Thus, the prevailing theory of fertility of these last thirty years, the so-called demographic transition theory, associated a decline of fertility rates with the process of modernization.[1] The view was taken up by policy-makers around the developing world, as epitomized by Indira Gandhi's claim, made in 1972 as Prime Minister of India, that 'development is the best contraceptive',[2] or as defended by the developing countries at the 1974 World Conference on Population in Bucharest.

Second, it underlines the split between developed and developing countries, and is therefore a highly political topic. Since 1960, almost 90 per cent of world population growth occurred in developing countries, and the trend will be even more accentuated in the future decades (UN 1991). As a potential factor of environmental degradation, population growth becomes therefore a topic of international negotiations. But even without referring to the global environmental crisis, population growth in the South is seen as a destabilizing factor in the world. At the extreme, it is presented as the cause of all ills. Consider, for instance, the following

---

1 The theory was set to explain and/or describe how societies move from high to low fertility rates. In a first stage, mortality rates were supposed to decline due to improvements in health, notably in the wake of the introduction of modern medicine. Population growth would stem mechanically from the ensuing gap between mortality and fertility rates. Finally, with development and an improvement in the conditions of life, fertility rates would decline, thereby ending the transition. Seminal works are Notenstein (1945), Davis (1955).
2 Cited in Keyfitz (1991).

declaration made in 1988 by the Club of Earth, whose members all belong to both the US National Academy of Sciences and the American Academy of Arts and Sciences:

> *Arresting population growth should be second in importance only to avoiding nuclear war on humanity's agenda. Overpopulation and rapid population growth are intimately connected with most aspects of the current human predicament, including rapid depletion of non-renewable resources, deterioration of the environment (including rapid climate change), and increasing international tensions.*

Cited in Ehrlich and Ehrlich 1990: 18

This vision of the issue by the scientific community is not isolated. The famous Heidelberg Declaration signed by 425 prominent scientists, including 52 Nobel prize laureates, at the time of the end of the conference in Rio called overpopulation a 'plague' comparable to 'hunger and pandemics'.

This vision is, in part, purely egoistic. In Rufin's words it is the fear of the 'new barbarians' (Rufin 1989), that a degradation of the situation in the South will threaten the North's welfare. As Lorimer, a leading demographer, bluntly put it:

> *trends which threaten the national aspirations of more than half the world's population present a problem to all nations.*
> *Frustration breeds envy, suspicion and violence. The security of the lucky nations with large national resources, accumulated wealth and advanced techniques may be critically affected by the progress or reverse experienced in the less fortunate nations during the next few decades.*

Lorimer 1963: 145

In response, Southern countries have imposed the view that Northern lifestyles, and not Southern population growth, was the central cause of the global environmental crisis (see the chapter in this book by Lipietz). The absence of any official debate on population growth in Rio – although the topic was on everybody's lips in the corridors – can be seen as a diplomatic victory of the South... and of the Vatican.

But the North–South divide is not that clear, because population growth also underlines the split between the westernized elites of the South and the vast majority of the people living in those countries. To have a large number of children is often the best strategy for the poor : children are rapidly productive; they are an insurance for old age; indeed, each child is an additional chance of economic success for the family. But for the governing bodies of developing countries, population growth is increasingly perceived as hindering economic development. It raises the demand for capital so as to increase the capital available per worker; it increases the demand for social services, notably in education, and thereby diverts some resources from more directly productive investments (see Lewis 1955; Coale and Hoover 1958). Population policies are thus designed in the perspective of a race between population growth and economic development. Note that the long-term effects of population growth – notably population density – are given little attention (Stamper 1977). Today, many developing countries have official population planning policies geared at slowing down the rate of population growth. These include China, the nations of South Asia, Central America, South-East Asia and parts of Africa. Conversely, most states of South America, West Asia and some of Africa do not have any population programme (UN 1990). Altogether, about 61 per cent of people in the world live under a government which incites them to have fewer children. The North – from the point of view of sustainability – and the westernized elites of the South – from the point of view of development – could thus find a common interest in controlling population growth from the perspective of 'sustainable development'. Already in the 1984 World Conference on Population in Mexico, the South was asking for financial aid from the North to run population planning policies. In these conditions, who will protect the basic reproductive rights of the poor ?

For these different reasons, population growth may seem a very convenient and (statistically) highly visible cause of environmental degradation. Because it stems from non-modern behaviours, it does question the modern ideology. Furthermore, it appeals to common sense: environmentalists consider that the level of human activities on earth is reaching unsustainable limits. Since the total of human activities is the sum of each person's activity, it would appear intuitively correct to say that the more persons there are, the greater the total activity. Thus population growth is often held, notably by biologists and international organizations, as an important factor, if not the main one, of environmental degradation (Ehrlich and Ehrlich 1990; WCED 1987; UNEP 1990; Myers 1991).

But the reality is much more complex because different people have varying impacts on the environment. Lifestyles is the other main possible factor of environmental degradation. If sustainability puts some constraints on the total level of human activity, it does not, at least initially, determine how this activity is to be distributed. In theory, a sustainable society could equally be characterized by a small number of people with a high level of consumption per person, or by a large number of people consuming little resources but enjoying long periods of leisure. In this respect, a number of authors have argued that modern institutions are the real culprit, and that population growth has only a marginal impact on the environment. Inegalitarian market relations would displace subsistence agriculture for export crops nourishing the luxury demands of the rich (Lappé and Collins 1980). Indeed a number of recent famines have been explained, not as an absolute scarcity in food, but as a scarcity of *entitlements* to food (Sen, 1981). Environmental problems linked to agriculture – desertification, deforestation, erosion of soils due to over use, pollution due to the over use of pesticides and fertilizers – would thus stem from a misuse of land under the pressure of market forces. Another important factor would be modern technology, oriented toward economic efficiency at the cost of environmental degradation (Commoner 1971).

THE 'EHRLICH' EQUATION : THE IMPOSSIBLE SYNTHESIS

In response to this chorus of conflicting views, there has been a number of attempts to arrive at a synthesis and to measure the contribution of each factor. This required a theoretical framework, often referred to as the 'Ehrlich equation'.[3] The equation combines total impact on the environment, population and consumption in the following way:

$$\text{total impact} = \text{population} \times (\text{total consumption}/\text{population}) \times (\text{total impact}/\text{total consumption}) \tag{1}$$

To simplify, we shall henceforth write:

$$I = P \times C' \times T.$$

C' is consumption per capita and must be distinguished from C, total consumption.

This equation is merely an identity and is therefore always valid. In fact, C' and T are never observed directly. I, T, and C are the independent variables, in the sense that we can usually get direct data for them, and straightforwardly

$$C' = C/P, T = I/C \tag{2}$$

The goals of the equation are :

- to propose a synthesis of the conflicting theories of the causes of environmental degradation;
- and to provide a framework that can guide policy-makers in their dealing with the environmental crisis.

The value of the equation must be gauged by its capacity to meet these two goals, the former of which is dealt with in this section, the latter one in the next section.

We cannot derive directly from the Ehrlich equation any indication as to the contribution of population growth to the total environmental impact. What is usually done is to compare the levels of impact at two different points in time; what is then assessed is the contribution of population growth to the increase in the total impact. But to do so, it is

---

3 The equation has been presented as the theoretical framework of the debate (Ehrlich and Holdren 1971; Ehrlich and Ehrlich 1990; Harrison 1992), and applied empirically (sometimes in a simplified form) to measure the contribution of population growth to global warming (Bongaarts 1992, Myers 1991), land use (Harrison 1992), energy consumption (Pearce 1991), and use of pesticides, nitrogenous fertilizers and motor vehicles (Commoner 1988).

necessary to make three assumptions. First, to choose one definition, among many possible, of such contribution. Second, to consider the groups as homogenous in terms of consumption and technology. Third, to suppose that the variables P, T and C' are independent. These assumptions are repeatedly made in the literature without much explanation or empirical support. Yet they are problematic in many ways, as we shall now see.

What Definition ?

To examine this issue, we can use a simplified version of equation [2][4]

total impact = population x impact per person, or I = P x F   [3]

With this equation, there is a number of possible definitions of the contribution of population growth to a change in total impact. This is merely a new version of the old index-number problem which arises each time we attempt to split changes up into contributions. A simple numerical example will make the point :

Date 1:	P=100	I=100	F=1
Date 2:	P=200	I=400	F=2

Total increase of environmental impact is therefore 300. There are two extreme methods of defining the contribution of population growth. One is to look at what would have been the impact of population growth if there had not been any increase in the level of impact per person. Under this hypothesis, the contribution would have been 100. Thus the contribution of population growth would be 33 per cent. Another way, rarely used, is to take the increase in impact per person as a given, and look at what would have been the impact had there not been any population growth. In this case, the contribution of population growth is assessed at 200 or 66 per cent of the total.

Perhaps the more commonly used method is to define this contribution as the ratio of the rate of population growth to the rate of growth of the environmental impact. In our two period example, this third method is equivalent to the first one. But to use rates of growth is itself not very satisfactory because the result will depend on the number of sub-periods considered. It is theoretically more appropriate to suppose that there is an infinity of sub-periods. In this case, the contribution will be determined by the logarithms of the variables. This definition has the important advantage of being independent of the initial level of impact per person (F_0).

We have therefore three competing definitions (assuming that P, F and I move in the same direction):

---

4 This is the form used by Ehrlich and Holdren (1971).

1     $Sp = (P_2-P_1)/(I_2-I_1) \times F_1$
2     $Sp = (P_2-P_1)/(I_2-I_1) \times F_2$
3     $Sp = (\text{Log } P_2-\text{Log } P_1)/(\text{Log } I_2-\text{Log } I_1)$

where Sp stands for the 'share of population growth'.

Still others could be proposed, and each definition will yield very different results. Thus, in our numerical example, we get: Sp (1) = 33 %; Sp (2) = 67 %; Sp (3) = 50 %. The variability of the results is illustrated in the case of world carbon dioxide emissions between 1960 and 1988 in Tables 5.1.

Table 5.1 Regional carbon dioxide emissions, 1960–1988

	Carbon dioxide		Population (mil)		Population impact %			(3) % total
	1960	1988	1960	1988	1	2	3	
Africa	40	170	279	605	36	70	53	2
Asia (dev)	297	1193	1574	2876	27	60	43	12
Latin America	82	267	218	430	43	71	57	3
North America	852	1430	199	272	54	66	60	11
Europe	732	1180	425	496	27	38	32	5
USSR	396	1086	214	284	19	39	28	6
Japan	64	270	94	122	9	28	18	1
Oceania	28	75	16	26	37	61	49	1
Developing countries	418	1630	2072	3911	31	63	46	17
Developed countries	2072	4040	948	1200	28	43	35	22
World	2490	5670	3020	5111	[29]	[51]	[41]	

Source: Harrison (1992).
Notes: 3 corresponds to Harrison's results. Contributions at the world level are calculated indirectly, weighted by increases in emissions.
The last column is the share of population growth to total world increase in emissions using definition 3.

Definition 1 (respectively 2) considers implicitly F_1 (respectively F_2) as the 'normal' level of impact per person. The difference between 1 and 2 stems therefore from a difference in what level of consumption per person is taken as a reference. Definition 3, by contrast, assesses the impact of population growth as dependent on the impact level when each bit of the population growth occurred. It is therefore independent of any fixed level of reference of impact per person. But it does not mean that it is free of any reference. In fact, its reference is dynamic. Under definition 1, each 'additional' person has a 'right' to an impact of F1. Under definition 3, each additional person has a right to an impact which corresponds to the average impact when the person comes into the world.

By a similar argument, but considering now the contribution of the growth in consumption per person with the constraint that the sum of the two contributions must be equal to one or 100 per cent, we derive that the different definitions also take implicitly as a reference a certain size of population: P_2 for definition 1, P_1 for definition 2, and a dynamic reference for definition 3. Saying, with definition 1, that population growth accounts for 33 per cent of the increase of total impact means that, if there had not been any growth in impact per person, then total impact would have risen only by 33 per cent.

There is no overriding reason to favour one definition over the other. Definition 3 has indeed the advantage of being independent of any *a priori* choice of a level of reference. Yet this is a choice in itself. And if it is mathematically convenient, it should however be supported on other grounds. The point is that it is impossible to measure the 'contribution' of population growth to the environmental impact of human activities without adopting references for both population size and consumption per person. And different references will yield very different results.

Heterogeneity

It is again useful to start with a simple numerical example, still using the simplified version of the Ehrlich equation. Suppose that a country is composed of two groups, A and B, with the characteristics at date 1 and 2 as shown in Table 5.2.

Table 5.2 Population groups and environmental impact

Date 1	Group A	Group B	Total
Population	90	10	100
Total impact	0	10	10
Impact per person	0	1	0.1

Date 2	Group A	Group B	Total
Population	190	10	200
Total impact	0	20	20
Impact per person	0	2	0.1

If decomposition of the country between group A and group B is impossible, that is if the levels of population and consumption are only observable at the country level, than it will appear that the contribution of population growth to the increase in environmental impact is 100 per cent (whatever the definition used), since there is no increase of the average impact per person. But this result is clearly not satisfactory since the group which grows in size has no impact on the environment.

The problem is sometimes acknowledged, for instance by Harrison (1992: 313), and such studies disaggregate between developing and developed countries or between continents. But others are much less careful. Thus, in an UNFPA publication, Myers (1991) could argue that population growth is responsible for about two thirds of the increase in the emissions of carbon dioxide between 1950 and 1985, simply because during the period, the emissions of carbon dioxide grew by 3.1 per cent a year and world population by 1.9 per cent. But since the population of developing countries grows fast in size but consumes very little resources, whereas the reverse is true for developed countries, there is a problem of heterogeneity. A simple disaggregation between developed and developing countries reveals the oversight. In doing so, Harrison found that population growth would account for 41 per cent of the increase in emissions between 1960 and 1988 using the same definition as Myers (definition 3).

Myers is not an isolated example. Pearce (1991) makes a similar assumption while assessing the contribution of population growth to the increase of energy consumption between 1960 and 1984 using the first definition (ie consumption per person of reference is that of 1960). At the world level, when calculated directly as Pearce does, this contribution would be 46 per cent. Simply using the disaggregated results by continent and weighting them by the respective increases of consumption yields a very different result indeed: 23 per cent.

Disaggregating between North and South yields other quite paradoxical results. When we speak about population growth, it is 'obvious' that we speak about population growth in the South. This is indeed where 90 per cent of population growth took place during the last three decades. Yet, according to Harrison's calculation (using definition 3), population growth in the *North* would have accounted for a greater share of the global increase in the emission of CO_2 than population growth in the South : 22 as against 17 per cent. This is because the consumption per person factor is so much greater in the North, a point indeed stressed by Ehrlich and Ehrlich (1992 : 58). Thus, with the same definition and the same data, if we speak about the contribution of population growth at the world level, we find 64 per cent. But if we speak about the contribution of population growth taking place in developing countries, we find only 17 per cent!

This problem of aggregation is particularly critical because consumption per person and fertility rates are negatively correlated around the world. That is, because the poor tend to have more children and the rich less, in any aggregate, the equation will overestimate the contribution of population growth. This is true at the world level, as revealed in the preceeding examples. But it is also true at a continent or country level, although none of the studies reviewed take the issue into account. The 17 per cent above is therefore already a large overestimation of the environmental impact of population growth among the poor in developing countries. If we could statistically distinguish between the 10 per cent richest in developing countries, and the rest of the population, then we would certainly find that 80 per cent of world population growth has contributed less than 10 per cent of the increase in total emissions of CO_2. Table 5.3 illustrates how misleading are results not taking into account the issue of heterogeneity. Finally, it must be noted that heterogeneity in the technologies used introduces yet another bias in the calculation of the different contributions.

We must however be cautious while disaggregating the data, when statistically feasible, to take into account use of natural resources for exports, as not doing so might give very misleading results. For instance, looking at

Table 5.3 World carbon dioxode emissions, 1960–1988: contribution of
population growth

	Contribution of population growth (%)	*% of total population growth*
Crude world calculation	64	100
Disaggregated world calculation	41	100
LDC contribution to DWG	17	89
Contribution of the 'poor' in LDC	<10?	80

Note: Definition 3 used for calculation of respective shares.

changes in farms' areas (area of arable and permanent crops) between 1961
and 1985, Harrison found that population growth would account for 72 per
cent of the change in developing countries. The technological factor, here
the inverse of yield, would have had a negative impact, that is it would
have tended towards reducing the area under cultivation by 2.6 per cent per
year. Put another way, the demand for land has risen by 3.2 per cent per
year (population growth 2.3 per cent, per capita consumption growth 0.9
per cent), and this demand was met by a greater productivity (2.6 per cent)
and by an extension of land area under cultivation (0.6 per cent).

These results are of course open to the critique of heterogeneity, the
more so as access to land is particularly inegalitarian. Inequality in land
distribution is therefore not considered as a potential factor of
environmental degradation. But even more importantly, the whole effect
of commercialization and the use of land for exports to developed countries
is not taken into account, although this is held as a main cause of
environmental degradation (Lappé and Collins 1980; Repetto and Holmes
1983). For instance, commercial logging for the export market has been a
main force behind deforestation; another important force, notably in Brazil,
has been the establishment of cattle ranches, again turned towards exports.
But this demand is not taken into account because of the separation
between developing and developed countries.

Are the Variables Independent?

Applying the Ehrlich equation supposes that the three variables P, T and
C' are independent. That is, it is assumed that an increase in P (population
growth) will have no effect on the technology used or on the level of
consumption per person. This is a very strong assumption, and one that
the authors have adopted perhaps without stopping to gauge its
significance. Yet it openly conflicts with a number of theories on the
consequences of population growth.

In their seminal article Ehrlich and Holdren (1971) had discussed why,
in the case of industrialized countries, an increase in population could
have a positive effect on T, thereby reinforcing its impact on the
environment. In general, and notably in developing countries, the inverse
might well be true. For instance, it has been argued that population

growth was itself a main cause of technological innovation (Boserup 1965). A higher density of population not only permits the implemention of new methods of production, such as a greater division of labour, but also creates the need for new methods when the environmental constraint is binding. For Boserup, it is therefore both a condition and an incentive for innovation. A number of studies on the subject have shown that greater population pressure led to the adoption of labour-intensive farming methods, without necessarily degrading the environment (Hayami and Ruttan 1971; Binswanger and Ruttan 1978). In other cases, the environmental constraint may be stringent, and population growth will lead to a reduction of levels of consumption per person. In any case, each individual addition to the population brings with him or herself a new capacity to innovate, and this will possibly more than compensate what he or she will take from the world, as forcefully argued by Simon (1981).

It has also been argued that population growth could have a negative effect on consumption per capita. This is in fact a central argument put forward by those who view population growth as a problem. 'A population problem exists', argues Demeny (1986: 481), 'when my preference for children diminishes your access to steak. . We have a population problem, in other words, when externalities are attached to demographic behaviours.' That is, although it may be in a couple's immediate interest to have many children, if all couples behave similarly, and because some resources are finite, eventually everybody will be worse off, a process often referred to as the 'poverty trap'. In fact, if all resources have been appropriated (whether held privately or in common), the impact of population growth on these resources will not be direct, but transmitted through the institutional framework. Taken to extremes, if the management of a resource is independent of the demand for this resource (I = constant), an increase in the size of the population will automatically lead to a decrease in consumption per capita if T is assumed fixed. Not taking into account this sort of mechanism will lead again to an overestimation of the impact of population growth on the environment.

Conversely, and according to demographic transition theory, an increase in consumption per capita will possibly have an impact on fertility rates, and thus on the level of population in the long term. Under this argument, the contribution of the consumption factor would be overestimated.

The point is that population growth can be accommodated in different ways. How it is accommodated, and therefore what will be the consequences of population growth, will largely depend upon the institutional framework (Repetto and Holmes 1983; Cain and McNicoll 1988; McNicoll 1989; Ghimire 1993). It follows that assuming the variables P, T, and C' independent is far from neutral : it supposes a certain organization of society and of the world, typically one in which resources are freely and/or openly accessible. It is in such a context that Hardin wrote on the 'tragedy of the commons', although what he really meant by commons was open-access resources (Hardin 1968). In such a setting indeed the impact of the growing population will theoretically be at its maximum. Classic examples for such open-access resources are the atmosphere and the oceans. But paradoxically, it is with respect to these resources that the case of population growth as a main cause of environmental degradation is empirically the weakest. Extending this framework to resources like land or forest is very problematic because it does not take into account institutions that do exist, and the role of which is precisely to render interdependent the variables P, T and C'. The effect of land tenure, of community structures, of governmental intervention are not taken into account, although it is repeatedly argued that they play a crucial role. Indeed, in the static framework, Ehrlich's equation has the validity of an identity. But through the institutional framework, including the market system, the variables P, T and C' are made interdependent and the use of the equation to assess the contribution of population growth to environmental degradation becomes highly problematic.

REMEMBERING THE PAST

The other goal of the Ehrlich equation is to guide environmental policies. By assessing the respective contributions of the different factors, it implicitly points to where adjustments are needed. Yet, when applied, the equation assesses the contribution of each factor during a limited period of time only, without taking into account the historical process that led to the environmental crisis. Considering the environmental impact at a given point in time, say 1960, it can only gauge the contribution of each factor at that time to a subsequent increase in this impact. This methodology is again very problematic. For instance, even if population growth had been the main factor leading to an increase in additional emissions of CO_2 thereafter, the reason why this constitutes a problem is because the 1960 level of emission was already unsustainable, and this possibly for reasons quite independent of past population growth. The results obtained from applying the Ehrlich equation during a short time span cannot therefore guide directly future policies.

In this respect, an interesting distinction has been made by Shaw (1989). To contrast the intellectual roots of Commoner's position – that 'environmental impact is not correlated with the rate of population growth' (cited in Shaw) – with that of the other extreme and apparently opposite one of Nafis Sadik (1988, cited in Shaw) who claims that 'high fertility and population growth are contributing to the damaging of the natural resource base', Shaw introduces the distinction between 'ultimate' versus 'proximate' causes of environmental degradation. He then suggests that Commoner's claim is one of ultimate causality in which the major contributor to environmental degradation is the high and wasteful consumption of countries with low population growth rates, while Sadik's claim is one of proximate causality, where the question is not about the factors that produce a particular outcome, but those that aggravate, trigger or catalyse the incidence in a specific situation.

The conclusion Shaw draws from this distinction is quite typical. His argument is that Sadik's position has become particularly important today because the control of ultimate causes of environmental degradation have remained out of reach. In other words, between the two forms of expansion of human activity, demographic and economic, Shaw sees the former as easier to tackle than the latter, and concludes that it should therefore be given priority. This view is not an isolated one. We find it, for instance, in the conclusion of Ehrlich et al(1993), where their discussion of the difficulties to meet future food demand is quite convincing. Yet they fail to address directly the issue of distribution, and only emphasize the population growth factor. As they conclude:

> *It is impossible to avoid the conclusion that the prudent course for humanity, facing the population-food-environment trap, must above all be to reduce humane fertility and halt population growth as soon as humanely possible (pp 24–5)... In theory much could be done to reduce the maldistribution of food, although doing so is certain to be very difficult in practice (p 26).*

A last example is Bongaarts (1992) on the emissions of CO_2: 'Since few governments are likely to adopt policies that deliberately reduce the growth in GDP per capita, any reduction in [growth of fossil fuel consumption] must preferably be brought about by reducing population growth or energy and carbon intensities' (pp 25–6).

The picture is now quite clear : under the assumption that ultimate causes of environmental degradation are out of reach, proximate causes like population growth are put at the forefront. The cynism of this view is striking : it calls for putting yet another limit on the poor who supposedly have too many children, whereas they already face limitations in all directions. It is thus those who have benefited least and suffered most from all the past experiences of development and of globalization who should make the necessary adjustments to the environmental crisis. Note that the assumption that 'nothing can be done about the ultimate causes' is in accordance with assuming that the variables P, T, and C' are independent.

But if this 'pragmatic' assumption is dropped, Shaw's distinction leads to a very different conclusion and points out another failure of usual applications of the Ehrlich equation. Ultimate causes are what created the environmental crisis in the first place. Those social groups or countries behind those causes should therefore bear the cost of finding and implementing a solution. Such a solution would be an institutional structure regulating the use of certain resources. To clarify the issue, we have to come back to the general causes of environmental degradation. The environmental crisis stems from the convergence of three factors : the finiteness of the natural resource base; a growing demand for natural resources; and inadequate institutions to regulate the use of these resources. Typically, the form of management of the resources should respond to the tension between a sustainable supply of resources and demand for these resources. And if demand is low compared to the resources available, there is no need for formal management.

Both the Ehrlich equation and the view that nothing can be done about the ultimate causes suppose that there is no regulating mechanism, and thus that all the blame for environmental degradation should be put on the growing demand. This absence of regulating mechanism is clearly a cause of environmental degradation, and it seems suprising to suppose that sustainability could be attained without doing something about it. It follows that the contribution of different factors to the environmental crisis cannot be gauged according to their direct impact on the environment. A different methodology must be used, one which distinguishes between two stages:

1. Total demand is inferior to the sustainable threshold. In this case, there is no specific need to regulate the use of the resources. Different factors (population, consumption, technology) will affect total demand. To measure the contribution of each factor to an increase in total demand, the Ehrlich equation can be used with the proviso made in the preceding section.
2. Total demand is above the sustainable threshold. If sustainability is held as a first priority on the political agenda, then the only cause of environmental degradation is the absence of an efficient regulating mechanism. That is, environmental degradation should be attributed entirely to a lack of political commitment to find an appropriate solution.The impact of such factors as population, consumption or technology should no more be assessed in terms of environmental degradation, but rather should be assessed with respect to the stress they put on the regulating mechanism, whether it exists or not.

The point is that the impact of population growth – or, for that matter, of increases in consumption per capita – cannot be assessed in the same way whether it takes place in an open world or whether it takes place in a closed one. For example, if A is the impact of population growth in the absence of an institutional framework, and B is its impact when there is an adequate institutional framework (A>B), B is the blame that should be attributed to population growth, A minus B being attributed to the absence of institutional framework. The polluter should be held responsible, not only for polluting, but also for creating the conditions in which others will pollute more if no solution is implemented. It does not make sense to denounce the unsustainability of population growth in societies which are unsustainable for altogether different reasons.

In this perspective, it makes little sense to speak about the relative contributions of population or consumption to increases in CO_2 emissions in a country like the United States. The fundamental problem is that total demand has risen above the threshold under which no form of management is compatible with sustainability. Thus, the main cause of environmental degradation is that emissions of CO_2 are not regulated.

Taking this approach, all the increase in emissions of CO_2 in developed countries since 1960 would be due to a lack of political intervention, since in 1960 emissions per capita in those countries were already above the sustainable level with respect to the 1960 population. In these conditions, the contribution of population growth to the increase of world emissions would be 17 per cent (the share of developing countries, see (Table 5.3), whereas the blame for a lack of political intervention would be 62 per cent (total share of developed countries in the increase, see Table 5.1)).

CONCLUSION

A first goal of the Ehrlich equation was to clarify the controversy around the causes of environmental degradation. Is this goal achieved? At a purely numerical level, the index number problem leads to some ambiguities that should be clarified. At a more theoretical level, the equation leaves out a number of factors bearing on the environment; notably commercialization and the breakdown of traditional resource management systems. Finally, the heterogeneity problem leads to numerical results which are wholly misleading. This was very clearly illustrated by Table 5.3 : we showed that population growth in Southern countries could not account for more than 17 per cent of the increase in CO_2 emissions since 1960, instead of 64 per cent if the heterogeneity issue is not considered! And even 17 per cent is an overestimate since it does not take into account the problem of heterogeneity within the South. Speaking about population growth at the world level can only bring confusion, because it associates people with radically different life-styles. When we speak about population growth at the world level, it is obvious we speak first and foremost about population growth in the South. Yet when we calculate the contribution to the environmental crisis of population growth taking place in different regions of the world, the share of that in the North turns out to be greater than that in the South. There is therefore an important problem of semantics, which can only be solved through great cautiousness in the use of different terms. A first step towards clarifying the debate will be to fully acknowledge that it is meaningless to speak about the impact of population growth at the world level.

A second goal was to help design policies toward sustainability. The problem here is that the Ehrlich equation tends to blame the 'proximate' rather than the 'ultimate' causes of environmental degradation, to use Shaw's terminology. But this is again very misleading. The logic that says 'we cannot do anything about the ultimate cause, so let us do something about the proximate ones' supposes that there is a 'we'. It supposes the existence of a political community confronted with a series of different issues. By contrast, the global environmental crisis will require the *creation* of a global community. Certainly not a world government; but a community of states which recognize that they are addressing a common issue. Ever since the publication of the Brundtland Report entitled *Our Common Future*, it is more and more argued that we all share one world, and thus a common future. This, supposedly, creates some duties for all of us with respect to one another. It is also clearly a call for responsibility. Since we *all* share the same world, we *all* have to make some efforts to save it, and thus, implicitly, we *all* have to make some sacrifices for it. This world we share is a world of limited natural resources, of limited global commons. In other words, what we share is a common problem, the global environmental crisis, because it may affect the lives of us all. Furthermore, through this crisis, we all become supposedly interdependent : each person's behaviour and well-being is connected to other people's behaviours through the global biospheric system.

For the North, this sense of interdependence is perhaps quite new. Certainly not so for the South who has felt dependent upon the North for many years, notably through economic relationships. What this means is that the 'ecological' interdependency revealed by the global environmental crisis cannot be perceived in its own terms only. It must be recast in the history of international relations, and within the context of another form of interdependency, namely economic interdependency. In this perspective, addressing first the issue of economic relations appears a much more promising route to building some form of international cooperation, than speaking about population growth.

REFERENCES

Binswanger, H and Ruttan, V (1978) *Induced Innovation: Technology, Institutions and Development* Johns Hopkins University Press, Baltimore

Bongaarts, J (1992) 'Population growth and global warming' *Population and Development Review*, vol 18, pp 299–319

Boserup, E (1965) *The Conditions of Agricultural Growth* George Allen and Unwin, London

Cain, M and McNicoll G (1988) 'Population growth and agrarian outcomes' in Lee et al (eds) *Population, Food and Rural Development* Clarendon Press, Oxford

Coale, A and Hoover, E (1958) *Population Growth and Economic Development in Low-Income Countries* Princeton University Press, Princeton, New Jersey

Commoner, B (1971) *The Closing Circle* Alfred A. Knopf New York

Commoner, B (1988) 'Rapid population growth and environmental stress' paper presented to the United Nations Expert Group on Consequences of Rapid Population Growth, United Nations, New York

Demeny, P (1986) 'Population and the invisible hand' *Demography* vol 23

Ehrlich P and Ehrlich A (1990) *The Population Explosion* Touchstone, New York

Ehrlich P, Ehrlich, A and Daily, G (1993) 'Food security, population and environment' *Population and Development Review*, vol 19

Ehrlich P and Holdren, J (1971) 'Impact of population growth' *Science*, vol 171, pp 1212–17

Ghimire, K (1993) *Linkages Between Population, Environment and Development* UNRISD, Geneva

Hardin, G (1968) 'The tragedy of the commons' *Science*, vol 162, pp 1243–48

Harrison, P (1992) *The Third Revolution: Environment, Population and a Sustainable World* I B Tauris, London

Hayami, Y and Ruttan, V (1971) *Agricultural Development: an International Perspective* Johns Hopkins University Press, Baltimore

Keyfitz, N (1991) 'Population and development within the ecosphere: one view of the literature' *Population Index*, vol 57, pp 5–22

Lappé, F and Collins, J (1980) *Food First, the Myth of Scarcity* Candor Book Souvenir Press, London

Lewis, A (1955) *The Theory of Economic Growth* Allen and Unwin, London

Lorimer, F (1963) 'Issues of population policy' in P Hauser (ed) *The Population Dilemma* A Spectrum Book, Englewood Cliffs, New Jersey

McNicoll, G (1989) 'Social organization and ecological stability under demographic stress' in McNicoll and Cain (eds) *Rural Development and Population: Institutions and Policy*. The Population Council, Oxford University Press, New York

McNicoll, G Y and Cain M (eds) (1989) *Rural Development and Population: Institutions and Policy* The Population Council Oxford University Press, New York

Myers, N (1991) *Population, Resources and the Environment: the Critical Challenges* United Nations Population Fund, New York

Notenstein, F W (1945) 'Population: the long view' in T Schultz (ed) *Food for the World* Chicago University Press, Chicago

Pearce, D (1991) 'Population growth' in D Pearce, E Barbier, A Markandya, S Barrett S, K Turner, T Swanson (eds) *Blueprint 2: Greening the World Economy* Earthscan, London

Repetto, R and Holmes, T (1983) 'The role of population in resource depletion in developing countries' *Population and Development Review*, vol 9, pp 609–32

Rufin, J-C (1989) *L'Empire et les Nouveaux Barbares* Pluriel, Paris

Sadik, N (1988) *1988 State of the World Population Report: Safeguarding the Future* United Nations Fund for Population, New York

Sen, A (1981) *Poverty and Famines* Clarendon Press, Oxford

Shaw, P (1989) 'Rapid population growth and environmental degradation: ultimate versus proximate factors' *Environmental Conservation*, vol 16, pp 199–208

Simon, J (1981) *The Ultimate Resource* Martin Robertson, Oxford

Stamper, M (1977) *Population and Planning in Developing Countries: a Review of Sixty Development Plans for the 1970s* The Population Council, New York

United Nations (1991) *World Population Prospects* 1990 United Nations, New York

United Nations (1990) *Result of Sixth Population Inquiry Among Governments* United Nations, New York

UNEP (1990) *Unep Profile* Unep, Nairobi

WCED (1987) *Our Common Future* Oxford University Press, New York

Chapter Six

Distributive Justice and the Control of Global Warming

V Bhaskar

INTRODUCTION

'Global warming raises unique questions about our responsibilities to future generations.' – Thus begins John Broome's recent book, *Counting the Cost of Global Warming*, which argues that we have a responsibility to take action today so that the welfare of future generations is not adversely affected. The argument that Broome makes is a moral one, not one based on self-interest – after all, you and I will be dead and gone by the time that the greenhouse effect makes the oceans rise and alters our planet's climate in unforeseeable ways. The unborn are powerless, and if we choose to be guided purely by self-interest, we could bequeath them a wasteland without even being around to hear their reproach. Broome argues that our actions must be guided by ethical criteria, and that we must take remedial action to curb the emissions of greenhouse gases. The precise extent to which we do so depends upon how we morally evaluate alternative distributions of 'well-being' across generations. Broome does not provide any answers to the question of how much we must curtail greenhouse gas emissions. His purpose instead is to set out a framework, an ethical framework, within which such questions may be addressed.

Broome's dissection of inter-generational distributional questions is insightful and valuable. It establishes clearly that global warming is a *moral* issue. No discussion of it can be divorced from ethics, and from the ethical responsibility of today's denizens of the globe towards their descendants. However, one omission is striking – there is no mention of the heterogeneity of today's generation, of the different standards of living between the typical American and the typical Sudanese, or indeed between the Japanese and Bangladeshis of tomorrow. Nor is there any discussion of the different degrees to which these societies have exploited the global commons to date. What implication do these large differences have for the division of responsibilities? Do a Sudanese and an American have equal responsibility to future generations? What does 'equal responsibility' mean in the context of global warming?

Of all issues which impinge upon the welfare of future generations, global warming is perhaps the one which explicitly requires a treatment of intra-generational distributional issues. The global environment is a global public good, and greenhouse gases, which contribute to global warming, are an archetypal public bad. It does not matter whether a unit of carbon dioxide is emitted in Bangladesh or the United States – it contributes equally to global warming in either case. Consequently we must define, in global terms, the responsibility of current generations the world over to future generations. Inevitably in doing so, we confront the division of the burden of this responsibility within the current generation.

This paper begins where Broome's book ends. Given that we have a moral responsibility towards future generations, we have to consider what is the moral basis for distributing the burden of our responsibility within the current generation. How, in particular, this burden should be distributed between nation states (although in principle one can go further, and allow for heterogeneity within nations).

The primary concern of this paper, based on the ethical distribution of the burden of emission control, has been questioned. It is argued that questions of ethics are irrelevant, and the distribution of international burdens across countries will inevitably be determined by power-politics. I do not believe that this is entirely correct. The outcome of international negotiations may be determined by bargaining power; however, bargaining power is not determined *entirely* by material factors – it is also influenced by the perceived morality of one's position. The importance of ethical considerations may be greater than usual in the case of global warming, since we will feel a need to undertake any emission control only if we are concerned about future generations.

The remainder of the paper deals with a number of interrelated issues. The empirical evidence on the current distribution of global emissions of greenhouse gases is detailed. Next we ask whether there is a conflict between an efficient programme of emission reductions and an equitable one, and argue that tradeable emission permits can ensure efficiency, allowing us to base the allocation of emission entitlements on grounds of equity. The next section sets out a simple model which explains how earlier generations may use the global environment in order to affect the intra-generational distribution of welfare in the future. The rest of the paper focuses on the moral issues. First we consider welfare-based theories and theories based on rights, and suggest that in the case of global warming, both theories give similar answers. A discussion follows of some of the specific criteria which have been suggested for allocating emission entitlements. Finally we address the question of historical responsibility: since the stock of greenhouse gases is due to past emissions, which are overwhelmingly by the North, should we correct for this differential exploitation of the global environment in the past, or should we let bygones be bygones?

THE DISTRIBUTION OF GREENHOUSE GAS EMISSIONS WORLDWIDE

Human economic activity has, in the last 100 years, contributed to an increase in the concentration of 'greenhouse gases' – of which carbon dioxide (CO_2), methane, nitrous oxide and chlorofluorocarbons (CFCs) are the most important. The increased atmospheric concentration of these gases gives rise to the 'greenhouse effect', whereby a larger proportion of solar energy is trapped by the atmosphere instead of being reflected back into space. This has the effect of raising global temperatures, which could have major effects upon global climate. The consequent melting of the polar ice-caps would raise sea levels, and could adversely affect low-lying areas such as Bangladesh, the Netherlands and island states. The precise size of the greenhouse effect and its impact is a matter for scientific debate, and far from settled. The economic costs of global warming are also a matter of controversy – Nordhaus (1991) for example argues that the costs are small whereas Cline (1992) is less sanguine. Nevertheless, the issue is too serious to be dismissed given the magnitude of projected increases in CO_2 concentration. Carbon dioxide emissions increase rapidly with industrialization and the burning of fossil fuels. As developing countries industrialize, one can expect their levels of CO_2 emissions per capita to gradually 'catch-up' with current levels in the developed world. If the situation continues unchanged, the Intergovernmental Panel on Climate Change (IPCC) estimates that CO_2 concentrations will double (as compared to pre-industrial concentrations) by the year 2020, and will be more than quadrupled by the end of the 21st century. These large changes are likely to have non-linear impacts upon the global environment and the economy, which we can predict only approximately. Carbon dioxide exists in the atmosphere for a very long period of time. Consequently, changes in CO_2 concentration will be long-lasting, and can only be reversed gradually. For these reasons it appears that precautionary measures to control the emissions of greenhouse gas emissions are warranted, and indeed the issue is on the international agenda today, although coordinated action to tackle the problem may yet be a long way off.

Of the greenhouse gases, carbon dioxide and methane are the most significant – the role of nitrous oxide in global warming has been down-graded in recent years, and agreement has been reached on the phasing out of CFCs. Carbon dioxide is resident in the atmosphere for an estimated period of between 50–200 years, while methane has a shorter time span of about ten years. Consequently, the long-term effects of emissions are substantially greater in the case of carbon dioxide. The primary source of CO_2 emissions is industry, due mainly to the combustion of fossil fuels. Second in importance are emissions from biota sources, due to deforestation and other changes in land use pattern, which are mainly concentrated in developing countries. Estimates of emissions from biota sources are extremely divergent, and for individual developing countries total emissions can vary by a factor of two to four depending upon the estimate used. Table 6.1 gives an estimate of the distribution of industrial

Table 6.1 Percentage shares in CO_2 emissions, population, GNP, 1988

	1988 emissions[1]	*Cumulative emissions[2]*	*Population*	*GNP*
North America	25.2	33.2		
Western Europe	15.0	26.1		
Eastern Europe + USSR	25.6	19.6		
Japan + Oceania	6.1	4.8		
Developed countries	71.9	83.7	23	84
LDCs	28.1	15.0	77	16

Notes:
1. Industrial CO_2 emissions.
2. contribution to current concentration of CO_2 in the atmosphere, based on cumulative emissions since 1800, adjusted for decay.
Sources: Grubler and Nakicenovic (1992), Young (1991)

CO_2 emissions world-wide, as well as an assessment of the contribution of various regions to current concentrations.

There is substantial uncertainty about the extent of anthropogenic methane emissions. Methane emissions in developed countries are relatively small, and are due to the use of fossil fuels and livestock/animal waste. In LDCs, methane emissions are due principally to livestock waste and rice cultivation. The extent of these emissions is extremely difficult to calculate, and there are a range of estimates in the literature. Table 6.2 presents the 1988 emissions of CO_2 and methane in terms of gigatons/tons of carbon equivalent. It shows that the distribution of carbon emissions per head of population is highly uneven. The basic asymmetry is that the 'North' has a level of per capita emissions over four times that of the 'South'. There are further variations within the North, with North America having a level of per capita emissions over twice as large as Western Europe and Japan. The USSR and Eastern Europe have higher per capita emissions than Western Europe/Japan. Within the South, Brazil has a

Table 6.2 Regional CO_2 and methane emissions 1988

	1988 emissions[1]	*Per capita emissions[2]*	*Emissions per unit GDP[3]*
North America	1.64	6.06	0.34
Western Europe	1.00	2.62	0.21
Japan + Oceania	0.40	2.82	0.22
Eastern Europe + USSR	1.70	4.25	0.75
Developed countries	4.73	3.97	0.35
LDCs	3.39	0.87	0.45

Notes:
1. Total emissions in gigatons of carbon equivalent
2. Tons of carbon equivalent per head of population
3. Tons of carbon equivalent per $1000 PPP equivalent
Source: Grubler and Nakicenovic (1992)

relatively high level of per capita emissions, and the exact figure could be higher due to uncertainties about the detrimental effects of deforestation.

It is also instructive to consider emissions per unit of GDP, not so much because this is an appropriate way for allocating emission rights, but because this measures, very crudely, the efficiency with which output is produced relative to the global cost in terms of emissions. GDP is measured in dollars, and the conversion can be made either at the market/official exchange rate, or in purchasing power parity units. We have chosen the latter, which is a better measure of real income. Table 6.2 shows that the South has a higher rate of emissions per unit of GDP than the North, but this difference is not as large as one might imagine, being about one third higher. Eastern Europe and the USSR have very high emission/GDP ratios, more than double that of the OECD countries. There is also substantial divergence between OECD countries, with North America having an emission/GDP ratio of 1.5–2 times that of Japan/Western Europe.

EFFICIENCY VS EQUITY IN EMISSION CONTROL

Is there a conflict between efficiency and equity in the distribution of emission entitlements? Prima facie, there indeed seems to be some conflict. Many of the developing countries have a low level of overall emissions – as we saw in Table 6.2, per capita emissions are much lower in the developing world as compared to the developed world. However, the industries in these countries are often energy inefficient, use older technologies and are hence more polluting. This is illustrated by the higher level of emissions per unit of GDP in the developing world – a crude measure only since the composition of GDP is very different in different countries. Countries with a high ratio of emissions to GDP, and in particular with a high ratio of fossil fuel CO_2 emissions relative to GDP, will tend to have lower costs of abatement. This is because their current technologies/practices are often energy inefficient relative to alternative technologies which are available. It is argued that this is the case in the former USSR/Eastern Europe and China and India, where the greater use of coal also contributes. Many developing countries could also reduce emissions by controlling deforestation; a measure which may be warranted independently, quite apart from its impact upon the greenhouse effect. Since greenhouse gases are a truly global pollutant, it matters not, from the point of view of global warming potential, where emission reductions are brought about. If it is cheaper to reduce emissions in developing countries rather than in developed countries, this would be an efficiency argument for focusing on reducing emissions in the former. However, would this not conflict with egalitarianism?

It is indeed the case that any system of non-tradeable emission entitlement will bring about a conflict between equity and efficiency. There is no reason for these two principles to coincide, and indeed, for some very plausible principles of equity, such as equal per capita entitlements, the divergence can be very large. This criterion implies that developing countries could increase emissions, while developed countries make substantial reductions. However, an efficient system of emission reduction is one where emissions are reduced at lowest cost, in terms of output. If emission entitlements are distributed on a per capita basis, targets which are acceptable to developed countries will be well above what developing countries need, and hence the latter will be under no pressure to reduce the GHG emissions in the process of development.

Barrett (1991) estimates costs of reaching a given emission target for the European Community under alternative schemes for distributing this target among member states. He finds that uniform obligations are very cost inefficient, and in an illustrative calculation, finds that their total cost is almost 50 times greater than a cost effective policy. The cost difference is likely to be even larger in the case of the world as a whole, where differences in the marginal costs of reducing emissions are likely to be substantially larger than within the European Community.

A second problem with non-tradeable emission entitlements is that distributional considerations will influence the global emission target. To illustrate this point, consider the case of equal percentage reductions. This will be extremely costly for low polluters and for the developing countries, and consequently they will press for higher global emission targets. Considerations of equity will therefore dictate a higher global target than that indicated by our earlier analysis. Take another case, of equal per capita emissions. This may be more equitable; however, countries with low levels of per capita income, but with a high level of emissions relative to income (such as many developing countries including China), will have no incentive to reduce emissions, even when these can be acheived at relatively low cost. Opportunities for cheap emission reductions will be foregone as a consequence.

This conflict between efficiency and equity can however be avoided by allowing emission entitlements to be traded. With tradeable entitlements, a country which is obliged to reduce emissions must either do so itself, or persuade another country to do so, and buy its entitlement. A country such as the United States which has a high level of emissions, but which may also have a high marginal cost of reducing emissions, has the option of persuading China to control its emissions in exchange for monetary compensation. Indeed, if the market for tradeable entitlements is competitive, it can be shown that the resulting distribution of emissions will be efficient – a target level of emissions will be achieved at minimum cost. Consequently the entitlements may be distributed on an equitable principle, since trade allows us to achieve efficiency independent of the initial distribution of entitlements. The system we refer to is of course one of tradeable emission quotas. Each country is allocated a quota of permissible emissions on some distributional principle. Countries may however trade their quotas, so that a country which would like to emit more CO_2 than its quota can buy quotas from a country which has a surplus of quota relative to emissions. If the market for quotas is competitive, the price of one unit of emission quota is the opportunity cost of one unit of emissions in terms of convertible currency, and this is the same for all countries. Consequently this system achieves an efficient allocation of emission reductions.

It must be noted here that a global target for emissions can also be achieved efficiently via a uniform global tax on emissions, which would be levied upon individual countries by an international authority. This is the carbon tax which has been discussed by a number of authors (Epstein and Gupta 1990; Hoel 1992; Whalley and Wigle 1991). This tax revenue can be redistributed to countries in ways consistent with distributional criteria. It can then be shown that the global tax achieves an efficient allocation of emission reductions provided that no country has a large share in tax revenues *at the margin*. A system of tradeable entitlements is similar to a global carbon tax – indeed, in the absence of uncertainty and with an appropriate distribution of tax revenue the two systems are equivalent. We shall focus on quotas since they can be naturally related to our discussion of equitable entitlements.

INTER- AND INTRA-GENERATIONAL DISTRIBUTION

Greenhouse gas emissions are an example of market failure, and indeed of the failure of individual nation states, which requires remedial action at the international level. Individuals in the course of economic activity emit greenhouse gases which contribute to global warming. The costs of their economic activity are incurred by future generations worldwide. Although each individual may be concerned about the welfare of future generations, he/she cannot make sufficient impact as an individual to be able to take corrective action unilaterally. Indeed, since the greenhouse effect is a global problem even nation states are too small to internalize this negative externality. The global environment is perhaps best seen as a public good, which will be collectively bequeathed to future generations. Individual nations, by reducing their emissions, leave a safer environment for future generations worldwide. However, emission reductions in any one nation may be too small to have a significant global effect, and furthermore, can be offset by increased emissions by other nations. *Collective* international action in order to solve this problem is therefore imperative.

Consider the following stylized representation of the problem, which may clarify the interaction between inter-generational and intra-generational issues. Let there be N countries, with countries indexed by the superscript i. Current national income, y^i, is assumed to be a increasing, strictly concave function of the level of GHG emissions in country i, g^i – this reflects the fact that control of greenhouse gas emissions is costly, and the marginal cost of emission control is increasing, the more we reduce emissions. National income may either be consumed or saved; in the latter case t^i is transferred to the future generation. U^i represents the utility of the current generation in country i. This depends both upon the current generation's consumption, and upon the utility of its descendants, V^i. V^i is increasing in the transfer received by the tomorrow's generation, t^i, and decreasing in the total level of global emissions, G.

$$G \quad = \quad \Sigma_i \, g^i \qquad\qquad\qquad\qquad\qquad\qquad [1]$$
$$U^i \quad = \quad U^i \, (y^i - t^i \,, V^i) \qquad\qquad\qquad\qquad [2]$$
$$y^i \quad = \quad f^i \, (g^i) \qquad\qquad\qquad\qquad\qquad\quad [3]$$
$$V^i \quad = \quad V^i \, (t^i \,, G) \qquad\qquad\qquad\qquad\qquad [4]$$

This stylized model incorporates two significant features. The current generation in each country is 'partially altruistic' in two senses. First, it cares only about its own descendants, and not the future generation the world over, so that its utility depends only on V^i. Second, its concern about its own descendants could be limited, so that V^i could affect U^i only weakly.

Each country maximizes its utility function with respect to the level of emissions, g^i, and the level of transfers, t^i. This gives rise to the first-order conditions:

$$dU/dg^i \quad = \quad U_y(.) \, f_y(.) + U_v(.) V_G(.) \; = \quad 0 \qquad [5]$$
$$dU/dt^i \quad = \quad -U_y(.) \, f_y(.) + U_v(.) V_y(.) = \quad 0 \qquad [6]$$

[5] and [6] must be satisfied at an optimum for each country. From [4] we know that the partial derivatives of V depend upon G, the total level of global emissions. Hence each country's optimal choice depends upon the sum of emissions of every other country. A non-cooperative equilibrium is a pair (g^i, t^i), i =1,2,...N, such that [5] and [6] are simultaneously satisfied for each country. It is instructive to re-write the first order conditions as [7]

$$V_G(.)/V_y(.) \quad = \quad -f_g(.) \qquad\qquad\qquad\qquad [7]$$

This has a ready intuitive explanation. Each country chooses g^i to equate the marginal rate of substitution of its descendants between income and emissions, to the marginal cost of reducing emissions, in terms of income.

It is easy to see that such an equilibrium is inefficient, because emissions are a public bad. Each country's emissions decrease the welfare of future generations everywhere, but the country only takes into account the effect on its own descendants while making its choice. However, our primary concern is with the ethical aspect of this problem. What are the implications of this doubly partial altruism for intra- and inter-generational distribution?

Consider first the implications of the fact that each country cares only for its own descendants. Its concern is expressed through a transfer in two forms – a transfer of the private good, t^i, and a transfer of the public good, the global environment. The former can be directed exclusively to its own descendants, while the latter necessarily accrues to the future generation the world over. Since the country is concerned only about its own descendants, the transfer of the private good is more effective for this purpose. Consequently, partial altruism results in an excessive level of emissions. Each country will over-exploit the environment, thereby adversely affecting future generations in other countries. It compensates (or in fact, over-compensates) its own descendants for this adverse affect by transferring the private good. In effect, each country uses the global environment to alter the distribution of welfare within the future generation – it takes welfare away from the other countries and gives to its own descendants.

If all countries are symmetrically placed, the redistributive effect cancels out. The inefficiency still remains since the level of emissions is too high, being used for this redistributive purpose. The redistributive effects do not cancel out if countries are asymmetrically placed. To take a simple example, consider two countries which are otherwise identical, except for the fact that the first (the affluent country) generates more income from each unit of emissions than the second (the less affluent country). In equilibrium, the first country will have a higher level of emissions than the second, and will also transfer more income to its descendants. In effect, the present generation in the first country can effectively redistribute welfare within the future generation, from country two to country one.

Although we may care for the future generation, we may do so insufficiently, so that V may carry very little weight in our utility function. What are the implications of this sort of limited altruism? The first is that we may transfer too little to the future generation, both in terms of the private transfer and by degrading the global environment. An ethically adequate altruism will imply that we would have to increase both transfers. In other words, we would be called upon to reduce emissions of greenhouse gases to a level which is consistent with the future generation having a level of welfare to which they are morally entitled, rather than that which we deign to give them.

MORAL THEORIES IN THE CONTEXT OF GLOBAL WARMING

As the introduction of this paper stresses, concern about global warming is essentially a moral concern. There are two quite different ways in which a moral concern for future generations can be expressed. The first, which is the route taken by welfarism, is a concern with the well-being of the future generations, so that their welfare is incorporated along with that of the current generation in the social calculus. A welfarist concern suggests that the uncontrolled emission of greenhouse gases would reduce the (expected) welfare of future generations below acceptable limits. It asks us to place ourselves in a neutral position, to divorce ourselves from our position in the current generation, and to ask whether the distribution of welfare between us and our descendants is morally defensible. An alternative moral position concerns itself not with the welfare, but the rights, of future generations. From this point of view, the global environment is a common resource for us now and in the future. We can justifiably appropriate a part of it for our purposes only if there be, in Locke's words, 'enough and as good left in common for others'.

Let us begin by examining the implications of a welfarist position. There are, of course, several variants of welfarism. Utilitarianism gives us a choice between alternative social states so as to maximize the sum of individual utilities. Rawls' difference principle (1972) asks us to maximize the welfare of the worst-off person. Broome (1993) favours critical-level utilitarianism, which was first proposed by Blackorby and Donaldson (1984) – this states that we should seek to ensure that everyone has a critical minimum level of welfare, and having achieved this, we should be utilitarian. These welfarist principles, although very different, in the context of global warming and on the question of intra-generational distribution, may however give very similar conclusions.

How is this possible? After all, Rawls requires that we maximize the welfare of the least well off, whereas utilitarianism simply looks at the total sum of utility, irrespective of its distribution. These different theories may have similar practical implications because the distribution of welfare in the world today is so far removed from any utilitarian optimum. Given the widespread inequalities in the world today, it seems very likely that the marginal utility of one dollar to a poor Bangladeshi is substantially greater, and in fact of a different order of magnitude, than the marginal utility of one dollar to an average American. Utilitarianism would, in this context, require a redistribution of dollars towards the Bangladeshi until marginal utilities were equalized. Until that point, the practical difference between utilitarianism and the difference principle may be slight.

One may of course dispute the claim regarding the relative sizes of the marginal utility of one dollar. However, the only reasonable way to dispute this appears to be by denying that one can compare utilities across persons. If we do not allow for inter-personal comparisons of utility, we do not allow for the possibility of any utility-based moral theory. To the extent that we want to use any welfarist moral theory, we must allow for inter-personal comparisons of utility, and having allowed that, it seems unreasonable to dispute the conclusion regarding marginal utilities.

To conclude, any welfarist theory suggests that the burden of global warming should be put squarely upon the shoulders of the North. Of course, the qualititative conclusion is quite independent of the issue of global warming. The above argument would suggest a large transfer of wealth from the North to the South even if global warming was not a problem.

The welfarist theory of justice is disputed by rights based theories, such as those advanced by Locke, and more recently, by Nozick (1974). Nozick argues that the justice or otherwise of a social state cannot be evaluated by simply looking at the well-being of individuals in that state. Individuals have rights, including the right to appropriate what they have produced or acquired justly, and any redistribution on welfarist grounds would infringe those rights. Nozick's theory would argue that the difference in well-being between the American and the Bangladeshi is irrelevant, and may be consistent with justice. What matters is whether the resources which allowed the former to be well off are justly appropriated or not. If the condition of just appropriation is satisfied, redistribution is uncalled for. If the original appropriation is unjust, redistribution may be called for in order to ensure 'justice in rectification'.

There are two questions which arise in the context of the exploitation of global environmental resources. First, what does a rights based theory imply for the obligations of the current generation towards future generations? Second, if differences in well-being in the world today are related to unjust past appropriation of global environmental resources, is redistribution called for on the grounds of 'justice in rectification'? We address the first question in the remainder of this section, and deal with the second question later in the chapter.

Locke suggested that private appropriation of a resource was just if there be 'enough and as good left in common for others'. In the context of a scarce resource (such as the global environment), it is clearly literally impossible to leave enough behind for others if one uses it at all. Nozick therefore reinterprets the proviso: my appropriation is just if 'the situation of others is not worsened' (Nozick: 1974, 175). Nozick's proviso is very weak, as Cohen (1986) argues, since it allows the appropriator to retain all the benefits of acquisition. Nevertheless, even this weak proviso has some relevance. If we contribute to the greenhouse effect, thereby adversely affecting future generations, it is incumbent upon us to compensate them for this adverse effect. Our exploitation of the global environment allows us to enjoy a higher level of real income than would be possible in the absence of such exploitation. We should save a part of this real income, and transfer it to future generations, say as capital.

The future generation is however heterogeneous, and will be differentially affected by global warming – land-locked Switzerland may not suffer any adverse effects from global warming and may even benefit whereas a rise is the sea level could be disastrous for an island state such as Tahiti, or low-lying Bangladesh. Here the Nozickian proviso, that no one be worse off, requires us to make *differential* transfers – more to tomorrow's Tahitians and less to the Swiss. A given level of global emissions today entails a distribution (across countries or regions) of ill-effects in the future. These adverse effects must be compensated for by transferring resources from today's generation to those affected in the future.

The above discussion makes clear that current emission entitlements also entail a corresponding liability, for compensating future generations. How are the emission entitlements to be distributed within the current generation? The Lockean proviso suggests that each individual in the current generation has an equal share in this global resource. It suggests that countries should be distributed emission entitlements on the basis of their populations. Further, the liability to compensate future generations should be based upon the emission entitlement.

CRITERIA FOR DISTRIBUTING EMISSION ENTITLEMENTS

A number of criteria have been proposed as bases for distributing emission entitlements, which we can examine in the light of the preceding discussion.

Entitlements Based on 'Grandfathering'

Grandfathering refers to the establishment of a property right through use. In the context of the global environment, this criterion implies that entitlements to emit in the future will be equal to current emissions. In other words, those who are currently polluting excessively have thereby established a right to continue polluting in the future. If total emissions are to be reduced, this principle implies that emission entitlements will be proportionately reduced, so that each country will be called upon to make *equal percentage reductions* in emissions. In either case, this criterion favours the developed countries, which have a high level of current emissions, and adversely affects developing countries. On this basis, Table 6.2 suggests that developed countries with 23 per cent of the world's population will be allotted 58 per cent of the world's emission entitlements, whereas developing countries with 77 per cent of the world's population will be allotted 42 per cent of entitlements. Per capita entitlements in the North will be, on average, 4.6 times as large as those in the South. Since this doctrine is unfavourable to the South, it is sometimes sought to be tempered by requiring deeper cuts for countries which have had a greater historical contribution to emissions. Extending this, it may also be possible to allow for *negative cuts*, ie to allow developing countries to increase emissions. However, the underlying basis on which rights to the global commons are sought to be defined is the same in all these variants – the right is established through usage.

Grandfathering is based upon the *status quo* doctrine : the current rate of emissions confers a *status quo* property right that is established by the use of the right in the past. Consequently, if reductions are to be made, each country must be dispossessed from its *status quo* right equally. This is grossly inequitable, since developing countries, whose emissions will surely rise from their extremely low levels at present, are penalized. Even among developed countries, it punishes those countries which have made the greatest efforts at energy efficiency such as Japan. Such countries have lower levels of emissions as compared to the US, and the costs of additional emission reductions are substantially greater for them.

Recall our earlier discussion, where we argued that a rich country could use the global environment as a way of transferring welfare to its descendants. Grandfathering is doubly dubious: not only is this transfer not addressed, a further benefit is conferred upon those who over-exploit the environment.

Emission Quotas Proportional to GDP

The logic of this allocation is that all production should be required to be equally clean. This may seem an efficient way of achieving any global target, but this is not the case if quotas are not tradeable. The scheme without tradeable quotas requires countries to achieve the same *average* level of GDP to emissions. This is not the same as equating the marginal cost of emissions in terms of international currency. The latter can be shown to be the appropriate criterion for an efficient allocation of emission reductions. Distributionally, this scheme would be most favourable to Japan and Western Europe, and least favourable to Eastern Europe/former USSR and the developing countries. Given that there is no efficiency requirement for operating this scheme, the distributional criteria are based on the idea that the richer countries should have more of the world's common resource.

Equal Per Capita Emission Quotas

The basis for this principle is that the world's environment belongs equally to all human beings, and each one is entitled to an equal share. In other words, whatever the target level of emissions, permits should be shared out between countries on the basis of their share in world population. This principle entails a distribution of emission entitlements which is very different from the distribution of actual emissions, since the LDCs have a greater share of world population than of emissions. Opposition to this principle is essentially on 'pragmatic' grounds, that this would be unacceptable to developed countries.

With equal per capita entitlements, each country would have an aggregate entitlement proportional to its population. The question arises, should the aggregate entitlement in a particular year be based on the population in that year, or should it be based on population in some base year, say 1994? Several writers (Grubb 1989, for example) have argued in favour of the latter. They suggest that if entitlements were based on current population, poor countries, which would trade some of their entitlements for foreign exchange, would have a positive incentive to increase population so as to increase their foreign exchange earnings. The emission entitlements scheme would therefore have the undesirable effect of increasing population. However, on the assumption that governments are concerned with per capita income (or per capita welfare), this argument seems incorrect. An increase in population which raises total entitlements may increase the total foreign exchange earned by selling entitlements. It will not increase per capita foreign exchange earnings, and will therefore not raise per capita income. Per capita income is likely to fall due to the rise in population, given the scarcity of other factors such as land and capital. Consequently, a tradeable entitlements scheme based on current population will be neutral in its effect on population – it creates no additional incentive for higher or lower population size. Of course, if entitlements are based on population in the base year, this creates an additional incentive to reduce population growth.

If we start from the position that each individual has an equal right to global environment, the allocation of emission quotas is straightforward. Given the global emission target, this is simply divided by the global population, and each country is allocated quotas in proportion to its share of the world population. It is immediately obvious that most developed countries would then have a deficit of allocated emission quotas relative to their desired level of emissions, whereas developing countries would have a surplus. Consequently, trade in quotas would bring about transfers between countries. An equivalent allocation can be brought about by an international carbon tax; a specific tax which would be levied on each ton of equivalent carbon.

RECTIFYING HISTORICAL INJUSTICE AND GLOBAL WARMING

The discussion hitherto has been based an allocating entitlements to current emissions, without reference to the historical record of contribution to current concentrations of greenhouse gases in the atmosphere. But the greenhouse effect must take into account the contribution of past generations for reasons already stated; those of the cumulative build up of CO_2 in the atmosphere and its long-term effects. Fujii (1990) and Smith (1991) have attempted to calculate the overall responsibility of different countries for current CO_2 concentrations. This involves calculating the cumulative effect of emissions since 1800 (emissions at an earlier date are discounted by the rate of CO_2 decay). In the case of methane, the residence time in the atmosphere is short, so that the difference between current emissions and cumulative emissions is not very large. Table 6.1 shows current emission shares and the overall contribution to concentration, region-wise. The contribution of Western Europe and North America to the concentration was much greater than their share of current emissions. Historical emissions from LDCs have been extremely low, and hence their low share in contributing to overall CO_2 concentration.

Fujii (1990) argues that each individual in each generation has the same emission entitlement. He divides each region's contribution to current GHG concentration by the total population of the region, past and present, in order to derive the contribution per capita. This is even more unequal across countries than the distribution of current emissions per capita. Fujii argues that developed countries owe LDCs a debt because of their excessive emissions in the past. This point is also made by Smith (1991, 1993), who calculates a *natural debt index* – an index of how much each country has 'borrowed' from the natural environment. Both Fujii and Smith argue that this debt should be repaid, and that emission entitlements should be adjusted to correct this imbalance. Consequently, equitable allocation would require that LDCs have greater emissions per capita as compared to developed countries, reflecting the difference in natural debt.

What is the validity of this argument, which holds current generations in the North responsible for the emissions of their ancestors? Are Fujii and Smith right to argue that the North must today repay those natural historical debts? Or can one take an individualist stance, and argue that the natural debts incurred by past generations in the North have perished along with those who incurred them?

To take a welfarist moral position, one can argue that history is irrelevant. One can argue for a redistribution between North and South on welfarist criteria, given the enormous inequalities that exist in the world today. However, the question of precisely how these inequalities came about is irrelevant for a welfarist, and the fact of past exploitation of the environment by the North makes no difference to the argument. However, for a rights-based moral position, the question of the historical responsibility is indeed critical. Can one then take a purely individualist position, and argue that nations as such bear no responsibility, and it is merely the individuals who lived in the past who bear responsibility? If current generations in any country are not responsible for the acts of their predecessors, why should they have to repay a debt which they played no part in incurring? On this reckoning, developed countries may have indulged in excessive emissions of greenhouse gases in the past, but there is no way they can be held responsible for this, since the individuals who were responsible no longer exist.

This argument does not stand for several reasons. The first, and rather obvious, reason is that much of the carbon dioxide currently in the atmosphere has been emitted in the lifetime of the current generation. However, more importantly, it can be argued that the current generation may also have to take responsibility for past emissions, even if we do not want to attach any moral opprobrium upon them for this. The current generation is the beneficiary of *resource transfers* from previous generations. These resource transfers take various forms, including physical capital, human capital investments, and knowledge, as well as natural and environmental resources within developed countries. They have been possible only because of past exploitation of global environmental resources. If the earlier generations in the developed world had been constrained from degrading the global environment to the extent they have actually done, they would have suffered through lower level of per capita income. In consequence, they would have been less able to save and invest in productive capital, and less able to transfer productive assets to the current generation. Developing countries have a claim to a part of these transfers, simply because they were made possible by the excessive use of global environmental resources by previous generations in the developed countries. Put somewhat differently, if current generations in the North accept *assets* from their parents, then it is incumbent upon them to also accept the corresponding *liabilities*.

There are two caveats in applying this argument. First, if the past generation has transferred more liabilities than assets, the current generation in the North could well be justified in accepting neither – although however, this is in fact not the case. Second, excessive Northern exploitation of environmental resources may have also enabled a greater stock of global *public* goods to be transferred. Scientific knowledge is one example. These public goods may benefit all countries today, albeit to different degrees, and to the extent that they benefit the South, the North today has to compensate the South less.

What about the argument that the natural debt idea is invalid since the North was unaware of the possible harmful effects of emissions of greenhouse gases? It seems to us that this argument is misplaced. Ignorance of the harmful effects simply means that we cannot attach any moral blame on previous generations. However, no matter what motivated them, the effect was to benefit their children by permitting a larger extent of transfers of assets, and to the detriment of the global stock of environmental resources. Ignorance does not undo the case for corrective action today. An analogy would be if I take an object, not knowing that it belongs to you, and give it to my daughter, you are surely entitled to reclaim it, even though neither my daughter nor I may be a thief.

CONCLUSION

We have argued that questions of inter-generational as well as intra-generational equity must necessarily be confronted if we are to have a meaningful discussion of global warming. These questions of distribution can be addressed from a number of divergent viewpoints. Nevertheless, we find all these viewpoints seem to give qualititatively similar conclusions – that current generations have a responsibility to the future, and the burden of this responsibility must be borne largely by the North.

REFERENCES

Agarwal, A and Narain, S (1991) *Global Warming in an Unequal World: A Case of Environmental Colonialism* Centre for Science and Environment, New Delhi

Barrett, S (1991) *Reaching a CO_2 Emission Limitation Agreement for the Community: Implications for Equity and Cost-Effectiveness* Commission of the European Communities, Directorate-General for Economic and Financial Affairs

Blackorby, C and Donaldson, D (1984) 'Social criteria for evaluating population change' *Journal of Public Economics*, vol 25, pp 13–33

Broome, J (1992) *Counting the Cost of Global Warming* The White Horse Press, Cambridge

Cline, W (1992) *The Economics of Global Warming* Institute for International Economics, Washington DC

Cohen, G A (1986) 'Self-Ownership, World-Ownership and Equality' in F S Lucash (ed) *Justice and Equality Here and Now* Cornell University Press, Ithaca, NY

Epstein, J and Gupta, R (1990) 'Controlling the Greenhouse Effect: Five Global Regimes Compared' Brookings Occasional Paper, Washington DC.

Fujii, Y (1990) 'An Assessment of the Responsibility for the Increase in CO_2 Concentration and Inter-generational Carbon Accounts' WP-90-55, International Institute for Applied Systems Analysis, Laxenburg, Austria

Grubler, A and Fujii, Y (1991) 'Inter-generational and Spatial Equity Issues of Carbon Accounts' *Energy – The International Journal*, vol 16 , pp 1397–1416

Grubler, A and Nakicenovic, N (1992) 'International Burden Sharing in Greenhouse Gas Reduction' Environment Working Paper no 55, The World Bank, Washington DC.

Hoel, M (1991) 'How should International Greenhouse Gas Agreements be Designed' in P Dasgupta, K G Maler and A Vercelli (eds) *The Economics of Transnational Commons* Oxford University Press, Oxford (forthcoming)

Locke, J (1967) *Two Treatises of Government* edited by P Laslett, Cambridge University Press, Cambridge

Nordhaus, W (1991) 'Economic Approaches to Global Warming' in R Dornbusch and J Poterba (eds) *Global Warming: Economic Policy Responses* MIT Press, Cambridge MA

Nozick, R (1974) *Anarchy, State, and Utopia* Basic Books, New York

Rawls, J (1972) *A Theory of Justice* Oxford University Press, Oxford

Smith, K (1991) 'Allocating Responsibility for Global Warming: The Natural Debt Index' *Ambio* vol 20, pp 95–96

Smith, K (1993) 'The Basics of Greenhouse Gas Indices' in P Hayes and K Smith (eds) *The Global Greenhouse Regime: Who Pays* Earthscan, London

Young, H P (1991) 'Sharing the Burden of Global Warming' mimeo, School of Public Affairs, University of Maryland, College Park

Chapter Seven

Enclosing the Global Commons: Global Environmental Negotiations in a North–South Conflictual Approach*

Alain Lipietz

With the ongoing negotiations around the international agreements on climate change and biodiversity, humankind is entering a new area. For the first time, we are involved in the collective management of *global* ecological crises.

A 'global ecological crisis'is a crisis the causes of which are diffuse and the effects of which are universal. From the economic point of view, a global crisis differs greatly from *local* crises. In local crises, such as river pollution, traffic jams or soil erosion, local agents are usually directly accountable for damages to local victims (frequently the same individuals). Thus the economics of externalities, moral hazard and other microeconomic concepts are suitable to deal with the problem, at least theoretically, and even practically, for monetary compensation may be organized. We are dealing here with a 'stabilized universe', where people agree upon basic goals, duties and rights (Godard 1993). By contrast, in the ecological global crisis, the 'culprit' may be nothing less than a *model of development* encompassing whole continents, and 'victims' may be in other continents with different lifestyles. We are here in a 'controversial universe', involving debates about national models and international justice.

In this chapter, the climate agreement negotiation will be used as a life-size experiment, with some consideration given to other contrasting experiments: the ozone layer crisis and the biodiversity negotiations. The focus will be on the aspect of 'North–South' conflict, and we will consider economic tools not only as theoretical means to deal with our subject, but also as objects for our study. In fact, we are witnessing the birth of a social object: the political economy of global environment.

---

*This paper draws on research financed by UNESCO and the French Minister of Environment (Program ECLAT) – see Lipietz 1992a.

THE OZONE LAYER NEGOTIATIONS AS MODEL

The 'acid rains' problem may appear as the first global ecological crisis dealt with in international relations. In fact, the problem was merely international, and could be considered as a peculiarly long-distance example of local pollution. It was discussed at the Berlin G7 Summit (1985) and led to international agreements implying national regulations covering the height of chimneys, catalytic converters and so on.

The ozone layer depletion problem was the first real global ecological problem *stricto sensu* – or at least it was the first to be seriously considered. This may be because the first potential and actual victims were Australians – that is to say, people living in an advanced capitalist country. From the sociological and economic point of view, Australia is a northern country. Once the cause of the Antarctic ozone hole was identified as the dispersion of CFC and other gases in the atmosphere, mainly in the geographic North of the planet, the crisis became an international North–North conflict. Moreover, the appearance of Antartic ozone layer depletion increased consciousness of the absolute necessity to 'do something'. As a result, since the first Vienna agreement (1985) new international decisions are being taken yearly to counter this threat (Montreal 1987, London 1990, Copenhagen 1992). This life-size experiment proposed a kind of model for subsequent negotiations:

1. Attention to a global environmental crisis is first aroused by voices in the scientific community. Actually, the threat of a crisis is not perceived before it is voiced by scientists. Moreover, scientists do not immediately agree either on the causes or the effects. The point (in the ozone layer depletion crisis) is the fact that the very scientists who agree that CFC emissions are the causes of Antarctic ozone hole insist that some twenty years are needed between the emission of CFC in the northern hemisphere and its arrival above the Antarctic. Thus, hard decisions are to be taken with a weak knowledge of the potential consequences. We are thus in the realm of Limited Rationality *à la* Herbert Simon. In this case, Limited Rationality implies the implementation of the *Precaution Principle*: When the future effect of a present cause is uncertain but may be highly damaging and then irreversible, it is wiser to act immediately in order to suppress the cause until we know better.
2. The Precaution Principle is not a standard cost-benefit analysis: the cost of doing something is uncertain, the benefit is between null and gigantic, with a radical uncertainty *à la* Knight. Moreover, the benefit (in that case avoiding general exposure to skin cancers) is mainly a benefit to other generations. Thus the subjective aversion to the specific risk (for oneself or for one's children) weighs on the decision. (Future) victims have to find a speaker before a first move may be undertaken. And these speakers must have a voice that may be heard.
3. It is not sufficient that victims complain; it is necessary that 'culprits' feel accountable. Contrary to the 'no-bridge' principle of general

equilibrium theory,[1] the authors of global externalities have to feel
sorry for the unfortunate and unwanted effects of their practices. The
acknowledgement that future generations of Australians have a right
to be protected from UV-rays is a social innovation, for, as Coase
would put it, they had no explicit property right to a protective ozone
layer. Of course, this new 'human right'is more easily acknowledged
by Europeans and North Americans when they realize that they are
affected by the same problems.

4. Since there exists no 'market' between generations and not even
   between nations for a global common such as the ozone layer, since
   there exists no world regulation and no world government, the
   solution appears as an agreement between nations about their
   commitment to avoid environmentally damaging practices at the
   national level. Since, in the present case, the 'culprits' are all likely to
   be in the 'sociological North' of the planet, the agreement is
   negotiated between economically advanced countries.

   Here is the rub. Most, if not all, less developed countries have no
   other dream than to imitate the model of development that precisely
   led to the global crisis. The difference is that the agreement is signed
   before they may have enjoyed the benefits of the now prohibited
   practices (in this case refrigeration). Hence their objection: it may be
   necessary that we (southern nations) feel 'accountable' when we are
   as developed as you (northern countries) are now, but there is no
   reason why we should have to accept at once this new regulation
   which you ignored at the time of your take-off and industrialization.
   In the ozone layer protection debate, India and China lost no time in
   raising this objection, as they will do later. Here again, the ozone case
   proposes the following model.

5. Once the agreement is reached in the North, the South protests, and a
   new negotiation begins. We enter the realm of international relations.
   The power of the North (military, technological, financial) may be
   tremendously superior to that of the South, but it is not easily
   mobilizable in the specific conflict.[2] Countries such as China and India
   have a powerful weapon: their power to obstruct. They may refuse to
   sign, so they have to be induced to sign, for example, through some
   financial proposal, such as technology transfers at concessional
   conditions.

6. It must be emphasized that the problem arises from the principle of
   sovereignty. The State, the national State, is the only effective power
   that can create new entitlements, new regulations where natural or
   traditional property rights do not exist and may not exist. Even if an
   ecological crisis could be solved through market regulation of a new

1 In the standard microeconomics of GET, preference sets of agents are independent of the
satisfaction of the other agents : there is 'no bridge' between various *homo oeconomicus* other
than exchanges of commodities and money.
2 The concept of 'issue-specific power' was introduced in the field of International
Relations by W M Habeeb (1988). It was introduced in the analysis of environment
international negotiations by de Campos Mello (1992).

field of property rights (and this is far from obvious), the market and the rights have to be created. Up to now there is no possibility for this to occur other than by sovereign decisions of the States concerning their own citizens and territories *and* a 'free' agreement between sovereign states about the global commons.

The 'North–South' aspect of the problem then arises from the fact that, when a 'Universal' principle is agreed upon between sovereign States, the economic consequences may differ in the extreme according to the initial positions of different States, and more precisely according to their historical level of development.

Since we are talking of 'Commons', let us recall the great European crisis of the 14th century. At that time, given a particular technological paradigm and a particular set of social relations in the countryside, demographic pressure appeared to exceed the productive capacities of the land: hence the extreme sensitivity of the whole population to a new epidemic of the plague. Europe lost more than half of its population and, when two centuries later it recovered its 1340 level, the social and technological system of land use had dramatically changed. A new entrepreneurship had developed among new direct land holders (not necessarily land 'owners'). In order to secure a more efficient use of the land, village commons had been 'enclosed' and efficient farmers had the titles. The problem was that non-efficient peasants, who used to have the commons at their (inefficient !) disposal, were merely 'proletarianized'.

The European crisis of the 14–16th centuries may be understood as an economic, social, demographic and ecological crisis, and the 'enclosure movement' (origin of the 'bourgeois revolution') as a part of its solution. The present global ecological crises, which are crises of global commons, may imply some 'global enclosure' as part of the solution. A proletarianization of 'less efficient nations', that is an exclusion from access to world market and modernity as a result of this new barrier to entry, may then appear as a counterpart of that solution. Hence the North–South aspect of the political economy of global commons.

THE BIODIVERSITY NEGOTIATION

Much less discussed than climate change in the process on the way to Rio, the Biodiversity convention suffered from a fuzzy definition of its scope. Yet it turned out in Rio to be the unexpected battlefield which witnessed the complete defeat of US Administration by the coalition of all other countries, from the closest (Canada) to the farthest (Malaysia) but in such a way that it appeared as a victory of the latest... In fact, the Biodiversity battle expressed in a caricatured way the North–South character of the global environmental negotiations.

Biodiversity is *not* the diversity of 'big'animals. This diversity is already dealt with under the Washington Convention (1975). The biodiversity here considered is the diversity of living stock, that is diversity of microscopic species, and diversity of genetic stock within species, both of them constituting the 'germoplasm', the raw material of the pharmaceutical and seed industries, and of biotechnologies. By extension, the debate on biodiversity has to deal with the diversity of the ecosystems in which 'biodiversity' can exist.

The concept of 'diversity' itself has to be qualified. Since we are not concerned here with aesthetics (once again, this is the scope of Washington Convention), the 'value of existence' of biodiversity is based on *unknown* diversity, or more precisely on the diversity (and proliferation) of unknown germoplasm. The fact that the scope of what is to be protected is unknown is not a weakness, but constitutes the very value of this 'global common'. In fact, biodiversity is the common immunization system of global life and of life-connected industries. Just as the human immunization system creates randomly at any minute antidotes for external aggression which are not yet existing, and selects from its stock an available response when a specific aggression appears, in the same way unknown biodiversity is a preexisting condition for stabilizing reactions within global life, organized or not by humankind. Of course, biodiversity becomes an economic common good when this reaction is organised by human activity.

Take as an example maize seeds, the basis for corn cropping. Maize was selected in a centuries-long process, thousands of years ago, in the area of Tehuacan in Mexico (Gay 1984). This process of selection was the result of the *techne* of Mexican peasants, but its precondition was the huge unknown variety of the genetic stock in the meso-American countryside.[3] Though the varieties of maize selected by peasants were highly specialized by comparison to the wild ancestors of maize, the biodiversity within 'peasants maize' remained very wide. Moreover, the maize of the Indians'crops went on interfering with wild seeds of the same family, within a half-wild, half-cultivated (but 'handicraftly' cultivated) ecosystem.

By contrast, maize seeds produced by agribusiness and pharmaceutical firms are highly selected. In the 'edge-varieties' (the type of seeds with highest performance) which are used in the majority of modern cornfields in advanced capitalist countries, the biodiversity is extremely narrow. When a new aggression arrives (as has occurred) such as bacterial or viral aggression, the few selected seeds may be unable to react, and the only solution is to find, in a 'rich' ecosystem (from the biodiversity viewpoint), the genetic element which, by being added to the edge-seed, could solve the new problem. These 'rich' ecosystems are by definition in the *non-industrialized* areas where peasants' maize and wild maize still survive.

As we may notice, tropical rainforests are not the only reservoirs of biodiversity. Any area where there used to exist natural biodiversity *and* which was only exploited through picking or peasants' agriculture, but not through standardized and industrialized agriculture, is likely to present unknown useful germoplasm. Surviving biodiversity is thus the by-product

---

3 The difference between *techne* and *logos* as two forms of social knowledge (*techne*: empirical, implicit ; *logos*: systematized, explicit) is developed in Marglin and Marglin (1990)

of surviving ethnodiversity. Thus it is not by some geo-historical luck that most biodiversity reservoirs, just like copper mines, are in the 'geographical South'. It is by the definition of biodiversity that these reservoirs are mainly in the sociological South (that is, the less developed countries). And it is quite likely that the useful aspects of this unknown biodiversity could only be detected by the R & D activities of pharmaceutical firms in advanced capitalist countries. In one sentence: biodiversity, as a raw material, is in the South and the industries that use it are in the North. We are back to the crudest, sixties-style dependency theory type, North–South conflict. Hence the very simple position of US Administration, presented in the Rio negotiation and in the GATT 'intellectual property protection' negotiation: *any molecule in a forest or a peasant's field is free, any molecule identified by a laboratory is subject to royalties.* And of course the South's position was just the reverse: *biodiversity being a localized natural resource belongs to the country in which it is present* (like oilfields). *The identification of the use-value of a molecule being a product of science, it should become a human common good.*[4]

In this debate, Europe was quasi absent. The EC report to UNCED did not address the real issue, and confused it with some enlarged Washington Convention. France proposed the constitution of some 'world natural parks' protected by some Green Helmets of UNO. This was an unacceptable proposal for 'enclosure' of biodiversity, subtracting such parks from common use and from the sovereignty of nations without any financial compensation. The proposal was the more unacceptable because France proved itself to be unable to protect its own 'rich' ecosystems (Marais Poitevin, Pyrennean Bears Reserve) against powerful lobbies (intensive agriculture, hunting, motorways).

Here there appears to be some paradoxical contrasts with our real 'enclosure' parallel. 'Enclosing biodiversity' means forbid 'efficient' modernized agriculture on some territories in order to protect the capacity of adaptation of all the rest ! But clearly peasants and capitalist timber firms may think of other uses for these territories. A global regulation protecting biodiversity appears to deny the right to modernize. Thus the strongest opponents in the South will be the 'productivist elites' of newly industrializing countries: timber exporting Malaysia, the ranching-supporting governors of Brazilian Amazonia. On the other hand, indigenous people, who 'protect biodiversity at the risk of their own life'(according to a leitmotiv of Rio Global Forum of the NGOs), represented a potential ally for conservationist proponents in the North: either ecologists... or pharmaceutical firms (Hetch 1992, Hetch and Cockburn 1989a, 1989b).

These strange systems of alliances (quite noticeable in the support of the British singer Sting for the Amazonian friends of Chico Mendes) blurred the debate, until it finished in Rio with United States refusing to sign a convention tailored to a productivist compromise between elites of North and South. The convention acknowledged some property rights of

---

4 A joke heard around the GATT negotiation and the NGOs was that alternatively patents on maize should be paid to Mexicans with compound interest over 3000 years!

States over 'their' biodiversity and the necessity for biotechnological transfers to the South at concessionary conditions. Thus, it represented a 'victory' of the South. But in reality it was an acceptable compromise for the elites of both side:

■ The firms in the North were acknowledged to have the right to put a patent on living stock, as a condition for financing R & D on biotechnologies.
■ The States in the South were acknowledged to have a right to a new kind of royalties on their territory, on condition they agreed not to 'exploit' designated areas.

The losers were indigenous people (who were not recognized as the 'gardeners' of biodiversity[5]) and the most radical ecologists who were dubious about the development of biotechnologies. Actually, that issue was the occasion for the only major split in Rio in the Global Forum of the NGOs. But the George Bush administration refused to sign! As a result, all the choreography of 1970s anti-imperialism arose in favour of the Convention. Demonstrations raged in Rio streets against 'patents on living' and imperialist offences against sovereignty over 'our' forests. Canada signed, then Japan, Great Britain, and all Europe. The Rio Conference turned out to be a diplomatic Viet Nam for the Bush administration. Later, the Clinton administration signed the convention. A great deal, however, remains to be interpreted in this rather fuzzy text, in particuliar its consistency with the conclusions of the Uruguay Round regarding intellectual property.

THE CLIMATE CONFLICT

The Greenhouse Effect is certainly the clearest, the most spectacular, the best studied, and alas the most dangerous of North–South conflicts around global commons. It clearly illuminates most features of the 'ozone model' of a Controversial Universe which we presented earlier in the chapter.

■ The first warnings came from scientists (in fact, from Arrhenius at the end of 19th century) much before any effect could be felt.
■ When some indicators that *could* be associated with global warming appeared (spectacular droughts, typhoons, together with a small increase in average temperature in the last decade), some 'victims' were able to associate their problems with the scientists'warnings.
■ The global crisis was addressed when ecological movements developed in industrialized countries, criticizing the northern way of life as the cause of the crisis.
■ The 'solutions' proposed to the debate implied an agreement between sovereign States, involving national policies. The agreement seemed

5 In fact, indigenous people may be granted part of their rights through private agreements, such as in the negotiations between US pharmaceutical firms and Chamans in Guatemala.

to be within reach between northern countries, but soon it appeared that some proposals had an 'anti-South' bias.

Yet there are important differences with our two first examples:

- Contrary to the ozone crisis, the victims are mainly in the 'social South'.
- Contrary to the biodiversity crisis the burden of necessary policies would lie mainly on northern countries.

As a result, the North–South conflict will present a very strange picture: some northern states will try to convince other northern states and some southern elites to take measures mainly in favour of southern people !

We shall insist first on the 'in favour of whom?' aspect of the debate, for it was hidden by the more pragmatic debate 'who is to take the biggest share of the burden?' Yet neither economics nor international relations could ignore the question of 'interest'. In order to outline this, let us have a brief summary of the scientific aspect of the debate.

There was a quasi consensus in the International Panel on Climate Change (IPCC 1991) that, for a doubling of CO_2 concentration in the atmosphere (or equivalent quantities of other green house gases – GHGs), the rise in average temperature would be 3°C ±1.5°C. This large uncertainty for a physicist is not so relevant for international relations, because a rise of +1.5°C would already be a major problem (and +4.5°C an inconceivable crisis) !

Uncertainty also exists on *when* such a concentration would be reached, but, at the present rate of emissions, it is agreed that it was a question of more or less half a century.

What would be the effects of a +3°C increase ?

We do not know exactly, and it is better so. As in Rawls' *Theory of Justice*, we are in a situation of distributing initial endowments and setting up the new rules of the game.[6] According to Rawls, at this stage of the collective search for a 'fair' mode of regulation, it is better not to know who would gain the most, and stay under a 'veil of ignorance' (Rawls 1971).

For instance, for a doubling of CO_2 concentration, the increase in temperature during the northern summer on the Baltic sea would be less than 4°C (and less than world average) according to the numerical simulation of the French *Laboratoire de Meteorologie Dynamique*, and it would be more than 8°C (much more than world average) according to

---

6 The reference to Rawls is not artificial. The Rio debate was really an attempt to define an international ecological regime as fair as possible, and the words 'fair' and 'fairness' were certainly among the most frequently used. Here we need a terminological definition. In the International Relations theories *à la* Keohane-Krasner, the word 'regime' is used as a set of 'rules of the game', or 'mode of regulation', according to the usual terminology of the French Regulation Approach and sometimes of WIDER papers (eg Marglin and Schor 1990), while 'regime' usualy denotes the *resulting trajectories* of the working of rules of the game. Since the languages of International Relations is invading global ecological debates (see Porter and Brown 1991), we shall use indifferently 'regime', 'mode of regulation' or 'rules of the game'.

the British Meteorological Office. Rain would increase in the Mediterranean basin according to the Geophysical Fluid Dynamics Laboratory at Princeton, and it would decrease according to the BMO! Philippe Roqueplo, who monitored the scientific debate with the eyes of the model-maker and of the sociologist, outlines the reluctance of many policy makers to clarify the regional distributions of global warming. In fact, the 'veil of ignorance' induces global *preventive* policies (involving North and South). On the contrary, the knowledge of who would be 'the winners and the losers' (from global warming) would foster an *adaptative* strategy of the losers and may exempt the winners from any solidarity (Roqueplo 1993:140).

Yet the fact that we don't know the *physical* effects does not entail our not knowing who would be economicaly the relatively 'worse losers'. In fact:

- First, weather will be globally wetter, but water will be less useful on the ground, for it will evaporate faster, or will erode the soil more violently. This 'tropicalization' of the world is likely to be detrimental to countries of the geographical South relying heavily on agriculture and with a large peasant population.
- The sea level will increase (through dilatation) by some 30–50 cm – a disaster for countries with large seashore populations: deltas, islands and so on.

Clearly, most victims are *de facto* in the 'social South': India, China, Bangladesh, the Maldives because of the sea-level rise; Southern America and Africa would join the list because of changes in conditions for agriculture.

By contrast, a country of the North like the US, though being a powerful agricultural country but with only one semi-desert delta, has a weak 'interest' in fighting the greenhouse effect. That was perfectly illustrated in a quite standard economic analysis by Nordhaus (1990). Admitting a doubling of CO_2 in 40 years with a green house effect of $+3°C$, Nordhaus first identifies its cost (for the US) with the fall in production in various sectors, principally agriculture. The latter being of less and less importance in US economy, the cost will be very low (–0.25 per cent in expected GDP). Then he discounts this cost at a rate of 4 per cent. Not surprisingly, such a low cost will justify few anti-GHG actions, even in the US where marginal economies are exceptionally cheap, as we shall see. Nordhaus evaluates the curve of cost of reduction of GHG emissions as rapidly growing: US$5 per ton of carbon at the level of -13 per cent (by comparison to the baseline), US$100 per ton at the level of –45 per cent. In his words, it would be 'unwise' to seek for more than a marginal reduction (–13 per cent). An ecotax of US$5 per ton of carbon, that is 58 cents per barrel of oil, would be 'cost-effective'.

Nordhaus' argument is extremely interesting. By characterizing any effort greater that this very low level as 'foolish' and 'unwise', he laid the basis for the future position of the United States. Moreover, he indicates in a caricatured way the flawed approach of classical economics.

- He assumes a 'no bridge principle' between the 'satisfactions curves' of states, as microeconomists do between individuals. Thus, eco-

126

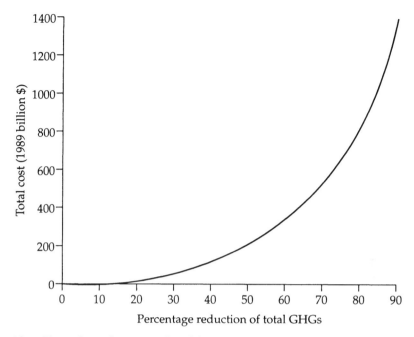

Note: Figure shows the estimated total long-run cost of different levels of GHG reductions. The calculations assume 1989 levels of world output and prices and 1989 levels of GHG emissions per unit output.
Source: Nordhaus, 1990

Figure 7.1 *Cost of greenhouse gas reduction*

demographic crises at the southern borders of the North are considered as 'no-cost' for northern countries. Such a statement is the more surprising in that Nordhaus proposes migrations as normal forms of adjustment to climate changes, as if ignoring the fact that 'economic migrants' are currently fired on at borders such as Tijuana. The 'No bridge principle' (that is, the idea that a country, and especially a leading country, should or may ignore the interests of its neighbours) is certainly unsuitable for international relations. Nordhaus clearly underestimates the costs *in the North* of a crisis in the South.

- He also overestimates the costs of prevention from global warming. His figures rely upon the instantaneous cost of GHG and energy saving policies, ignoring the economies of scale induced by a global regulation policy and the autonomous energy efficiency improvement.[7]
- The discount rate is an acceptable index for one individual's preference for the present. Is it an acceptable rule *between* present and future generations, that is, when there is no possible market with a co-contractor? This is precisely what is denied by ecologists and social philosophers such as Hans Jonas (1990). Their *Responsibility Principle*

7 On this debate about the long-term energy (or GHG) efficiency of techniques, see Hourcade 1993.

implies that the rights of future generations are not relegated beyond the horizon of economic computation.

■ The Polluter Pays Principle, when understood that 'a polluter agent should pay for the economic damage it causes' , is not equivalent to an incentive policy. At the level of 58 cents per barrel, the 'price-signal' will be lost in the noise of random variations of the price of oil on the spot market. The price of energy *may* be an incentive, as we shall see, but not below a higher threshold.

Anyway, Nordhaus illustrates quite well one possible theorization for a possible attitude of northern states: 'Do Nothing'. Up to now, it could seem that the normal attitude of southern states should be 'Do Something'. The 'enclosure conflict' should present itself as the South trying to protect its climate against the northern pollution by GHG. But the reality of negotiation on climate was and is still quite different. In order to understand this paradox, we have to introduce a more realistic representation of North and South.

A CARTOGRAPHY OF GHG POLITICS

The first elaboration we may propose is a closer scrutiny of the costs of 'Doing Something', and not only to its advantages (that is, to the damages of 'Doing Nothing').To my knowledge the most impressive systematic attempt is the study by Benhaim, Caron and Levarlet (1991) (later BCL). They classify 50 countries (including most of OECD and Eastern Europe, the main Third World countries) by automatic taxonomic methods according to 20 criteria. The result is quite interesting, both when it confirms *actual* similarities of attitudes in the climate negotiation and when it contrasts with reality.[8]

The BCL Methodology

The first group of indicators includes GDP per capita and the Index of Human Development (PNUD 1988). They are static indicators (by contrast to rates of growth), neutral with respect to population. All other indicators are linked to the energy system: type of energy used, indices of consumption of primary energy, of energy efficiency, of energy reserves, of CO_2 emissions, per capita, per unit of GDP, per country.

Note that the last one is not neutral with respect to the size of population, just as energy reserves are not neutral with respect to the surface of the country.[9] Also note that there is no index of 'advantages in doing something' (such as share of peasantry, share of population living at sea level).

8 For detailed criticisms of BCL's study, see Lipietz 1992a.
9 Consider, for instance, that USSR is counted as one country! This may seem a major methodological flaw. Yet the *compound* nuisance capacity of a country is a real parameter of its diplomacy.

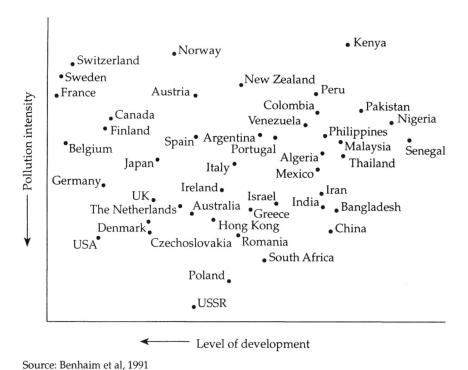

Figure 7.2 *Level of development and pollution intensity*

In Figure 7.2 BCL present a classification of countries via principal components analysis. The horizontal axis in the analysis presents an opposition between 'development' (on the left) and 'underdevelopment'. Development is positively correlated to:

- energy-consumption per capita;
- CO_2 per capita;
- share of nuclear energy;

and negatively to:

- coefficient of CO_2 per unit of GDP (measured at exchange rates);
- share of hydrocarbons;
- reserves of hydrocarbons.

In other words, the more a country is developed, the more it consumes energy per capita and thus the more it emits CO_2 though the more GHG-efficiently it produces its energy.

On the vertical axis, the criterion of 'cleanness' of production is illustrated, opposing GHG-efficient use of electricity at the top to GHG-polluting use of carbon at the bottom.

Combining these two axes, a 'virtuous' hierarchy, from the top-left to the bottom-right appears. The 'GHG virtuous' are, on the first line, Switzerland, Sweden, France, then other Scandinavian countries, Canada, Belgium, then Germany and Japan, then the US and UK, Spain...

Further investigation separated out 'open frontier countries' (the US, USSR, China, Brazil) with large populations, as opposed to all others, including Bangladesh.[10]

In a very graphic way this chart isolates, in the (sociological) North West of the world, countries which are both rich *and* GHG-efficient in the production of their energy: the 'super-virtuous' of European Free Trade Area (EFTA), the 'virtuous' Japan and EEC (less so in the cases of UK and Spain). These countries are ready to implement the *precaution* principle: they have or can get the technologies, they are already at a relatively low (yet unsustainable) level of emissions.

By contrast, the US appears in the South West of the chart, along with fossil energy wasters: ex-Socialist countries, South Africa and China. In these countries, along with Petromonarchies, welfare is correlated to GHG wasting. They are in favour of what BCL label the *blockage strategy*. Georges Bush, with his Rio statement 'Our way of life is not subject to negotiation', illustrates this position.

Very different in appearance are the countries at the South East of the 'GHG-virtuous' North West: India, Brazil, Mexico, China, Malaysia. These countries are too poor to be already GHG-dangerous and to be GHG-efficient. But clearly they aspire to be as 'developed' as western countries, and consider that up to now these precursors never implemented any precaution principle. These countries are pushed into an *accusation strategy*: denouncing the responsibility of the North West *in the past* for the concentration of GHG in the atmosphere, such a strategy contends that it is not yet time to implement a precaution principle in developing countries.

The Concrete Positions in the Debate

If we now cross the two criteria (advantages of 'Doing something' discussed earlier, and costs of 'Doing something' analysed above), the North–South conflict appears now much more complex.

Along the two criteria, the position of the US is clearly in favour of 'doing nothing': the dangers from greenhouse effects are weak, the cost of fighting it may be very high, even if the low GHG-efficiency of their energy production makes the marginal improvements quite inexpensive (as for ex-Socialist countries). The problem is that, from a *global sustainability* point of view, the improvements required from the US are far from marginal.

Here we have to anticipate what a global sustainability criterion would be. World development would be GHG-sustainable if the total amount of anthropgenic GHG-emissions were equal to the capacity of the world 'sinks'

---

10 The 'open frontière' criterion was introduced as an explainatory factor in the debate by Banuri 1992.

for GHG.[11] Assuming a world population of 10 billion (in 2040), the average sustainable quantity of emissions would be 500 kg of carbon per capita. At present, the US production is 10 times this figure ! It is thus perfectly clear that the 'selfish' interest of the US is the blockage strategy (Do Nothing).

The radical *accusation* strategy seems to be the opposite, and indeed its glamour in a North–South conflict is very attractive: 'You are the culprits, you have to do something'. The problem is that this position is also a blockage position, since it is subordinated to the implementation of a precaution strategy by foreign countries which are in favour of blockage. It is quite appealing for elites who desire to emulate the US model of development (a savage capitalism in an open frontierland) *and* which are not too much worried by the consequences of the greenhouse effect on their own population. Here it is important to note that international negotiation involves *governments,* that is elites, and not people. The position of a government may be quite different from its people interests if the political regime is rather independent from a civil society it purports to represent.

Malaysia provides a good example of satisfying these criteria. As the Prime minister Mahathur Muhammad did not hesitate to put it in the *Asian Society Forum* 1991: 'Democracy, human rights, ecology, union rights, are but obstacles that advanced countries try to put on the road of their future competitors'.

So we have in fact two types of 'Do Nothing' positions: the one of the North (fighting the greenhouse effect is too expensive and useless for us) and the one of the South (fighting the greenhouse effect would unfairly hinder our development, and the results of global warming are irrelevant to us).

But our discussion indicates two classes of potential followers of a precaution strategy. The first one includes the nations which have serious reasons to believe that they would be the first victims of global warming: Bangladesh, Maldives India, Africa, South America. When, moreover, they are countries which are both low producers of GHG (much less than the 'sustainable' 500 kg/capita) and quite GHG-inefficient, they may assume that they have a wide margin for globally GHG-sustainable development: their contribution to the world production of GHG may increase for a while without being a real problem, and their very development will induce a more GHG-efficient production of energy.

Symmetrically, we noticed that there exist northern countries which may think of increasing their GHG-efficiency faster than their production of energy (for example EFTA, France). Producing less than two tons per capita, and evolving towards a 'service society' with a steady population, they may think that the 500 kg target is within their scope. When, moreover, they are countries particularly sensitive to their leadership responsibilities *vis-à-vis* southern countries, or to the dangers stemming from demographic and ecological turmoil at their southern borders, they may assume that a precaution strategy is relatively inexpensive and really

---

11 At present, the power of absorption by the sinks is about half the anthropgenic emissions of CO_2. But it may be argued that efficiency of the sinks could be dependent on the growth of CO_2 concentration in the atmosphere, according to some retroaction principle *à la* Le Chatelier.

useful. EEC countries are the most representative of this position. Moreover, domestic ecological militancy begins to frame their politics.

So we have in fact two types of 'Do Something' position: the one of the South (we need to fight the greenhouse effect, and we could afford it with some help from the North) and the one of the North (we have the capacities to fight the greenhouse effect and it is in our interests to offer it to the world).

So the North/South divide is crossed by another divide: Do Nothing/Do Something (see Figure 7.3)

Figure 7.3 *Environmental strategies*

WHAT IS TO BE DONE?

In the years leading up to Rio, blockage positions could less and less express themselves in a crude way. On the contrary, the years 1990–1992 were punctuated by conferences, reports of IPCC, books, TV programmes, ecologists' mobilizations, stressing more and more clearly the necessity to 'do something'. The debate was less and less 'should we do something?', more and more 'is it so urgent to do something ? and who should take the biggest share of the burden ?'.

The debate on burden-sharing followed two interwoven paths: a technical debate on the sources of GHG emissions and a policy debate on targets and instruments. The interweaving is so tight than it would be counterproductive to isolate the two aspects: in fact, the debate on the sources ('who is the culprit ?') was a debate on targets ('who has to reduce its emissions?').

The WRI–CSE Controversy

That was very clear when, in 1991, in the times of *Prep Com* II (and of Gulf War II[12]), Anil Agarwal and Sunita Nerain of the Centre for Science and Environment (New Delhi) launched their polemics against the apparently 'technical' report 1990–1991 of the *World Resources Institute,* an independent Washington think-tank connected to the US administration. Up to this time, there were few questions about the absolute responsibility of CO_2 emitted by industrial countries for the growth of the greenhouse effect. The WRI report (1990) brought two new elements in the discussion.

- It attempted a *comprehensive* evaluation of all GHG emissions including the CO_2 emitted through deforestation (especially spectacular in Brazil in 1987, the year on which the report relies), and above all methane, which is a by-product of fermentation of organic matters in cattle digestion and in paddy fields. Methane is a more dangerous gas than CO_2: each molecule of methane (CH_4) has 40 times more effect in capturing infra-red rays than one CO_2 molecule.[13] Through such indices of conversion, the WRI was able to evaluate the gross production of GHG by country.
- The report took into account the fact that the gross flow of emissions of GHG to the atmosphere is not equal to the change of their stock in the atmosphere. The oceans and earth reabsorb about half of it. These natural sinks are the real 'global commons', given by Nature to Humankind. The WRI report allocates these sinks to countries proportionally to their gross emissions: thus it yields the *net* emissions by country.

The rating is then unexpected. The contribution of the South is nearly equal to that of the North (which, at the time, included Socialist countries). The major polluters are the: US, USSR, Brazil, China, India

The WRI report was important. Apart from more detailed arguments, it provided a first survey of all GHG emissions, and drew attention to gases other than carbon dioxide. And it identified clearly the sinks, and not the atmosphere, as the global common which was to be 'enclosed', allotted and regulated for the safety of humankind. Yet, in doing this, the report included two major flaws from the theoretical point of view, with very important policy implications.

---

12 The Gulf War II context was certainly of great importance in the pre-Rio 'ecological order' debate, since the 'New International Order' appeared as a 'double-standard' order (Lipietz 1992b, Postscript)
13 CFC and other halons are thousands of times more dangerous, but are under another international agreement.

1. All the gases are not equally subject to the 'precaution principle'. CO_2 remains in the atmosphere from 50 to 150 years. Thus the concentration of CO_2 in 2050 will depend on the sum of emissions over the proceeding century. By contrast, methane is very unstable and remains in the atmosphere for around three years. The control of the methane cycle can wait. While the 'comprehensive approach' implies as a *target* the reduction of all GHGs, the precaution principle implies only the reduction of CO_2.
2. The distribution of the sinks according to the gross emissions implies a peculiar form of enclosure (or entitlement): it is according to the acquired contribution to global pollution. Since we are at the dawn of an initial entitlement or endowment process *à la* Rawls, it is clear that such a deal is far from fair: the poorest, the less developed, the less accountable for present pollution and the more likely to increase their population, are offered the smallest possibility to increase their emissions!

The reply by Agarwal and Nerain (1991) was devastating and focused mainly on the second point.

First of all, the CSE criticizes the data of the WRI: 1987 was exceptional for forest fires in Amazonia, the emissions of methane by southern cattle are overestimated, etc. But, being unable to propose another quantitative basis for the discussion, the CSE criticizes the two methodological points of the WRI. The comprehensive approach is rejected on the basis of an ethical argument: the production of methane (in food production) is a necessity, the production of CO_2 (in industries and car driving) is a luxury. Clearly, such a critique is most appealing in a North–South confrontation, when 'South' means the LDCs (and not the NICs), and their peasants (not their elites...).

More constructively the CSE opposes the WRI allocation of the global common (the sinks for CO_2) between nations. Arguing that all human beings are born equals in rights, the CSE proposes an egalitarian allocation, that is an initial endowment between countries proportional to their population at present time. The structure of 'net emissions' changes completely, hence the 'burden sharing' scheme.

This powerful proposition was extremely welcome in the international negotiation. Soon it became the unifying position of the southern environment and development NGOs in the process up to Rio. In North–South meetings between NGOs (the *Prep Com* III and IV, the Ya Wananchi conference in Paris, December 1991), this position became hegemonic. But it also influenced the governments of Southern Asia (India, Pakistan, Bangladesh) which relied upon such NGOs as the International Union for Conservation of Nature for the writing of their national report to UNCED. These more official positions were frequently based on the more academic work of Grubb (1990) in favour of the principle of tradeable permits. Hence it became the unifying position of India and all the group of the '77', of China, of UNCTAD. The advantages of the proposal are indeed impressive:

■ The permits are distributed according to base-year population, so it is an incentive for each country to control its own birth rate.

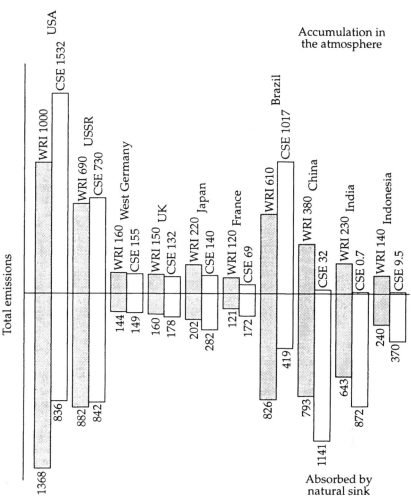

Source: Agarwal and Nerain, 1991

Figure 7.4 *Allocation of responsibility for greenhouse gas emissions (in million tonnes of carbon equivalent) as calculated by CSE*

- Countries exceeding their permissible emissions are all northern countries. A levy should be put on this excess in order to finance GHG-efficient technologies.
- Countries with emissions in excess could also *buy* permits from countries which have excess permits. All these countries are in the South. Thus, even with excess permits, economies in emissions would be profitable for southern countries. In turn, this price for tradeable permits would finance the sustainable development in the South.

We are not going here to discuss the economics of tradeable permits. In fact, once the initial endowment is given, the market for tradeable permits would be much like the oil market.[14] The world could experience a situation of 'atmosphere peonage' (with southern countries selling their permits to breath at very low price, in order to pay for their debt), or, on the contrary, the constitution of a strong oligopolistic market controlled by two 'Saudi Arabia of permits': India and China.Up to now, all this is no more than fancy economics, since obviously, by the time of the 1992 Rio Conference, humankind was not ready for such a sophisticated enclosure process.

The Debate on Ecotax

It is not sufficient to distribute permits between nations and fix with them the collective target of GHG-sustainable development: how could states induce the population of their own nation to restrict their emissions ?

Here we enter the debate 'target policy *vs* instrument policy'. Policies presented in the previous paragraphs are target policies: the CSE distribution of permits fixes a target-amount for each nation, the WRI implies a general and common target for a rate of reduction. Yet the CSE proposal includes also *instruments:* a market for permits, a levy (a world ecotax) on the excess. That was precisely its constructivist weakness: the negotiation and, worse, the implementation of instruments, imply that the capacity to control and regulate is given to some international body. The very technical capacity to measure the effective emissions country by country is questionable. A body that could organize the market, implement and redistribute the levy, would have to be a real world government....

On the contrary, it seems that a *subsidiarity principle* could be easier to implement: once the world community has agreed upon a target (differentiated or not according to countries), it would be the responsibility of national states to choose their own instruments. If we accept this subsidiarity divide, it seems that a target policy, possibly mitigated with the tradeable permits instrument, is more suitable at the international level (because agents – the states – are tailored to negotiate on norms and quantities, and because they are few enough to organize a market for permits). On the contrary, tax instruments are more suitable at national level, because here the agents – firms and households – are so heterogenous that no market could be organized, and so numerous that no control could be organized on real emissions.[15] But things are not so simple.

On the one hand, in a globalized economy, instrument policy cannot and should not be under the discretionary sovereignty of governments. Neither norms nor ecotaxes nor subsidies are neutral *vis-à-vis* competitiveness. Either they hinder competitiveness and are rejected by business lobbies, or they foster competitiveness, and are subject to contests at the GATT. And precisely, a market-oriented Uruguay Round was negotiated in parallel with the Rio Conference.

On the other hand, instrument policies may be negotiated at an international level *without* an agreement on the target, and in the

---

14 In fact, there is a difference : the level of the levy is an upper limit to the price of tradeable permits, for any country may prefer to pay the levy instead of buying permits.
15 On the tax vs tradeable permits, see Hourcade et Baron (1992), Godard (1992).

ignorance of what should be the target, hence how far one is from the target.[16] Instrument policies seem in line with the precaution principle: we don' t know if they are really necessary and sufficient, but if (later) they appear to have been necessary (sufficient or not) then it was a step in the right direction, and if they appear to have been unnecessary, they may have been useful in some other respect (this last argument indicates the possibility of 'no-regret' strategies).

Thus, concrete diplomacy is likely to wind up as some policy mix of targets and instruments at national *and* international level. The capacity of leadership consists, for a single country or group of countries, to propose such an international regime, both suitable for its own internal policy and acceptable by others in the name of general interest. The Rooseveltian New Deal (between capital and labour) was the expression of this kind of 'hegemony': it was both an internal 'grand compromise', and it was a model for all nations, fostered by the victory over Nazism and by the Marshall and MacArthur plans (Lipietz 1992b).

The only real attempt to reach the hegemony accross the UNCED process came from the European Community. The Rooseveltian ambition of the EC (labelled 'the *Environment Imperative*') was explicitly expressed in the *EC Report to UNCED*, and the challenge was presented in a report of the DG XI (the 'Ministry of Environment' of EC) to the Commission (the Government of EC), later adopted by the Commission itself and then presented as a *Communication to the European Council*:

> *With the completion of the internal Market, the European Community will be the biggest economic/trading partner in the world with the potential to exercise an important level of moral, economic and political influence and authority. As such the Community owes it to both present and future generations to put its own house in order and to provide both leadership and example to developed and developing countries alike in relation to protection of the environment and the sustainable use of natural resources (...). The willingness of the Community to fulfill its responsibilities offers an important opportunity to fill a current vacuum in global foreign policy and a catalytic role in regard to the Global Climate Convention to be adopted at the UNCED Earth Summit in June 1992.*[17]

Concretely, the deal was many-sided.

1. Rejecting the 'comprehensive approach' of US Administration, the report focused on carbon dioxide.
2. The developed countries would commit themselves to reverse the

---

16 In the perfect world of General Equilibrium, there is a duality between instrument and targets, as implied in the Nordhaus curve, Fig 1.
17 'Community Strategy to limit Carbon Dioxide emissions and to improve energy efficiency', communication from the Commission to the Council, SEC(91) 1744 final, Brussels, 14 October 1991, mimeo. (The Council is the assembly of EC members-governments, which acts as a legislative body for the European Community).

growth of their CO_2 emissions, so that the level in the year 2000 would be back to that of 1990.

3. The developing countries would be free to increase their emissions of CO_2 as they grew, provided that they would commit themselves to increase their CO_2 and energy-efficiency.
4. In order to reach their target, the developed countries would introduce a carbon-energy ecotax. This ecotax would be levied at the national level, it would be budget-neutral (compensated by reductions in other taxes). But the level of the tax would be internationally coordinated, and would progressively reach the level of US$10 per equivalent of a barrel of oil.
5. The tax would be differentiated according to the CO_2-efficiency of the energy system: five dollars for any energy (including CO_2-clean ones: nuclear, hydrolic), plus an amount dependent on the CO_2 emissions: lower for natural gas than for oil, higher for carbon.
6. In addition, research and development of CO_2-efficient technologies would be subsidized.
7. Technological and financial transfers would help the South to match.

The three first points of the deal represent the 'target' part of the mix. They are in line with the South's objections to an early implementation of the precaution principle (and thus to meet Agarwal's goal, if by different means).

The last four points represent the 'instrument' set. The level of tax in year 2000 seems to be approximately in accordance with the emission target, considering the expected level of increase in GDP and the price-emissions relationship of the Nordhaus curve. The budget-neutrality is in line with the anti-tax bias of the late eighties, the uniformity of the rate of tax in industrialized countries is in line with the Urugay Round spirit (admitting that less developed countries deserve a privilege) and the choice of a tax as the instrument is probably the most cost-effective. Moreover, the level proposed for the tax makes it a real incentive for economic agents, since it is verified that real differences on price have a serious effect on CO_2 emission (Figure 7.5).

Point five reflects the fear that a shift from fossil energies would increase nuclear energy.[18] Moreover, it induces a shift *between* fossile energies towards the cleanest ones. Points six and seven take into account the importance given to the autonomous increase in energy efficiency, especially in the South (Goldemberg et al 1987).

NOT TO CONCLUDE

In sum, the *European Commission Communication to the Council* represented probably the best obtainable compromise between North and South, about one year before the Rio Conference. More precisely, it implied an alliance

---

18 It may also reflect a compromise between Germany (relying heavily on carbon for its energy production) and France (relying heavily on nuclear plants). Yet the German-French summit of May 29–30 1991 agreed upon a pure CO_2-tax.

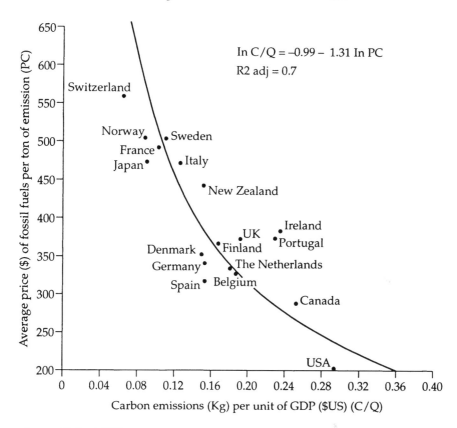

Source: Godard, 1992

Figure 7.5 *Carbon emissions and the price of energy*

between the 'North-Do Something' group and the 'South-Do Something' group of nations, between Western Europe and Southern Asia. Yet this compromise failed.

The first reason is that it expresses an hegemonic regime which is still controversial. In fact, it expresses the ecological superiority of the technical paradigm of Japan and Northern Europe (Germany plus Scandinavia), that is the North-West of the BCL chart (Figure 7.2).[19] But this superiority is not yet sufficient to result in a political leadership imposed on the US which would be a loser in this compromise.

Maybe a Euro-Japanese initiative for the implementation of an ecotax could have obliged the US to meet the challenge. But another reason of the failure was the inner weakness of the candidate to leadership: the European Community. In fact, the EC comprises a 'core' with advanced social and ecological compromises (the North of the continent) and an Atlantic and Mediterranean periphery, with 'flexible' capital-labour

---

19 In turn the superiority of this paradigm relies on a more efficient capital-labour compromise. See Lipietz (1992b and forthcoming).

relations and loose environmental regulations (Lipietz 1992a). Only the demographic weight of the core could impose the ecotax to the periphery. But in December 1991, the Maastricht meeting proposed a reform of the European constitution, increasing economic competition within Europe, but submitting ecological and social regulation to the rule of unanimity between governments. Thus, any single government was given a *veto* right on the ecotax. While some North European countries (in EC and in EFTA) had already engaged themselves in a unilateral implementation of a CO_2-energy ecotax, the United Kingdom and Spain did not hide their intention to practise ecological (and social) dumping.

In sum, the carbon-energy ecotax was the first victim of the Maastricht conference. The reaction of the Commissioner in charge of Environment, Carlos Ripa de Meana, was bitter. Next morning he stated to the French newspaper *Liberation* (10 December 1991):

> *Maastricht is a real treachery on environmental issues. We are going towards a two-speed environmental Europe. Environment policies, their costs, their regulation will differ according to country. That will be a big joke! We are preaching, we are making sermons on tropical rainforests, we cannot go to Rio with only words about the greenhouse effect!*

Ripa de Meana's prophecy was to be fulfilled perfectly. In April 1992, the European Council failed to adopt the ecotax. In May, the International Negotiation Group on Climate Convention adopted an half-empty compromise. Combined with the failure of the biodiversity negotiation, it closed any possibility for the emergence of a strong 'Do Something' alliance on Rio: the Europe-India axis was broken, the Rio Conference turned out to be an ordinary North–South conflict, with a China-India-Malaysia axis petrified in an 'accusing' position.

Could we conclude that the Rio Conference and the whole negotiation on climate was a failure ? Not really. In fact, the compromise was half full, and captured many southern requirements and European proposals. Refusing 'eco-colonialism', it was a step forward and a real commitment for the North:

- It was admitted that only carbon dioxide had to be controlled immediately. Southern rice and cows were given another chance.
- It was assessed that only developed countries had to make a first step: return by 2000 to a 'previous' level of emissions.[20]
- The word 'previous' was associated with the year 1990 in another paragraph.

This subtle language (a masterpiece of former vice-general secretary of United Nations, Jean Ripert) allowed the United States to sign without really committing themselves, while Europe proclaimed that it considered 1990 as the benchmark for a programme of reduction.

---

20 Technically, the committed countries were the ones signing and 'Annex I list'.

Where are we now? Not surprisingly, the ecotax is still not implemented in the post-Maastricht European Union. But negotiations are still advancing. Facing a general fiscal crisis (due to the German unification and the recession), the states in Europe are seeking new sources of revenues, as is the US. Tax on gas and ecotaxes are more and more appealing. Moreover, the December 1993 report by a group of economists headed by Edmond Malinvaud proposed the carbon-energy ecotax as a substitute to Social Security taxes levied on labour (Dreze et al 1994).

Thus, in the name of fighting unemployment through a decrease in labour cost, the ecotax is vindicated while governments increase taxes on gas. This implementation of the 'no-regret strategy' expresses the common wisdom that even if it may not be time to put a halt to the tide of cars in circulation and their CO_2 emissions, it may still be a good precaution not to foster it. In Hourcade's (1993) terms, the American way of life (Fordism) appears of 'contestable legitimacy'.[21]

Yet, the no-regret strategy, this weakest form of the precaution principle, ignores that it may be later than we think.

REFERENCES

Agarwal, A, Nerain, S (1991) *Global Warming in an Unequal World: a Case of Environmental Colonialism* Center for Science and Environment, New Delhi

Banuri, T (1992) *Decision Making on Sustainable Development in Asia* Report to UNESCO, mimeo

Benhaim, J, Caron, A, Levarlet, F (1991) '*Analyse économique des propositions des acteurs face au problème du CO_2*', *Cahiers du C3E*, Univ Paris I, mimeo

de Campos Mello, V (1992) *La puissance du faible. Les rapports Nord-Sud dans les négociations Forêt de la CNUED* Mémoire DEA, Univ Paris I, mimeo

Commissariat General du Plan (1993) *L' économie face à l' écologie* La Découverte/La Documentation Française, Paris

Gay, J P (1984) *Fabuleux maïs: histoire et avenir d' une plante*, AGPM, Paris

Godard, O (1992) *La réduction des émissions de gaz à effet de serre au moyen de taxes*, OECD, Paris

Godard, O (1993) 'Strategies industrielles et convention d' environnement: de l' univers stabilisé aux univers controversés', *Economie et Statistiques* n°258–59, Oct 1992

Goldemberg et al (1987) *Energy for a Sustainable World* WRI, Washington

Grubb, M (1990) *Energy Policies and the Greenhouse Effect* Royal Institute of International Affairs, Darmouth

Habeeb W M (1988) *Power and Tactics in International Negotiations* The Johns Hopkins Press, Baltimore

Hetch, S (1992) *Eco 92 as a negotiation process. The debates in the Americas* Report to UNESCO, mimeo

Hetch, S & Cockburn, A (1989a) *The fate of the forest. Developers, destroyers and defender of the Amazon* Verso, London-New York

Hetch, S & Cockburn, A. (1989b) 'Defenders of the Amazon' *The Nation*, May 22

Hourcade, J C (1993) 'Les arguments économiques de la négociation internationale autour de l'effet de serre' in CGP

---

21 Obviously a joke on the theory of 'contestable markets'.

Hourcade, J C, Baron, R (1992) *Réduire les émissions de gaz à effet de serre au moyen de permis négociables* OECD, Paris

International Panel on Climate Change (1992) *Climate Change: the IPCC Response Strategies* World Meteorological Organization/UNEP

Jonas, H (1991) *Le principe de responsabilité: une éthique pour la civilisation technologique* Cerf, Paris

Lipietz, A (1992a) *La préparation de la Conférence des Nations Unies sur l'Environnement et le Développement comme processus de négociation* Rapport à l'UNESCO, mimeo

Lipietz, A (1992b) *Towards a New Economic Order. Postfordism, Ecology and Democracy* Polity-O UP, London-New York

Lipietz, A (forthcoming) 'Capital-Labour relations at the dawn of the 21st century' in J Schor and J You (eds) *The Transformation of Capital–Labour Relations: A Global Perspective* Edward Elgar, Aldershot

Lipietz, A, Radanne, P (1993) *'Energie: élargir les marges de liberté'* in CGP

Marglin, F A (1990) *Dominating Knowledge ; development, culture, assistance* Oxford University Press, Oxford

Marglin, S, Schor, J (1990) *The Golden Age of Capitalism. Reinterpreting the Postwar Experience* University Press, Oxford.

Nordhaus, W D (1990) 'Economic Approach to Greenhouse Warming' présentation to the Conférence *Economic Policy Response to Global Warming* Rome, 4-6 Octobre

Porter, G, Brown, J W (1991) *Global Environmental Politics* Boulder, Westview Press

Rawls, J (1971) *A Theory of Justice* Oxford University Press, Oxford

Roqueplo, P (1993) *Climats sous surveillance. Limites et conditions de l' expertise scientifique* Economica, Paris

Stoffaes, C (1993) 'Energie nucléaire, économie, écologie' in CGP

World Resources Institute (1990) *World Resources 1990-1991: a Guide to the Global Environment* OUP, Oxford

Chapter Eight

Environmental Policies
and North–South Trade:
A Selected Survey of the Issues

Partha Sen

INTRODUCTION

C oncern over environmental issues has come a long way. From being regarded as the preserve of 'cranks', it has been taken up even by those sections of business whose interests apparently clash with any notion of regulation in the name of the environment. How, within such a short time, such a sea change has occurred is still an enigma, but the fact remains that these issues have become popular and where business has to respond to organized public pressures (however imperfectly) it, at least, has to pay lip service to the cause.

If this trend continues then environmental regulation is going to feature more prominently on the economic agenda in the near future. The problem with this – even for those who welcome the turnaround in public thinking – is that we do not have either enough factual information about the problems, nor can we conceptualize the way society should respond to the challenges posed by these issues. Traditional economic theory would view the problem as one of externalities and public goods. Nordhaus refers to the environmental problem as the 'grand-daddy of all public goods' (see Nordhaus 1991). The intergenerational aspects of the problems would also be recognized by economists. But, as will become clear later, when we try to go beyond this to the specifics of the issues involved we have almost no guidance from conventional wisdom.

The purpose of this chapter is to look at the interaction between environmental and other policies in the North and the pattern and the level of production and trade throughout the world. Because this is too vast an area to survey, we shall restrict ourselves to a selective study of some of the more important issues involved. The topics that are covered are:

- a discussion of the intertemporal issues involved (these are, of course, discussed at length elsewhere in this volume);
- a brief history of the pattern of North–South trade since the Second World War;
- the relation between pollution and growth;
- the role of the GATT;
- alternative tax policies and the gainers and the losers from these;
- the environmental implications of NAFTA; and
- the implications of a freer trade in food and coal on world welfare and pollution.

INTERTEMPORAL ISSUES

Let us first look at the intertemporal issues involved in designing and implementing policies to protect the environment. We begin by thinking of the world as a closed economy (which it undoubtedly is!) and posing the question: how would we design policies, assuming for the moment that we can, which trade off our well-being (broadly defined) with those of the future generations? Here we would need a lot of information about the magnitude and the timing of environmental degradation that is supposed to be taking place. *Ceteris paribus*, one would take more seriously those actions whose deleterious effects are going to be felt relatively soon. If this is accepted, then deforestation in the Third World due to population pressures, for instance, is probably more of a pressing problem than global warming or the disappearance of the ozone layer. This is not to deny for a moment the grave implications of the continued use of CFCs and other polluting gases, but just to remind ourselves that the 'cottage industry' of pollution associated with underdevelopment is as important as the 'large-scale industry'of pollution associated with a mature economy, mainly because its costs (and the timings of these) are better documented – though they may not make headlines like the depletion of the ozone layer. One should not overlook the fact that to reverse the deforestation that has occurred in the Third World is going to be a longer drawn-out process than, say, the ease with which CFC substitutes have been developed. As we shall see later the Third World countries are very inefficient in their use of energy – the carbon content per unit of GDP there is much higher than the OECD countries. Since the environment is inextricably linked to development in the Third World, any attempt to tackle one of them at a time is bound to fail.

Most environmental issues involve a society trading-off present production and welfare vis-à-vis the future. Some kind of a calculation has to be made about the gain to the future generations from reducing prodution today. How pure should the environment that is to be handed down be? Remember the environment can be left as it is if all production ceases but surely that is not the aim. The task of evaluating the trade-offs involved and designing policy responses to these cannot be done by the market mechanism even under the most favourable assumptions because firms would then maximize expected (discounted) profits without regard to the negative production externality. In addition, future generations are not enfranchised except through the altruistic motives of the present generation towards their descendants.

Now if we move to a world of nations which do not trade with one another, but each with a policy plan of the type discussed above, it does not require a very sophisticated analysis to see that a poor economy with a large population at or near subsistence levels would find it more difficult to ignore the needs of those currently alive and thus would discount the future more than would an economy which is relatively better off. It has a subsistence constraint which is truly binding. This brings us to the fairly important conclusion that, even without the complications arising from trade and payments, a relatively equitable distribution of initial endowments would make the task of environmental safeguard easier. For the relatively rich, a small transfer of resources would not make much of a difference, whereas for the poor it would allow them to at least think of the future. The *sine qua non* for this is a recognition on the part of the donor countries that such a transfer is twice blessed. Whether such a transfer is possible and if possible how it might be effected is discussed below.

To summarize, we see that to achieve meaningful discussion of environmental protection we need the following:

1. some notion of intergenerational trade-offs;
2. a more equitable distribution of the world's resources which is likely to make the task of giving some weight to the future easier;
3. this in turn needs a recognition of interdependence; and
4. it would require state intervention since the market cannot be expected to produce efficient outcomes.

A BRIEF OVERVIEW OF NORTH–SOUTH TRADE

We are quite accustomed to talk about the nations in the South being a homogeneous undifferentiated entity, even though in reality it is not clear that they share many common attributes except a history of being colonized (though even here backgrounds vary). Even for a limited exercise like North–South trade, what is common between India and Somalia, South Korea and Saudi Arabia? The debt experience of the various countries in the South has been very different. Their agricultural histories and responses have been diverse. As discussed in the next section, their use of polluting inputs is also very different. An ideal disaggregation for the kinds of problems discussed in this paper would be to treat the NICs (including China) separately. Two other possible distinct blocs would be the OPEC countries and sub-saharan Africa.

Still we shall not follow the preferred route outlined above and talk of a homogeneous South. The crucial distinguishing feature of the South as a bloc is that it is a net importer of manufactured goods and an exporter of primary goods. Even here the trend is towards a decline in the share of food and agricultural raw materials as a share of the South's exports (this fell from 77 per cent in 1955 to 55 per cent in 1970 to 45 per cent in 1978).

The share of manufacturing now constitutes well over half (58 per cent in 1988) of the South's exports (rising from 10 per cent in 1955 to 27 per cent in 1970 to 45 per cent in 1978). Over 90 per cent of South Korea's exports are manufactured goods. But the South as a whole still remains a net importer of manufactured goods – in 1980 the EC exported 124 per cent more of manufactured goods than it imported (the corresponding figures for the US were 34 per cent and for Japan 241 per cent). Geographical location also matters. For instance in the export of capital goods the North has 'divided up' the South among its various members – Japan exporting to the Asian NICs, the US to Latin America and Europe to Africa. The slow growth of Africa helps to explain the slow growth of the European capital goods industry (see van Wijnbergen 1985).

In all the studies of North–South interaction the basic asymmetry about the size of the North and the South is highlighted – namely in economic size the North is very large compared to the South and that changes in the South have negligible effects on the North while the converse is not true. This implies that a Southern expansion on its own is likely to peter out, while a coordinated Northern expansion is expansionary worldwide.

It is by now well documented that in the last four decades there has been a secular deterioration in the terms of trade of primary goods producers in the South – the *Prebisch hypothesis*. This of crucial importance to some parts of the South, like Africa, but increasingly less so for the South as a whole with its expanding export of industrial goods.

ECONOMIC DEVELOPMENT AND THE ENVIRONMENT

Now we come to the main question to be addressed in this paper: what are the implications for Southern production and trade of environmental policies in the North? Before attempting to answer this question we shall look at three points which will serve as a background for the discussion which follows. First we shall look at the emission figures for greenhouse gases by various countries. The other points are related. Any discussion of the environmental consequences of relocation of production usually leads us to what we might loosely describe as the 'cautious' view and the 'optimistic' view. The optimists point to the ease with which progress has been achieved in some international fora and also the relatively painless adoption of environmentally-friendly new technology by a few countries. The best example of the former is the Montreal protocol on the use of CFCs. A good example of the adoption of new technology is Japan. We will look at these two examples in turn.

First let us briefly look at the pollution profile of various countries. These figures are taken from Whalley (1991) and are the fossil fuel emissions of various countries in 1987. Note that these are not the only sources of environmental degradation (see the discussion on the trade-offs facing various countries and the discussion below on pollution and growth). These figures are however extremely important if the issue of global warming is to be addressed at all.

In emission per capita the US leads with a figure of 5.03 tons per capita (the world average being 1.08 tons per capita), followed by Canada, Australia etc.Saudi Arabia is the highest among the non-North countries, followed by Poland and South Korea (which at 1.14 tons per capita is just above the world average). Three countries, the US, the USSR and China, together accounted for over 50 per cent of the total world emissions. But in terms of inefficiency of fuel use, calculated as grams of carbon/\$ of GNP, China is way ahead of the rest at 2024 (world average 327) followed by Egypt and India. What is obvious from these figures is that the North is the villain in terms of current consumption but that any unregulated transfer of industry to the South could have disastrous environmental consequences. The only thing that seems to be preventing the South from contributing to global pollution more is its poverty.

Second there is the ease with which the major players reached an agreement on the use of CFCs.The Montreal protocol signed in September 1987 provided for a timetable for a reduction and an ultimate ban on the use of these ozone-layer depleting gases. Can this example be emulated elsewhere? The answer is almost certainly 'no'. One reason is that the market for CFCs is controlled by a few firms who also produce CFC substitutes. Also, the ozone depleting nature of CFCs is scientifically well-established. Faced with the prospect of being sued by skin cancer patients the companies were not unwilling for a switch in technology. A global ban is a facilitating device in that no one then would be able to use CFCs.

Finally there is the example of the remarkable ease, that is, without loss of competitiveness, with which Japan has been able to switch to 'clean' technology. Japan imports 99.6 per cent of all its oil and 81 per cent of all energy (1987 figures). For the US the figures are 38 per cent and 14 per cent respectively (all figures are taken from Institute of Energy Economics (1992)). In 1987 energy consumption per capita and per unit of GNP was 3.04 tons of oil/person/year and 0.262 tons of oil/\$1000 of GNP for Japan. The corresponding figures for the US are 7.65 and 0.441, the OECD averages being 4.74 and 0.41. Only the Netherlands fares better than Japan on these counts. To get an idea of Japanese improvements in fuel efficiency over time, we note that the energy intensity of GDP fell by more than one third between the first oil price shock in 1990.

Japan's position in Asia is also worthy of some comment. China and Nepal have an energy to GNP ratio which is seven times that of Japan. Thailand and India use 2.5 times energy per unit of GNP than Japan, while South Korea and Malaysia use about twice the amount. In crude steel production Chinese energy consumption is three times that of Japan, whereas India uses 75 per cent more but South Korea is more efficient by 20 per cent (1986 figures). In cement production China consumes twice the amount of energy per unit of output and India 60 per cent more than Japan.

There are however two factors which make it unlikely that the Japanese experience can be emulated by other industrial countries:

1. The almost total dependence on imported oil and the wild gyrations in its price that forced the Japanese to look for energy saving methods

long before the environment became important. To the extent that other countries have some of their own sources of energy this becomes less pressing.
2. Japan is uniquely placed among OECD countries in terms of its growth rate of output and the level of investment. A high rate of investment implies a high (or potentially high) rate of scrapping and the installation of new machinery. This can be seen from any simple model of vintage capital where a faster growing economy would have a higher proportion of new machines using cleaner technology. Western European investment, on the other hand, has been relatively sluggish and thus the introduction of a clean technology has been more painful.

Let us now turn to the main question, that of economic development and the environment. In an internal World Bank memorandum Larry Summers, the then Vice-President of that organization, wanted to support a migration of dirty industries from the North to the South. Three reasons were suggested why this should be encouraged. First, wages were lower in the South so that lost earnings from death and injury from environmental hazards would be lower. Second, richer countries valued their environment more than the poorer countries. And finally, the capital-poor South was less polluted than the capital-rich North. So it was felt the countries in the South had a better capacity to absorb the dirty industries.

Ignoring for the time being the racist overtones in these remarks, this suggestion seems a good starting point to begin an analysis of economic growth, trade and the environment. *En passant*, we note that all three reasons advanced cause complications for explantions based on the traditional Heckscher-Ohlin model. Obviously factor returns are different and factor flows occur in response to these. Tastes are also internationally different. And of course, environmental externalities are obviously present.

If dirty industries moved to the South and exported their products to the North then the arguments about eco-dumping become relevant. Eco-dumping occurs when one country (the importing one) forces its producers to internalize the environmental costs whereas the others (the exporting ones) do not.

Further, a number of multinationals have in any case produced and sold products which are banned in the North, eg DDT and asbestos. There is also some evidence that multinational firms located in the developing countries observe lower levels of safeguards compared to their units located in the OECD countries. We shall give three examples. The first and the most publicized one is the Bhopal disaster. On the night of 2–3 December 1984, a gas leak (vapours of methylisocyanate (MIC))from the plant of Union Carbide killed between 2000 and 5000 people and permanently damaged the lungs of 86,000 people. Union Carbide's plant in India had lower standards compared to their plant in West Virginia in the US. These included inferior vapour detection equipment and a lack of adequately sized and automatically operated emergency equipment.

In the second example in 1982 Mitsubishi, a Japanese chemical company, set up a plant in a small town in Malaysia. This company disposed of its radioactive thorium waste in plastic bags. Following protests, Mitsubishi initially denied any wrongdoing but public and legal pressure forced it to backtrack.

The third example concerns the production and sale of asbestos products. It is a legal requirement in many countries that the seller bears the responsibility for any failure to warn potential consumers about non-obvious hazards associated with its use. In the US many people had in fact sued sellers of asbestos products, but the sale of asbestos products continued without proper warning in other countries (see Castleman 1987 for many other examples).

This discussion shows that the mutinational firms which may have been motivated to move to the South for a variety of reasons such as low wages, tariff protected domestic markets and so on also enjoy a lower environmental cost. This is a source of worry for trade unionists and others in the OECD countries that domestic firms might move to less environmentally regulated countries (see the discussion on the GATT below).

Recently a number of US multinationals have tried to ensure the same safety standards at home and abroad. This sometimes can be self-defeating, for example, in the absence of similar conditions of waste-disposal in a LDC, a multinational decides not to undertake the project at all (see Cairncross 1992:9).

This brings us to another aspect of Larry Summers' argument. Is it really the case that the Southern countries have a greater ability to absorb pollution? There are two distinct points to be made here. First, the urban centres in the South where these industries are likely to move are as polluted as the northern cities (of course, life is cheaper in the South!). Delhi, Mexico City or Bangkok are hardly examples of clean air. Second, different kinds of pollution are associated with different stages of development. Lack of urban sanitation, concentration of lead and cadmium in river basins (95 per cent of urban sewage in LDCs is untreated) and high levels of ambient particles and lead are inversely related to the level of income. At a middle level of per capita income we find sulphur dioxide, nitrates, chemical oxygen demand, biological oxygen demand reaching a maximum (ie, these have an inverted u-shaped relationship with per capita income). Here also the turning points vary between pollutants. The very rich dirty their economies differently. Average per capita carbon dioxide emissions, which are much less life threatening, peak at very high levels of per capita income (see Cairncross 1992 and Grossman 1993 for some figures). It is undoubtedly true that most developing countries are likely to be more tolerant of pollution than developed countries. Most of the environmental degradation in the South is non-traded and the North is quite content to live with that. It is only when pollution crosses over to the South either in traded goods or in terms of the global warming potential of deforestation of tropical forests that the North takes notice.

The southern countries which have embarked on a path of industrialization face a dilemma. Initially they cannot choose the environment over growth. So a clean environment has to wait for them to attain a certain standard of living (see the discussion on Japan). But the world just would not be able to bear, environmentally, all the developing countries following the northern path of growing first. Imagine the amount of CO_2 emissions before China and India attain a per capita income of $15,000. Whatever other quibbles one may have with the notion of sustainable development, on this issue, at least, it is difficult to argue against. There has to be some recognition '... of biophysical constraints on growth from the side of finite environmental sources of raw materials and energy or finite environmental sinks for waste matter and energy.' (Daly 1992: 2).

Environment in the context of the previous paragraph has to be interpreted in a wide sense. There is ample evidence that incomes per capita have to grow before population growth slows down (in the absence of coercion). Since population growth is associated with environmental degradation in poorer countries, eg deforestation, lack of sanitation, use of chemical fertilizers due to the pressure on land etc, this constitutes a potential threat to the environment in the South.

GATT AND THE ENVIRONMENT

We now move on to look at the relationship between the environment and institutional arrangements governing trade. In particular, what would happen in the case of an environment-related trade dispute? What mechanisms exist to ensure that eco-dumping does not occur? Who will set standards related to the environment?

The GATT aims to provide a framework for freer trade. It seeks for its signatories equal treatment (the most favoured nation status and non-discrimination) and the gradual removal of barriers to free trade (quotas, tariffs, export subsidies etc).The leading players have, however, not been sufficiently committed to free trade to want to give up all control over trade policy. GATT, therefore, allows for exceptions to the most favoured nation status (eg in its treatment of countries with a balance of payments problem) and also allows for situations where the rules can be superseded by 'waivers'. This reluctance to cede policy autonomy on the part of the leading players also makes GATT relatively toothless. It cannot, for instance, initiate action against non-compliance.

Non-discrimination is a principle, as we shall see later, which is likely to clash with the likely use of trade policy for environmental ends. A country can impose whatever rules or taxes it likes on its imports as long as domestic production is subjected to the same taxes. It can set product quality but it cannot, as a rule, set process requirements.

There are three areas where trade liberalization espoused by GATT could run foul of environmental considerations.

1. Countries are concerned about their trading partners being lax in implementing stringent environmental policies, ie 'eco-dumping'. As mentioned above this causes costs of production to be lower in the countries where the cost of pollution is not internalized. An import

duty would be seen to be correcting this distortion if the extent of non-internalization could somehow be calculated. This is, however, in violation of GATT which does not recognize eco-dumping as a valid reason for the suspension of the non-discrimination principle (see Wiemann 1993).

Internalizing environmental costs is easier said than done. They have not been incorporated in national income accounts. At the micro level the problem is even more difficult. From an international perspective there is the added complication that different countries may have different preferences for a clean environment (see Daly 1992).

2. Countries could impose very detailed product standards. A few years ago the EC decided that the hormone content of US beef was too high – to which the US reacted by banning the import of EC agricultural products. In 1991, Germany passed a law requiring companies to take back and recycle their packaging. Cars in Germany may be required to be sent back to their manufacturers at the end of their economic lives. This puts foreign companies at a disadvantage in that their transportation costs are almost doubled. Some other examples of product standards are the toxic chemical contents of leather goods and garments and emission standards regulations of motor cars.

If these product standards are applied on domestic and foreign goods (ie without discrimination) then these do not violate GATT rules. GATT, however, does forbid setting process standards, ie specifying how a good is to be manufactured. In some cases one can infer process standards from product standards. Examples of these are the hormone content of meat and the toxic content of leather goods. But in most cases such an inference is not possible.

It is of some interest whether within a trading bloc, for instance the EC, whether harmonization of product standards takes place and at what level. If such harmonization takes place around the high standard countries then it augurs well for a world where some countries set high environmental standards. In the EC for most products because of disagreements harmonization has not been achieved and the member states have settled for mutual recognition of standards. Thus Denmark is allowed to insist on soft drinks bottles to be returnable whereas other countries do not (this decision was upheld by the European Court in 1988). In other cases there has been agreement at the EC level for example on the Large Combustion Plant directive requiring power stations to reduce emission of gases which contribute to acid rain. This movement originated in Germany but was extended to the whole of the EC in order to ensure Germany did not lose out as a consequence of its green preferences.

3 Another area where trade policy may be used in violation of GATT is when countries use such policies to protect Global Commons. Can a country concerned about global environmental damage use trade

restrictions for non-compliers? From the perspective of GATT this is not permissible. To quote from a recent GATT document:

> *...it is not possible under GATT's rules to make access to one's market dependent on the domestic environmental policies or practices of the exporting country... [This] protects trade relations from degenerating into anarchy through unilateral actions in pursuit of unilaterally defined objectives... however valid they may appear.*

GATT 1992, vol 1:24

Seventeen of the 127 environmental agreements examined by the GATT contain trade provisions. The Montreal protocol, the Basle convention on trade in hazardous waste and the Convention of Trade in Endangered Species (CITES) all rely on trade sanctions as the primary deterrent for the countries violating the agreement.

It should be pointed out that trade restrictions need not solve the problem. First, it does not help if the country concerned does not import the good in question (unless an across-the board embargo is envisaged). The US does not buy any fish from a country in violation of the International Whaling Convention. It could not have limited itself to a ban on whale meat since it does not import any whale meat anyway. Second, an import ban, unless imposed by all importers, could just divert the banned products elsewhere. This happened in the tuna–dolphin case (discussed below). As a consequence of the US refusal to buy Mexican tuna, the Italian and Japanese consumers benefited from the fall in its price. Third, a country subject to a trade embargo might switch to producing other products which are not necessarily environmentally friendly. An example of this is the clearing of rainforests for cultivation following the ban on the sale of timber. Finally (a point related to the previous one), a country may begin to process a raw material whose import has been banned. Instead of selling timber the country concerned could start exporting furniture – processing mills in Cote d'Ivoire are estimated to be 30 per cent less efficient than in developed countries.

Given these reasons it is obvious that for the Third World countries to conform to environmental sentiments of the North they have to be adequately compensated. Under the Montreal protocol, for instance, a Global Environment Facility has been set up to compensate developing countries for abstaining from the use of CFCs and other greenhouse gases. Still '...there must at least be an appreciable increase in appropriations for development aid as has been repeatedly promised at international conferences.' (Weimann 1993:15) Currently OECD countries give about $50 billion in official development assistance for all purposes which is about 0.35 per cent of their GNP. Their defence expenditure is 5–6 per cent of GNP. There is a lot of scope for an environmental/peace dividend here.

To prevent trade sanctions from being used for environmental reasons some other cooperative moves have been suggested. One of them is to provide environment-related debt relief so that the pollution associated with exports to service debt are kept in check. Obviously this should be conditional on the receiving country taking steps to desist from degrading the environment. A second possibility is technology transfer from the North to the South. It goes without saying that the larger is the membership coverage of a treaty the lower the number of non-signatories and the importance of trade sanctions etc diminishes.

Before moving on to the next issue, let us look briefly at one case which illustrates the conflict between national environmental policies and the GATT. This is the tuna–dolphin case mentioned above.

In the eastern tropical Pacific, yellow fin tuna is found. To catch the tuna, however, dolphins also have to be caught, since the tuna congregate under dolphins. The Americans love to eat tuna but they also adore dolphins. The US has a law called the Marine Mammals Protection Act (MMPA) which forbids it to import tuna from a country whose fleets kill on average 25 per cent more dolphins than do the US fleets, ie the requirement is to be (almost) as careful about not killing the dolphins as the Americans. The MMPA, to prevent recycling of dolphin-unfriendly tuna catch, requires that no tuna be imported from any country buying tuna from a country which does not meet the standards stipulated in the MMPA.

Under pressure from an environmental pressure group in 1991 the US government reluctantly (because it recognized that this would violate the GATT rules) imposed a ban on tuna imports from Mexico, Venezuela and Vanuatu. To prevent 'tuna-laundering' Thailand, Japan and the EC were added to the list. Mexico appealed to a GATT panel which found that the US had violated the non-discrimination principle. One of the possible exemptions under Article XX of GATT would apply if this ban was to protect a resource if it lay within US territory. This was not the case with the Mexican exports of tuna. The GATT panel, however, allowed the US to insist on labelling tuna 'dolphin-friendly' if they were indeed caught that way. This, the panel felt, was product information applied without discrimination.

TAXES ON CARBON EMISSIONS

We now turn to a different issue. If some global agreement was indeed possible on the control of emissions of greenhouse gases, what would be the distribution of costs and benefits? Three kinds of taxes have been proposed and used in simulations in traditional trade models (see Whalley 1991). The simulations are based on a target reduction of greenhouse gases by 50 per cent.

1. The first tax proposed is a national-based production tax. Not surprisingly the gainers here are the oil exporters (their GDP goes up by 10.8 per cent) and the South is the biggest loser (GDP falls by 4.76 per cent).
2. The second tax is a national-based consumption tax. This benefits the

North the most (their losses are minimized – their GDP falls by 0.63 per cent only) and hurts the oil exporters the most (24.8 per cent decline in GDP).

3. Finally a global tax is going to hurt the North the most because they are the biggest consumers of oil per capita (2.4 per cent of GDP), while the GDP of the South actually rises (by 2.9 per cent).

All these taxes imply an overall reduction of world GDP of about 2 per cent. Note the production-based tax recreates the memories of the 1970s oil price shocks. Also note that a production-based tax increases the welfare of the exporter. Why then cannot nations who have some monopoly power implement this unilaterally? The answer probably lies in the nature of OPEC's exports and the inability of oil production to move across national boundaries. In general, in a short-run trade framework a nation's terms of trade improve following a unilateral tax only if income effects arising from the disbursement of revenues are fairly strong (For details see Table 8.1 and Winters 1992 for further discussion).

Table 8.1 Welface effects of carbon taxes by regions

	Producer tax	*Consumer tax*	*Global tax*
Average tax rate ($/ton of carbon)	448	448	448
Welfare change (% GDP)			
EC (12)	–4.0	–1.0	–3.8
US and Canada	–4.3	–3.6	–9.8
Japan	–3.7	0.5	0.9
Oil exporters	4.5	–18.7	–13.8
Rest of the world	–7.1	-6.8	1.8
World	–4.4	–4.4	–4.2

Source: Whalley and Wigle (1991)

TRADE LIBERALIZATION AND ITS ENVIRONMENTAL CONSEQUENCES

Two examples of the environmental consequences of trade liberalization are discussed here. The first one is the North American Free Trade Agreement (NAFTA) and the second is, as is likely in the light of the recently concluded GATT negotiations, a liberalization of world trade in food and coal.

Let us turn to NAFTA first. It raises the usual (ie similar to the EC) problems associated with harmonization of standards, dispute resolution mechanism, questions of sovereignty etc (see Debellevue et al 1994). In addition from the perspective of this chapter we have some possibly interesting projections. Since Mexico, a developing country, is joining an already existing free trade area between two northern countries, the US and Canada, it may well hold some lessons for the formation of similar blocs elsewhere. The industrial relocation implications of such a union are of concern to both trade unionists in the US and Canada and the policy authorities in Mexico. However we shall confine ourselves to the environmental implications for Mexican agriculture.

Agricultural income is distributed in a very skewed manner in Mexico. Twelve per cent of Mexican farmers receive 54 per cent of the total output. To ease a land shortage the government encourages migration to the tropical forest areas. It is estimated that in the 1980s a quarter of a million acres of forest land was lost as a consequence. But rainforests cannot support agricultural activity for more than five years at a time. Therefore when productivity of these lands falls, people move again. Such land is often converted into cattle ranches, though land is often directly cleared for raising cattle. It is estimated that about two million hectares of land were cleared every year in the 1980s for conversion into cattle pastures.

Mexican cattle-raising is much more profitable compared to its US counterpart. It is expected that NAFTA will give a fillip to Mexico's ranching sector thereby accelerating the process of deforestation. Currently only about 10 per cent of land is used for agriculture, while about 45 per cent is used for cattle-raising.

Another important by-product of NAFTA is the expected increase in monoculture agriculture with the attendant increase in the use of pesticides. US appearance quality standards are very high and this increases the amount of pesticides sprayed. Over the last two decades organochlorine pesticides (eg DDT) which were found to be detrimental to the environment have been replaced by organophosphorus, carbamates and piretrine products. There is a trade-off involved in this switch. It reduces the risk to the consumers but the newer pesticides are more toxic and so increase the risk to the farmers. With NAFTA in place this risk to the Mexican farmer is expected to increase unless some major breakthrough is made on the technological side (see DeBellevue et al 1994: 58).

Overall, at least according to one study, Mexico's economic fortunes after joining NAFTA will not witness a major turnaround. Mexico's trade balance is seen to be deteriorating by about 10 per cent, while its GNP will fall by 0.04 per cent and its unemployment rate will fall by 0.6 per cent. From an environmental perspective this implies that it is unlikely that Mexico is going to see its economic condition improve so much that it will be in a position to implement tighter environmental standards (DeBellevue et al 1994: 56).

The other example of trade liberalization which has major implications for world welfare is the pattern of trade and the environment. The question we ask is: what would be the effect of a liberalization of some of the markets where the North has hitherto adopted a very aggressive protectionist stance? Food is a good example. Another good which is important from an environmental perspective is coal.

Anderson (1992) looks at the world food market in a partial equilibrium framework. His model suggests an increase in world food prices of the order of 25 per cent if only the advanced countries liberalized. This would lead to the food-producing developing countries gaining $17 billion annually, in addition to the liberalizing countries gaining $47 billion annually. World grain production is expected to fall and resources would move into meat and dairy products.

What would be the environmental consequences of such a relocation? Chemical fertilizer and pesticide use is positively related to the producer price. One would expect the use of these to fall in the North but increase in the South. Labour migration out of agriculture would fall as a consequence of rising incomes, which should also reduce deforestation for fuel.

Liberalization of world coal trade would raise the price of coal and thus contribute to a switch to other less carbon-intensive fuels. In so far as protected northern coal has a high sulphur content a reduction in its production is desirable.

CONCLUSIONS

In an attempt to answer the question 'What would be the implications of a tighter environmental regulation in the North on the distribution of production and trade in the world ?', we first looked at the problem in an explicitly intertemporal setting and tried to argue that a more equitable distribution of world resources is conducive to the preservation of the environment globally and that the problem encompasses many items which come under the heading of development economics, eg population control, unemployment. All these contribute directly to a worsening of the environment. It is, however, true that to determine the intertemporal trade-offs we need much better data on the likely effects of pollution than we have at the moment.

Next we briefly reviewed the pattern of growth of North–South trade since the Second World War. Here we saw that notwithstanding the secular deterioration of the South's terms of trade and its debt problem, the South's exports to the North have, over time, increasingly taken the form of manufactured goods. This trend would only be reinforced by an environment-based relocation of northern industry.

We then reviewed (some of) the issues involved in the growth process of developing countries, the trading pattern and the implication of these for the environment. It seems likely that higher growth would cause a deterioration in the global environment under the historically known paths of growth.

This then lead us to try and understand what institutions, if any, exist to ensure orderly growth of trade without environmental degradation. The answer here seems to be that the GATT has to be modified drastically if such a requirement is to be fulfilled.

In the context of the emissions of greenhouse gases we looked at the alternative taxes proposed. Given the different effects on different sections of the world's population it seems unlikely that an agreement would be reached soon.

Finally we looked at two types of trade liberalizations and the implications for the environment. The first of these is the formation of NAFTA.

This would bring some elements of the North and the South together. Here we saw that Mexico is unlikely to benefit much either in terms of its macroeconomic indicators or in terms of the quality of its environment. The second scenario discussed was that relating to a liberalization of world trade in a few goods and its implication for the environment. Here it seems that a liberalization by the North of its market for food and coal would both raise welfare and improve the environment quality in most parts of the world.

REFERENCES

Anderson, K (1992) 'Effects on the environment and welfare of liberalized world trade: the cases of coal and food' in Anderson and Blackhurst (1992) *The Greening of World Trade Issues*, Harvester Wheatsheaf, Hemel Hempstead, UK

Anderson, K and Blackhurst, R (1992) *The Greening of World Trade Issues*, Harvester Wheatsheaf, Hemel Hempstead, UK

Cairncross, F (1992) The environment survey, *The Economist*, 5–20

Castleman, B (1987) 'Corporate standards applied internationally in global development and environment crisis – Has humankind a future?' *Pacific Peoples Environment Network*, Sahabat Alam, Malaysia

Daly, H E (1992) 'From adjustment to sustainable development: the obstacle of free trade' paper presented at the Loyola Law School conference

DeBellevue, E B, Hitzel, E, Cline, K, Benitez, J A, Ramos-Miranda, J and Segura, O (1994) 'The North American Free Trade Agreement: an ecological–economic synthesis for the United States and Mexico' *Ecological Economics* 9, pp 53–71

GATT, International trade 1990-91, Geneva, Switzerland

Grossman, G M (1993) 'Pollution and growth: what do we know?' Paper presented at CEPR/OECD conference

The Institute of Energy Economics (1992) Report on the global environmental issues in Japan, Tokyo, Japan

Nordhaus, W D (1991) A sketch of the economics of the greenhouse effect *American Economic Review*, Papers and Proceedings 81, pp 146–150

Piggot, J, Whalley, J and Wigle, R (1992) 'International linkages and carbon reduction initiatives' in Anderson and Blackhurst (1992), op cit

van Wijnbergen, S (1985) 'Interdependence revisited: a developing countries perspective on macroeconomic management and trade' *Economic Policy* 1, pp 85–137

Whalley, J (1991) 'The interface between environmental and trade policies' *Economic Journal* 101, pp 180–189

Whalley, J and Wigle, R (1991) 'The international incidence of carbon taxes' in Dornbusch, R and J Poterba (eds) *Economic policy responses to global warming* MIT Press, Cambridge

Wiemann, J (1993) '*Environmentally-oriented trade policy: a new area of conflict between North and South*' German Development Institute, Berlin, Germany

Winters, L A (1992) 'The trade and welfare effects of greenhouse gas abatement: a survey of empirical estimates' in Anderson and Blackhurst (1992) op cit

Chapter Nine

The Korean Model of Development and its Environmental Implications

Jong-Il You

In March of 1991 eight officials of the Doosan Electro-Materials company, a member of the Doosan *chaebol*, were arrested for dumping some 300 tons of phenol – known to cause cancer and damage the nervous system – into the Nakdong river which supplies drinking water to around 10 million people. Seven government officials were also arrested for trying to cover up for the company. A month later, the environment minister was forced to resign. Not an unusual story in many countries but very much so in South Korea (hereafter simply Korea) where anything that was seen as a hindrance to growth maximization – be it political freedom, labour rights and social equity, or protection of the environment – used to be ruthlessly suppressed or wilfully neglected. What has changed is the political climate since democratization began in 1987. In an unprecedented reaction to industrial pollution the citizens of Taegu, where the plant was located, took to the streets and the environmental protest movement spread like wildfire, leading, for instance, to the closure of three factories in Taejon charged with polluting the Kuem river. And a successful boycott of the Doosan products, ranging from circuit boards to the most popular beer, Coca Cola and Kentucky Fried Chicken, forced its chairman to resign (Merson 1991).

Koreans are not prepared to tolerate the enormous environmental damage and the extreme levels of pollution any more. In this, they are challenging nothing less than the foundation on which the Korean economic miracle has been created even as it is being touted as the model to be emulated. Amazingly, I have not been able to find a single scholarly journal article on the economic analysis of the environmental issues in Korea. Both the left and the right seem to love the Korean model of development, albeit for different reasons, and not much attention has been paid to the social ills and the environmental degradation it has entailed. Are they a price well worth paying for the 'good life' in terms of material consumption the rapid growth has brought about? Is the Korean model the best way to development? How many Koreas can the fragile Earth afford?

This chapter investigates the environmental implications of the Korean model of development. First we look at the political economy of development in Korea and draw the connection between political freedom, social equity and the environment as victims of growth maximization. The next section documents the environmental consequences of development in Korea – population growth and urbanization, natural resources and environmental pollution. It will be seen that environmental pollution is a much more serious problem than resource depletion in Korea. Next the relationship between growth and environmental depletion in Korea is analysed. The final section attempts to make a judgement on the Korean model of growth in light of its environmental implications.

The central claim of this chapter is that the Korean model of development should not be regarded as 'the model' to be followed by the rest of the South once environmental considerations are brought into account. Korea pursued maximization of growth rather than maximization of welfare, one aspect of which is that the welfare cost of environmental degradation was virtually ignored. It does not seem to be prepared to commit itself to environment-friendly growth in the foreseeable future. After decades of economic growth at the expense of grave environmental degradation, the government and the people of Korea are addicted to growth that has an increasingly tenuous relationship with enhancing the quality of life. The world would be on a dangerous course if the entire South were to emulate Korea.

I wish to make it clear that, far from there being no lessons to be learned from the Korean model, on the contrary, there is a great deal to be learned from the Korean experience about what sort of policies and institutions work successfully in achieving rapid economic development. And I have nothing against rapid economic development in the poor South which is probably necessary for sustainability of the world economy for demographic reasons (see Baldwin 1993). What I *am* saying is that the proper model of development must be one of 'growth with environmental care' instead of 'growth at the expense of the environment' as in the case of the Korean model.

THE POLITICAL ECONOMY OF DEVELOPMENT AND ENVIRONMENT IN KOREA

The Political Economy of Growth Maximization

During the last three decades Korea has undergone a remarkable transformation from one of the poorest countries in the world to a 'new giant' of East Asia. Its GDP growth rate averaged 8.8 per cent during 1963–1990. GDP per capita reached $6250 in 1991 and is expected to exceed $10000 in 1996 according to the seventh 5-Year Economic Development Plan. Key statistics regarding the growth performance are presented in Table 9.1. Structural change has been equally rapid: the employment and

Table 9.1 Growth performance in Korea 1963–1990

Growth rates (% pa)	1963–73	1973–81	1981–86	1986–90	1963–90
GDP	9.3	8.2	8.4	10.2	8.8
Population	2.3	1.6	1.4	1.2	1.8
GDP per capita	6.8	6.5	6.9	9.0	7.0
Real wage*	7.7	8.6	7.5	12.2	8.6
Labour force	3.4	3.2	1.8	3.5	3.1
Investment	18.5	12.4	10.4	16.2	14.9
Manufact. GDP	20.3	13.9	10.4	12.5	15.4
Agricultural GDP	3.3	1.0	3.7	0.2	2.2
Exports	32.9	15.6	11.1	12.4	20.7
Imports	22.8	13.8	7.4	16.0	16.3

Note: * manufacturing wage
Sources: Bank of Korea and Economic Planning Board

the GDP shares of agriculture declined from 63 per cent and 43 per cent in 1963 to 16 per cent and 9 per cent in 1990, while those of the manufacturing sector rose from 8 per cent and 15 per cent in 1963 to 27 per cent and 29 per cent in 1990.

While there are disputes about the secret of the fantastic growth performance of Korea, with the orthodoxy stressing the importance of the neutral trading regime and free-market competition and its opponents highlighting the role of import substitution and a heavy dose of government intervention, what is clearly beyond dispute is the ability of the Korean state to impose its policies with little resistance from either the capitalist or the working classes. Not only was it free to pursue relentless growth-maximization policies, but it was able to discipline errant capitalists or trouble-making workers who deviated from the course of action set out by the economic development plans. This rather unusual state of affairs is, more than anything else, the central ingredient of Korea's economic success, except perhaps for its special geo-political status as an anti-communist garrison state in the Cold War which earned Korea huge amounts of aid and access to the US markets.

Why was the Korean state so strong in terms of both its relative autonomy in defining goals (ie growth maximization) and its capacity to mobilize resources and implement policies? The autonomy of the state can be explained by the fact that the social classes were very weak and in no position to oppose the agenda of the developmental state organized by President Park who assumed power through a military coup in 1961. Capitalists were dependent on the state, with their meagre economic base having originated from the disposal of the industrial assets left by the Japanese and the US aid in the 1950s under the Rhee government (1948–1960). Landlords were stripped of their political might and economic base through the land reform in the early 1950s. Organized labour and other popular movements were ruthlessly destroyed by the US military government (1945–1948) which considered them obstacles to erecting an anti-communist regime in South Korea. The middle class was practically non-existent.

The extraordinary administrative and coercive capacity of the Korean state has such historical origins as the long tradition of centralized bureaucratic state, the inheritance from the colonial period of a strong military-administrative apparatus, and the massive build-up of the military and the national police following WWII and the Korean War (Choi 1983). On top of this, the military junta led by Park nationalized the commercial banking system and seized control over the entire financial system, gaining an extraordinary leverage over the private sector.

Not all strong states are developmentalist, although in the postwar era most of the states pursued economic development to a greater or lesser extent. The Korean state was highly committed to development for two reasons. First, the military leadership perceived that economic development was an imperative for national survival and dignity. For them, economic development was a national security issue as North Korea was ahead of the South in economic strength in the early 1960s. The military leadership also felt threatened by declining US aid and humiliated by their dependence on US support; thus the slogan 'nation-building through exportation'. Second, it attempted to erase the illegitimacy of the coup by fostering rapid economic development. In a country where the military class were subordinated to the literary class for centuries the military-dominated state led successively by Park (1961–79) and Chun (1980–87) never gained wholehearted acceptance by the populace. Rapid economic development was offered as a compensation for the loss of political rights (Bello and Rosenfeld 1990).

The military leadership did not need to look far to discover a secret formula for rapid economic development. Park, a former official in the Japanese army, knew only too well how the Japanese colonial government quickly built an impressive industrial base in Korea during the 1930s to prop up its war aims. This episode featured extensive state intervention in the economy, a peculiar developmental banking system, enlisting of *zaibatsu* groups for crash industrialization and their reward with heavy subsidies, and mobilization of the entire population to achieve the objectives of the state – all featured again in the 1960s and 1970s (Woo 1991).[1] The model worked once again. State intervention, developmental banking, reliance on big business, these are all quite typical of late industrialization. What set Korea apart from the less successful countries was the immense effectiveness with which these instruments were used to carry out the development plans, owing to the strength of the Korean state. In particular, the state in Korea imposed performance standards on the businesses in return for subsidies more successfully than other states (Amsden 1989).

---

1 After seizing power Park quickly lined up *chaebol* (Korean transliteration of *zaibatsu*) for the economic development programme of the state by arresting its leaders for illicit accumulation of wealth and then extracting promises of cooperation in return for leniency. He then confiscated the banks and lined up all the financial intermediaries under the direction of the Ministry of France, establishing a powerful instrument of industrial policy.

For all its economic successes the military-dominated regime could not hold on to power forever. In fact, in the long run, it was the very success of the regime in delivering rapid economic development that undermined the foundation of the regime. For the rapid economic development meant increasing power for social classes: the gigantic *chaebols* amassed enormous economic power, the newly prosperous middle class increasingly resented the arbitrary use of the state power, and the numerical and organizational strength of the working class was growing. The response of the state, especially in the early 1980s, was to accommodate the *chaebols'* needs – for example, by selling the commercial banks to the *chaebols* in the name of liberalization – in return for illicit political contributions on the one hand, and, on the other, to forcefully suppress the labour movement and political dissent. The growth coalition between the state and *chaebol* looked increasingly suspect and this undermined the implicit social compact in which the state would harness the social forces and mobilize the economic resources to the goals of economic development and the citizenry would tolerate authoritarian politics. In the minds of the younger generation of Koreans, with no living memory of wars and starvation, the military-dominated state had outlived its purpose. Such was the political reality which, along with the increased strength of the popular classes, led to the demise of authoritarian politics and the beginning of democratization in 1987.

Victims of Growth Maximization: Political Freedom, Equity, Environment

More or less absent in the large literature on Korean development is a sober assessment of what it meant for the well-being of the people. True, many noted the rise in the material standard of living, including health and education, that accompanied the rapid rise in income. Moreover, these benefits of growth have been widely, if not equally, shared by the majority of population as ample employment opportunities were created by the rapid growth of the economy. However impressive these achievements may seem in comparison to what has happened in many other parts of the developing world, they should not blind us to the deep social discontents that have persisted within Korea. The costs which the hyper-rapid growth has imposed on the population are as real as its benefits, and we need to ask if the benefits justify the costs and, more importantly, if some of the costs could have been avoided.

The first casualties of the Korean-style development were political freedom and human rights under the military-dominated authoritarian state. Any profound social change is bound to have traumatic aspects, especially when it occurs as fast as it did in Korea. The breakdown of traditional values and social ties and rapid structural changes inevitably bring about heightened social conflict. In Korea such changes were engineered by the powerful state machinery which, with its unusual capacity for repression, suppressed any dissent on the path of development, producing thousands of political prisoners and provoking self-immolation by many protesters. Striking workers, protesting farmers and communities seeking to protect themselves from destructive development projects were ruthlessly put down by the security-police apparatus.

The very fact of political repression suggests that not all was well in spite of rapid economic growth. In fact, in the name of growth maximization, distributional equity and social welfare were neglected and the environment was actively sacrificed. In the minds of the leaders of the state economic growth was a collective good serving the 'nation' and was not to be constrained by mere individual welfare considerations. In the 1970s the government officially proclaimed its policy priority to be 'growth first, distribution later'.

It has been widely publicized that the income distribution in Korea is one of the most equal among the developing countries and that it did not experience the typical worsening implied by Kuznets' U-shaped curve. For casual observers inside Korea, however, the inequality of income distribution was plainly excessive and worsening over time as even the government acknowledged in the 1980s. Why the difference in perceptions? Besides the obvious point that there is no reason why Koreans should be satisfied with the fact that their income distribution is better than the Brazilian one, it is important to note that the international economists' perception was shaped largely by what happened up to the early 1970s, when the rapid reduction in unemployment did improve income distribution. Few took in the subsequent deterioration. Moreover, the data from which earlier calculations were made are seriously flawed as they exclude a large segment of population including the very rich and the very poor, the 'imputed income' from housing and of course the unreported income (Yoo 1990). Corrections for the unrepresented households (Kim and Ahn 1987) reveal an unmistakable trend of rising inequality from the early 1970s, even though it still underestimates the degree of inequality due to the importance of the imputed income and unreported income in wealthy households.[2]

A more visible and acutely felt inequality, which is not captured by the household income distribution data, is the enormous concentration of power and financial resources in the hands of *chaebol* whose explosive growth has been underwritten by the state. In a loan market characterized perennially by excess demand they had nearly monopolized access to preferential loans and low-interest rate bank financing, crowding out small and medium-sized businesses into the unorganized money markets. Regional inequalities created by concentration of industrial facilities in Seoul area and the South-east have also been an important

---

2 One estimate shows that the capital gains from the real estate in 1988 and the first half of 1989 was about 2.2 times the nominal GNP during the same period (Kim and Lee 1989:58). Needless to say, these enormous capital gains are distributed in a highly uneven way: the Gini coefficient for the ownership of land is over 0.9 in most big cities (ibid:44). Also, the practice of holding financial assets under assumed names is an important cause of large unreported incomes of the rich.

source of conflict.[3] Not only was the growth maximization by the state engendering growing social disparities, but the state, in keeping with the 'growth first, distribution later' policy, did little to ameliorate them through social spending. The share of government spending on social welfare has been one of the lowest in the world (You, forthcoming).

Not surprisingly, the environment also fell victim to growth maximization policies. There have been positive developments such as the sharp decline in the population growth rate from above 3 per cent in the fifties to below 1 per cent in 1991 and the successful reforestation, but they pale in comparison to the massive environmental degradation brought about by the rapid industrialization and urbanization in a milieu where polluting smoke was hailed as a symbol of development. The state had no inclination to protect the environment lest it hurt business profits and growth. The victims of toxic pollution were viewed, if they protested, as antisocial enemies of the national drive toward economic growth. Faced with the government's unwavering pro-industry stance, the victims of pollution – usually the most powerless members of the society like farmers and fishermen – opted to bring their cases directly to the polluters and usually received only a small fraction of their original claims (Auer 1991).

On paper, there was the Public Nuisance Prevention Law (PNPL) of 1963 which empowered the government to set emission and effluent standards and required pollution-abatement facilities in all new factories. But as the responsibilities for enforcement of PNPL were assigned to an understaffed Environmental Division under the Ministry of Health and Social Affairs, itself the ministry with the least clout in the government, there was no systematic monitoring and rarely have polluters faced any penalties (Cha 1976). As public concern with the environmental degradation grew, the PNPL was replaced by the Korean Environmental Preservation Act in 1977 and the Environmental Division was upgraded to the Environmental Administration in 1980. In the early 1980s the government, for the first time, began to take some actions to tackle the most politically sensitive pollution problems – the unbreathable air in Seoul and the filthy water in the Han river. But even after the Environment Administration was upgraded to the Ministry of Environment in 1990, in the wake of democratization, its regulation of pollution discharge remains mostly cosmetic as it lacks both the judicial power and the necessary enforcement personnel (Chung et al. 1990).

The next part of this chapter will document the details of the environmental degradation caused by decades of neglect. What I want to stress here is the connection between the political freedom, social equity and environmental protection as the victims of the growth maximizing Korean model of development. Already democratization has brought into question the obsession with growth-maximization as the national goal

---

3 All the leaders of the military-dominated regime have come from the southeastern region, and they allocated a disproportionate share of investment in that region as well as assigning key government and military posts to their fellow southeasterners. The thoroughly neglected southwestern region, where the long-time opposition leader Kim Dae Jung came from, has been the bastion of opposition to the regime.

under the military-dominated regimes, although rapid growth remains the primary objective of the long-term economic policy. The government of Roh (1988–1993), which represented a halfway house to democracy, began to relax labour repression in the aftermath of the giant eruption of strike waves in 1987 and to pay attention to the long-neglected welfare needs by introducing the minimum wage law, national health insurance and the national pension system (You, forthcoming). Korea may never again enjoy the frantic economic growth rates of the late 1980s. The inevitable erosion of competitiveness due to rising labour costs has slowed down the growth machine in the 1990s. As Koreans wrestle to imagine a new political economy which balances growth and social needs, environmental issues have also come to the fore.

THE ENVIRONMENTAL CONSEQUENCES OF DEVELOPMENT

Population Growth and Urbanization

Korea is one of the most densely populated countries in the world, second only to Bangladesh if we exclude city states, with the population density of 438.4 persons per km^2 in 1990. The total population increased from 25.0 million in 1960 to 43.5 million in 1990. But the population growth rate steadily decreased from 2.9 per cent per annum in 1960 to 0.98 per cent in 1990. The total fertility rate dropped from 6.0 to 1.6, considerably below the replacement rate, during the same period. The population projection based on the 1990 census estimates that the population will stabilize at around 50.6 million by the year 2021 (Ministry of Environment 1991). Due to the reduction in the fertility rate and increased life expectancy the population structure has changed from a pyramid shape to a bell shape, with the percentage population aged 14 or less decreasing from 42.3 per cent in 1960 to 25.8 per cent in 1990.

The rapid reduction in the population growth rate can be attributed to the rapid rise in income as well as to the vigorous promotion of the national family planning programme. Adopted in 1962 as a part of the economic development plans, it succeeded in raising the rate of contraceptive use from 9 per cent in 1964 to 77 per cent in 1988, the highest in the developing world (see Table 16.6 in WRI 1992). It is worth noting that the population policy was carried out by subtle advertising and free provision of family planning services rather than in a repressive way.

While Korea has done well in curbing population growth, it has been unable to solve excessive urbanization. The process of urbanization in Korea has been extremely rapid. The percentage of urban population (those living in the cities of at least 50,000 residents) increased from 28.3 per cent in 1960 to 71.6 per cent in 1990. The percentage of population living in cities of one million or more increased from 17.3 per cent in 1965 to 50 per cent in 1990. The growth of the Seoul metropolitan area has been especially explosive. The population of Seoul, the land size of which is only 0.6 per cent of Korea, reached 10.6 million or 24.4 per cent of the total population.

The population of the Seoul metropolitan area was 18.6 million or 42.7 per cent of the total population (Ministry of Environment 1991).

The chief cause of the heavy concentration of population is the concentration of the social infrastructure and industrial facilities in large metropolitan areas and industrial complexes, which was promoted on grounds of economies of scale and growth maximization. Seoul, in particular, is not only the political centre as the capital city of the country but the centre of industry, commerce, finance, education and culture. In the face of such overwhelming attractions, government policies to disperse population away from Seoul region have been ineffective.

The rapid urbanization has inevitably caused serious problems in the natural and living environment in urban areas. In addition to the pollution of ambient air and water near cities and the generation of solid wastes, which will be discussed below, there are incredible traffic congestion and housing problems.

Table 9.2 Number of motor vehicles (000s)

Year	Total	Passenger cars	Buses	Trucks
1965	39	13	9	17
1970	126	60	16	50
1975	194	84	22	87
1980	528	249	42	236
1985	1113	557	128	429
1988	2035	1118	260	658
1990	3395	2075	1320	
2000*	12650	9200	3450	

Note: Excludes 2-wheeled motor vehicles * projection
Source: Ministry of Transportation

As can be seen in Table 9.2 the growth of the number of motor vehicles has been extremely rapid, roughly doubling every four years or so, and is expected to continue at a similar pace for the foreseeable future. In recent years, especially, the increase in the number of passenger cars has been explosive: it almost doubled in just two years between 1988 and 1990. Apart from rising incomes and falling automobile prices, government policy to promote the car industry by expanding the domestic market has been at work.[4] Compared to the increase in the number of cars, the expansion of the road system has been totally inadequate. For example, between 1970 and 1985, the length of city roads in Seoul increased only twofold whereas the vehicle fleet increased tenfold. To keep the expansion of the road system in line with the rise in the number of cars seems near

---

4 The government aims to establish Korea as the world's fifth-largest maker of cars, with the annual output reaching three million vehicles by the mid-1990s (*Far Eastern Economic Review*, 18 January 1990, pp 35–36)

impossible due to the skyrocketing cost of land.[5] As a result traffic congestion in large cities is expected to get worse from an already intolerable situation. The average speed of motor vehicles during the peak hour was measured at about 15 km/hour in Seoul and 18 km/hour in Pusan in 1987, but is expected to fall to about 7–8 km/hour in both cities by 1996 (KTI 1989). In addition to the huge inconvenience, the traffic congestion causes enormous economic losses in terms of the additional fuel consumption, the loss of additional driving time, the environmental cost of additional automobile emissions, increased accidents, and so on. The cost of additional fuel consumption due to congestion in Seoul during 1987 was estimated to be over $500 million and is expected to increase up to $8 billion by the year 2001 (KTI 1987).

The housing problem in urban areas is one of the most serious social problems in Korea. The rapid growth in urban population, coupled with the trend towards nuclear families resulted in ever-growing demand for urban housing with which supply of housing has been unable to keep up. Thus, between 1960 and 1988, the ratio of the number of housing units to the total number of households declined from 82.5 per cent to 69.8 per cent nationally and from 64.8 per cent to 58.2 per cent in urban areas. Since some households own multiple housing units, the actual supply condition is even worse: for example, in Seoul only 28 per cent of the households own any land at all.

Energy and Other Natural Resources

Energy

Industrialization and economic growth in Korea have been literally fuelled by increasing energy consumption. As shown in Table 9.3, the total consumption of primary energy in Korea increased more than tenfold and the per capita consumption more than sixfold during 1961–1991. The elasticity of energy consumption with respect to GDP was below unity in the 1960s, but exceeded unity in the 1970s despite the oil shocks, as Korea pushed its Heavy and Chemical Industrialization programme which changed the industrial structure toward energy-intensive industries such as steel and petrochemicals. Energy efficiency was taken more seriously in the 1980s and it improved substantially up to 1987. More recently, however, energy consumption increased much more rapidly than GDP as energy prices declined considerably. A sectoral analysis shows that this was mainly due to the deterioration of energy efficiency in the highly energy-intensive industries and the rapid increase in energy consumption in the transportation sector (Chu 1991).

The increase of energy consumption, well over 10 per cent per annum

---

5 The land price in Korea is phenomenal. One estimate suggests that the ratio of total value land to GNP was over 9 in 1989 which is higher than even the Japanese ratio of 6.5 (Kim and Lee 1989).

Table 9.3 Energy consumption in Korea 1961–91

	1961	*1971*	*1981*	*1988*	*1991*
Primary energy Consumption (million TOE)	9.7	20.9	45.7	75.4	103.4
Per capita energy Consumption (TOE)	0.38	0.63	1.18	1.80	2.37
Average annual GDP growth (% pa)	9.1	7.5	10.6	8.1	
Energy consumption growth (% pa)	8.0	8.1	7.4	11.1	
Elasticity (energy/GDP)	0.88	1.08	0.70	1.37	

Source: Ministry of Energy and Resources

since 1988, is ringing alarm bells in Korea. In the absence of drastic measures, however, rapidly expanding energy consumption is expected to continue: the conservative estimate in the Sixth Five-Year Plan forecasts 7.1 per cent annual growth rate during 1992–1996. This is on top of already high energy-intensity of the economy. Even at the low point of 1987, the ratio of energy consumption to GDP in Korea was about 40 per cent above that of the OECD average and more than twice that of Japan (per capita energy consumption is roughly half of the OECD level, while per capita GDP is roughly a third).[6] The main reason for this is the inefficient energy use in the industrial sector, whose share of the energy consumption rose from 38.5 per cent in 1975 to 46.3 per cent in 1988 which is considerably higher than that of the OECD countries.

Due to insufficient domestic energy resources Korea has increasingly relied on imports from overseas to meet the growing energy demand. In the earlier stage of the development the bulk of the energy consumption derived from anthracite and firewood, which are the only indigenous energy resources in Korea besides hydropower. But firewood has been rapidly phased out as a source of energy (from 43 per cent in 1965 to 6 per cent in 1980) and the supply of anthracite could not keep up with the rapidly growing energy demand. Since the 1970s Korea has heavily depended on oil and, to a lesser extent, bituminous coal, both of which are imported. In the 1980s, nuclear energy and liquified natural gas, which are also imported, were introduced and their relative importance

6 See Table 21.2 in WRI 1990. While the energy requirement per unit of GDP is known to be negatively correlated to the level of per capita income, the relationship practically disappears or even is reversed when the exchange rate-based GDP figures are replaced by the PPP-based figures. But the Korean figure is relatively high even by this measure: the energy requirement in 1989 (from Table 21.2, WRI 1992) per dollar of PPP-based GDP in 1990 (from UNDP 1993) is 11.2 megajoules in Korea, 7.7 megajoules in Japan, 9.0 megajoules in France, 10.0 megajoules in the UK and 15.1 megajoules in the US.

is growing in recent years. As a result dependence on imported energy rose from 8.6 per cent in 1961 to 91.9 per cent in 1991. In 1991 imports of mineral fuels amounted to 12.8 billion dollars which was 15.6 per cent of total imports or 5.4 per cent of GNP.

The rapid increase of energy consumption has had its predictable consequences on the environment. On a favourable note, destruction of forest for firewood ceased to be a problem as the government prohibited the use of firewood in the early 1960s. However, air pollution from burning of fossil fuels has become serious and there are concerns about the safety of the nuclear power plants. Concerned with the dependence on imported oil, the government made a strategic decision to go nuclear in the 1970s.[7] After the first reactor was built in 1978, Korea has continued to build new reactors and by 1999 will have 14. Nine reactors currently operating are already supplying half of electricity demand. The public is apprehensive after it was reported in 1989 that the wife of a worker in a nuclear plant had two miscarriages of brainless fetuses and that there were many deformed animals born in the area.

Land, water and forestry

Korea's land area is about 99 thousand square kilometres, of which around two-thirds is mountains and slopes. Poorly endowed with mineral resources, Korea depends on foreign imports for every major mineral except tungsten. About 65 per cent of the land area is forest, about 21 per cent is farmland, and the rest is used for housing, industry, etc. Since 1972 the government has tried to organize land use through the Comprehensive National Physical Development Plans. The first plan, which covered 1972–1981, aimed to establish growth-poles by concentrating industrial and social infrastructure investment in a few chosen areas. This growth-pole policy has contributed to population concentration, regional disparities and environmental degradation. The second plan (1982–1991) introduced the concept of Integrated Regional Settlement Areas, aiming to reduce urbanization and regional disparities, but has met with little success.

The annual renewable water resources in Korea are estimated to be about 63 km^3. The annual withdrawal in 1976 was 10.7 km^3, of which 75 per cent was taken up by the agricultural sector 14 per cent by the industrial sector, and 11 per cent for domestic use (Table 22.1, WRI 1992). Despite relatively plentiful water resources, there are growing concerns about availability of water due to pollution.

Even though 65 per cent of its land is forest, Korea imports large amounts of forestry products (about 1.4 billion dollars worth or 1.7 per cent of total imports in 1991). Massive tree cutting by the Japanese during the colonial period and centuries of firewood collection, especially during the period after the liberation to the Korean War when there was no effective government protection of forest, left most of the hillsides denuded in the

---

7 There are reasons to believe that the desire to develop nuclear weapons, as a response to Carter's human rights policy and a partial withdrawal of the US troops stationed in Korea, was also a motivating factor (Park, 1990).

1950s except in remote areas. The consequences were dire: massive land-slides, severe flooding and soil erosion inflicted heavy economic losses. As the demand for marginal land increased, the problem was further exacerbated. This vicious cycle of poverty continued until early 1960s.

In the 1960s the government banned the use of firewood and concentrated on erosion control. But the real turning point was the Ten-Year Forest Development Plan instituted in 1973 which called for rapid reforestation of the entire country. It was completed in just six years and a total of over 1 million hectares (15 per cent of the forest land) was planted. While this was an impressive achievement, the emphasis on fast-growing trees to achieve rapid reforestation meant low quality forest. This problem was addressed by the second Ten-Year Plan (1979–1988) under which 80 large-scale commercial plantations on 0.4 million hectares have been created and a total of over 1 million hectares have been planted. As a result of these efforts, the forest growing stock increased from 61.7 million m^3 in 1970 to 216.4 million m^3 in 1988 and the average stock volume rose from 10.4 m^3 to 33.3 m^3 per hectare during the same period (Chung et al 1990). However, since the newly planted trees are yet to mature, so far timber production has not increased.

The success of the reforestation campaign is a result of both vigorous government action and the rapid economic growth. The government mobilized the entire nation, from school children to corporate executives, for the tree-planting campaign as well as increasing its expenditures on the forest sector. It also designated private land as forest area and required the owner of the designated land to replant the land (as if it had never heard that establishing clear property rights can solve the problem of environmental externalities!). These forceful government actions might not have been as successful had it not been for rapid economic development which allowed substitution of firewood by other fuels and imports of timber and wooden materials. But of course the substitution of fuel means substitution of one kind of environmental problem for another, and wood imports from Malaysia and the US mean trees cut down there instead of in Korea.

Agriculture

Agricultural production in Korea increased 3.0 per cent per annum during 1965–1980 and 2.8 per cent per annum during 1980–1990; in per capita terms 0.8 per cent and 1.7 per cent, respectively. Nonetheless its share in GDP declined from 38 per cent in 1965 to 9 per cent in 1990, since the growth in the industrial and the service sector was far higher. Over the years the key policy goals in agriculture have been self-sufficiency in rice and the expanding production of vegetables, fruits, meat and milk products to accommodate changing food consumption patterns due to rising incomes. These goals have been successfully achieved, but Korea still remains a major importer of such agricultural products as wheat, corn and soybeans.

Due to the high population density Korean agriculture is characterized by extremely intensive utilization of land. The average cultivated area per farm household is only 1.2 hectare. The increase in rice production was achieved by extracting one of the highest rice yields through rapid increases in the application of chemicals along with the introduction of high-yield varieties. Fertilizer consumption in 1990 was 425 kg/ha, one of the highest in the world (Table 18.2, WRI 1992). It grew rapidly until early 1970s, at around 8 per cent a year, but since 1973 its growth rate slowed down to 1 per cent. Consumption of pesticides grew much faster in the earlier periods – around 26 per cent per year up till 1973 (Ban et al 1980) – and did not slow down by much later. Between the 1975–77 and 1982–84 period the average annual consumption of pesticides rose from 4675 tons to 12,273 tons, an annual growth rate of 14.8 per cent (ibid). The intensity of fertilizer and pesticide use has led to a severe contamination of groundwater, rice fields and crops with heavy metals like cadmium and mercury (Bello and Rosenfeld, 1990:96–98).

Rice cultivation depends a plentiful water supply. During the colonial rule the Japanese engaged in massive irrigation development and, as a result, over 40 per cent of rice paddy acreage in Korea was irrigated even in the early 1950s. By the mid-1970s this had risen to 70 per cent. While irrigation has contributed to increasing the agricultural production, construction of dams and salinization of soil present new problems.

Environmental Pollution

This section documents some of the salient aspects of the environmental pollution in Korea. The reliability of the data is a problem. Although the government publishes wide-ranging data on the environment, frequently there are significant discrepancies between the government figures and the figures reported by private researchers. For the sake of convenience I rely on the government figures.

Air pollution and acid rain

The two major air pollutants in Seoul and other big cities are sulphur dioxide and total suspended particulates as one might expect in a typical middle-income country. The existing data indicate that the concentration of these pollutants peaked around 1980 in most cities. The reduction in the concentration of SO_2 in the ambient air during the 1980s, by almost one half in Seoul, resulted from a belated government policy to require the use of low-sulphur oil in industries and liquefied natural gas in large buildings, and the enforcement of auto emission standards, etc (Chung et al 1990). But this is no cause for celebration. According to a WHO study Seoul had the highest SO_2 content in the ambient air among the major cities in the world (Hepinstall, 1985:70). More recent data reported in World Resources 1990–91 show Seoul still in the third place in terms of the average number of days in a year with SO_2 over 150 µg/m^3, trailing only

---

8 The problem can be more serious than is indicated by the average SO_2 concentration as there is wide variation depending on the site and the season. Since nearly half of air pollutants are generated by coal burning for heating, the problem is severe in winter. A recent study revealed that over 35 per cent of the measurements in Seoul during winter months showed SO_2 concentration levels over 0.22 ppm, the level which may increase the death rate according to WHO (Dong-A Ilbo, December 92).

Shenyang and Teheran (Table 24.5 in WRI 1990).[8] Besides, due to the extremely fast increase in the number of automobiles, concentrations of carbon monoxide and nitrous oxides are expected to rise rapidly. (Currently, they hover around the Korean environmental standards which are less stringent than the international standards).

Air pollution has caused a trend of acidification of the rainfall: for example, between 1985–87 the pH level of the rainfall declined from 5.5 to 5.1 in Seoul, 5.4 to 5.3 in Taegu, and 5.0 to 4.9 in Ulsan (Environment Administration 1988). As a result, there is a serious acidification of soil in Seoul and other large cities. The pH level within 20 km of the city centre in Seoul is below 4.5 and within 50 km is below 5.0. The industrial complex area in Ulsan shows a pH level between 4.0 and 4.5 (Lee 1992). Due to acid rain and acidification of soil there is a severe damage to forest in the entire Seoul metropolitan area. For example, about a half of the tree species in the Secret Garden, an old palace in downtown area, have disappeared in the last five years. The destruction of forest has also caused a drastic decline in insect species: the number of insect species collected in Seoul fell to 459 in 1970 and down to only 90 in 1980 from 510 in 1960 and 519 in 1950 (ibid).

CO_2 emissions in Korea increased at 9.0 per cent per annum during 1971–1982 and 7.3 per cent during 1983–1988, compared with 1.8 per cent and 2.3 per cent in the world during the same periods. Per capita CO_2 emissions in Korea reached 1.4 tons in 1988, surpassing the world average of 1.2 tons, and is expected to reach 3.6 tons by 2030 (Ryu et al 1991).

Pollution of water

Rivers and coastal seas in Korea are heavily contaminated from municipal sewage, industrial waste water and agricultural runoff, much of which is discharged without treatment. All the important rivers, which are the major source of drinking water, are of second rate or poorer quality in terms of biological oxygen deman level. There are grave concerns about the contamination of the tap water with toxic heavy metals, even as the proportion of the population receiving piped water is increasing fast (25 per cent in 1967 to 68 per cent in 1987; 98 per cent in Seoul).[9] The tributaries near the urban centres are so contaminated that their water cannot be used even for industrial purposes.

The water quality in the Han river, the water supply source for the Seoul metropolitan area, has been a major concern. Due to population concentration in the region, the Han river is heavily polluted there and the fish population disappeared long ago. The situation has improved somewhat after several sewage treatment plants were opened in 1987 and 1988 as part of the Han River Basin Environmental Master Project. Until then there was only one treatment plant in the area with the treatment capacity of less than half a million tons per day compared to 3–4 million

---

9 In 1989, for example, the admission by the Ministry of Construction that the treated water in ten water purification stations was found contaminated with heavy metals set off a panic, driving people to buy imported bottled water.

tons of daily waste water. Despite the expansion of the treatment capacity there are still problems due to the lack of a separate sewer system overflow of storm water into waste water (Chung et al 1990). Moreover, the water quality in the upstream Han river as well as in other major rivers is deteriorating. In the nation as a whole only about a third of the municipal sewage was being treated at the end of 1991. The government plans to raise the treatment rate up to 65 per cent by 1996 (The Government of ROK 1992).

While municipal sewage contains mostly organic materials, industrial wastewater contains much more toxic materials like heavy metals. Even though the government has set the standards for pollution-abatement facilities for industrial waste water, non-compliance is widespread: in 1989 the inspection by the Environment Administration found non-compliance in almost 20 per cent of the cases.[10] Industrial complex areas like Kuro and Ulsan are severely contaminated with cadmium, copper, lead, mercury and other heavy metals. As many industrial complexes are located near the coastal areas, coastal contamination has become a serious problem. In the coastal sea of Ulsan, for example, concentration of lead and mercury was found at three times the legal limit and concentration of copper 47 times the legal limit.

Solid and hazardous waste

Inside Korea it is often said that Koreans top the world in discharging domestic solid waste. According to the Environment Administration data, in 1989 per capita domestic solid waste in Korea was 2.2 kg/day. This is far greater than in most of the OECD countries (for example, 1.1 kg/day in Japan, 0.8 kg/day in France, 1.0 kg/day in the UK) with the sole exception of the US (2.4 kg/day), although due to variations in the definition of waste it cannot be regarded as a strictly valid comparison (Table 21.4, WRI 1992). From this already very high level, it is still increasing rapidly: during 1984–1989 the average annual growth rate was over 6 per cent, compared to 1.5 per cent during 1980–90 in OECD countries. The principal reason for the high level of municipal waste is the widespread use of coal briquettes for heating and cooking: burned coal briquettes accounted for 40 per cent of the total in the nation and 28 per cent in Seoul. But even after subtracting burned coal briquettes, per capita domestic waste in Korea is 1.3 kg/day, very high by the international standards. As coal briquettes are being replaced by substitutes such as liquefied natural gas, the increase in municipal waste is expected to slow down and perhaps stabilize around the year 2000.

Disposal of domestic solid waste in Korea poses an important environmental hazard. In 1989 94 per cent of the total was disposed by landfill, 1.9 per cent was incinerated and only 2.9 per cent was recycled. Both the landfill and incineration are carried out mostly without any measures to

---

10 The actual non-compliance rate is certain to be much higher, since often a cover-up goes on as the surveillance crew is obstructed at the entrance. Most of the small and medium-sized firms are not equipped with anti-pollution facilities, and even the large-scale firms frequently resort to illegal dumping as in the case of Doosan.

contain environmental damage. In addition, existing landfill sites are quickly used up due to increasing amount of waste, while it is getting increasingly difficult to find new ones.

Industrial solid waste is increasing even more rapidly: during 1984–1989 it increased by about 13 per cent per annum. The designated (hazardous) industrial waste, which accounts for about 4 per cent of the total industrial waste, increased by 23 per cent per annum. In addition, large quantities of toxic industrial waste, 560 thousand tons in 1989 according to the government figure, are imported as 'recyclables'. In 1989 when about 58 thousand tons of industrial waste was discharged daily, 53.9 per cent of it was recycled, 29.4 per cent dumped in landfills and 3.3 per cent incinerated. The low standards under which the industrial waste is disposed of and the widespread illegal dumping of toxic industrial wastes have created serious environmental hazards, the full extent of which is not known.

ECONOMIC GROWTH AND ENVIRONMENTAL DEGRADATION IN KOREA

In principle, economic development need not necessarily cause environmental degradation. Since economic growth is accompanied by structural and technical changes which have independent effects on the environment apart from the pure growth effect, if the structural and technical changes are in the right direction they can offset the adverse impact of growth on the environment. Moreover, environmental impact is not a scalar variable: during the course of economic growth certain environmental problems associated with poverty can be ameliorated even as new problems surface. In fact, countries at different stages of development show different patterns of environmental problems (World Bank, 1992:10–11; Beckerman 1992).

In low-income economies the main environmental problems concern natural resources, especially deforestation and soil erosion, and lack of access to safe water. These problems tend to decline as income increases. In middle-income economies the main environmental problems are those created by industrialization, airborne and water-discharged pollutants arising from power generation, land transportation and industrial production (TSP, SO_2, Pb, BOD, etc). These second-phase problems tend to worsen initially but then improve as income rises, although the improvement is not automatic. However, some environmental problems such as toxic wastes, municipal wastes, pesticide runoff and emissions of CO_2 and NO_x continue to worsen as income rises. These are the third-phase problems associated with developed countries.

Some of the indicators of environmental stress reviewed above suggest that Korea is no exception to the general pattern outlined above. The rapid rise in income allowed a great improvement in such first-phase problems as deforestation, safe water supply and sanitation. At the same time, the rapid industrialization has created menacing pollution problems which were unknown only a few decades ago. During the 1960s and the 1970s the discharge of the second-phase pollutants increased enormously due to the structural and technical changes associated with industrialization. For example, during 1965–1979 the emission of sulphur oxides increased by ninefold while GDP increased by three and a half times. In the 1980s the government began to address pollution problems, and as a result some local improvements, such as air quality in Seoul and water quality in the Han river, were achieved. At the same time, toxic wastes, municipal wastes and CO_2 emissions rose rapidly, indicating the advent of the third-phase environmental problems. In the late 1980s solid industrial waste and waste water increased at about 20 per cent per annum.

That the Korean experience with environmental problems broadly conforms to the 'succession' model does not mean that all is well. Some third-phase problems are already more severe than in the developed countries (eg municipal wastes) or expected to be so in the near future (eg CO_2 emissions), while the second-phase problems do not yet show signs of significant improvement. Table 9.4, which reports the results of an expanded input-output analysis by Rhee (1991), shows that such second-phase pollutants as SO_2, TSP and BOD increasing at a slightly faster pace than the already very high GDP growth rate during the period 1980–86. It is true that they are not increasing nearly as fast as they were in the earlier period, nor in comparison to third-phase pollutants like industrial and municipal wastes. However, it is also clear that Korea has yet to deal with the second-phase pollutants effectively.

Table 9.4 Causes of increasing emission of pollutants 1980–1986

| Pollutants | Industrial waste | | BOD | COD | SO_x | TSP | NO_x |
	Designated	General					
1980 emission (000, tons)	1053	10082	1048	896	422	291	136
1986 emission	2108	18947	1775	1571	696	512	228
% increase	100.0	87.9	69.4	75.4	65.0	76.1	67.9
growth effect	64.0	64.0	64.0	64.0	64.0	64.0	64.0
Structural change effect (%)							
(Domestic demand)	1.0	1.2	–3.5	2.5	–9.0	–4.7	–7.9
(Export demand)	23.7	6.8	0.9	13.9	7.5	7.3	7.3
(Import substution)	2.2	5.3	–2.6	–8.4	1.3	1.1	1.4
Technical change effect	9.1	10.4	10.5	3.2	1.2	8.2	3.0

Source: Rhee (1991)

What is most striking about the Korean experience with environmental problems is the contrast between the success in dealing with the first-phase resource problems and the failure in dealing with the second-phase or third-phase pollution problems. This can be explained by the fact that the primary objective of the government was growth maximization instead of welfare maximization. Restoring the resource base, both human and natural, was seen as an essential investment, while pollution abatement was considered as luxury consumption. Therefore the success of reforestation programmes, public health and population control programmes in Korea can be understood along the same lines as its success in educating its labour force. A relatively well educated and healthy labour force was to become the backbone of economic growth, while curbing population growth and controlling soil erosion were necessary to minimize foreign exchange drains on food imports. Korea's excellent achievements in these areas are a testimony to the capacity of its state. When necessary, the state went far beyond setting public spending policies and regulations, mobilizing public participation with massive campaigns and even riding rough-shod over individual rights as in the case of reforestation.

In contrast, pollution abatement was given little attention as the growth maximization dictated maximum support for industry and its profits. The engine of growth was not to be slowed down just because of some adverse side effects! The automobile industry provides a good example of this logic. As discussed earlier, the irrationality of a transportation system which relies heavily on passenger cars is painfully clear in Korea. However, rather than devising a rational transportation system that can move the people and goods most efficiently, the government enthusiastically supported the expansion of the automobile industry on the grounds that it is strategically important due to its backward linkage effects.[11]

Both the public sector and the private sector expenditure on environment show the extent of environmental neglect in Korea. As a share of GNP the government expenditure on environment was only 0.16 per cent in 1988 which is, while a sharp rise from 0.06 per cent in 1982 and virtually zero in earlier years, still negligible compared to 0.5–1.5 per cent in OECD countries. The investment in pollution abatement in the manufacturing sector represented only 0.8 per cent of the total capital investment in 1988 in comparison to 5–10 per cent in the OECD countries (Shin 1991).

Given the lack of effective environmental protection policies, Korea has developed an industrial structure which is intensive in materials and energy use and employs technologies that are highly polluting. This has nothing to do with comparative advantage based on endowment: Korea, as mentioned above, has very little energy and other natural resources. Rather, it has to do with the artificial comparative advantage created by the low valuation of 'environmental goods' at the time when increasing opposition to environmental pollution within the advanced countries led to rising environmental standards (see Sen, Chapter 8). This shows up in the pattern of foreign trade as well as the pattern of foreign direct investment.

The artificial comparative advantage is reflected in the fact that the export sector is responsible for a disproportionately large share of major pollutants. In 1986 the export sector accounted for 29.6 per cent of the final demand or 14.4 per cent of total sales. But it generated 30–50 per cent of many pollutants, 45.4 per cent of designated industrial waste and 50.6 per

---

11 The model of 'good life' sold by the government in the 1970s was a nuclear family with two children and a nice house with a television antenna on its roof top. In the 1980s one of the children was replaced by a car.

cent of solid industrial waste (Kim 1990). Another piece of evidence is that the changes in the structure of export demand are, along with the technological changes, the major cause of the growth of pollutants exceeding the growth rate of GDP, whereas the effects of the changes in the structure of domestic demand and imports are mostly pollution-reducing or only modestly pollution-increasing (Table 9.4).

The pattern of foreign direct investment in Korea tells the same story. Except for the electronics/electrical goods sector, the bulk of the foreign investment went to such pollution-intensive industries as chemical/petrochemical, including fertilizers and pesticides, and metallurgy in the 1960s. The same pattern continued in the 1970s and into the 1980s, with the addition of the transportation equipment sector as a major recipient of foreign investment in the manufacturing sector and a large increase in the share of the tertiary sector due to foreign investment in hotels and finance.[12] Foreign direct investment in pollution-intensive industries was concentrated in industrial complexes. Thus, for example, in the Ulsan/Onsan industrial complexes, there were 31 foreign-owned firms as of 1985; 25 of them in chemical/petrochemical industries and an additional three were metal refineries. Due to this heavy concentration in pollution-intensive industries the foreign firms were generating 55 per cent of the particulates and 80 per cent of the waste water containing designated hazardous pollutants, while accounting for 34 per cent of the total sales in the Ulsan/Onsan industrial complexes. They also accounted for 59 per cent of the compensation for pollution damages (Tables 4, 11, 12 & 16 in Kim 1991).

IS KOREAN GROWTH-MANIA RATIONAL?

Commenting on the NICs' (Korea, Taiwan, Singapore and Hong Kong) experience with economic development and environment, the World Resources Institute flatly says that they are 'not a model of sustainable development, even though they are often cited as a model of economic development' (WRI, 1992:43). This claim is based on the observation that the growth in these countries was achieved at the expense of severe environmental degradation. But this argument is less than compelling because of the possibilities of technological changes as well as the policy-induced or otherwise behavioural changes toward reducing the environmental impact of economic activities. Such changes, however modest, are already beginning to taking place in Korea as a result of political democratization, the rise in income and various environment-related trade regulations. In fact, the gist of the optimistic view on development and

---

12 Some environmentalists in Korea believe that one of the main motives of Japanese investment in Korea was to export pollution-intensive industries in the aftermath of the environmental catastrophes like Minimata Disease during the 1950s and 1960s. The so-called 'Yasuki Scheme' presented at the Korea–Japan Cooperation Committee in 1970 envisioned a division of the chemical industry between the two countries. At the time a Korean daily reported that the Korean cabinet discussed the idea of importing pollution-intensive industries (Kim 1991).

environment is that not only are such changes possible, perhaps with strong government action, without sacrificing growth, but that economic growth will make it easier to pay for such changes (for example, World Bank 1992). Many would even argue that economic growth is the only answer to environmental problems (for example, Beckerman 1992; Baldwin 1993). From such a point of view there is little to be concerned about in Korea's environmental record.

Given the tremendous uncertainty about the effects of environmental degradation and the future possibilities in clean technologies, it seems impossible to make any conclusive judgment on whether the Korean model of development is sustainable. The usual difficulties in assessing sustainability is, in the case of Korea, compounded by the lack of data on the effects of environmental degradation, not to mention any sophisticated economic valuation of such effects. While horror stories abound about chemical poisoning of workers and farmers, increasing respiratory diseases among urban residents breathing polluted air, damages to crops and fisheries near industrial complexes and so on, a comprehensive picture on the economic costs of pollution is not yet available.

The growth record of Korea so far does not show any evidence of environmental constraints: decade average growth rates are roughly the same over the last three decades (see Table 9.1). It may, however, be noted that the high growth rates have been maintained by devoting an increasing share of output to investment (implying a rise in the capital-output ratio). Gross domestic fixed capital formation as a share of GNP averaged 23.9 per cent during 1965–73, 29.8 per cent during 1973–81, and 30.6 per cent during 1981–90. The Seventh Five-Year Plan (1992–96) recognizes this trend and plans only(!) 7.5 per cent annual growth with the average investment share of 36.4 per cent during the plan period (The Government of ROK 1992). If this trend continues, the growth rate will inevitably decline in the future. It is, however, impossible to tell how important a role environmental degradation has been and will play in raising the capital-output ratio.

Although nothing definite can be said about the sustainability of the Korean model at the local level, one must not forget the *global* implications of extending the Korean model to the entire developing world.[13] Of course, it would be ludicrous to scapegoat Korea (for that matter, even China) for the global environmental threat. After all, most developed

---

13 For example, had the entire non-high-income economies had the Korean level of per capita emissions in 1989, the rate of increase of the atmospheric concentration and stock of carbon dioxide would have been about 0.8 per cent instead of the actual 0.5 per cent a year (calculated from the data in Table A9, World Bank 1992 and Table 24.1, WRI 1992). Even more alarming calculations could be made from the fact that the Korean growth rate of CO_2 emissions was 7.3 per cent during 1983–1988 while the world growth rate was 2.3 per cent. The consequences on resource depletion could be quite dramatic for some metals if the 1990 per capita consumption in Korea is assumed to be that of the world. The world reserve base life index at 1990 would then change from 62 to 17 years for copper, from 36 to 11 years for lead, from 40 to 10 years for zinc, and from 265 to 106 years for iron ore (calculated from Table 21.5, WRI 1992).

countries have followed a similar historical pattern and continue to put an enormous burden on the world's environmental resources and space. The global problem must be dealt with at a global level and there is no question that the North must take the bulk of the burden in any equitable solution. But at the same time, it is not conceivable that we can find a solution to the global problem without changing our notion of what a successful development is.

It is not primarily because of its implications on the global sustainability that we must reject the Korean model as the general model of development to be emulated by the less developed countries. There are other reasons to question the desirability, or indeed the rationality, of the Korean model. First and foremost, economic growth should not be taken as an end in itself. This is not to deny the tremendous contribution to the material well-being that the economic growth in Korea has made. Rather, the point is that the relentless pursuit of growth maximization in Korea resulted in sub-optimal welfare and, therefore, is irrational. Growth maximization plus lack of democracy meant that local needs were trampled upon, avoidably and senselessly. The persecution of environmentalists and the suppression of public discussion on environmental problems under the authoritarian government (even mentioning the pollution situation in public was monitored and regarded as treacherous) suggest that the welfare costs of environmental degradation were grossly undervalued to say the least (Kim 1991; Bello and Rosenfeld 1990). The fact that a number of environmental stress indicators in Korea are at the high end of the spectrum bolsters this argument.

It might be argued that clean environment is a luxury good, and, as such, should not be given importance at the early stages of development. However, given the wide scope of environmental externalities, the political conditions that determine whose voices will be heeded are as important as the level of income in deciding how a society will treat its environment. Since the beginning of democratization in the late 1980s, there has been a remarkable surge in environmental protests and environment-oriented organizations.[14] This suggests that the tolerance limit for environmental degradation was reached long ago but people were bulldozed into accepting the authoritarian state priorities.

The irrationality of untrammelled growth lies not only in its failure to maximize the welfare of the current generation. A strategy of 'growth first, environment later' can be cost inefficient, since 'it is often cheaper to prevent environmental degradation than to attempt to 'cure' it later', as the World Bank observes (1992:40). That is, if indeed Korea decides to clean up the mess. But the real problem is that the commitment to clean up is not easily forthcoming. Although as a consequence of growing environmental protests, narrow economic efficiency no longer reigns

---

14 This parallels events on the labour front (see You, forthcoming). The labour unrest and organization drive were more explosive, but they already lost momentum whereas the environmental protest movement continues to grow. Among the environmental movements, the most advanced is the anti-nuclear movement propelled by both safety concerns about nuclear power plants and military tension in the area.

supreme,[15] it is still true that the growth objective frequently overrides environmental concerns. For example, after ordering desulphurization facilities in the late 1970s, the government postponed its implementation until 1985 in the face of a threat from oil refineries that they would raise prices by 20 percent (Bello and Rosenfeld, 1990:99). Another example concerns regulation of foreign direct investment. On paper, there is a law that prohibits foreign investment in pollution-intensive industries specified by the Ministry of Environment. But it has remained just a piece of paper, because the official list has not been promulgated. Once the Environment Administration actually made up a list, but it was discarded by the cabinet meeting (Kim 1991).

The 'growth first, environment later' policy may be self-defeating. After decades of environmental degradation, a rather drastic change of priorities has become necessary in Korea. But the Korean people have become addicted to rapid growth (they talk of a 'total crisis' when the growth rate falls to 6–7 per cent a year!) and are deeply motivated to stay ahead of competition and catch up with the North. It is doubtful that they will accept in the near future any significant reduction in growth in exchange for a cleaner environment. An indication of this is the extremely poor market performance of the products sold with the 'green mark' in Korea. Decades of 'growth at the expense of the environment' does not make the best experience with which to begin 'growth with environmental care' or 'sustainable development'.

Many economists will find the expression 'addiction to growth' outrageously paternalistic, since it implies that there is an irrational element in the preference for growth. But that is precisely the situation. The case of automobiles is an excellent example. The government promotes domestic car sales in support of the industry and the country ends up with a totally irrational transportation system. People are flocking to buy cars even though they realize that they cannot commute by driving because of the incredible traffic congestion and the weekend getaways usually turn sour with aggravating struggles on the road. They have to have them, because everyone else has: because, without them, they feel inadequate, because that is the 'advanced' way of life. In a poor country there is no question that growth is of paramount importance in enhancing people's lives. But after a certain level of material necessities and comfort is achieved, growth may cease to be so. The rise of the environmental movement in Korea does give some hope that the 'growth addiction' may be cured in the future. At present, however, it is largely dominated by the

---

15 For instance, the construction of a Dupont plant in Onsan is being delayed due to the protest of the residents. In 1990 environmental and other civil organizations were able to stop the government from collecting construction materials from Paldang Dam, the principal water pumping station for the capital region, marking the first-ever victory against a large-scale government development project. In another instance, many factories had to curtail production in May of 1992 as the residents' sit-in protests closed down the solid waste dump site in Kimpo for more than a month after discovering illegal dumping of toxic wastes.

not-in-my-backyard (NIMBY) mentality rather than a deep questioning of the nature of growth in Korea.[16]

CONCLUSION

The Korean model of development was founded on a developmentalist authoritarian state which was able to pursue growth maximization forcing the Korean people to accept suppression of political and labour rights, growing social inequities and severe environmental degradation. Therefore, the laudable growth performance is found somewhat wanting when we look at its welfare consequences. Especially when we embrace the imperative of sustainable development, Korea can no longer be regarded as an unmitigated success.

Korea has developed an industrial structure which is intensive in materials and energy use and employs technologies that are highly polluting as a result of the virtual non-existence of environmental regulations. Consequently, the rate of increase in pollutants has been higher than the world record-setting growth rate. In addition, Korean agriculture is one of the most intensive in fertilizer and pesticide use. The problems of municipal waste, toxic waste and nuclear waste have become critical with increasing difficulties in finding new dump sites or storage facilities.

But Korea is not without successes even in its environmental record. Its record in curbing population growth is one of the best in the world, its reforestation programme one of the more spectacular successes, and it has done a decent job of providing safe water and sanitation. These successes in dealing with the first-phase resource problems contrast with their rather dismal record on the pollution problem. Both are, however, consistent with growth maximization at least within the time horizon the government has had. In so far as the success with the first-phase problem was just one facet of Korea's extraordinary ability to expand the economy, it cannot be taken as an indication that Korea will be successful in dealing with the second- and third-phase pollution problems. In fact, some third-phase problems are already extremely severe and rapidly worsening while the second-phase problems are not yet significantly improving.

It is true that the past growth in Korea has raised its ability to pay for the environmental protection. In addition, since the beginning of political democratization in 1987, the environmental movement is growing rapidly in Korea and has been able to force the government to be a little more attentive to the environment. However, economic growth ranks far above

---

16 Because of the prevalence of NIMBYism, an understandable feature of a nascent environmental movement, there are growing difficulties in locating waste sites. The problem is especially acute in finding a storage site for soon-to-be overflowing nuclear waste that is now stored at the nuclear plants. The government tried in 1990 to build a secret nuclear waste treatment plant on Anmyon island but was forced to back down after the villagers rioted for three days. Unable to persuade a single community to accept even a temporary storage facility, the government is providing villagers in the six targeted communities with overseas trips to see nuclear waste treatment facilities in other countries, while promising an unspecified amount of money as well as that the site will not become a permanent storage facility (Paisley 1993).

the hierarchy of government objectives and the Korean people are deeply addicted to growth. Even the environmental movement is mostly of NIMBY sort. It is difficult at present to imagine Korea getting serious about the environment in the near future.

Given the radical uncertainty about the effects of environmental degradation, it is not possible to make a firm judgment on whether the Korean model of development is locally sustainable. However, based on the observations made above, we can be quite confident in questioning its rationality. It is the conclusion of this chapter that the Korean model of development should not be 'the model' of development even though it can serve as a source of lessons for bringing economic growth to the South. Its growth maximization objective must be replaced by welfare maximization, which would mean, among other things, pursuing 'growth with environmental care' rather than 'growth at the expense of environmental degradation.'

REFERENCES

Amsden, A (1989) *Asia's Next Giant* Oxford University Press, Oxford

Auer, M (1990) 'Pollution Conflict Resolution in the Republic of Korea' *The Georgetown International Environmental Law Review* vol 3, pp 229–43

Baldwin, R (1993) 'Does sustainability require growth?' paper presented at the joint CEPR/OECD Development Centre conferernce on 'Sustainable economic development: Domestic and international policy' Paris, 24/25 May

Ban, S, Moon P and Perkins, D (eds) (1980) *Rural Development* Harvard University Press, Cambridge, Mass

Beckerman, W (1992) 'Economic growth and the environment: Whose growth? Whose environment?' *World Development*, vol 20, pp 481–96

Bello, W and Rosenfeld, S (1990) *Dragons in Distress: Asia's Miracle Economies in Crisis* Institute for Food and Development Policy, San Francisco

Cha, M (1976) 'An evaluation of environmental policy: With reference to the Public Nuisance Prevention Law in Korea' *Journal of East & West Studies*, vol 5, pp 43–62

Choi, J-J (1983) 'Interest conflict and political control in South Korea: A study of the labour movement in manufacturing industries, 1961-80' unpublished PhD dissertation, Department of Political Science, University of Chicago

Chu, H (1991) 'Energy efficiency in Korean manufacturing (in Korean)' Issue Paper 91-61, Korea Institute for Industrial Economics & Trade, Seoul

Chung, C, Koh, I-D and Kwack, I-C (1990) 'Economic policies for sustainable development' Korea Development Institute, Seoul

Environment Administration (1988) *Korea Environment Yearbook* (in Korean), Seoul

Government of the Republic of Korea (1992) *The Seventh 5-Year Plan for Economic and Social Development* (in Korean) Economic Planning Board, Seoul

Hepinstall, S (1985) 'A smell of success in the battle against pollution' *Far Eastern Economic Review*, 18 July 1985

Kim, D and Ahn, K (1987) *Korea's Income Distribution, Its Determinants and People's Perception of the Distribution Problem* (in Korean), Choong Ang University Press, Seoul

Kim, J W (1991) 'Environmental aspects of transnational corporation activities in Ulsan/Onsan   industrial complexes, Republic of Korea' *Konghae Yòn'gu*

(Pollution Studies), vol 21, pp 15–25

Kim, S W (1990) 'A study on the relationship of the structure of export industry and environmental pollution: Applying Leontief pollution model' (in Korean) Masters thesis, Graduate School of Environmental Studies, Seoul National University

Kim, T-D and Lee, K-S (1989) *Land, Object of Speculation or Place of Living* (in Korean) Pibong Press, Seoul

Korea Transport Institute (KTI) (1987) *Information on Transportation* (in Korean), Seoul

Korea Transport Institute (1989) *Proposals for Transportation Policies* (in Korean) Seoul

Lee, K-J (1992) 'Destruction of forest in Korea' mimeograph, City University of Seoul

Merson, J (1991) 'Korea wakes up to the environment' *New Scientist*, 8 June, pp 20–1

Ministry of Environment, Republic of Korea (1991) *National Report of the Republic of Korea to UNCED 1992* Seoul

Paisley, E (1993) 'Waste not, want not' *Far Eastern Economic Review*, 28 January 1993, pp 46–7

Park, T W (1990) 'South Korea' in R Thomas and B Ramberg (eds) *Energy and Security in the Industrializing World* University Press of Kentucky

Rhee, J J (1991) 'Policies to accelerate environmental improvement' (in Korean) Ministry of Environment, Seoul

Ryu, J-C et al (1991) 'Global warming and the direction of the energy policy in Korea' (in Korean) Energy Economics Institute, Seoul

Shin, E (1991) *Environmental Policy and the Sharing of Pollution Control Costs* (in Korean) The Korea Economic Research Centre, Seoul

United Nations Development Programme (UNDP) (1993) *Human Development Report 1993* Oxford University Press, New York

Woo, J-e (1991) *Race to the Swift: State and Finance in Korean Industrialization* Columbia University Press, New York

World Bank (1992) *World Development Report 1992* Oxford University Press, New York

World Resources Institute (WRI) (1990) *World Resources 1990-91*, Oxford University Press, New York

World Resources Institute (1992) *World Resources 1992-93* Oxford University Press, New York

Yoo, J G (1990) 'Income distribution in Korea' in J Kwon (ed) *Korean Economic Development* Greenwood Press, New York

You, J-I (forthcoming) 'Capital-labour relations in South Korea: Past, present and future' in J Schor and J-I You (eds) *The Transformation of Capital-Labour Relations: A Global Perspective* Edward Elgar, Aldershot

Chapter Ten

National Development and Local Environmental Action — the Case of the River Narmada

Gita Sen

No development project, however laudable, can possibly justify impoverishment of large sections of people and their utter destitution.

> Supreme Court of India in *Lalchand Mahto and Ors vs Coal India Ltd* Civil Original Jurisdiction, MP No 16331 of 1982; quoted in Vaswani (1992)

No trauma could be more painful for a family than to get uprooted from a place where it has lived for generations... Yet the uprooting has to be done. Because the land occupied by the family is required for a development project which holds promise of progress and prosperity for the country and the people in general. The family getting displaced thus makes a sacrifice for the sake of the community. It undergoes hardship and distress and faces an uncertain future so that others may live in happiness and be economically better off... If not handled properly, these human beings could even impede the progress of project building. They could constitute pockets of protest, unrest and dissatisfaction....

> S C Varma, former Chairman, Narmada Valley Development Agency; quoted in Alvares and Billorey (1988)

All those directly affected by a proposed project should be involved in developing the project concepts. Water resource planning and management are not battles to be won by a particular interest group, but are a matter of mutual problem solving.

> Jan Veltrop, President, International Commission on Large Dams; in *Civil Engineering*, (August 1991)

INTRODUCTION

Few problems of Third World development are as sharply contested as the displacement of local people by the building of large infrastructure projects. Primitive accumulation, ie, the separation of groups of people from their traditional means of livelihood by others more powerful than they, has occurred in history both gradually and in sharp, concentrated episodes. Infrastructure projects such as the building of large power or irrigation facilities are typical of the latter, though the effects (both positive and negative) are usually felt over many generations. As a result, the ensuing conflicts of interest also tend to be sharply focused, and frame the problems of national development in high relief.

This paper uses the controversy over large dams to explore the contradictions of defining and implementing national development in the face of competing local concerns and needs. The exploration is along three dimensions — national economic objectives, local livelihoods and ecological sustainability. The paper uses the current debate on the projects along the River Narmada, as well as the history of earlier dams built in India to illustrate its arguments.

The conflicts generated by a large hydroelectric project are multifaceted. At one level the issue appears to be the classic dilemma of environment versus development, pitting ecological concerns about the damage to local ecosystems as well as more global issues of warming and loss of carbon dioxide sinks against the drive for higher economic growth. 'Sustainable development', defined by the Brundtland Report as that pattern and pace of development which does not buy the welfare of the present generation at the expense of future generations, provides the solution in principle, however difficult to implement in practice.

In a Third World context, however, the problem is more complex. Ranged against environmentalist concerns are problems of poverty removal, the need to increase agricultural production, the growing energy and water needs of a number of productive sectors as well as domestic consumption. Economic growth has a qualitatively different premise and promise in such a case. The distribution problem is one *within* the current generation, and is not addressed even in principle by the Brundtland definition of sustainable development which focuses on trade-offs across generations.

How can or should such conflicts of interest be resolved? On the one hand are concerns that fall within the ambit of what has typically been understood as national development objectives; on the other are the fears of eroding livelihoods, loss of community, and the destruction of social institutions. In a Third World context, the environmental problem is in many ways subsumed under more fundamental disagreements over development itself.[1] What should the project of national development include, and who should define it? Certainly in the Indian case the major ecology movements, eg, the Chipko movement, the Narmada Bachao

---

1 Das (1992) discusses the differences between Western environmental groups and Third World ecology movements along these lines.

Andolan, the Western Ghats movement, the current struggle by farmers against multinational seed companies such as Cargill, have all posed environmental questions within a broader challenge to the pattern of national development itself. This paper examines the usefulness of the main framework used for this class of problems, and argues for alternatives.

NATIONAL DEVELOPMENT AND PRIVATE INTERESTS

In the public debate of most nation states, national development has generally been an unchallenged goal whose legitimacy in the general imagination overrides the conflicting claims of particular interests. Its dominant paradigm is one in which private interests are subordinate to and hence must be made compatible with the public good. Its analytical underpinnings include a combination of the economic theory of public goods/externalities and the political science concept of eminent domain. The underlying premise is that private interests and behaviour may generate externalities that are inimical to social welfare; the behaviour of individual agents has therefore to be modified so that their particularistic claims are induced to fall in line with social objectives.

The corresponding problem for policy is how to induce such changes in private behaviour. Under the principle of eminent domain, the state has the right not only to use and dispose of all commonly held resources, but to acquire even resources held privately under clear ownership titles upon payment of compensation, if such acquisition is deemed to be in the larger social interest. The assumption is that the state can compensate losers to induce them to accept the primacy of social goals.

Whether the actual operation of the dominant paradigm is generally perceived to be 'fair' or not in a particular case depends on the following:

- whether social goals have been defined taking *all* the significant private interests and concerns into account;
- whether all particular interests are given equal weight, or whether the concerns of the weak are given adequate weight; and
- whether all interests have equal access to representation in the domain of public discourse, ie equal citizenship rights and obligations *de jure* and *de facto*.

This does not deny that some particular interests may actually gain from the state's actions while others lose. But the implicit assumption is that, while some interests might win in this process, this is only because they happen to be in line with the objective social interest, and not because they can exercise special economic, political or social clout. Furthermore, the system must contain democratic checks that will ensure that all those affected can participate in the process of project formulation and decision making, or at least can obtain an impartial hearing of their concerns.

This issue of 'fairness' comes into sharper focus if we consider three sets of questions that challenge both the concept and the practice of national development:

1. **What constitutes the public interest?** All public policy is rife with divergences between public interest and private concerns. In most cases private interests can be defined relatively unambiguously even though there may be a multiplicity of them. But the definition of what constitutes the public interest is more tricky, since in theory it involves some amalgamation of private interests, and in practice this is in the hands of governments. The critical question when public goals are seen as being considerably at odds with at least some private interests is whether government can be trusted to be an impartial definer and arbiter of social welfare. In principle a democratic polity with separation of powers, and checks and balances on the functioning of the executive branch, may be the key to ensuring that governments are impartial in defining social goals. In practice, the developing world is full of post-colonial governments and state apparatuses that are far from democratic. Even in political democracies such as India, the actual functioning of the system's checks and balances leave much to be desired.[2]

2. **Whose interests are taken into account when social goals are defined by governments? (Or what is national about national development?)** There is considerable potential for bias when there are wide social, economic and gender disparities between government functionaries and the private agents whose interests are seen as being at cross-purposes, between different groups of agents, and within each sub-group itself. In the context of a large hydroelectric project, those whose land is likely to be submerged are often tribals, while those who are likely to consume the increased water or power are generally non-tribals – either farmers, industrialists or domestic consumers from other regions. Both economically and socially the losers and gainers are very different. Similar and wide differences are likely to separate government functionaries from those whose interests are at odds with the project. There may even be divergent interests within a particular group, ie gainers or losers, with differential perceptions of gain and loss, and different capacities to articulate interests and engage in public debate.

   Such divergences are important not only as pointers to the presence of multiple and competing interests, but also because they affect the very formulation of social objectives or national goals. It is highly likely in current political economic contexts that the concerns of those at the lower end of the economic and social scale will not weigh in very heavily in the formulation of social objectives. Their losses will be weighted lightly relative to the gains of others higher in the social order and closer to the formulators of social goals. The practice of national development in a context of wide disparity needs, therefore, to be examined since the distribution of its benefits and costs can be highly unequal. To what

---

2 In recent years the Supreme Court of India has become increasingly incensed at the extent to which even its dictates are ignored by different branches of the executive.

extent does it include the concerns and aspirations of those likely to be dispossessed? Or is national development a convenient abstraction for the domination of a subset of particular interests distinguished from the others by class, caste or regional identity? In particular, how does the concept address the security of livelihood systems of the very poor or those who are socially marginal? This brings us to a third critical set of issues.

There are, however, two fundamental differences between the first case and the latter two. In the first case, the regulation of individual behaviour is likely to benefit all those whose behaviour is being regulated by creating a safer and more orderly traffic environment. In the latter two cases, neither the sidewalk vendors nor the oustees are likely to share in the benefits from regulation. More importantly, what is being given up in the first case is not so fundamental a requirement of the individual's subsistence (at least in a Third World or Indian context) as in the other cases. Should the three cases then be treated on par? More specifically, should not the costs in (2) and (3) be weighted higher than otherwise? Secondly, should the compensation provided take into account not only the nominal value of what is lost (in the case of the pavement vendor such costs might be assessed at zero since the pavement did not belong to her/him in the first place, and no compensation may be offered) but a recognition of the disruption of livelihoods systems and security?

3. **What if the private interests that are viewed as conflicting with social objectives are driven not by some general perception of private advantage, but by basic survival needs which, furthermore, are not accorded much weight in social goals?** The implications of this question become clearer by considering the following. In what way is the problem of regulating the traffic behaviour of automobile owners different from the problem of regulating sidewalk hawkers who make a living from their sales, or from the problem of inducing the potential oustees of a large dam to give up their lands and systems of living? One might view all three cases as being equivalent on the grounds that all three involve the subordination of individual interests to the common good.

The next section uses the case of the hydroelectric projects along the River Narmada to illustrate some of the issues raised thus far.

CONFLICTS OVER THE RIVER NARMADA

The proposed hydroelectric projects on the Narmada river in central and western India are among the most hotly debated environment-development issues in India today. As we shall see below, the debate over the projects is by no means new. But while the 1950s and 1960s were a period of public optimism and faith in their economic and social value, this is no longer the case. Within the last decade a powerful movement of opposition to the projects (the Narmada Bachao Andolan) has marshalled arguments, evidence and support. Its relative success is evident from the fact that first Japanese foreign assistance, and more recently the World Bank's funding have been withdrawn. The World Bank did not actually withdraw funds but was near enough to doing so, following the adverse report submitted by its Morse Committee, so that the government itself pulled back. Under pressure from those who stand to gain from the projects, and given that considerable financial capital has already been invested, the government of Gujarat is trying to go ahead on its own. Bonds of the Sardar Sarovar Nigam (one of the two major projects) have been floated recently and the public response appears to have been positive since the issue has been oversubscribed. Whether this means that the government will actually go ahead and complete the projects is not clear, since finance is only one of the issues in the debate.

The three sets of issues raised in the previous section are central to the current debate over the hydroelectric projects on the River Narmada. Interestingly, ecosystem considerations, while important, are subsumed under fundamental questions relating to the meaning of development itself. Environmental effects have certainly been discussed extensively, particularly in the context of the benefit–cost analysis used for project evaluation. But although critics of the projects have argued that they are not ecologically sustainable, this is secondary to the principal concern, namely, the impact on the livelihoods of the large numbers of people whose land base will be submerged. Indeed, one might argue that a defining feature of many 'environmental' movements in the Third World is that ecological damage is evaluated through the lens of people's livelihoods. Human activity is viewed as *part* of the ecosystem rather than as an external force that alters the ecosystem. But human activity is not monolithic in that the activities of some can affect the livelihoods of others. Sustainability in this context means the ability of the system, including its livelihood aspects, to be reproduced over time.

The River Narmada is one of the largest Indian rivers and one of the few that flows from east to west with a basin area of about 100,000 square kilometres. The river originates in Shahdol district in the state of Madhya Pradesh and runs for a total of over 1300 kms before flowing into the Arabian Sea. The first 1000 kms are in Madhya Pradesh, after which the river forms the border between Madhya Pradesh and Maharashtra, and then between Madhya Pradesh and Gujarat, before flowing its last 160 kms through Gujarat to the sea. About 40 tributaries join its waters along the way, and some 20 million people, including large numbers of tribals such as the Bhils and the Gonds, cultivate the land in its basin.

Harnessing river waters through major hydroelectric schemes has been an important feature of India's development plans from their earliest phase. In the mid-1960s the government decided that the waters of the Narmada would be shared between the states of Madhya Pradesh, Maharashtra, Gujarat and the arid western border state of Rajasthan. In 1969 the Narmada Water Dispute Tribunal was set up. Its constitution itself set off a competitive spate of project formulation by each state attempting to maximize its share of the river's waters (Alvares and

Billorey 1988). The two largest and most important of these projects are the Sardar Sarovar and Narmada Sagar dams which the Indian government cleared for implementation in 1987.

The Narmada Sagar dam is to be built in East Nimar district of Madhya Pradesh to irrigate 123,000 hectares of land and generate initially 223 megawatts of electricity (which will later fall to 118MW). The Sardar Sarovar dam, currently under construction in Bharuch district of Gujarat, is expected to irrigate 1,792,000 hectares and generate 300 megawatts (dropping later to 150MW) (Alvares and Billorey 1988; Table 1).

The Case for the Projects

The most consistent case for the projects has been made by the Agricultural Division of the World Bank which, until the Morse Commission report of 1992, was a major funder for Sardar Sarovar.[3] Its argument was that the benefits from the projects considerably outweighed the costs. The benefits included, according to the Bank, significant potential increases in agricultural output, particularly food production, improvements in power availability during peak loads and for agricultural pump sets, and multiplier effects in increased investment and employment. It estimated the ratio of beneficiaries to those adversely affected as being 100:1 even without including the multiplier effects, and argued that the project has the potential to feed 20 million and to employ about 1 million people (World Bank 1991). The justification for these estimates was based particularly on the urgency of water needs in Gujarat, with food and domestic water scarcity, and the cost of relief efforts seen as a major and growing problem.

> *These people (ie those facing escalating shortages) can be seen as the resettlers of the future who will have to move, perhaps into city slums, to find food and employment, in the event that the irrigation does not come. They do not hold public meetings now, but in the year 2020, if you deprived them of their Sardar Sarovar dam, they would certainly be out on the streets.*

(World Bank 1991)

Furthermore, proponents of the projects argue that the costs have been exaggerated in a number of ways. First, they hold that the number of persons adversely affected by dam construction will be lower than the estimates of opponents, since many of the villages and much of the land classified as 'affected' will only partially be affected, not permanently

---

3 In 1985 the World Bank approved $450 million for the Sardar Sarovar project. In 1992 the Morse commission, appointed by the Bank in response to considerable internal and international pressure, submitted a report which was highly critical of the project, especially the poor quality of its rehabilitation plans. The Indian government, seeing the writing on the wall, decided not to request further disbursement of Bank funds. In 1990 the Japanese government, until then another major funder along with the Bank, had also withdrawn funding.

inundated. Second, they argue that while there may be some negative environmental impacts due to loss of forests, wildlife habitat, consequent increased pressure of men and animals on surrounding areas, and loss of religious and/or cultural sites, these costs will be offset by environmental gains as well. The latter will include better micro-climates due to increased evaporation, more habitats for waterfowl, and possibilities for fisheries, and more photosynthesis in the irrigated areas. Third, proponents hold that, while problems of resettlement and compensation are important, it would be wrong to romanticize the current living conditions of the tribals. Many of those whose lands are likely to be affected do not live currently in pristine forests, but in poor quality and highly degraded lands.

The Case Against

Critics of the Narmada projects hold, first of all, that the cost–benefit calculations used to justify the projects are of dubious quality (Alvares and Billorey 1988). For example, the benefit–cost ratio for Narmada Sagar have been revised at least thrice. In the first two sets of calculations (in 1982 and 1984) neither the capital costs of the project nor environmental costs were included. These two calculations generated a benefit–cost ratio of 1.88 and 1.52 respectively as against the Planning Commission's norm of 1.5 for such projects. Thereafter the Government of India's own Department of Environment and Forests estimated the environmental costs as a colossal Rs30,000 crores. In response to this the Narmada Valley Development Authority generated a new set of benefit figures which are quite dubious since they appear to involve double counting of benefits, as well as questionable calculations of opportunity costs. Similar problems appear to beset the calculations for Sardar Sarovar. Alvares and Billorey (1988) estimate the benefit–cost ratio of Narmada Sagar to be only 0.17 and of Sardar Sarovar to be 0.38, ie well below the figure of unity which would be required for benefits to exceed costs.[4]

Differences on the cost–benefit calculations are, however, a proxy for more fundamental disagreements. Critics of the projects argue along four main lines.

Loss of land and livelihood systems

The loss of land and destruction of the livelihood systems of large numbers of people, many of them tribals, currently living in the proposed catchment areas is the most important of these. According to the Department of Environment and Forests of the Government of India (as quoted in Alvares and Billorey 1988; Tables 2 and 3) the Sardar Sarovar project will submerge 240 villages with a population of 100,000 people, 70 per cent of them living in the state of Madhya Pradesh. The Narmada Sagar project will submerge an additional 254 villages, the homes of

---

4 I do not in this paper subject the widely divergent cost–benefit estimates that have been generated by different parties to the debate to any kind of scrutiny. That would require more technical information than is currently at my disposal, and would in any case be somewhat outside the main arguments of the paper.

170,000 people, all in Madhya Pradesh. Of these, 60 per cent in the case of Sardar Sarovar and 34 per cent in the case of Narmada Sagar belong to 'scheduled castes and tribes', acknowledged to be the poorest and most socially and economically exploited in the country – the former (and in many instances, current) 'untouchables'. These figures do not include those who may be partially or indirectly adversely affected such as by the backwaters of the Sardar Sarovar dam. The total eventual numbers of displaced persons may be upwards of a million people. The high proportion of 'scheduled tribes' among those whose land will be submerged (as high as 51 per cent in Sardar Sarovar) arises from the fact that the hilly area for the proposed project is heavily populated by tribals who have lived there for long periods of time.

It would be wrong, however, to imagine that current tribal living conditions represent a balance with their environment. 'The romantic image of the "tribal" does not match the reality of adivasi existence as variously experienced in the Narmada valley' (Baviskar 1991). It is all too simple to counterpose an image of tribal livelihoods as deriving from a traditionally harmonious relationship with their environment. But the history of primitive accumulation in the valley goes back at least two hundred years.[5] Tribal resistance to the depletion of forest resources by outsiders (largely from Gujarat) led the British during the colonial period to repress them in a variety of ways including military force, and to encourage non-tribal settlement in the region. Tribal peoples were thus increasingly pushed onto marginal lands in ecologically fragile forest areas. In the following era the exploitation of both timber and non-timber products continued; the growing impoverishment of the tribals led to their increasing transformation into wage-labourers, both within the forests themselves and as migrants to the plains. With their growing involvement in market-oriented production came social and class differentiation among the tribals themselves. They now include both land-owning, settled peasants as well as landless labourers. Some of these peasants, particularly in the districts of Dhar and Khargone, are actually participants in the Green Revolution in the region, using high yielding seeds, fertilizer, pesticides and water. In other districts, tribal labourers are predominant but hardly conform to a romantic image of sustainable livelihoods, even though their survival is heavily dependent on whatever marginal access they continue to have to forest resources. Interestingly, as Baviskar notes, tribal landowners tend to be stronger supporters of the movement against the projects.

As Baviskar (1991) points out, the tribals do not themselves have a romantic conception of 'Nature', the forests or of land. For them, land and forests are a resource, a critical basis of their livelihoods. This is not to

---

5 Baviskar (1991) provides a thoughtful self-critique of the Narmada Bachao Andolan itself arguing, *inter alia*, that middle class activism tends to view 'the 'tribal'... (as)... a cultural resource from which we have picked aspects that seem to fit our patchwork ideology...' This serves the purpose of positing tribal livelihood systems as an alternative to the ecologically damaging and inequitable process of 'development'. Baviskar herself argues that the Andolan needs to go considerably beyond such a critique if it is to fulfil its potential, and if it is to treat tribal peoples as subjects of their own destinies.

deny that their cultural and spiritual beliefs and practices are profoundly rooted in their physical environment; such practices provide the cultural mortar that holds their livelihood systems together. But it does mean that they may not be averse to change, provided the transformation of their livelihood base was in their favour and did not further impoverish them. This includes the dynamic preservation of the cultural practices and social institutions that are the bedrock of their self-image. If economic gain for some among them were linked to the destruction of social institutions and a consequent disorientation and anomie for the majority, then this may well be resisted.

The proposed projects are likely, nevertheless, to overwhelm the existing class differences among the tribals in the region since the scale of proposed land loss is so great.

Poor quality governmental plans

The second source of opposition and controversy surrounding the projects (including the Morse Report) is based on the poor quality of the governments' plans for rehabilitation and resettlement of the proposed oustees. Legal provisions by which the state in India handles the claims of those ousted by development projects are complicated by the federal structure of administration, and by the fact that different states have entirely different laws under which they handle claims. The original law under which the central government addressed the compensation of those affected by its claims on their land was the Land Acquisition Act of 1894.[6] Enacted during the colonial period, the original Act only provided cash compensation (but not alternative land) for those whose land was taken over compulsorily by the state. It was only as late as 1984 that the Act was amended to allow the government to provide alternative land in compensation, but even this was an enabling provision and not a legal requirement. Neither the amendment nor the original Act acknowledged the rights of the landless including labourers and service workers within a community, or of those without formal land-titles but with customary use-rights to land such as women. Although the central Ministry of Home Affairs recommended in 1985 that a comprehensive and legally binding national policy should be evolved to include all those displaced by public, private, or joint sector projects, little progress has been made in this direction.

Three state governments, Maharashtra, Madhya Pradesh and Karnataka have, in the meantime, framed laws in this regard. In other states, all that exists are government guidelines which have no legally binding force, and which are arbitrary and often inconsistent from project to project. They typically cover only those with land, excluding not only landless labourers but also artisans and other service workers, as well as adult women, and those without formal titles to land (other than legal tenants). Most provide for cash compensation and a few for alternative land or employment. The Maharashtra Act includes male landless persons

---

6 For a detailed discussion of various central and state government laws see Vaswani (1992).

among those considered affected, but the Madhya Pradesh Act does not. Neither Act recognizes the claims of adult women outside the family, but both provide for resettlement and rehabilitation of the entire community of oustees and not just of individuals.

In principle three types of compensation mechanisms are possible — cash, land, or income schemes. Of these, cash is generally recognized as the worst. Typically the land of the oustees tends to be undervalued while the prices of comparable land in resettlement areas tends to be much higher, either because of increased demand (consequent on resettlement itself) or because middlemen take advantage of the ignorance or desparation of the oustees. Alternative land as compensation is in principle much better, and may well be the ideal so far as landed oustees themselves are concerned. In practice, however, it is only marginally better than cash, largely because enough land of comparable quality is rarely available, and because the rights of those without clear land titles remain questionable. Alternative income generation schemes such as jobs training or credit for small enterprises rarely seem to work well in India because of poor programme quality, and also because of the inherent difficulty of converting large numbers of land-oriented people overnight to non-agricultural skills. Compensatory employment probably benefits those who actually obtain jobs especially if these are in the public sector, but few displaced persons actually get such jobs. Nor can public enterprises shoulder the costs involved indefinitely. Thus, no existing compensation scheme reasonably meets the needs of the situation (Mankodi 1992, Viegas 1992). Perhaps the problem has less to do with the type of compensation than with the overall situation which pits unprepared rural or hill people against the vagaries of markets, or the indifference and rigidity of bureaucracies.[7]

In the case of Narmada Sagar and Sardar Sarovar, the Narmada Tribunal's recommendations of land-for-land and resettlement of villages rather than individuals have been observed largely in the breach. There is little likelihood of the Narmada Sagar oustees getting land since it is generally known that little unoccupied land of cultivable quality is available in Madhya Pradesh. Sardar Sarovar oustees have been given the option of either moving to Gujarat to get land or getting only cash if they stay in Madhya Pradesh. But even the land available in Gujarat has been meagre and of very poor quality.

The absence of a coherent plan for resettlement was a major reason for the adverse opinion of the Morse Report to the World Bank. The Bank's

---

7 What may be needed is the involvement of service intermediaries who can mediate between the oustees and the government and provide essential services and support to the former. Vaswani (1992) suggests that an acceptable compensation policy requires the creation of a separate line ministry for rehabilitation in both the central and state governments, and the flexibility to take regional variations and project specifics into account. It should have the following features: adequate planning well before the project itself; inclusion of all those affected and not only those with clear land titles; if cash compensation is given, it should be compelemented by income generation, jobs training and alternative employment; strong focus on the needs of women and children; and group rehabilitation to minimize community disruption.

own policies require that a resettlement plan be in place prior to the approval of a project. Although Bank staff had been requesting partial or complete plans from the states of Madhya Pradesh, Maharashtra and Gujarat, the response was to produce ad hoc and piecemeal documents. As a consequence the Bank began to lower its sights and settle for whatever it could get, contravening its own stated goals and procedures. Where resettlement has begun, the oustees face considerable conflicts of interest with existing villagers over land titles, as well as problems of water, wood for fuel, and community disintegration. The apathetic response of the Indian state to the growing discontent about the quality of its resettlement programmes was criticized by the Commissioner of Scheduled Castes and Scheduled Tribes of the Government of India in a letter to the then Prime Minister V P Singh (B D Sharma 1991).

Unfortunately, so far as the Indian state's treatment of those displaced by large hydroelectric projects is concerned, past experience with a number of other large dams does not generate optimism.[8] The construction of the Ukai dam which submerged 170 villages (100 of them completely) in Gujarat is a case in point (Mankodi 1992). In that case not only were there the usual problems of bureaucratic insensitivity and lack of a cogent plan for rehabilitation, but compensatory land was made available after extensive and indiscriminate deforestation. Rapid soil erosion resulted in quick deterioration in land quality, adding to the problems of the oustees. The net result of Ukai was that the downstream area, which was already richer, better serviced by transport and communications, and more densely populated, benefited the most from the irrigation and power generated by the dam. The upstream areas were impoverished and ecologically devastated, leading to seasonal distress migration to the downstream areas, which thereby benefited further from the availability of a regular supply of cheap wage labour for new cash crops.

Uneven distribution of costs and benefits

Although each large dam has had its own specific costs and benefits, this kind of lopsided distribution between upstream and downstream areas seems to be a general phenomenon. Uneven distribution of costs and benefits cloaked in the language of national development goals is the third major source of criticism of the projects. In the case of the Narmada projects, particularly Sardar Sarovar, the differential distribution is further complicated by the fact that it crosses state boundaries, with Madhya Pradesh bearing much of the cost, and Gujarat obtaining most of the benefits. Gujarat is a relatively prosperous state, but one with relatively little fresh water resources particularly for intensively irrigated agriculture; Madhya Pradesh on the other hand is a poorer state with a large tribal population. As already discussed earlier, most of the submerged villages and population will belong to Madhya Pradesh. Corresponding losses of biological species and agricultural land will also be high. Under the projects as currently conceived, Madhya Pradesh will

---

8 For a number of cases of the impact of large dams on those displaced see Thukral (1992).

only get a share of the power generated, while most of the water and power will go to Gujarat.

R C Singh Deo, former Irrigation Minister of the state of Madhya Pradesh, argues that reducing the height of the Narmada Sagar and Sardar Sarovar dams will not only significantly reduce the numbers of people ousted, but will also make it possible to increase the share of the water to the middle reaches of the river. In this way more water can be used in the dry areas of Madhya Pradesh, but this would reduce water to Gujarat. Singh Deo believes that the Narmada Development Authority has not been interested in such alternatives because of the greater political clout of Gujarat's farmers and industrialists. The political importance of Gujarat to the Congress party (which has been increasingly threatened since the 1980s by the growing power of the Bharatiya Janata Party) and the fact that a former chief minister of Gujarat was inducted as central minister for Planning ensured rapid environmental clearance and planning approval for the current projects.

But Singh Deo also argues that, without significant external assistance, it will be impossible for Madhya Pradesh to complete Narmada Sagar (Singh Deo 1991). Gujarat, on the other hand, is attempting to press ahead with Sardar Sarovar despite the withdrawal of the World Bank, and hopes to tap private capital markets. It has also been constructing a massive canal system to irrigate around six million acres, an amount far in excess of what could be irrigated through its share of the river waters as awarded by the Narmada Tribunal (Singh Deo 1991). But for Gujarat to receive the benefits it hopes for, not only Sardar Sarovar but also Narmada Sagar must be built. Otherwise not enough of a steady discharge of water will be available to allow Sardar Sarovar to operate at its expected capacity. Given the scarcity of resources at the disposal of the Madhya Pradesh government, and given that there is growing opposition to Narmada Sagar within Madhya Pradesh because it threatens to divert those resources (not to mention water) from other smaller projects higher up the river (such as the Bargi reservoir), the end result of all of the expenditure being incurred appears dubious.[9]

The irony, according to opponents of the projects, is that the most drought-prone areas of Gujarat – Saurashtra and Kutch – will receive very little of the water from the Narmada projects. Some estimate that only 28 per cent of the state's drought-prone talukas (subdivisions of districts) will receive water from Sardar Sarovar (Paranjpye 1990). The principal

9 M N Buch, a former officer in the Indian Administrative Service, argues that, '...In fact, investment on the Narmada will deprive millions of farmers in the State of the resources which could create localised irrigation systems for them, thus perpetually condemning them to poverty. Tawa [another project in Madhya Pradesh — my note] is a very good example of how a large dam could enhance disparities. So much money has been invested in this project that nothing was left in the State exchequer to invest in the upland district of Betul. Despite the problems with Tawa, irrigation from the reservoir has certainly helped farmers in Hoshangabad district to become richer. At the same time the farmers of Betul have remained stagnant and, by comparison, have become poorer than their cousins in Hoshangabad because Tawa has taken away all the investible resources in the state....' (Buch 1991).

beneficiaries are expected to be cash-cropping farmers in the wealthier districts of Gujarat, as well as industry, services and domestic consumers in these areas. The differential distribution of costs and benefits of the two projects is therefore along three axes: upstream oustees versus downstream beneficiaries, the state of Madhya Pradesh versus the state of Gujarat,[10] and differential access among those downstream.

Ecological impact

The fourth important criticism of the projects is their ecological impact. As far back as 1901, the Irrigation Commission appointed by the British Governor-General of India opposed any major irrigation projects in the Narmada valley because of its black-cotton soil which drains poorly and has a tendency towards waterlogging (Paranjpye 1991). Critics of the projects argue that the government of India has overridden the concerns of its own Ministry of Environment and Forests in attempting to go ahead with the projects. As early as 1985, the Ministry had refused to clear Sardar Sarovar because environmental studies had not even begun in some cases and were unfinished in others. But with approval of the project by the World Bank in the same year and under considerable pressure, the Ministry backed down on the understanding that environmental studies would be completed simultaneously with the project itself. This is patently absurd for most of the environmental issues of concern, since project construction would render it impossible to make any other than very minor and marginal changes in design on the basis of the environmental studies. It meant in fact that the project implementers had been given virtual carte blanche.[11]

The absence of serious environmental evaluation and impact studies *prior* to project implementation is made more serious because almost every aspect of the projects appears fraught with environmental risks. Although many parts of the project area itself are considerably eroded and have already high human and livestock densities, there is still much biodiversity in the area which will be submerged. Of the total area of around 145,000 hectares that will be submerged by the Narmada projects, it has been estimated that about half will be agricultural land and the other half forests. While much of the latter is already under intensive human

---

10 It should be clear that the differential distribution across states is more than a spatial matter; the states in India are agents of both administration and development, and have differential resources they can draw on and different problems to cope with. An additional feature currently complicating the divide between Gujarat and Madhya Pradesh is the fact that major political parties have different strengths in each. Gujarat, despite the growing power of the Hindu fundamentalist BJP (Bharatiya Janata Party) is still run by the Congress Party, while Madhya Pradesh has voted for the BJP in recent elections. Party politics may become an additional factor in state attitudes towards the projects. The ABVP (Akhil Bharatiya Vidyarthi Parishad, the youth wing of the BJP) has expressed strong reservations about the projects (Lokayan 1991).
11 It is in this context that the alliance between the indigenous Narmada Bachao Andolan and external NGOs such as the Environmental Defense Fund became important in launching a successful effort to pressure the World Bank to withdraw funding. This culminated in the Morse Report which was highly critical of the environmental aspects of the project.

and animal use, large stands of teak, salai and anjan remain. Wildlife species such as panther, tigers, bears, wolves, antelopes and a number of threatened species are also to be found. Worst of all, no comprehensive study of the region's species has been undertaken, and the actual biodiversity loss of insects, plant strains and genetic resources will be unknown. With submergence of the dam areas, and without proper corridors for movement, there may well be considerable loss of fauna. Submergence will also undeniably increase the pressure on surrounding forests, particularly given the poor quality of rehabilitation plans. Soil conservation plans to cope with problems of silting, waterlogging, salinity and waste-water drainage have also been weak.

Opponents of the projects are also concerned over the earthquake risks in the region which is of moderate seismicity (Alvares and Billorey 1988). Reservoir-induced seismicity has been known to occur in other moderately seismic areas such as Koyna in India with considerable loss of life. Nor have the health risks from new diseases such as malaria, schistosomiasis, and other vector- and non vector-borne diseases that have been experienced in the area of other large dams in India, including the Tawa dam in Madhya Pradesh itself, been assessed.

Are there Alternatives?

Among opponents of the Narmada projects there seem to be two different opinions about alternatives. One starts by asking whether national development goals could be met through other, more humane and environmentally responsible, means. Buch and others[12] argue that reducing the height of the dams would considerably reduce the financial, human and environmental costs of the projects while still meeting the needs they are supposed to fulfil. Supplementing this with methods less wasteful of water such as lift, sprinkler and drip irrigation would further improve the benefits. While this would reduce the power generated, reduction in transmission losses (which are known to be very high) might partially offset this problem.

The other approach questions the validity of the concept of national development itself. In a powerful critique Esteva and Prakash (1991) argue that popular movements that challenge current patterns of development will fail to effect genuine change if they fall prey to the seduction of 'universal' goals:

> ...*No genuine consensus is possible when abstract national plans or dreams replace people's real hopes: always concrete, localized expressions of their cultures... It has taken time for people at the bottom of India's social hierarchy to start perceiving that their real concrete worlds will continue to be sacrificed at the altar of national goals monitored by increasingly faceless bureaucracies, distant from the people they are supposed to protect and defend... In more recent years, people's initiatives... are returning people*

---

12 See Alvares and Billorey (1988), Chapter 5.

*once again to their roots, to their local spaces, to the regeneration
of their concrete hopes, expressed in concrete contexts, intended to
change the real life of concrete people...*

While acknowledging that the weakness of a concrete focus is precisely
that it is local compared to the forces it confronts, Esteva and Prakash
argue for flexible coalitions of different local issue-based movements as
the answer. In my opinion this approach has three flaws:

1. Its own espousal of the 'local' and 'concrete' appears to be overly
   universal. In many instances local aspirations may be laudable; but
   they do not become so simply by virtue of being local. They can
   become so only on some ethical basis (possibly axiomatic) that serves
   as the touchstone not only for national goals but equally for local
   ones. One cannot avoid this by appealing to the universal legitimacy
   of local aspirations.
2. Local aspirations are not innocent of gender, class, caste or other
   biases; this point reinforces the first.
3. This alternative entirely sidesteps any possible principles on the basis
   of which national objectives can be formulated. While this may not be
   a problem in many instances, it is unavoidable precisely in the case of
   'public goods', ie, those where externalities are involved. Thus, it is
   precisely the question at issue in riparian disputes; more generally, it
   is central to many ecological problems where resources, costs and
   benefits spill over local boundaries. In such cases, concepts of
   collective welfare (more inclusive and sensitive to distribution than
   the current paradigm) are essential as a basis for conflict resolution.
   Otherwise one is left with purely political resolutions which may be
   quite arbitrary in their outcomes.

PUBLIC INTEREST — THE PROBLEM OF DEFINITION

It should be clear from the previous section that I believe that the
alternatives must be framed on the basis of some principles of collective
well-being that centrally address the twin problems of *distribution* and
inclusivity. Our review of the Narmada case shows that all three requisites
for a perception of fair process have been violated. Social objectives have
been defined without taking account of the concerns of large numbers of
those who are likely to be affected. The interests of the weak have been
given less weight than those of the powerful: all interests have not had
equal access to the domain of public discourse.

I would suggest instead that assessments of projects like Narmada
should examine the distribution of benefits, costs and access along various
dimensions at the very outset. Second, they should particularly address
the concerns of those who are socially or economically without privilege,
weighting their concerns about livelihoods and survival higher than the
concerns of the more advantaged. Third, the actual formulation of projects
should put in place mechanisms to give special voice to the under-

privileged and draw them into the domain of public discourse. This may mean in some instances that even projects with otherwise laudable goals might have to be shelved or rejected altogether. But this will be an essential requirement if the project of national development is to be politically and ethically viable in the end.

In some ways the battle over the Narmada appears to have come to precisely such a juncture. After the withdrawal of World Bank funding, and in the aftermath of the threatened collective drowning by anti-dam activists during the monsoons of 1993, the government of India appointed a special commission of public enquiry to review the issues. As is to be expected, the enquiry has itself become hotly contested; nor is it clear what standing its report will have. But the appointment of the commission itself is a kind of hallmark, being the first time in India that problems of distribution and inclusion have come to the centre stage of the debate over environment and development.

REFERENCES

Alvares, C and Billorey, R (1988) *Damming the Narmada: India's Greatest Planned Environmental Disaster* Third World Network / Asia-Pacific People's Environment Network, Penang

Baviskar, A (1991) 'The researcher as pilgrim' *Lokayan Bulletin* 9:3/4 May-August, pp 91–7

Buch, M N (1991) 'And all the boards did shrink' *Lokayan Bulletin* 9:3/4 May-August, pp 47–53

Das, M (1992) 'The internationalization of the Narmada dam: do Western environmental groups have a role in Third World ecology movements?' Harvard Centre for Population and Development Studies Working Paper Series no 1, Cambridge

Esteva, G and Prakash M S (1991) 'Re-routing and re-rooting grassroots initiatives: escaping the impasse of sustainable development for the Narmada' *Lokayan Bulletin* 9:3/4 May-August, pp 113–25

Lokayan (1991) Akhil Bharati Vidyarthi Parishad Resolution–Narmada Valley project–plan of development or destruction? *Lokayan Bulletin* 9:3/4 May–August, pp 139–44

Mankodi, K (1992) 'Resettlement and rehabilitation of dam oustees: a case-study of Ukai dam' in EG Thukral E G (ed) *Big Dams, Displaced People* Sage Publishers, New Delhi

Paranjpye, V (1990) *High Dams on the Narmada* INTACH, New Delhi

Sharma, B D (1991) 'Letter to Prime Minister V.P.Singh' *Lokayan Bulletin* 9:3/4 May–August, pp 126–33

Singh Deo, R C (1991) 'Venting ire upon the Narmada' *Lokayan Bulletin* 9:3/4 May–August, pp 60–4

Thukral, E G (ed) (1992) *Big Dams, Displaced People* Sage Publishers, New Delhi

Vaswani, K (1992) 'Rehabilitation laws and policies: a critical look' in Thukral, E G (ed) *Big Dams, Displaced People* Sage Publishers, New Delhi, pp 155–68.

Veltrop, J (1991) 'The case for' in 'The debate over large dams' *Civil Engineering* August, pp 42–8

World Bank (1991) Extract in *Lokayan Bulletin* 9:3/4 May–August, pp 98–103

Chapter Eleven

Economics and Ecosystems: the Case of Zimbabwean Peasant Households

Will Cavendish

INTRODUCTION

In the past decade, bold claims have been made about actual or impending environmental crises in Africa, such as desertification, deforestation and soil erosion. Aside from the environmental cost of such crises, it is argued that these crises are serious because they are contribute to the pauperization of peasant households by undermining agriculture and increasing the scarcity of rural resources (for example fuelwood). Explanation of these grave developments has focused on the peasant as the agent of change, whether as a consequence of peasant characteristics (eg poverty, rapid population growth), historical processes (eg confinement on marginal lands) or poor incentives (eg distorted pricing, inadequate property rights). Given the strength of statements about these issues, it is surprising to find that there has been little in-depth work examining the interaction of peasant economy and environment — indeed, the study of African peasant households has been untouched by a serious integration of economic and environmental analysis. It would therefore seem important to conduct such analysis in order to scrutinise such claims.

This chapter takes as a case study the economically marginal households of the majority of Zimbabwe's Communal Areas, and examines the interrelations between peasant economy and the environment. From this examination, three main themes are developed. The first stresses the importance of an integrated analysis of economics and ecosystems: only through such work will meaningful analysis be possible both of Zimbabwean peasant production and of environmental change and/or degradation. On the one hand, traditional economic work, by ignoring the critical role of environmental resources both as generators of household welfare and determinants of household decision-making, has failed to understand adequately the economic systems it is analysing. On the other hand, comprehending the economic factors impinging on natural resources leads to a quite different perception both of the definition of environmental degradation and its causes from that commonly presented. Second, government policies, through faulty understanding of these economic and environmental interactions, have largely failed to ameliorate the problems they were intended to solve, and sometimes have even undermined the peasant economic production system and the survival of natural resources. Finally, it will be argued that 'sustainability' is in practice an extremely difficult concept to utilize: as a result, grandiose statements concerning environmental degradation and unsustainability should be regarded with some scepticism.

This paper is organized as follows. The next section outlines the production system (and in particular the agropastoral production function) of Communal Area farmers, emphasizing both their highly income- and asset-constrained status and their economic remoteness. As a consequence, these households rely heavily on the goods and services offered to them by natural habitats/environmental resources, a reliance explored (on pages 208–14). Given the pervasive interactions between economy and environment, it is then argued that the characteristics of local ecosystems have an important role to play in explaining household decision-making. As a consequence, it is unsurprising to find that peasant households have substantial environmental knowledge, and indeed are involved in managing their local ecosystem to retain flows of important natural habitat goods and services (see pages 218–22). In the light of this analysis, the final section discusses and concludes the main themes of the paper.

PEASANT HOUSEHOLDS IN COMMUNAL AREAS: LOW-INCOME AND HIGHLY CONSTRAINED

Zimbabwe's agricultural areas can be basically divided into two zones. The first zone comprises the Commercial Farming Areas — large, white-owned farms located in favourable Natural Regions[1] — while the second zone comprises the Communal Areas (CAs), the region of interest for this paper. These areas, and the agricultural system within them, are a colonial creation whereby the African population of Zimbabwe was relocated in agriculturally more marginal areas. As a result, peasant households in Zimbabwe's Communal Areas are characterized by features common to small peasant producers across southern Africa. There are relatively high population densities and the average farm household is large (circa 10 members), while the average farm is not large, consisting of three hectares of arable land, often located more than one km from the household. Communal Area farms are generally located

---

1 Zimbabwe is divided into five Natural Regions (NRs), calibrated by annual rainfall levels, with NR I representing the highest rainfall region, and NR V the lowest. The agricultural potential of the land is considered by and large to follow the same classification (Whitlow 1980, Whitlow 1982).

in less favourable regions for agriculture: 74.2 per cent of CA farms are in Natural Regions IV and V, which — on account of their low rainfall levels (less than 650 mm pa) — are officially described as suitable for only extensive and semi-extensive farming.

The Agricultural Production Function

The characteristic of the agricultural production system usually emphasized is that it is *agropastoral:* in other words, the production system comprises a combination of crops, livestock and natural resources. Thus, while crops and vegetables are grown on the three areas that can, by and large, be considered to be under the private control of the household (namely arable fields, gardens and the homestead), another critical component of agricultural production is the livestocks' grazing lands, which are characterized by communal tenure. The characteristic emphasized here, however, is the heavy reliance of the agropastoral system on non-marketed transactions, and in particular the role played by natural habitats. Not only are these natural habitats used as the communal grazing lands and thus underpin the entire agropastoral production system, but also they contain the woodland, mountain and riverine areas from which most environmental utilizations are derived.

In this section, though, we focus on the agropastoral system. First, consider the role of livestock: their importance lies chiefly in their provision of draft power and manure. Draft power is a critical input into crop production, as ploughing at the optimal time has a marked impact on crop yield (around 50 per cent) (Ashworth 1990, Cumming and Bond 1991). Households without livestock generally rely either on hand-hoeing or wait to hire/borrow livestock for ploughing after the optimal time. Manure is also an important resource: for Communal Area farms, mostly located on arid, nutrient-poor soils, regular fertilization of fields is necessary if adequate yields are to be obtained. Manure is the most common fertilizer used by Communal Area farmers (Dewees 1992). Indeed, this is the point of the agropastoral system, which involves the close interaction between cropping and livestock activities, and where the value of livestock primarily comes from its role in providing inputs to the agricultural system. Ownership of livestock — and in particular cattle — hence becomes crucial to these households' agricultural production: for example, arable yields for households with large cattle herds are triple those of stockless households.

However, the uses of cattle are not just restricted to draught power and manure. Other services they offer the household include the supply of milk, the provision of power for transportation, the production of saleable offspring, transformation into consumption items (meat, hides, hooves etc), and a vehicle for savings and investment — in other words, multiple use assets (Scoones 1992). In fact, the key role of cattle is to provide the household with non-market substitutes for inputs (draught, manure, work) and consumption goods (milk, meat) that the household chooses not to purchase in the market.

This point can be extended by considering inputs into livestock maintenance and the sources of fertilizer. With regard to the former, few households (especially those in NRs III to V) purchase livestock feed: instead, households rely primarily on forage and browse in the communal grazing areas in local natural habitats; and secondarily on the recycling of crop residues from their own fields to provide livestock sustenance (Campbell and Grundy 1991). Similarly, although (purchased) chemical fertilizer is available to households, in fact it is organic fertilizer that is more widely used, again especially in the less affluent farms of NRs III to V (Conroy 1990). The role of manure has already been mentioned.[2] The second most important source of fertilizer is leaf litter which households collect from woodlands in surrounding natural habitats. Again, use of this resource is widespread: Campbell et al (1991a) report that, in a survey spanning three Natural Regions of Zimbabwe, 68 per cent of respondents claimed to use leaf litter, making this utilization the most significant direct transfer of nutrients from woodlands to fields. Finally, households also use termitaria,[3] though this utilization is highly variable across Communal Areas (Campbell and Grundy 1991).

Thus, in the critical areas of agricultural production and livestock maintenance, households rely heavily on non-marketed goods — and in particular, goods that are derived from the natural habitats in the rural life space surrounding the household — despite the existence of marketed substitutes. What explains this pattern of consumption? Two overriding determinants are suggested:

1. the extremely low cash income status of most CA households, and
2. their economic remoteness implying the existence of pervasive market failures for poor rural households.

Communal Area Household Cash Incomes

The extremely low cash incomes of Communal Area households have been charted by a number of studies. The most insightful of these is a study by Jackson and Collier (1991), based on a survey during the 1984/85 season of 600 households spread over the five Natural Regions (Table 11.1). This establishes a household benchmark mean 'full income' figure of only Z$701 per year (US$437): converting using Adult Equivalent Units, this gives the extremely low mean per capita 'full income' figure of Z$227 pa (US$142). Even this, however, overstates average pure cash income, as both remittances and crop income include valuations of subsistence flows. Adjusting for these subsistence valuations, mean annual cash income

---

2 Note that livestock manure, ie essentially produced by natural habitats, with livestock as the production 'technology' converting forage and browse inputs from natural habitats into nutrient outputs (manure).
3 Termitaria are widely used since termite mounds can contain a significant proportion of the nutrients found in cultivated lands, so that use of these soils can raise yields significantly. Furthermore, termite mounds regenerate rapidly and are therefore a renewable resource (Dewees 1992).

Table 11.1 The income structure of rural households

	Households with income source (%)	Total household income (%)	Mean income from source (Z$)
Crop income	95.8	50.4	368
Remittances	37.0	18.5	348
Local off-farm wages	10.7	14.7	960
Self-employment	23.1	7.9	225
Livestock income	66.8	5.4	56
Estate wage	6.0	2.5	295
Local farm wage	12.8	<1.0	32

Mean aggregate annual income data	
(per household)	*(per adult equivalent)*
Z$701	Z$227

Median aggregate annual income data	
(per household)	*(per adult equivalent)*
Z$450	Z$138

Source: Jackson and Collier 1991.

becomes Z$421 per household (US$261), with mean per capita annual cash incomes a mere Z$130 (US$80).[4] Finally, these average income figures disguise considerable income inequality: median incomes are less than two-thirds of these mean income figures.

A corollary of these extremely low income levels is the very low asset levels of Communal Area households. While there is no comprehensive survey of assets levels in Communal Areas[5], Table 11.2 provides a summary of available data. There are two main points:

1. Cattle comprise as much as 80 per cent of total asset values: other than cattle, the average household owns only a few, mostly low value, agricultural implements, and some smaller livestock.
2. As we will see later, these assets are vulnerable, as livestock stocking strategies involve periodic die-offs. However it should be noted that, like income, the averages overstate the median asset level which is, in fact, significantly below that of Table11.2.[6]

---

4 These low figures are born out by a host of other studies, both country-wide and in specific locales (CSO 1988, Campbell et al 1989, MLARR 1990, Coudere and Marijse 1991, Mehretu and Mudimu 1991). Though carried out in different years with different methodologies, they all provide figures similar to those of Table 11.1.
5 This situation is replicated across Africa generally, despite the importance of assets in underpinning welfare and reducing household insecurity. However, see Deaton (1991) and Dercon (1992) for a start on this work.
6 Jackson 1989 provides data on the considerable inequalities in cattle ownership

Table 11.2 Household assets

	Households with item (%)	Average no. per household	Average value per item (Z$)	Average value per household
Scotch cart	34.9	0.4	314	126
Water cart	3.9	0.1	132	13
Bicycle	22.4	0.3	101	30
Ox-cultivator	31.6	0.3	68	20
Harrow	17.8	0.2	59	12
Wheelbarrow	39.7	0.5	43	22
Ox-plough	83.8	1.1	38	42
Yoke	82.2	2.1	8	17
Hoe	92.1	5.4	3	16
Sub-total				298
Cattle	n.a.	7.00	287	2,001
Goats	n.a.	6.67	30	202
Total				2,501

Source: Tables 1.5, 1.8, 5.1 and 5.2 in MLARR 1990 and author's own calculations

Why are income and asset levels so low? The work of Jackson and Collier (1991) demonstrated that rising incomes were directly connected to Communal Area households' ability to accumulate and diversify their number of income-generating activities. However, households are held back from accumulation and diversification by their highly-constrained nature. The economic effect, and severity, of these constraints is clearly indicated by high marginal returns to livestock accumulation: Scoones (1992) calculates the internal rate of return on cattle to be uniformly greater than 100 per cent. These constraints are obviously related in part to the low level from which these households are starting, a level which has been delineated above. However, as is discussed below, they are also a consequence of the economic remoteness of Communal Area households.

Communal Areas' Economic Remoteness

By economic remoteness, what is meant is economic distance (measured through proportional transactions costs) from markets in which significant income-raising trading can take place (ie. excluding markets within the rural life space, which have a much lower potential for raising incomes). Generally speaking, this economic remoteness is the cause of the widespread market failures that afflict peasant production and hence inflicts a substantial welfare loss on rural producers. While the literature on the existence of markets for Communal Area households is patchy, there are some characteristics affecting the existence of markets that are relevant to a majority of Communal Area households. The first is that Communal Area households are frequently physically distant from formal markets, shops, mills, clinics, roads and so on (MLARR 1990). Covering the distances from farm to services to carry out economic activities comprises considerable unit transactions costs as these trips must be undertaken mostly by foot: indeed, a study of one Communal Area found that the total energy costs of making key trips was over 25 per cent of the available household energy budget. Thus, the substantial distances separating Communal Areas from various amenities suggests market failure is a generic phenomenon (Mehretu and Mutambirwa 1992).

As far as specific markets are concerned, connections between Communal Area households and formal markets are weak (even though the same market in the rural life space may be active). For example, capital market failures are pervasive. Insurance markets for crop income failures do not exist, while less than 10 per cent of Communal Area farmers receive formal credit (World Bank 1991). Unsurprisingly, this minority is found in the better agricultural areas, meaning it is the resource-poor farmers for whom formal credit markets are failing (MLARR 1990). In order to compensate for this, informal credit mechanisms are common, but they exist firmly within the rural life space. Similarly, while on the surface the state marketing boards offer access to external markets for Communal Area farmers' agricultural outputs, in practice transportation costs to depots for poorer farmers are high, and it is households in NRs II and III that have mostly benefited from participation in these markets. If a poorer household does sell crops, this is usually to other households within the rural life space. The same pattern holds for non-agricultural goods: rural to urban sales are rare, but within-rural sales are common (McPherson 1991).

Labour markets are, in contrast, more active. Data on the components of household income demonstrated the importance of remittances from non-resident labour who, by definition, are involved in external markets. However, the potential of external labour markets to raise rural incomes is heavily circumscribed by Zimbabwe's critical unemployment problem. Within the rural area labour markets are widespread. For example, one study found 39 per cent of households hiring at least one permanent worker, while as many as 77 per cent of households had hired casual workers in the last year (Adams 1991). However, these rural labour markets do not raise incomes appreciably as wage rates are low, at Z$30 to Z$40 per month (Scoones 1992). Similarly, markets for the key agropastoral input, livestock services, are common — indeed, Muchena (1989) catalogues five payment mechanisms for ploughing services — but they are often costly and are overwhelmingly within the rural life space. In general, then, participation in income-raising markets is very limited.

Conclusion

Earlier, the surprisingly widespread reliance of Communal Area households on non-marketed goods and natural habitats for important inputs into the production system was noted. This has been explained by the extremely low-income, highly-constrained nature of Communal Area households, which renders them unable to purchase these inputs in the market. However these same constraints face households in all areas of economic activity: in the following section, then, the analysis is expanded to look at the wide range of natural habitat utilizations by Communal Area households. To motivate this discussion, consider the low cash incomes of Communal Area households. It is clear from the data above that if all household consumption had to paid for, income levels of these sorts would place Communal Area households near the bottom of a global poverty profile, with scarcely adequate incomes to purchase anything other than the most minimal consumption bundle. Hence, there is something missing from the conventional economist's description of these poor, economically remote, rural households: namely the pervasive dependence of Communal Area households on natural habitats.

NATURAL HABITATS AS A SOURCE OF GOODS AND SERVICES FOR COMMUNAL AREA HOUSEHOLDS

Evidence of the importance of wild resource use can be taken from Table 11.3, which lists the wide range of different natural habitat utilizations mentioned in various literatures. As will be shown, a fundamental problem in evaluating these utilizations is the lack of proper economic data on quantities used, prices, the pattern of household use and the like.[7] However, while not all households use all the wild resources listed, casual empirical evidence suggests most utilize many of these resources, hence the high valuation given to resources (see below) and efforts made to conserve them. Indeed, the fact that many of these resources offer multiple uses to households suggest they also provide considerable flexibility of use, in contrast to the constrained nature of agricultural production noted previously: this has not, however, been adequately researched.

The Consumption of Wild Foods

There is no definitive analysis of the consumption of wild foods. A comprehensive listing is presented in Gomez (1988), who lists species of wild cereals, legumes, vegetables, mushrooms, fruit, insects, fish and game known to be consumed by Communal Area households. However, there is no quantification of resource use and hence no indication of the significance of these items in rural diets.[8] As the evidence reviewed below includes a mere subset of the species listed in Gomez, it must be regarded as a preliminary analysis only.

First, there is evidence that wild meats can play a quite substantial role in rural diets despite the illegality of hunting. For example, de Vos (1978) suggests that hunting of wild animals yielded 2.5 million kgs of meat per annum in the mid-1970s, more than the local beef industry. More recently, Murindagomo's (1988) study of Angwa in the mid-Zambezi finds that adults consumed an annual average of 88 kg of bushmeat per person. Further,

---

7 This study is currently being undertaken and will appear in Cavendish (forthcoming).
8 Quantitative research of this type has been done in other African countries, where wild resources have been found not only to be critical in rural diets, but important also in urban areas as well (Asibey 1974, Sale 1981, Martin 1983, Eltringham 1984, Anadu et al 1988).

Table 11.3 A taxonomy of natural habitat utilizations by communal area households

Utilization or service	Source of item	Type of activity in household
Wild meat	State forest areas Wildlife areas	Consumption Income generation
Wild fruits and nuts	Local woodlands Trees in grazing areas Trees in fields Trees in homesteads	Consumption Interseasonal stock Income generation (sale) Input into income generation (wine brewing)
Fish	Local rivers and dams	Consumption Income generation
Other wild foods: Insects Honey Mushrooms Wild vegetables Birds	Local woodlands Local fields	Consumption Income generation
Natural medicines	Local woodlands	Consumption Income generation (for n'angas)
Other wild goods: Gum Glue Wild shampoo and soap Wild salt Tooth-cleaning materials 'African' snuff Dyes	Local woodlands Local grazing areas	Consumption
Fuelwood for: Cooking and heating Beer brewing Brick burning	Local woodlands Trees in grazing areas Leftover wood from other uses (especially construction)	Consumption Interseasonal stock Input into income generation (brewing, brickburning)
Construction wood: Hut walls Roofing poles and cross-poles Door frames Granaries Storage huts Livestock pens Storage racks Drying racks Fencing (live and dead) Tree protectors	Specific trees in local woodlands Local woodlots	Input into housing investment

Table 11.3 *continued*

Utilization or service	Source of item	Type of activity in household

Wood for making:
  Agricultural implements
  Furniture
  Household utensils
  Musical instruments
  Hunting and fishing
   implements
	Local woodlands
	Trees in grazing areas
		Input into consumer durables
		Input into production tools
		Input into income generation
		Input into consumption (hunting)

Reeds, Grasses, Cane, Bark etc:
  Thatching grass
  Sleeping mats
  Other mats
  Storage baskets
  Winnowing baskets
  Transport baskets
  Brooms
  Rope
  Herding whips
  Gourds and calabashes
	Contour ridges in fields
	Grazing areas
	River- and streambanks
	Trees in local woodlands
	Trees in resettlement areas
		Input into consumption items
		Input into income generation
		Input into production equipment
		Input into housing investment

Clays for pottery:
  Storage pots
  Cooking pots
	Rural life space	Input into consumption item
		Input into income generation

Leaf litter	Local woodlands Trees in fields Termitaria	Input into agricultural production
Termite mounds	Local grazing areas Crop fields	Input into agricultural production
Livestock fodder and browse	Local woodlands Grazing areas	Input into consumption item (milk) Maintenance of capital assets Indirect input into agricultural production (manure, draught power)
Shade	Trees in grazing areas Trees in fields	Input into agricultural production
Ecological services eg Higher soil organic matter better, soil moisture, reduced soil erosion	Trees in fields	Input into agricultural production

illegal poaching brought a return of Z$8.20 per hectare, far exceeding the estimated damage to crops incurred by the wildlife on whose presence such high consumption levels are predicated. Finally, an important role is played in rural diets by the consumption of smaller mammals such as rodents, birds etc, and of fish caught in local rivers and dams (Wilson 1989b).

There is more evidence concerning the prevalence of wild fruit consumption. For example, Campbell's (1987) study covering three natural regions and three tenure systems found wild fruit to be an important supplement to diets in all three regions and tenure systems. Ninety-five per cent of respondents stated that a member of their family regularly consumed wild fruit, with most consumed by young children. In a later survey, Campbell et al (1991a) found that an even higher percentage of rural households — 98 per cent — collected wild fruit. Further, wild fruits are used not just for immediate consumption, but are also stored for consumption in the dry season and can be sold in local markets, with 10 per cent of households raising income this way. This extensive use of wild fruits has been confirmed by the studies of Wilson (1990) and McGregor (1991), with evidence in the latter study that wild fruit is more heavily used by poorer households. Finally, the importance of wild fruit is confirmed by the considerable efforts undertaken to preserve wild fruit trees.

Quantitative evidence on the consumption of other wild foods is insubstantial. There is some work (Parent and Thoen 1977, McGregor 1991) indicating that wild mushrooms are used quite heavily, although evidence is scanty. Other important wild foods are honey, wild vegetables and edible insects such as termites, caterpillars and especially 'mopane worms' (Wilson 1990, Dewees 1992). These are shown in Wilson (1989b) to form the basis of most relishes (ie the accompaniment to the stiff cereal porridge made from maize). Many of these resources are dried and stored for consumption during the late dry season, when food shortages are common, and for a variety of them, urban markets exist.[9]

Wild species are also used commonly as medicines. Up to eighty per cent of both rural and urban populations consult traditional healers for treatment of illness and other maladies (McIvor 1989). This heavy utilization implies substantial wild resource demands, as traditional healers use these resources exclusively: indeed, over 500 species have been catalogued as having medicinal use by traditional healers in Zimbabwe (Gelfand et al 1985). However, many households also use wild resources for their own treatment of common complaints such as headaches, colds, indigestion and diarrhoea (Cavendish, forthcoming). Finally, there are a number of other known uses about which little has been written, for example, use of certain twigs for cleaning teeth; use of wild species for soap and shampoo; collecting wild salt; and extracting gum and glue.

---

9 Some wild resources have become heavily commercialized. Edible caterpillars (*madora*) are now tinned or dried and packaged and sold widely by Botswana, South African and Zimbabwean companies. Like many insects, madora have a high nutritional content: a meal of 20 fulfills an adult male's entire daily requirement of calcium, phosphorus, riboflavin and iron (Brandon 1987).

The Multiple Uses of Wood

The dominant direct utilization of natural habitats, however, is household use of wood. Wood has multiple uses for the CA household, and households' rate of use of wood is at the centre of the total valuation of natural habitats. The first and best-known of these multiple utilizations is fuelwood. It is well established that fuelwood as an energy resource is critical to rural households in Zimbabwe, since 95 to 100 per cent of these households use wood rather than any other fuel source for cooking and heating (du Toit et al 1984, MacGarry 1987). While cooking and heating is the single most important use, other major fuelwood uses include heating for special occasions, for beer brewing, and to fire brick kilns (Grundy et al 1993). Indeed, rural dependence on fuelwood as an energy source is well enough known for the imputation of fuelwood use values in household budget surveys (1985Z$70 pa, equivalent to 9 per cent of total cash expenditure) (CSO 1988). Note that, despite this dependence, successive researchers have found no general evidence either of wide-spread fuelwood scarcities or of fuelwood demands causing deforestation (Whitlow 1980, du Toit et al 1984, McGregor 1991, Grundy et al 1993).

Less well researched, but equally important, is the use by households of construction wood. The only thorough piece of research on this subject is reported in Grundy et al (1993). This paper, though reporting research conducted in a resettlement area which is likely to be better wooded than most Communal Areas and hence have higher values for wood use than the average household, demonstrates the central role wood plays in the household's creation of housing assets. This is on account of the range of structures for which households use wood — Grundy et al list thirteen separate structures as requiring construction wood. Though the annual household volume required (about 2.7 m³) is lower than fuelwood consumption, it is probably of higher value, as construction wood needs specific tree species as their source which will produce poles of adequate length, straightness, durability and resistance to termites (Grundy 1990). Indeed, scarcities in the availability of construction wood have led both to households searching intensively for good woods to use, and the emergence of markets (Dewees 1992).

Finally, wood offers the household a number of uses aside from fuelwood and construction material, for example in making agricultural implements, furniture, household utensils, musical instruments and weapons (Ellert 1984). Once again, use of these resources is widespread, with over 90 per cent of households using wood for these purposes (Campbell et al 1991b). Similarly, there is widespread use of other wild resources to make household goods — in particular, use of reeds, grasses, cane, bark and clay to make ubiquitous and essential items such as *inter alia* thatch, sleeping mats, winnowing baskets, rope and cooking pots. Indeed, high demand for all these items means that some households rely heavily on income from associated activities such as carpentry, thatching, weaving and pottery (Cavendish, forthcoming). However, accurate data on quantities used and values generated are not yet available.

The Indirect Input of Natural Habitats Into Production

Natural habitats also provide a range of indirect inputs into the agricultural production system. The role of leaf litter and termitaria in providing nutrients to Communal Area farmers has already been discussed. However, probably the most important indirect input is the provision of free fodder and browse to livestock. A detailed discussion of the woodland-livestock-crop production nexus is left until later, as it is in livestock herding strategies that the necessary adaptation of farmers' production strategies to the properties of the surrounding ecosystem are most clearly seen. For now, it suffices to note that it is the exploitation of natural habitats and their properties that enables households to maintain livestock stocking rates at their current — if economically inadequate — levels, and thus it is natural habitats that underpin the entire agropastoral production system.

Other indirect inputs exist, but their value is less clear. One such input is the shade offered by the existence of trees in fields, important to agricultural workers during the long hours worked in fields during the agricultural season. Although the density of trees needed to offer such shade is low (0.5 trees ha^{-1}), Wilson (1989a) found that some trees in fields were preserved solely for shade. This is confirmed by Campbell et al (1991c), who found that amongst non-fruiting trees left in fields, the primary motivation was the benefit of shade, and by the data on reasons for tree-planting that is presented in the section on natural resource management, where it is reported that shade is one of the leading reasons given for households' tree-planting activities.

Finally, there is a range of benefits that can be classed under the generic heading 'ecological services'. Trees have a number of local ecological benefits: these include improving soil organic matter, soil structure, soil moisture status and soil nutrient status under or near to tree canopies, and reducing soil erosion on a broader scale (Ingram 1990). The result of these ecological benefits is improved yields and reduced costs of production, a fact recognized by farmers who have been found both to deliberately crop under tree canopies, and reduce their fertilizer applications accordingly. Farmers also benefit from reduced soil erosion due to leaving trees in their fields, especially if these trees act to stabilize field contours and thereby reduce the labour needed to repair damage (Dewees 1992). However, it is also the case that trees can have some negative impacts on crops, through *inter alia* competition for water, excessive shading of crops, and the harbouring of pest populations (Campbell et al 1991a). Hence, the net ecological effect of trees in fields on crop production is not always positive.

The Total Valuation of Natural Habitats to Communal Area Households

The above discussion is clearly plagued by a lack of adequate data which would enable a detailed comparison to be made between environmental utilizations and more 'conventional' activities. However, one attempt has been made to provide a valuation of some natural habitat utilizations (those associated with trees and woodlands), namely Campbell et al

(1991a, 1991b), who tried two methods to elicit household valuations. The first assigned values to natural habitat utilizations on the basis of assumed consumption levels derived from the secondary literature, and used local market prices to convert quantities to values. The results of this exercise suggested that tree products and services have an annual imputed value of nearly Z$1,000 per household, a figure considerably higher than median cash income levels. The second study was methodologically more ambitious, in that it used a Contingent Valuation Methodology (CVM) to attempt a valuation of a broader set of utilizations than was covered in the first study (eg browse, shade, erosion control). While these second were (at reasonable discount rates) lower than those of the first study, it is likely that the CVM study underestimated the true willingness-to-pay of Communal Area households. However, whichever of the two studies is more accurate, the key point is that the value of natural habitat utilizations for just a subset of activities is of the same order of magnitude as that of income measured in conventional household surveys.

Conclusions

In conclusion, several points are noted. First, natural habitats offer services which generally have marketed substitutes: despite these substitutes' existence, though, households continue to depend heavily on natural habitats. Thus, this pattern of extensive natural habitat utilization is consistent with the picture presented earlier of highly-constrained Communal Area households, and in fact generalizes the pattern of choice seen in the agropastoral production function and fertilizer use. Second, natural habitat utilizations are important in almost all the major economic areas of the peasant household, viz. income, consumption, asset accumulation (housing; livestock), and agricultural production. Furthermore, studies show that they have a value to the household that is probably equal to the subset of activities that economists have traditionally focused on, such that their absence in past studies has rendered our knowledge of the type of peasant household featured in this paper flawed. Finally, the dependence of these rural households on environmental resources, and their inability to stabilize such dependence through financial or physical asset accumulation, implies that households' production and consumption levels are conditioned on the nature of the ecosystem in which they find themselves placed. It is these links that are explored next.

SAVANNA ECOLOGY AND PEASANT RESPONSES

Zimbabwe's Communal Areas are located in the savanna, and hence their ecology is best understood as a subsystem of savanna ecology. Generally speaking, while savannas are superficially highly diverse in terms of physical characteristics such as physiognomy, flora and fauna, it has increasingly been realized that they have a strong underlying regularity, principally relating to a division into two savanna biomes: the 'arid' savanna and the 'moist' savanna (Huntly 1982). As their names suggest, the key underlying determinant of savanna type is the level of rainfall. Arid savannas receive less than 650 mm rainfall pa, most of which falls in four summer months (with drought therefore frequent and severe), while moist savannas receive more than 650 mm annual rainfall. This primary distinction produces a host of secondary differentiations between the two biomes: for example, these biomes can be distinguished on the basis of floristic criteria, vegetation structure and faunal groups. With regard to Zimbabwe, it was seen above that the country has been classified into Natural Regions on the basis of rainfall level, precisely the primary determinant of the savanna.

However, there is an important secondary filter of savanna type, namely the availability of nutrients within soils. The availability of soil nutrients is obviously another key determinant of primary production (ie type and composition of herbage) in the savanna. As before, two broad soil types can be distinguished. The first are eutrophic soils, ie soils where there has been little leaching of important nutrients, so that the availability of calcium, magnesium, potassium and sodium is high. In contrast, the second are dystrophic, or highly leached soils, where nutrient availability is low. Again, this broad distinction has been widely applied to Zimbabwe, where there is a clear difference between the clayveld — soils with adequate nutrients — and the sandveld — soils which are nutrient poor.

While there is clearly some relationship between rainfall level and soil nutrients, in fact there is sufficient independence of the two variables that it is possible to think of savannas in terms of a 2x2 matrix defined by moisture and nutrient availability (Cumming and Bond 1991). Relating this to the Zimbabwean case study, for example, it is possible to locate the main woodland zones as shown in Table 11.4.

Table 11.4 Principal woodland zones

Soil Nutrient Availability		Low	High
	Low	Plateau grassland	Acacia savanna
		Sahelian desert	Mopane woodlands
Moisture Availability			
	High	Wet miombo	Valley/escarpment woodlands
			Dry miombo

Source: adapted from Frost et al (1986).

It is thus possible to classify the different ecological areas of the savanna, and hence also of Zimbabwe's Communal Areas, using rainfall levels and nutrient availabilities as the key stratifying variables. Most importantly, such a classification highlights two key characteristics of the local ecosystems in which Communal Area farmers find themselves located, characteristics which highly-constrained and resource-dependent peasants must respond to in their production strategies. These are the patchiness and extreme variability of savanna ecosystems. We discuss these attributes of the savanna in turn.

1. Each element in the savanna matrix — or 'patch' — offers the agropastoral household differing quantities and qualities of primary production for the various economic activities it is involved in (eg agricultural production, livestock maintenance, collection of wild foods, fuelwood collection and storage etc). For example, consider the availability of grass and browse for livestock in these different patches. In moist savannas, there will be a high and relatively stable level of primary production. However, if located on nutrient-poor soils, the herbage produced will be high in structural matter and low in nutrients, and is therefore of low value to herbivores. In contrast, arid savannas will have much lower levels of primary production, but if located on nutrient-rich soils, this herbage will be highly palatable, of great value to herbivores. Similar differentiations can be made by ecological niche for almost all the resource utilizations, with each patch offering a different vector of resource availabilities. Most important, though, is the fact that these different ecological zones are locally present in any given Communal Area, forming a 'small-scale vegetation mosaic' (Huntly 1982).

2. The characteristic of Communal Areas is their ecological variability. Savanna ecosystems generally are subject to high annual climatic variability (ie rainfall), as well as recurring shocks such as fire, drought and floods. Rainfall variability and such shocks are quickly reflected in changes in the amount of primary production (grass and trees): thus, savanna vegetation is characterized by sudden and unpredictable changes, leading also to explosions and crashes in the populations of dependent species (Caughley 1983). Despite this instability, though, savannas show impressive ecological resilience in that while a species' numbers might vary enormously, actual extinction is rare. Indeed — and this point will be important when discussing the issue of sustainability — it is argued by ecologists that such resilience is directly related to the flexibility of spatial, temporary and dietary niche brought about by the instability and diversity of savannas: not only have savanna components adapted to considerable and frequent disturbance by developing mechanisms which allow recovery from stress, but also they probably require such variability and shocks to maintain their resilience (Walker and Noy-Meir 1982).

These characteristics — patchiness and extreme variability — are the primary attributes of the environment in which Communal Area farmers find themselves located. How have peasants responded to these environmental characteristics? Given the agropastoral nature of Communal Area production, it seems clear that a major challenges facing peasants is the accumulation and maintenance of cattle (peasants' herbivores).[10] As it is the draft and manure functions of cattle that

---

10 Much of the following discussion of livestock management strategies is based on the studies of Sandford (1983) and Scoones (1990).

constitute their chief value, the farmers' main objective is to maximize over time the number of units of cattle available to the household (or agricultural unit). However, since farmers are in general too poor to purchase feedstuffs, a critical constraint facing agropastoralists is the highly variable quantity of fodder and browse (primary production) available to their cattle on an inter-annual basis. In this environment, as Sandford (1983) details, farmers can broadly adopt one of two stocking strategies: a conservative one, in which cattle numbers are kept consistent with the level of food available in natural habitats in drought years, or an opportunistic one, in which population levels are allowed to follow environmental fluctuations, implying cattle die-offs during droughts (or even other, less severe, low-rainfall periods). Each of these has its costs: the conservative, as environmental utilization by cattle is below its theoretical maximum for all but drought years; the opportunistic, as capital and labour invested in cattle in the period before a drought/low rainfall year has a very low return due to cattle deaths.

Communal Area farmers' desire to maximize cattle numbers means they adopt opportunistic stocking strategies, resulting in cattle build-ups during runs of good rain years, followed by drought-induced die-offs. This pattern was particularly clear in the 1980s and early 1990s, in which cattle numbers followed the pattern of drought and recovery. Thus, cattle numbers, which had reached 6.1 million by 1975, fell to 5.2 million following the 1981–4 drought, recovered to 6.5 million by 1989, and then collapsed to 4.3 million after the severe 1991/2 drought (Cumming and Bond 1991, Department of Veterinary Services pers comm). Many rangeland researchers have now charted and supported this opportunistic strategy as an economically optimal response to the instability of the savanna ecosystem surrounding Communal Area farmers (Sandford 1983, Abel and Blaikie 1990, Behnke and Scoones 1992).

However, in order to avoid purely reactive strategies to savanna variability (ie temporal heterogeneity of resources), and hence in order to minimize cattle die-offs, Communal Area farmers actively exploit, through livestock migration during herding, the patchiness of local ecosystems (ie spatial heterogeneity of resources). In particular, herders capitalize on the non-covariance between rainfall levels and the primary production of the clayveld and sandveld zones, following on from their differing nutrient status. This non-covariance can be substantial, both intra- and inter-annually. For example, Scoones (1989b) shows that the wet year grass standing crop on the clayveld is a multiple of that on the sandveld, whereas the reverse is the case in dry years. Further, his range production data demonstrates substantial within-zone variability of primary production, and also highlights the important role 'key resources' (ie vleis, drainage lines, river banks and contour ridges) play in both zones in producing high quality and/or reliable foodstuffs.

Thus, with patches offering differing resource opportunities at different times, maximizing cattle numbers involves migration across patches. Researchers have charted both local and regional migrations, depending on the severity of climatic stress. For example, intra-annual rainfall variation poses the problem of surviving the late dry season: in response, herders both migrate from local clayveld in the rainy season to local sandveld in the dry season and utilize heavily key resources (Scoones 1989b). During drought years, more ambitious migrations occur, with cattle moved up to 150 km from the homestead (Scoones 1989a). In general, the ability of herders to take advantage of the flexibility of dietary niches offered by local ecosystems, and their rights of access to these niches, is critical to the maintenance of livestock assets in the face of the rainfall variability noted above.

The focus thus far has been on the close relationship that exists between farmers' stocking strategies (opportunism and migration) and ecosystem properties. However, there are other ways as well in which the nature of the ecosystem and peasant strategies interact. For example, there is evidence that wild fruits — which suffer less during low rainfall periods than crops of the savanna — are used by households to smooth consumption. For example, Clarke (1983) found that one wild fruit alone (*Grewia flavescens*) comprised 25 per cent of the food items in the diet during the dry season after the 1981–82 drought, versus a much smaller proportion found by Campbell (1987) for wild fruit as a whole during better times. Furthermore, Campbell (1987) found fruit consumption predominated in the hot, dry season, which correlates well with shortages of cultivated foods but is out of phase with fruiting activity. However, it is not just wild fruits that have this role. During the severe 1991/92 drought, the price of wild meat actually fell, on account of the widespread adoption (despite its illegality) of hunting as a food-gathering and income-generating activity (Cavendish, forthcoming).

As a final example, the patchiness of soils is exploited and responded to by farmers in their agricultural activities. For example, Communal Area farmers understand the different nutrient characteristics of soils, and hence the differing value of fertilizers in those soils (Swift et al 1989, Scoones 1992). Indeed, fertilizer applications vary widely, depending on the soil type being treated, even when different soil types coexist in the same field (Cavendish forthcoming). Similarly, planting decisions are made in the light both of crop type and of soil characteristics, with the coexistence of patch types offering farmers an opportunity to spread production risk.

So far, then, the pervasive role that natural habitat resources play in farmers' lives has been established, and evidence has been presented linking particular strategies adopted to the underlying determinants of the Communal Areas' environment. Despite this, it is often asserted that peasants are both ignorant about environmental resources and poor managers of those resources. In the next section, the opposite is suggested: on account of their value, environmental resources are both understood by peasants, and managed in many different ways.

PEASANT KNOWLEDGE AND ENVIRONMENTAL MANAGEMENT

The issue of peasant knowledge of soils — especially the clayveld/sandveld distinction — has already been touched upon in the previous section. However, the full knowledge of farmers is much broader than this, with Scoones (1989b) claiming that farmer's environmental classification is dominated by soil differences (and according closely with ecological theory). Separate soils zones are clearly differentiated: not just sandveld and clayveld, but also red soils, sodic soils, rocky soils and so on, with each soil's properties (ie stability, nutrient status, water retention) known and understood. Furthermore, within this classification by soils, farmers distinguish separate habitats with reference *inter alia* to water movement, tree type and past use. For example, local woodlands are known by the prevalent tree type (eg *Colophospermum, Acacia, Julbernadia, Uapaca*); drainage pans, drainage lines, vleis and riverine areas are distinguished; separate categories are assigned to virgin land and abandoned fields (Wilson 1987).

Following the research embodied in Wilson (1987), there can be little doubt about the extensiveness of peasant knowledge of trees. This undoubtedly follows from the importance of trees and tree products in the household economy of Communal Area farmers. As Wilson writes:

> *People living in the rural areas start to learn about trees from a very early age... Knowing the trees [about seventy species] is seen as being a basic requisite of personhood... People not only learn to identify trees, but where they are found... This interest, and the many hours that people spend in the bush means that people develop a knowledge of tree ecology, and an acute awareness of the resource.*

Thus, the outstanding feature of peasant knowledge of such key resources as soils and trees is not its paucity, but its breadth. This knowledge and high resource values results in an array of resource management strategies in the Communal Areas, at both individual and community level. One well known strategy (noted earlier) has been the preservation of certain highly valued fruit trees during the process of woodland clearance, such that even in severely deforested areas, fruit trees are the last to be removed.[11] For example, Campbell (1987), working in Save, found that the availability of fruit was not statistically different between the most and the least forested parts of the study area. Selective cutting of the woodlands in his sample area meant that the three most frequently used fruit trees remained relatively constant in cover over the two different areas, while other, less highly valued species had disappeared in the deforested area. Similar results were found by Wilson (1989a). In this survey of trees left in fields, he found that all locally-valued fruit trees were found to be left in fields, and that in dioecious species, the non-fruiting sex had been removed from fields. Likewise, Gumbo et al (1990) reported in their survey of 24 villages that of all trees left in fields, 82 per cent were indigenous fruit trees. Most recently,

---

11 It might be felt that the preservation of individual trees is a trivial matter. However, it should be noted that even single trees can produce surprisingly large volumes of fruit and browse. For example, Malaisse et al (1975) report *Brachystegia spiciformis* producing 26.6 kgs dry weight of seeds and pods, and *Strychnos innocua* — a small tree — producing almost 10 kgs dry weight.

Grundy et al (1993) found that of 20 species left standing in newly-created fields, a majority were fruit trees, and this was the primary reason given by respondents for their selection. Fruit is not, however, the only reason respondents give for preserving trees. Trees in fields can also be preserved for spiritual reasons,[12] for leaf litter, for shade and (less frequently) for their positive impact on crops (Wilson 1989a, Matose 1992), though in many cases these uses overlap. Cavendish (forthcoming) finds that, for established fields, all surviving trees are claimed by respondents to have been deliberately preserved.

Another common — and more active — resource management strategy is the planting of trees by households in and around the homestead or garden (areas which are the closest to having unequivocally private resource rights). Much has been written about tree-planting in the Communal Areas of Zimbabwe (eg see Campbell et al 1993, Bradley and Dewees 1993), and the following summarizes recent writings. The profitability of tree planting in some cases rests on the multiple use that trees offer households. An example of this point is *Sclerocarya birrea* (*mupfura*): its fruit is eaten or used to make wine (*mukumbe*); its nuts are used either to make a local butter and cooking oil or are sold; its shade improves agriculture; its bark and leaves are used as medicines; and its wood is used for stools, drums, household implements and fuel (Gumbo et al 1991). However, other trees — especially exotic fruit trees — can be profitable even with the single use of fruit consumption, as establishment costs are low. Though there is little economic data in this area, Dewees (1992) shows that under reasonable assumptions, the rate of return on individual fruit trees is greater than 10 per cent.

As a result, tree planting is widespread. Among the different surveys in which tree planting practices have been examined, the per centages of households engaged in tree planting were 61 per cent in du Toit et al (1984), 70 per cent in Beijer Institute (1985), 74 per cent in Grundy et al (1993) and 88 to 97 per cent in Campbell et al (1991a). Thus, tree planting by peasant households is clearly a ubiquitous activity. The four main reasons for tree planting are fruit, shade, fencing and construction woods: with fruit the most important, the great majority of trees planted are fruit trees, whether indigenous or (more frequently) exotics. However, reasons for tree planting vary with woodland availability, such that in the more deforested areas, meeting household construction and fuelwood demands are more the prime motivations. Household members also devote considerable time and resources to managing planted trees, especially those around the homestead, with trees being watered, fertilized, mulched and protected from livestock. Finally, this widespread planting of trees has occurred by and large without encouragement from central government, which instead has concentrated on an ambitious but mostly inappropriate programme of rural afforestation via centralized nurseries

12 Certain species of trees are associated with rain-making rituals, with ceremonies for the dead, or with communication with a family's ancestral spirits. For a discussion see Bourdillon (1987) and Wilson (1987).

of eucalyptus seedlings. Tree planting, then, provides clear evidence of local people as responsible and dynamic resource managers.[13]

Preservation of trees in fields (rather than woodlands) and tree planting in homesteads represent individual resource management strategies over largely private resources. The situation with regard to the management of the communal grazing lands, from where most wood is obtained, is less clear. It is true that researchers have discovered many traditional resource management practices or rules. Some of these have already been noted: for example, the preservation of fruit trees in the woodlands or, with regard to fuelwood, the fact that acquisition occurs largely by gathering dead wood, or by using the wood left over from other uses (ie. construction, making handicrafts, fencing), thereby alleviating pressure on woodlands by avoiding unnecessary cutting. Another mechanism regulating tree cutting is the belief in the sacredness of certain trees (which are prohibited from being cut) and, more generally, the connection between trees and Shona culture. For example, Grundy (1990) reports respondents naming 18 species of tree as sacred in her research area, while Campbell et al (1991a) found that 64 per cent of their survey households stated that trees were important for the spiritual wellbeing of their households. In some areas, woodland blocks have been set aside (often around burial sites) where all tree cutting is forbidden (du Toit et al 1984). Finally, when tree cutting does take place, it should be spaced adequately (Grundy 1990).

Other communal rules concern specific resources. To regulate fruit use, and hence reduce damage to the tree of early or indiscriminate harvest, many wild fruits are allowed to be consumed by the individual, but not sold.[14] Communities also try to regulate hunting and fishing by restricting hunting periods, banning the killing of young animals, banning the use of (tree-derived) toxins in fishing, and banning post-drought fishing to allow stock recovery (Wilson 1989b, Cavendish, forthcoming). Harvesting techniques which minimize damage to resources also exist for rope from branches (Grundy et al 1993), for the wild vegetable *derere* and in particular for wild medicines, with bark taken from alternate sides of a tree, roots removed in small quantities and the remaining roots covered over, and overlap of plant collection areas avoided by harvesters (Campbell et al 1993).

However, many of these rules derive from a time of resource abundance. This situation is changing as a result of past government policy,[15] continued land clearance for agriculture, rising demands and a confusion

---

13 Another, more passive, individual tree management strategy is tree regrowth on contour ridges separating fields. McGregor (1991) suggests that this is a minimum-effort, effective way of establishing trees being used in more deforested areas. Once established, though, these resources can be quite intensively managed: Matose (1992), for example, records pruning of trees on contour ridges and other borders in order to improve pole production.
14 Wilson (1987) notes that for the highly popular fruit *mashuku* (*Uapaca kirkiana*), harvesting could be done only with one hand, critical comments about their sweetness could not be made, and picking was to be done in a reverential manner!
15 The way in which successive government reorganizations of Communal Area agriculture has contributed to woodland clearance is documented in Wilson (1987).

of authority over resource management in the rural areas.[16] With rising resource scarcities, many of the rules documented above are under pressure. Tree cutting for fuel is now more common; sacred trees are now cut; valuable large trees are being cut down completely; preserved woodland blocks are shrinking or disappearing; communities have failed to stop the commercialization of the wild fruit trade; hunting regulations are ignored; the stealing of wood resources has been documented; and the pressure of urban demand appears to have led to the diminution of traditional medicine-gathering practices (du Toit et al 1984, Wilson 1990, Campbell and Grundy 1991, Matose 1992, Campbell et al 1993).

In response, however, new resource management strategies are developing. First, communities themselves are instituting new rules concerning the use of valued resources. A common example of this is the institution of fines for illegal cutting of trees in the grazing areas and of a management systems whereby permission to cut must be sought from the headman or VIDCO (Wilson 1990, Fortmann and Nhira 1992, Cavendish, forthcoming). Second, resource privatization is occurring apace, particularly over resources in fields. Whereas in the past these were regarded as community resources, trees, tree products, grasses from contour ridges and other borders and other such resources are increasingly regarded as private property, and permission must be sought from the field 'owner' before using a resource. Resource privatization is also occurring through the creeping annexation of communal land and woodlands (Scoones and Wilson 1989). Finally, resource domestication has been observed, with Wilson (1989b) noting the domestication by women of three 'wild' vegetables that were important to diets.

In conclusion, this discussion of peasant knowledge and resource management does not pretend that a rural utopia exists. Problems in resource management exist and in some cases are serious. However, this section contradicts the common view of the ecologically-ignorant and environmentally degrading peasant. Instead, Zimbabwean Communal Area farmers emerge as aware of their surroundings and responding to various resource challenges. Another quote from Wilson (1987) neatly captures this view:

> ...the studies of deforestation were really an experience of how locals did not see the process as the simple, rather hopeless, march of population pressure. ... They saw it as a phenomenally complex pattern of distinct ecological processes with many different specific causal factors, and one that was weaving new, often unfortunate, patterns, but not a situation that should be abandoned. On the contrary, they have the technical ability to **manipulate** it.
> [emphasis as original]

---

16 The issue of problems of authority is critical, but too complex to be addressed within the space constraints of this chapter. An excellent discussion of these issues is found in Scoones and Matose (1993).

PEASANT ECONOMICS, GOVERNMENT POLICY, AND THE SUSTAINABILITY DEBATE

Following these analyses, the main points of the paper are now drawn out. First, it should be clear that standard economic analysis of these low-income rural households, which lacks both ecological awareness and appreciation of the extent of natural resource utilization, has ignored important sources of economic values and determinants of economic strategies. Natural habitats contribute to (and sometimes determine) household consumption, production, asset formation and management, and risk-spreading activities: most, indeed, of the areas that economic analysis of peasant households has sought to explore. Without an integration of economic and ecological analysis, then, a proper understanding both of peasant economics and environmental change is unlikely to emerge.

The second point concerns government environmental policy towards the Communal Areas. For a long time, government and technocrats have highlighted soil erosion as one of the main environmental problems of the Communal Areas. Before discussing policies concerning this problem, it is worth pointing out that the physical database concerning Communal Area soils is poor. Many sources have studied soil erosion and resulting soil nutrient losses (*inter alia* Elwell 1983, Elwell and Stocking 1988, Whitlow 1988, Whitlow and Campbell 1989), and the general consensus is that parts of the Communal Areas face serious erosion problems. Whitlow and Campbell (1989), for example, find that over 25 per cent of the Communal Areas are severely or very severely eroded, as against less than 2 per cent in Commercial Farming Areas. At times technocratic warnings about the incipient dangers of soil erosion have been apocalyptic: 'If soil erosion is not checked immediately by a dynamic policy based on reliable technical information, we will witness mass starvation within our lifetime' (Elwell 1983).

However, these studies all have methodological difficulties. Some are based on extrapolations from the Soil Loss Estimating Model for Southern Africa. Tests have shown, though, that such extrapolations overestimate the extent of erosion by at least a factor of two, and possibly up to a factor of 30 (Roberts and Lambert 1990). Other studies are based on aerial photographs: however, mapping from these to actual erosion is far from perfect and in general, extensive ground-truthing is a necessary component of such studies. No systematic study of this sort has been carried out in Zimbabwe. Finally, some studies have generalized from plot data, but these do not provide a reliable basis on which to draw broad conclusions. So, while erosion well may be a problem in some areas, the exact dimensions of the issue are unclear.

Despite this, a variety of policies have been enacted to tackle soil erosion. For soil erosion in fields, the government has concentrated since the 1930s on the construction and maintenance of contour ridges, and more recently has promoted tied ridging and shallow ploughing as anti-erosion measures. There is a debate as to the effectiveness of these measures (see Bradley and Dewees 1993). Here, however, the focus is on attempts to reduce erosion in the communal grazing lands. The government has argued for many years that the cause of soil erosion here is the overstocking of cattle, as this quote from the First Five-Year Development Plan (1986–90) demonstrates:

The most important aspect of livestock production which is occupying the mind of government is the accelerating and continuous deleterious effects of overstocking and overgrazing in the communal lands which are causing severe and potentially irreversible ecological degradation.

Cattle overstocking and overgrazing leads, it is argued, to the reduction of herbaceous cover, increasing the exposure of soils to rain and wind. This increased exposure results in the compaction of soils, an effect exacerbated by trampling by hooves: consequently, water infiltration is reduced, and soil run-off increases (Swift et al 1989). In order to judge the extent of overstocking, governments both before and after Independence have developed recommended per hectare stocking rates for livestock in the Communal Areas, stocking rates which they believe are consistent with an non-degraded environment. However, actual stocking rates have been persistently above these levels, often exceeding recommended rates by factors of two or three (Cumming and Bond 1991). In the government's view, this overstocking is due to the property rights system of the grazing lands, with open access leading to a classic 'tragedy of the commons' (Abel and Blaikie 1990).

In response, the government has periodically attempted to reduce cattle numbers, either through forcible destocking, or through incentives to send cattle for slaughter. This reduction has been attempted despite the critical importance of cattle to the agropastoral system, and hence the considerable welfare loss destocking inflicts on Communal Area farmers. However, the whole overstocking hypothesis, by which these actions are justified, is based on two fallacies. The first is economic. Recommended stocking rates for Communal Areas are derived from research carried out on Commercial Farming Areas (Scoones 1989a). But (beef-producing) commercial farms have quite singular economic objectives for cattle, namely the maximization of quality meat production. This requires well-fed cattle. As a result, for a given hectarage, such producers will choose to have a smaller number of cattle with a resultingly more abundant standing crop of grass. In contrast, cattle in the Communal Areas are multiple-use assets, and farmer objectives are to maximize cattle numbers. They will therefore choose, for a given hectarage, to have a higher number of less well-fed cattle, the reason for the much higher stocking rates of the Communal Areas. Further, as stocking rates for commercial farms are well within ecological carrying capacity, these higher stocking rates — well above official rates — can be maintained without inflicting irreversible ecological damage (Behnke and Scoones 1992).

The second fallacy is ecological. The 'stocking rates' argument depends on there being a stable function relating cattle numbers to grass cover, with the animal-plant interaction the chief determinant of both populations. However, this is at odds with savanna ecology, which stresses rainfall variability as the key determinant of primary productivity and therefore also of herbivore numbers. In this schema, scarcities in grass cover are caused by droughts, not grazing pressure: these droughts then cause reductions in livestock numbers, which reduces grazing pressure in subsequent years, allowing recovery of grazing lands and an eventual recovery in cattle numbers until the next drought intervenes. Livestock numbers and grass cover are not determined endogenously, but exogenously by rainfall levels: attempting to revive grassland through manipulating livestock numbers is thus misguided. Furthermore, in savanna systems marked by instabilities and unpredictabilities, sticking to a single stocking rate is an inappropriate management goal (Ellis and Swift 1988, Mentis et al 1989).

This view of Communal Area cattle numbers is borne out in the study by Scoones (1990) of 60 years of livestock data. This found that cattle numbers, following a run of good years, do come close to ecological carrying capacity, but that this is rarely attained due to the intervention of drought, which results in cattle die-offs. In general, the study confirmed that cattle numbers are determined by rainfall variability, thus undermining the ecological basis of the stocking rate policy. In conclusion, then, one can say that destocking policies, which reduce agricultural incomes and household assets, have been implemented as a result of an inadequate understanding of peasant economics, and a lack on the part of policy makers both of ecological knowledge and a comprehension of the interactions between peasant production and the environment.

This is not the only government policy about which the same conclusion could be reached. For example, in an attempt to improve the open access 'problem', the government has spent considerable time and resources trying to promote the formation of fenced grazing schemes in the Communal Areas. These schemes have largely failed, primarily because administrators were ignorant of the importance of spatial movements of livestock and the role of 'key resources' discussed earlier. Schemes were designed which failed to guarantee access by pastoralists to different ecological patches, and thereby, if implemented, would have undermined the livestock system rather than supporting it (Cousins 1992). As a result, these grazing management schemes were largely ignored or subverted if actually put into practice.

Similar issues arose in the World Bank-funded Rural Afforestation Project, which was an attempt to reverse the continuing clearance of woodlands in the Communal Areas. This project focused on the planting of the rapid-growing eucalyptus tree, with seedlings provided from 48 nurseries in 16 Communal Area districts. The basis of the project was the belief that the Communal Areas faced increasingly critical fuelwood shortages, and that such shortages were the cause of deforestation. Little research was done before the start of the project to test these propositions: however, as noted previously, the assumptions were largely incorrect.[17] Furthermore, the project made little progress in meeting other, more

---

17 Indeed, eucalyptus is widely regarded as an extremely poor fuelwood, although people are more enthusiastic about using eucalyptus poles for roofing.

critical wood demands; farmers' interest in and demand for indigenous trees were not addressed; and no attempt was made to set up viable institutions for the management of remaining woodlands (Bradley and McNamara 1993).

A final example of environmentally-suspect government policy is attempts to get farmers to destump the trees from their crop fields.[18] This policy has been promoted by successive governments since the 1930s. Pressure has been put on farmers to destump — despite the immense labour involved — both by extension agencies, and by making it a requirement for granting an individual the certificate of 'Master Farmer', possession of which brings considerable benefits (eg cheap inputs, free ploughing, extension advice). Little attention has been paid by the technocratic agencies to farmers' own justifications for leaving trees in fields, such as fruits, improved crops and woodland conservation, and indeed the preservation of such trees is an example of peasant conservation activity undertaken in spite of the direction of state policy.

This review of government policy thus suggests a direct parallel with the conclusions drawn earlier for the discipline of economics. Both have ignored the importance of environmental resources in the household economy, and the need to understand environmental dynamics for an adequate comprehension of rural strategies and behaviour. Further, in the case of government, policies aimed at improving environmental resources have sometimes undermined household welfare or have had little identifiable environmental benefit.

Finally, there is the question of sustainability. Underlying much work on environmental management is an attempt to analyse whether communities are using resources sustainably. Underlying this paper is the contention that, in the system analysed, little useful can be said on the subject. Three problems are paramount.

1. **Any analysis of sustainability must specify accurately what unsustainability (resource degradation) is.** It is clear from the discussion of savanna ecology that such a specification is absent and is in principle difficult to establish. Most applications of sustainability to renewable resources emphasize non-decreasing resource stocks as a key indicator. This is inappropriate for savanna ecosystems, which could be characterized as 'density-vague' (ie where dynamics are bounded but where the system shows little preference for individual values — the grass/livestock interaction is an example), and indeed where the resilience (sustainability) of the ecosystem is believed to be tied to the maintenance of continual shocks and hence stock variability. As a result, many researchers have warned about the difficulty of deriving any reliable indicators of environmental degradation in these types of ecosystems (Abel and Blaikie 1988, Scoones and Wilson 1989, Walker 1989, Cumming and Bond 1991, Behnke and Scoones 1992).

---

18 The material in this paragraph derives from Wilson (1989).

2. **As indicators of degradation are not forthcoming, statements concerning environmental degradation require careful scrutiny.** For example, in the Zimbabwe context it is often implicitly assumed that woodland clearance represents degradation: however, such clearance may actually raise the economic productivity of an area, by increasing browse and fuelwood availability (Scoones and Matose 1993) and by augmenting the population numbers of species (eg grazing mammals, certain insect species) which are valued in local diets (Wilson 1989b). Both these studies stress that there is no intrinsic reason to label the agro-ecological change they chart as 'degradation', despite such labelling by government and technocrats. Another example is given in Cavendish (forthcoming). In his research area, before the 1991/92 drought, cattle numbers were high and range condition was poor, leading to concerns about environmental degradation. Following the cattle die-off and reduction in grazing pressure, rangelands recovered dramatically, with a result that local informants were unable to remember a time of equivalent grass abundance. The conclusion is, then, that any evaluations of sustainability must be made within a framework that adequately integrates both the complexity of ecosystem relationships and the economic goals of resource managers. Such work is rare.

3. **Even if this framework was available, there is a paucity of reliable data on which to make defensible judgements about sustainability.** Data problems have already been discussed for soils: suffice it to point out that for similar reasons, equivalent difficulties exist in analysing both the extent of woodland cover and its rate of change (Bradley and Dewees 1993). In this context of data uncertainty, there are great dangers in making assumptions about environmental degradation and consequently implementing 'pro-environment' policies, as these policies can be irrelevant or at worst exacerbate the problem they were intended to solve.

For these three reasons, then, extreme care should be used both in making and judging claims of environmental sustainability.

REFERENCES

Abel, N O J and Blaikie, P M (1990) *Land degradation, stocking rates and conservation policy in the communal rangelands of Botswana and Zimbabwe* ODI Pastoral Development Network Paper no 29a, 23pp

Adams, J (1991) 'The rural labour market in Zimbabwe' *Development and Change* 22, pp 297–320

Anadu, P A, Elamah, P O and Oates, J F (1988) 'The bushmeat trade in South-Western Nigeria: a case study' *Human Ecology* 16(2), pp 199–208

Ashworth, V A (1990) *Agricultural technology and the communal farm sector* mimeo, World Bank, Washington DC

Asibey, E A O (1974) 'Wildlife as a source of protein in Africa south of the Sahara' *Biological Conservation* 6, pp 32–9

Behnke, R H and Scoones, I (1992) *Rethinking range ecology: implications for rangeland management in Africa* World Bank Environment Working Paper no 53, World Bank, Washington DC, 33pp

Beijer Institute (1985) *Policy options for energy and development in Zimbabwe* Zimbabwe Energy Accounting Project, Harare, 251pp

Bourdillon, M (1987) *The Shona peoples* Mambo Press, Gweru, 3rd edition, 357pp

Bradley, P N and Dewees, P (1993) 'Indigenous woodland, agricultural production and household economy in the Communal Areas' in P N Bradley, and J McNamara, (eds) *Living with trees: policies for forestry management in Zimbabwe* World Bank Technical Paper no 210, World Bank, Washington DC, pp 63–138

Bradley, P N and McNamara, K (1993) *Living with trees: policies for forestry management in Zimbabwe* World Bank Technical Paper no 210, World Bank, Washington DC, 329pp

Brandon (1987) 'The snack that crawls' *International Wildlife*, pp 16-21

Campbell, B M (1987) 'The use of wild fruit in Zimbabwe' *Economic Botany* 41, pp 375–85

Campbell, B M and Grundy, I (1991) *Tree and woodland resources – the technical practices of small-scale farmers* Working Paper, Forestry Commission of Zimbabwe, Harare, 93pp

Campbell, B M, Du Toit, R F and Attwell, C A M. (eds) (1989) *The Save study: relationships between the environment and basic needs satisfaction in the Save catchment, Zimbabwe* University of Zimbabwe, Harare, 119pp

Campbell, B M, Vermeulen, S J and Lynam, T (1991a) *The role and value of trees in the small-scale farming sector of Zimbabwe* mimeo, University of Zimbabwe, Harare, pp.41

Campbell, B M, Vermeulen, S J and Lynam, T (1991b) *Value of trees in the small-scale farming sector of Zimbabwe* IDRC-MR302e, International Development Research Centre, Ottawa

Campbell, B M, Clarke, J M and Gumbo, D J (1991c) 'Traditional agroforestry practices in Zimbabwe' *Agroforestry Systems* 14, 99-111

Campbell, B M, Grundy, I and Matose, F (1993) 'Tree and woodland resources – the technical practices of small-scale farmers' in P N Bradley, and K McNamara, (eds) *Living with trees: policies for forestry management in Zimbabwe*. World Bank Technical Paper no 210, World Bank, Washington DC, pp 29-62

Caughley, G (1983) 'Dynamics of large mammals and their relevance to culling' in R N Owen-Smith, (ed) *Management of large mammals in African conservation areas* Haum, Pretoria, pp 115–26

Cavendish, W P (forthcoming) PhD Thesis, University of Oxford, Oxford

Clarke, J M (1983) *A socio-ecological study of a rural community in the Northern Sebungwe* MSc Thesis, University of Zimbabwe, Harare

Conroy, A (1990) *Fertilizer use and distribution in Zimbabwe* mimeo, World Bank, Washington DC

Coudere, H and Marijse, S (1991) 'Rich and poor in Mutoko communal area' in N D Mutizwa-Mangiza and A J Helmsing (eds) *Rural development and planning in Zimbabwe* Avebury, Aldershot, pp 70–91

Central Statistical Office (1988) *The economy of households in Zimbabwe 1985: main preliminary results from the Income, Consumption and Expenditure Survey 1984/85* CSO, Harare, 27pp

Cousins, B (1992) *Managing communal rangeland in Zimbabwe: experiences and lessons* Commonwealth Secretariat, London, 154pp

Cumming, D H M and Bond, I (1991) *Animal production in southern Africa: present practice and opportunities for farmers in arid lands* Multispecies Animal Production Systems Project Paper no 22, World Wide Fund For Nature, Harare, 142pp

Deaton, A (1991) 'Savings and liquidity constraints' *Econometrica* 59 (5), pp 1221–248

Dercon, S (1992) *The role of assets in coping with household income fluctuations: some simulation results* mimeo, Centre for the Study of African Economies, University of Oxford, 57pp

Dewees, P A (1992) *Household economy, trees and woodland resources in Communal Areas of Zimbabwe* mimeo, Oxford Forestry Institute, University of Oxford, Oxford, 85pp

du Toit, R F, Campbell, B M, Haney, R A and Dore, D (1984) *Wood usage and tree planting in Zimbabwe's Communal Lands* Forestry Commission of Zimbabwe, Harare

Ellert, H (1984) *The material culture of Zimbabwe* Longman Zimbabwe, Harare, 133pp

Ellis, J E and Swift, D M (1988) 'Stability of African pastoral ecosystems: alternate paradigms and implications for development' *Journal of Range Management* 4, pp 450–59

Eltringham, S K (1984) *Wildlife resources and economic development* John Wiley and Sons, New York

Elwell, H A (1983) 'The degrading soil and water resources of the Communal Areas' *The Zimbabwe Science News* 17(9/10), pp 145–47

Elwell, H A and Stocking, M A (1988) 'Loss of soil nutrients by sheet erosion is a major hidden farming cost' *The Zimbabwe Science News* 22(7/8), pp 79–92

Frost, P G H, Menaut, J-C, Walker, B H, Medina, E, Solbrig, O T and Swift, M J (1986) *Reponses of savannas to stress and disturbance: a proposal for a collaborative programme of research* Biology International Special Issue 10, IUBS, Paris

Fortmann, L and Nhira, C (1992) *Local management of trees and woodland resources in Zimbabwe: a tenurial niche approach* OFI Occasional Working Paper, Oxford Forestry Institute, University of Oxford. 34pp

Gelfand, M, Mavi, S, Drummond, R B and Ndemera, B (1985) *The traditional medical practitioner in Zimbabwe* Mambo Press, Gweru, p.411

Gomez, M I (1988) 'A resource inventory of indigenous and traditional foods in Zimbabwe' *Zambezia* 15(i), pp 53–73

Grundy, I (1990) *The potential for management of the indigeno us woodland in Communal Farming Areas in Zimbabwe, with reference to the regeneration of Brachystegia spiciformis and Julbernadia globiflora* MSc Thesis, University of Zimbabwe

Grundy, I M, Campbell, B M, Balebereho, S, Cunliffe, R, Tafangenyasha, C, Fergusson, R and Parry, D (1993) 'Availability and use of trees in Mutanda Resettlement Area, Zimbabwe' *Forest Ecology and Management* 56, pp 243–66

Gumbo, D J, Mukamuri, B B, Muzondo, M I and Scoones, I C (1990) 'Indigenous and exotic fruit trees: why do people want to grow them?' in R T Prinsely (ed) *Agroforestry for sustainable production: economic implications* Commonwealth Science Council, London, pp.185–214

Huntly, B J (1982) 'Southern African savannas' in B J Huntly and B H Walker (eds) *Ecological studies 42: ecology of tropical savannas* Springer-Verlag, New York, pp 101–9

Ingram, J (1990) 'The role of trees in maintaining and improving soil productivity - a review of the literature' in R T Prinsely (ed) *Agroforestry for sustainable production: economic implications* Commonwealth Science Council, London, pp 243–304

Jackson, J C (1989) 'Exploring livestock incomes in Zimbabwe's Communal Lands' in Cousins, B (ed) *People, land and livestock* Centre for Applied Social Studies, University of Zimbabwe, Harare, pp 183–212

Jackson, J C and Collier, P (1991) 'Incomes, poverty and food security in the Communal Lands of Zimbabwe' in N D Mutizwa-Mangiza and A J Helmsing (eds) *Rural development and planning in Zimbabwe* Avebury, Aldershot, pp 21–69

MacGarry, B (1987) *Biomass resource assessment: measuring family fuelwood con-
sumption in Zimbabwe* Commonwealth Science Council Technical Publication
Series no 217, London, p 54
McGregor, J (1991) *Woodland resources: ecology, policy and ideology* unpublished
PhD thesis, Loughborough University of Techno logy, Loughborough
McIvor, C (1989) 'Traditional medicine in Zimbabwe' *The Courier* 115, pp 19–20
Malaisse, F, Freson, R, Goffinet, G and Malaisse-Mousset, M (1975) 'Litter fall
and breakdown in miombo' in F B Golley and E Medina (eds) *Ecological studies
11: tropical ecological systems* Springer-Verlag, New York, pp 137–152
Matose, F (1992) 'Villagers as woodland managers' in G D Pierce and P Shaw
(eds) *Forestry research in Zimbabwe* Forestry Commission of Zimbabwe, Harare
Martin, G H G (1983) 'Bushmeat in Nigeria as a natural resource with
environmental implications' *Environmental Conservation* 10, pp 125–32
McPherson, M A (1991) *Micro-and small-scale enterprises in Zimbabwe: results of a
country-wide survey* GEMINI Report no 25, Michigan State University, Michigan
Mehretu, A and Mudimu, G (1991) *Patterns in land utilization and cognitive
behaviour in resource stewardship in Communal Areas of Zimbabwe: toward a
comprehensive design for land use policy* Working Paper, Department of
Agricultural Economics and Extension, University of Zimbabwe, Harare
Mehretu, A and Mutambirwa, C (1992) 'Time and energy costs of distance in
rural life space of Zimbabwe: case study in the Chiduku Communal Area'
Social Science and Medicine 34(1), pp 17–24
Mentis, M T, Grossman, D, Hardy, M B, O'Connor, T G and O'Reagain, P J (1989)
'Paradigm shifts in South African range science, management and
administration' *South African Journal of Science* 85, pp 684–87
Ministry of Lands, Agriculture and Rural Resettlement (1990) *Farm management
data for Communal Area farm units 1988/89* Farm Management Research Section,
Economics and Markets Branch, Ministry of Lands, Agriculture and Rural
Resettlement, Harare, 85pp
Muchena, M (1989) 'The effect of ox-sharing arrangements on the supply and use
of draught animals in the Communal Areas on Zimbabwe – preliminary
findings' in B Cousins (ed) *People, land and livestock* Centre for Applied Social
Studies, University of Zimbabwe, Harare, pp 253–75
Murindagomo, F (1988) *Preliminary investigations into wildlife utilization and land
use in Angwa, mid-Zambezi valley* M Phil Thesis, Department of Agricultural
Economics and Extension, University of Zimbabwe, Harare
Parent, G and Thoen, D (1977) 'Food value of edible mushrooms from Upper
Shaba region' *Economic Botany* 31, pp 436–45
Roberts, N and Lambert, R (1990) 'Degradation of dambo soils and peasant
agriculture in Zimbabwe' in J Boardman, I Foster and J Dearing (eds) *Soil
erosion on agricultural land* John Wiley and Sons, Chichester
Sale, J B (1981) *The importance and values of wild plants and animals in Africa* IUCN,
Gland, Switzerland
Sandford, S (1982) *Livestock in the Communal Areas of Zimbabwe* ODI, London
Scoones, I (1989a) 'Economic and ecological carrying capacity – implications for
livestock development in the dryland Communal Areas of Zimabwe' Pastoral
Development Network Paper 27b, Overseas Development Institute, London,
26pp
Scoones, I (1989b) 'Patch use by cattle in a dryland environment: farmer know-
ledge and ecological theory' in B Cousins (ed) *People, land and livestock* Centre
for Applied Social Studies, University of Zimbabwe, Harare, pp 277–309
Scoones, I (1990) *Livestock populations and the household economy: a case study from
southern Zimbabwe* PhD Thesis, University of London
Scoones, I (1992) 'The economic value of livestock in the Communal Areas of

southern Zimbabwe' *Agricultural Systems* 39, pp 339–59

Scoones, I and Wilson, K (1989) 'Households, lineage groups and ecological dynamics: issues for livestock research and development in Zimbabwe's Communal Lands' in B Cousins (ed) *People, land and livestock* Centre for Applied Social Studies, University of Zimbabwe, Harare, pp 17–123

Scoones, I and Matose, F (1993) 'Local woodland management: constraints and opportunities for sustainable resource use' in P N Bradley and K McNamara (eds) *Living with trees: policies for forestry management in Zimbabwe* World Bank Technical Paper no 210, World Bank, Washington DC pp 157–98

Swift, M J, Frost, P G H, Campbell, B M, Hatton, J C and Wilson, K B (1989) 'Nitrogen cycling in farming systems derived from savanna: perspectives and challenges' in M Clarholm and L Bergström (eds) *Ecology of arable lands* Kluwer Academic Publishers, pp 63–76

de Vos, A (1978) 'Game as food' *Unasylva* 29

Walker, B H (1989) 'Diversity and stability in ecosystem conservation' in D Western and M Pearl (eds) *Conservation for the twenty-first century* Oxford University Press, Oxford, pp .121–130

Whitlow, J R (1980) 'Agricultural potential in Zimbabwe – a factorized survey' *Zimbabwe Agriculture Journal* 77(3), pp 97–106

Whitlow, J R (1982) 'Marginality and remoteness in Zimbabwe – some factors influencing development potential' *Zimbabwe Agriculture Journal* 77(3), pp 97–106

Whitlow, J R (1988) *Land degradation in Zimbabwe* University of Zimbabwe, Harare

Whitlow, R and Campbell, B (1989) 'Factors influencing soil erosion in Zimbabwe: a statistical analysis' *Journal of Environmental Analysis* 29(1), pp 17–29

Wilson, K B (1987) *Research on trees in the Mazvihwa and surrounding areas* report prepared for ENDA, Zimbabwe, 69pp

Wilson, K B (1989a) 'Trees in fields in southern Zimbabwe' *Journal of Southern African Studies* 15(2), pp 369–83

Wilson, K B (1989b) *The ecology of wild resource use for food by rural Southern Africans: why it remains so important* mimeo, University College, London, pp.23

Wilson, K B (1990) *Ecological dynamics and human welfare: a case study of population, health and nutrition in southern Zimbabwe* unpublished PhD Thesis, University of London, London

World Bank (1991) *Zimbabwe: agricultural sector memorandum, vols. I-III* report no 9429-ZIM, World Bank, Washington DC, 263pp

Chapter Twelve

Development after Ecology

Bob Sutcliffe

It was during the period roughly between the first Indian Five Year Plan and the first oil shock that the time came for the idea that the whole world, including the poorer countries, should be developed. The great majority of those in governments, international organizations, universities and the media who became specialists in the field agreed that the journey to development for the economically backward countries involved following in the path of the more advanced ones until they caught up. It was assumed also that the majority of the people of the poorer countries had (or would acquire) needs and wants which were consistent with this end.

THE GREAT DEVELOPMENT DEBATE

Debates About the Vehicle...

The specialists disagreed frequently and vigorously among themselves about the best mode of transport or vehicle to use for the trip: planning or the market, protectionist or openness to the world economy and to trade and investment, using labour or capital intensive technology, giving priority to agriculture or industry; through balanced or unbalanced growth. The central issue in these major vehicular disputes was about what was to be the relative role of the state as an agent of development. What were seen as the successes of Soviet planning and Keynesian management encouraged those who saw the state as important, though the proponents of the free market as an agent of development were never lacking. A bold economist's simplification of these disputes is to say that they boiled down to the correctness of two key prices, that of foreign exchange and that of labour.[1] A common argument was that labour tended to be overvalued and foreign exchange undervalued by the wage and the exchange rate respectively; and this was judged to justify state

---

1 This simplification was suggested in a recent review by Albert Fishlow (1991).

intervention, labour intensity and protectionism.

Few of the participants in these debates doubted that the journey would take not-yet-developed countries past the same landmarks as the earlier travellers: increased saving and investment, higher material productivity, industrialization and the decline of agricultural employment, urbanization, the use of modern technology and eventually high mass consumption. Some thought that the stages[2] of the journey were clearly marked; for others, progress on all these fronts would be more intertwined. For some the journey would be gradual; for others progress would depend on a big push, a critical minimum effort, and an investment programme for balanced (or for unbalanced) growth. Acceleration metaphors abounded.

The development journey was seen as a limitless sum game and, in a phrase suggested by Albert Hirschman as a touchstone, could bring 'mutual benefit'[3] to all countries, developed and developing. Sometimes implicitly, sometimes explicitly, the acceptors of mutual benefit assumed that development could and would take place in basically capitalist economies, even though some of them advocated a very high level of state activity and intervention. Not all of them excluded the possibility that the journey could even be made under socialism, but they did not see it as necessary. Often development policies were recommended regardless of the social and political system.[4] A catching up (or modernizing) perspective dominated the vast development 'industry' which grew up during the years after 1950 and which included national aid agencies in the developed countries, national ministries of planning and development in the underdeveloped countries, and a vast array of international institutions nominally dedicated to the fomentation of development. But, as time went by, such a multitude of writers, administrators, politicians and institutions naturally engendered an opposition.

...and the Route

It is often difficult to say where one debate ends and another begins. But during the 1960s, coinciding with a revival of critical social thinking in general in the West, a new deeper level of difference began to appear in development debates. Differences about exchange rates, protectionism, the price of labour, the need for state investment and so on had all been, to begin with, about policies within an assumed socio-economic system. Increasingly they shaded over into a deeper difference about the relationship between development and the socio-economic system itself.[5]

The key difference in this more basic debate was over the question of

---

2 Classically, the influential W W Rostow with his five stages of economic growth (Rostow 1960).
3 This is the vocabulary used by Albert Hirschman in his famous and important article on 'The rise and decline of development economics' (Hirschman 1981).
4 Rostow, for instance, accepted with little comment that China was passing through its 'take-off'.
5 These two dimensions of debate are well caught in the analysis by Hirschman (1981).

mutual benefit. For some, the development of poorer countries was in no way contradictory to the interests of the developed ones: a rising tide would raise all boats. Others, however, denied the possibility of this mutual benefit. They believed that the development road map was either out-of-date or falsified. They thought that the developed countries had destroyed behind them the (capitalist) road by which they travelled to their development so that it was no longer passable. Some of them said that major reforms to the world economy (a New International Economic Order) might still enable them to travel the road. But many, including myself, agreed with Andre Gunder Frank that the underdeveloped countries had been made underdeveloped by the success of the developed ones;[6] so, since they were not starting from the same point, they could hardly travel the same road. Meanwhile, the continuing under-development of the 'South' was complementary to the continuing development of the countries of the 'North'. For sceptics about mutual benefit economic relations between developed and underdeveloped countries were seen as necessarily unequal,[7] so they tended to see development of the underdeveloped countries as requiring some degree of disconnection[8] from the world (economic) system[9] headed by the developed countries and from the social system (capitalism) which dominated it.

This collection of ideas, all of which reject mutual benefit in one way or another has been given many names: world systems theory, dependency theory, neo-Marxism, structuralism and many more. For some purposes it would be useful to give very precise definitions of these terms and theories and to draw fine distinctions between them; but for my purpose, as for others (Frank 1992), they can be bundled together and seen as a broad church with different detailed ideas but a common thread in the rejection of mutual benefit and of development as a possibility by way of the capitalist road and integration in the world economy.

Those who held these ideas, however, still thought that the under-developed countries could reach development, but by a different route. If the capitalist road was blocked or inaccessible they would have to build a

---

6 Andre Gunder Frank first used underdevelopment in this sense, not as a state but as a historical process, in his seminal article 'The development of underdevelopment' (Frank 1966).

7 Among the most important ideas about inequality was the idea of a secular adverse shift in the underdeveloped countries' terms of trade, developed by Raúl Prebisch, Hans Singer and others (Love 1980). Those who held these ideas did not necessarily deny mutual benefit but they provided important ideas and analysis for some of those who did. Paul Baran, however, a pioneer of the rejection of mutual benefit, dismissed the deterioration of the terms of trade as a non-phenomenon since the figures on which it was based were simply the distorted transfer prices of international corporations (Baran 1962). And later Baran and Paul Sweezy in various publications laid much more stress on the pumping out of the surplus in the form of profits by foreign corporations than on trade problems. Arghiri Emmanuel later developed a sophisticated and much debated theory of unequal exchange using Marxist theoretical categories (Emmanuel 1972).

8 The theme of the disconnection is present in many writers but has been most explicitly developed by Samir Amin (1988).

9 The 'world-system' vocabulary has been developed by Immanuel Wallerstein (1979) and his followers.

new socialist highway to development, but they could all get there in the end. So, to the differences about the vehicle (the policy mix) were added more profound differences about the route (the social system).

Here there were additional differences: over the kind of socialist system necessary to produce development, over what political changes were necessary to bring it about, over whether one country could attain socialist development in isolation, and, if not, over how many would need to adopt socialist systems for a really viable alternative to exist, and over whether development of the poorer countries was thinkable without socialism in the developed countries as well. There were, then, various alternative routes envisaged.

The debate about the social system, unlike earlier disputes over development policies, spread out far beyond the development specialists and was reflected at many levels in world politics. If we call the two sides in the debate the acceptors and rejectors of mutual benefit, then it is not an oversimplification to say that just about everybody (except left wing extremists) who pondered about the question in the developed countries were acceptors. And just about everybody (except fairly right wing people) who thought about the question in the underdeveloped countries became rejectors.

The different theories were points of reference in social and international conflicts. Governments who professed themselves acceptors of mutual benefit mined the harbours of, or refused to buy the products of, or financed opposition movements of, or plotted the assassination of leaders of countries ruled by governments rejecting it.

After 1973, however, the clean lines of this debate became more wavy. A third group (called the Warrenites, after their founder) were also left wing but seemed to agree with the acceptors of mutual benefit (Warren 1980). They dismissed what the rejectionists called the socialist road as a nationalist blind alley. For the Warrenites socialism was not a road to development but something attainable only when approaching the destination. Like most of the acceptors of mutual benefit they believed that the capitalist road remained open. Their arrival on the scene produced a slightly different debate which more or less petered out since some Warrenites accepted the seriousness of impediments on the old capitalist road and some rejectionists began to argue that some countries could travel along part of the road to produce 'dependent development' (Cardoso and Faletto 1979 and Evans 1979), or that some countries attained intermediate positions between the developed and the underdeveloped (the semi-periphery) (Wallerstein 1979). Many people concluded that the positions of the initially opposed sides in the debate thus eventually tended to converge (Sklair 1988, Leys 1986, Slater 1987).

But all in all it certainly had been a great debate. It polarized the discussions of development for a generation. Political leaders and intellectuals concentrated their actions and thoughts within the space defined by the debate. And there seems, even today, no doubt that the debate was about really important and still vital issues. But I will return to that later.

Tacit Accords

Today the echoes of that great debate have become fainter. What became of it? Why did it recede? Part of the answer is that the world threw up facts and problems which seemed important but which could not be easily explained or answered by either side in the great debate. The growth of the NICs seemingly violated the expectations of the rejectionists and helped to throw their paradigm into crisis. And the accumulation of development disasters, especially in Africa, along with the reverses associated with the debt crisis and worsening terms of trade seemed to confound the optimism of the proponents of mutual benefit. But, with the benefit of hindsight, we can also see that there was another reason that the debate receded: although at the time it had seemed to be based on profound disagreement, there was much more common ground than appeared. In debates, things on which both sides agree don't seem to be important at the time and so are ignored. Yet they may in the end turn out to be more significant than the matters which are debated. And so, in my view, it proved with the great development debate.

What was it that all the sides agreed on? First, there was an idea of what development would be like. It was, roughly speaking, thought to be similar to the situation which existed in the developed countries, which of course is why they were so called. Development was a place on the conceptual map somewhere between the United States, Western Europe and Japan. These countries might not be perfect but no one questioned most aspects of their (especially economic) characteristics: industrialization, the use of modern, highly productive technology, high levels of employment of productive workers working with machines for about eight hours a day, high average standards of living, efficiency, punctuality, longevity, the elimination of most deaths from infectious diseases... the familiar list can be long.

The second shared idea was that there was a close or even automatic connection between these economic aspects of development (especially rising production and productivity) and the meeting of basic needs and human welfare. Some held that development would after a time automatically equalize benefits, others believed that the state might have to intervene, still others thought that the best that the poor could expect was what trickled down from the rich. But all believed that national material riches (development) would or could result in greater human welfare.[10] In other words, they believed that development was desirable.

The third issue they all seemed to agree on was that the idea of development applied first and foremost to countries or nations. That is why the characteristics of development already listed refer basically to the

---

10 Of his own important contributions to thinking on development Andre Gunder Frank has recently written '..although I turned orthodoxy on its head, I maintained the essence of the thesis that economic growth through capital accumulation equals development. Thereby, the socialist and dependence heterodoxies were caught in the same trap as development orthodoxy, and any real alternative definitions, policy and praxis of "development" were precluded' (Frank 1992:136).

structure of national economies. It also explains why the predominant attitude to human welfare was that it was a sub-product of national development.

The fourth clause of the tacit accords was that, if there were obstacles to the universalization of development, then these were social, economic and political (domestic or international) but not natural. It seldom occurred to any participant in the great debate that universal development to European/Japanese/United States levels might not be materially possible. If everyone had some conception (sometimes implicit) of the relation between development and welfare almost no one thought about the connection between development and the physical environment.

The fifth clause is closely related to the fourth. Universal development was implicitly expected to produce an equalization between countries. This would be through a levelling up. So equalization did not imply redistribution (ie those at the top being brought down so that those at the bottom could gain). The famous aid target of 0.7 per cent of GNP was the most daring redistribution that anyone proposed. And the rejectors of mutual benefit in general saw deliberate redistribution through aid as a fraud or a poisoned chalice.

The sixth accord was that development was seen as a permanent state. There was a kind of socio-economic ratchet and countries were not expected to revert to underdevelopment once development had been attained.

Not everyone who was interested in development and under-development thought that the great debate over mutual benefit was the most important one. Some people didn't hold the six shared assumptions and so tried to launch different debates. But for a long time they were regarded as fairly marginal to the real issues; the time for their ideas was still to come.[11]

DOUBTS ABOUT THE DESTINATION AND THE VALIDITY OF THE MAP

The great debate receded because events and research exposed the dubious nature of these shared opinions. It was not that the problem of route, the fundamental issue in the great debate, was resolved or disappeared; but rather that, as the journey proceeded, problems of destination (the subject of the tacit accords) which previously seemed trivial began to appear ever more problematic.

Despite repeated efforts to move along the old road or to locate the new one, and even make some apparent progress, an unexpectedly large proportion of the population continued to suffer from extreme material and cultural deprivations. The assumption that the pursuit and even the attainment of a measure of development would increase human welfare seemed ever more shaky. On the one hand empirical data which

---

11 Among these can be placed ideas about the basic needs approach to development (Streeten 1979), urban bias (Lipton 1977), intermediate or appropriate technology (Stewart 1978 and various publications of the Intermediate Technology Development Group), and male bias in development economics (Elson 1991).

emphasized the persistence and even growth of poverty, hunger and disease: positive rates of growth of income coincided with worsening distribution; the statistics for Africa and South Asia lagged obstinately behind those for the successes of East Asia, those for women behind men, those for rural areas behind urban; in Asia the green revolution increased food production but did not reduce hunger to the same extent; in Africa the 1970s saw a return to major famines; the success of eliminating smallpox and the spread of child vaccination was followed by the chilling threat of AIDS. On the other hand there was a growing mobilization of groups demanding the fulfilment of their basic needs and rights which they saw as either not met by development or actually threatened by it. Such groups included women, indigenous movements, people threatened with forced removal from their land because of the arrival of commercial agriculture or the building of dams, and many others. As long as development was regarded as progressive it was assumed that people on the whole would want it. But when increasing numbers of people made it clear that they did not want it, it began to seem less evidently progressive.[12] The map, so it appeared to many, gave a false idea of the nature of the terrain in the region of development.

In addition, ideas from various sources converged to fortify the increasingly critical approach to actually existing development. To a re-examination of fundamentals among disillusioned, or at least disappointed, development specialists[13] were added:

- the criticism by the so-called new social movements of materially defined modernizing goals;
- the progress made by philosophers in defining such concepts as rights and justice (Rawls 1972);
- new approaches to history which emphasized the experience of the victims of previous experiences of development;[14]
- some economists' critique of the pursuit of economic growth;[15]
- the analysis by anthropologists of the culturally destructive aspects of modernizing development (Hobart 1993 and Marglin and Marglin 1990);
- and a growing tendency to question the values of modernism and its assumptions of linear progress and to equate these values in many cases with Eurocentrism (Tucker 1992).

So a new debate began to take shape: not so much about how to attain a known goal of development but rather about whether development as

---

12 For a discussion of a well known example of this, see Sen 1990.
13 A series of articles by Dudley Seers were an important part of this (Seers 1977 and Seers 1979).
14 A particularly important influence here has been E P Thompson (especially Thompson 1969) as well as the work of Raphael Samuel and other writers in the *History Workshop Journal*.
15 The pioneer in this was Tibor Skitovsky in a recently republished book (Skitovsky 1992). E J Mishan (1969) was also influential, though its ambiguous political and moral stance is illustrated by the fact that its latest edition (1993) lists gay bars (which I take to be a move towards human liberation) alongside drugs and other social evils as part of the costs of growth.

hitherto conceived was a worthwhile destination. What, by analogy with debates about socialism, we might call actually existing development[16] was a destination which to many looked less and less desirable. Many development specialists began to advocate the attainment of basic human needs as a primary rather than secondary objective (Streeten 1981 and Stewart 1985); others searched for a more appropriate technology;[17] others concentrated more on the problem of the poverty of individuals and groups rather than the underdevelopment of nations.[18] The common feature of these approaches was an attempt to see development in terms of what happens to *people* rather than to abstractions like nations. One of the best summaries of this approach can be found in a recent comment by two of the key contributors to it. The important questions to ask in assessing development, they say, are:

> *Do [people] have the capacity to live long? Can they avoid mortality during infancy and childhood? Do they avoid illiteracy? Are they free from hunger and undernourishment? Do they enjoy personal liberty and freedom?*
>
> *These are the basic features of well-being which derive from looking at people as the centre of all development activity. Enhancing their capabilities to function in these elementary ways is what lies at the core of human development. The achievements of people be it in terms of long life or functional literacy are valued as ends in themselves. This should be contrasted with more mainstream economic approaches which discuss human resource development. Here the focus is on human beings as a resource an input into production activities. The development of human resources is seen in terms of their contribution to income generation as an investment, like any other, in enhancing the productive potential.*
>
> (Anand and Sen 1993)

It is in this context that the environment makes its first appearance. An important facet of this many-sided destinational critique of development arose out of the sudden growth in awareness of the effect of human activities on the environment and the resulting impact on the conditions of human existence. Development produces pollution of many kinds and this means that any benefits of development can be partly or wholly offset by worse conditions of life. Many of these disadvantages (air and water quality, for instance) were only too obvious; others (like the health effects

---

16 Rudolf Bahro (1978) and many others used the phrase 'actually existing socialism' to refer to the now collapsed socio-economic system of eastern Europe. It holds open the possibility that there might be some other form of socialism which does not yet exist.
17 Fritz Schumacher (1973) was a crucial influence here. See also Stewart (1985).
18 A pioneering work here was Lipton (1977). Much recent feminist writing on development concentrates on the particular causes of women's poverty or the non-fulfilment of their needs.

of asbestos, electric fields, nuclear power, noise, diet) were revealed by scientific research. In this sense growing ecological awareness was no more than one more strand in the critique of the desirability of the previously unquestioned development destination.

Environmental consciousness and research, however, also gave rise to a different concern which often appears to transcend the others, not because it is intrinsically more important but because it portends happenings which would make the other debates redundant. In the early 1970s many people began to foretell the imminent exhaustion of the material resources on which development had been based (Meadows and others 1972); later came the predictions of climatic and other changes resulting from actually existing development which would at best shortly inflict profound changes on the physical conditions of human life and might at worst rapidly make it impossible, through the overuse of resources or the overproduction of wastes. Here the concern is not merely that development has undesirable side-effects on human life but rather that it, and in particular its generalization, might make human life impossible.

The influence of environmental questions in the development debate is new. Until very recently authoritative texts on development appeared which made no reference to it.[19] And, once incorporated into the debate, it produced very varying reactions regarding its practical and methodological importance. Even for those who regard environmental questions as important in development there are some who see them as factors which must be taken account of within a basically unchanged, if slightly more complicated, methodology (for example, Mikesell 1992 and Pierce, Barbier and Markandya 1990) and others who see them as demanding a drastic methodological change.[20] Some see the environmental problem as confirming the need for rapid economic growth (World Bank 1992) while others see it as demanding a cessation of growth and a radical reorganization of human social life (Daly 1991, Trainer 1985 and 1989).

Thus the great debate about the route to development, which displaced debates about the appropriate vehicle, has itself been to a great extent displaced by two different ones about, respectively, the desirability and the possibility of the previously posited destination. From now on I will refer to these as being about the welfare critique and the environmental critique. The welfare critique asks if a destination of development different from the one normally posited would not be better. The environmental critique questions whether the normally posited destination actually exists if it is pursued by all. In other words it argues that the current state of the world, or at least the state towards which it is heading, is materially unsustainable.

---

19 For instance, there is still no reference to the environment in Chenery and Srinivasan 1988-89, nor in Ranis and Schultz 1989); and only a very brief mention in Stern 1989. And the first World Bank *World Development Report* to really dicuss it was that of 1992, produced to coincide with the Rio Conference.
20 For instance, the work of Daly (1991) who is influenced by the ideas of Georgescu-Roegen (1971).

So, we might say that the welfare critique is about destination and the environmental critique is more about the validity of the map. It is in these areas that we now find the most challenging and original contributions to the discussion of development and the future of poor countries, at least at the intellectual but partly at the political level too.

COMMON FEATURES OF EXISTING DEVELOPMENT CRITIQUES

These two critiques of actually existing development (the welfare critique and the environmental critique) have a number of important features in common. In the first place, both of them, in different ways, see actually existing development as a partly contradictory process. The proponents of the welfare critique question the assumed positive relation between development and welfare and even suggest that actually existing development may produce negative consequences for human welfare and thus be undesirable.

The environmental critique embodies an even sharper notion of the contradictory nature of actually existing development. It sees the possibility or probability that such development will undermine its own material base and so become impossible to maintain. So, a phenomenon whose global generalization was previously regarded, almost axiomatically, as both desirable and possible is seen as neither: attempting to produce something regarded as good produces something else which is to a significant extent bad and which progressively destroys the chance of producing anything at all.

The second common feature of the welfare and environmental critiques, largely a by-product of the first, is their rejection of the most commonly used indicators of development, especially the national product (GNP) or national income. As a measure of welfare or development this concept has received so many criticisms during its history that it is really surprising that it continues to be economists' most successful export to the rest of the world. Nonetheless, national income and national product continue to be the most commonly employed economic statistics: a remarkable violation of the economists' principle of the virtues of the market!

The proponents of the welfare critique point out two drawbacks to using the well known measures of national income or product as indicators of economic welfare. First, they assign equal value to a dollar's worth of production of arms or untruthful advertising on the one hand as to a dollar's worth of medicines or literature on the other. This means that there is a relative undervaluation of those activities which contribute to human welfare. Second, they value a dollar of income of a millionaire on a par with a dollar of income of a poor person when the latter is obviously 'worth' more.

The proponents of the environmental critique also make two main criticisms of the calculation of the national income or product. The first refers to its way of dealing with pollution and its ill effects. Nothing is subtracted from the figure for national income to take into account the 'negative externalities' of pollution. (Hence, assuming these are greater than positive externalities, the national income is overestimated). Even more absurd, if action is taken to rectify the bad effects of pollution (for example, expenditure on cleaning up a river polluted by industrial waste) such expenditures appear as positive in the national income figures. In other words it is possible for the *cost* of contamination to appear as a *benefit* in the national income, not only once but in some cases twice!

The second criticism refers to the conversion of the national income or product figures from 'gross' value to 'net' value in order to take into account the part of the capital stock which is used up in the production process; but the capital considered here is only capital created by human investment and, wrongly, does not include the natural resources used up (see Daly 1988). These criticisms, like those from the side of the welfare critique, lead to the conclusion that the national income or product figures tend to overvalue enormously what is really 'produced' by human economies and what is really 'earned' by their participants.

The two critiques coincide on a third point. Both reject the idea, one of the main characteristics of earlier development thinking, that development is a process in which the 'underdeveloped' progressively approach the state of the 'developed'. This coincidence leads to a fourth: both see development not so much as a problem of some countries (underdeveloped ones) which the developed countries have overcome but rather as a problem for the world. The environmental critique emphasizes global interdependence, while the welfare critique draws attention to deficiencies in meeting needs in both rich and poor countries.

A fifth point which the critiques have in common is their concern with distribution and equity — between rich and poor, both within and between nations (welfare) and between present and future, or between generations (environmental), a point to which I will return later.

Finally the critiques share a sixth characteristic that they are not at all new. Every one of the arguments mentioned up to now was present in economic debates more than a century ago.[21] The modern critique of development is as much a revivalist as an original phenomenon.

There is a parallel between the beginning of the great debate about mutual benefit and these new development debates which has aided their impact. Rejectors of mutual benefit argued that the previous debates about development policy were all but irrelevant if they took place in the context of an unequal global socio-economic environment which prevented development. Those who advocated major social change as a necessary preliminary to development, therefore, seemed to be positing something more basic as the main discussion. Economic policy debates seemed trivial in comparison with the choice between capitalism and socialism. Now, similarly, both the welfare and the environmental critiques of develop-

---

21 As, for the ecological arguments, Juan Martinez Alier has shown us in his magnificent work in the archaeology of ideas (Martinez Alier 1987). An equivalent history of the welfare critique does not, as far as I know, exist. Amartya Sen, however, has written some of it (Sen 1990). He traces it back to Aristotle and Kant; and in the realm of social theory to Adam Smith and the early Marx. A full history would have to include the thinking of two centuries of welfare and social reformers, novelists, poets and playwrights in countries which have experienced development.

ment appear to define a problem which is in some way logically prior to the question of the socio-economic system. If humans do not benefit from it, and if it is materially impossible, it hardly seems to matter under what social system generalized development takes place. If such a line of thinking helps to explain the present interest in these issues, they are not, as I shall reassert later, soluble in isolation from the question of the socio-economic and political system.

DIFFERENCES BETWEEN THE WELFARE CRITIQUE AND THE ENVIRONMENTAL CRITIQUE

Although the two critiques overlap and share many arguments against actually existing development it is important to insist that they are different from each other, both conceptually and in terms of the problems they identify and the remedies to which they point. Theoretically it is possible to imagine a process which reduces or even eliminates the environmental damage of human activity but which does not advance the welfare of the deprived. There is an important current of opinion in ecological thinking which argues that too much concern with human welfare is 'soft' while ecological rationality requires hard unsentimental decisions.[22]

Equally, it is possible theoretically to imagine meeting current human needs more widely yet doing so in a way which is not at all sustainable and which may even add to existing environmental damage. The two critiques have discovered not one but *two* things wrong with actually existing development.

This difference is closely related to, if not identical with, a difference suggested by Ekins and Jacobs in their chapter in this book. They use three concepts to clarify the relationships involved: throughput (physical use of resources), GDP (the value of output) and welfare. The ecological critique of development is concerned with the relationship between throughput and GDP; the welfare critique with the relationship between GDP and welfare.

Since both these separate critiques point to the need for important changes in human activity, it seems important to look at the ways in which the changes they demand can be integrated, and to see the conditions under which they are consistent and inconsistent with each other.

Once again oversimplifying grossly, I will call the kind of changes advocated by those who have been most concerned with the welfare critique 'human development', and that advocated by those who have emphasized the environmental critique 'sustainable development'. These terms have their dangers in that they have recently come to be used positively by people of such a wide range of different and conflicting persuasions and interests that it is not possible that all of them mean the same thing by using these terms.

22 For instance, Garret Harding (1992) argues for rigid controls against immigration to the US (as has the pioneer US environmentalist group The Sierra Club) and against spending large sums on intensive care of new-born babies with serious health problems.

The terms also have the disadvantage that they are both enshrined in and closely associated with different prestigious international reports. These reports use the terms with a very concrete definition which is not necessarily an ideal one.[23] The two concepts of human and sustainable development have for the most part arisen separately and from different preoccupations, movements, writers and organizations. There is, therefore, no reason to think that they will necessarily coincide or even be entirely consistent with each other. Reports, books and articles devoted to one often neglect the other. When the ideas are presented jointly it usually reflects the good intentions of the author rather than analytical equality and unity. Sometimes, however, it does mean that a combined positive reponse to the problems suggested by both critiques is being defined, as in the case of Ekins and Jacobs' 'strong sustainability' (see Ekins and Jacobs, Chapter 2).

I do not want to enter in detail here into the problem of defining human and sustainable development. But I believe that, despite the problems mentioned, the terms are useful shorthands for two distinct sets of ideas which need to be unified. In general terms 'human development' can be taken to mean a process of social and economic change whose main motive is to produce a radical improvement in the material and cultural standard of living (or perhaps capability[24]) of people now suffering deprivation and which judges the utility of other aspects of development (production, technology and so on) by the criterion of their contribution to this improvement. This is the reverse of the traditional idea that welfare is a by-product or necessary result of economic development; needed economic development should be justified by its contribution to welfare.[25]

In similar terms, 'sustainable development' can be defined as changes in human material activities which radically lessen the depletion of non-renewable and not easily renewable resources and the harmful pollution of the environment, which thus radically lengthen the time over which human material needs can be met.

If there is no logical reason why these two things should coincide and yet both of them seem self-evidently desirable, it seems a logical next step to try to combine them and see the conditions which will aid and impede their common achievement.

A FUSION: SUSTAINABLE HUMAN DEVELOPMENT

The combination of these two critical concepts of development and some of their consequences may be pictured more easily by means of a simple

---

23 I refer, of course, to the Brundtland Report (World Commission on Environment and Development 1987) and the Human Development Report (United Nations Development Programme 1990-1993). For a critique of these see, respectively, Martinez Alier 1992 and Sutcliffe 1993b.

24 This refers to the important discussion of the nature of human development by A K Sen who is persuasively anxious to find a definition which emphasizes the means, freedom and capability to achieve cultural and material improvement rather than one which regards such improvement as embodied in certain concrete improvements (Sen 1990).

25 I owe this way of expressing it to Koldo Unceta of the Universidad del País Vasco.

visual model (Figure 12.1). Imagine a space which contains all possible human activities randomly distributed in a state of chaos. As a first step towards organizing this, imagine that activities are divided into those which do and those which do not contribute to human welfare. If we go further and arrange these according to some quantity of welfare which they add or subtract, then we can produce a vertical axis, which in principle measures welfare and can be called the *welfare* or *human development axis*. As a further step we can go back to the initial chaos and perform a parallel exercise using the criterion not of welfare but of the positive or negative effects of an activity on the environment. This gives us the *horizontal environment* or *sustainability axis*.

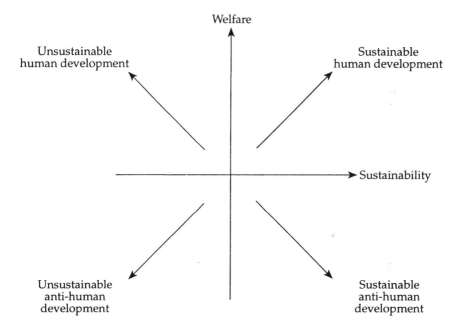

Figure 12.1 *Sustainable human development*

Figure 12.1 combines the two axes to produce a categorization of possible human activities into four types. In the SW quadrant are those activities which have negative impacts both on welfare and the environment; in the NW are activities which contribute to welfare but damage the environment; in the SE are those which improve the environment but at the cost of lower human welfare; and finally the NE quadrant contains those doubly blessed activities which have positive effects on both criteria.

Assuming that the axes are measurable, each human activity can in principle be located on this chart. The collection of activities in which human beings collectively engage today would be an area on the chart (or a point representing their average impact on welfare and the environment) as would be another set of potential activities which would be more in tune with the needs of sustainable human development. Any change of activities can be described as a direction of movement on the chart.

For the collection of human activities to correspond more closely than now to sustainable human development the desirable direction of movement is towards the North East. Actual movements may be the net result of numerous changes, each of which may go in a different direction on the chart. If more welfare for one deprived group inevitably also involves more pollution or the use of non-renewable resources (a NW movement) then for it to be consistent with sustainable human development there must be other compensating movements whose net effect is to produce change in a SE direction (lower welfare for others and measures to repair the environment). Many discussions about global environmental change have a frightening tendency to conclude that it is moving in terms of this chart towards the South West.

This model could only become more than a heuristic device to communicate concepts, relationships and stimulate debate if it were possible to quantify the axes in an operational way. Although I do not share all of the pessimism of some writers on the creation of complex indices which are meaningful (Jacobs 1991), I acknowledge that at present it is probably better to try to judge reality through many indicators rather than bundling them up into one. Exercises in the production of indices, however — such as a recent one to produce an index of sustainable welfare for the US in which each assumption is clearly explained so that, even if the final index is hard to interpret, at least it is clear what has gone into it — have produced interesting results which, if nothing else, may have some polemical value (Daly 1989 and Daly and Cobb 1990).

The model or map also suggests a four-way categorization of the appropriate fate of existing activities in a future pattern of sustainable human development:

1. activities which produce welfare in environmentally benign ways (NE quadrant) should be *maintained*, as should activities which produce necessary welfare by environmentally damaging means (NW quadrant) but for which no other method of production yet exists;
2. activities necessary to produce an adequate level of welfare for deprived people (some of which might necessarily be in the NW quadrant), also new, environmentally friendly, welfare-creating activities in the NE quadrant and perhaps some environmental repair measures in the SE quadrant should be *initiated*; such activities might even include some which have in the past been abandoned but which now can be seen to have positive effects according to both criteria (for instance, forms of public transport and diet discarded in favour of the cars and beef);
3. activities which produce no welfare and damage the environment (SE quadrant) should be *suppressed*, as should those NW quadrant whose welfare contribution is low or which could be carried out in other less damaging ways. The task of identifying activities which reduce welfare is often said to be too subjective to be possible; almost certainly, however, many activities would be condemned on these criteria with virtual unanimity;

4. finally many activities should be *transformed* (almost entirely in the NW quadrant) so that their positive welfare contribution is not lost but they are carried out with less environmental damage; the role of new or neglected environmentally friendly technologies will be important in many of these cases.

The initial letters of this categorization spell MIST (rather the opposite of the effect intended). A clearer location of activities on this map and the application of the MIST principles are an exercise in Utopianism which is necessary if the sum total of human activities is to become simultaneously more productive of human welfare and less unsustainable. To carry out this exercise only in theory, however, is to have a kind of technocratic, experts' environmentalism. For principles to be translated into practice implies that people, communities and societies get results when they try to act on the principles. That outcome will surely require a radical redistribution both of economic and political power.

THE IMPORTANCE OF REDISTRIBUTION

Defined as they have been here, both critical concepts (human and sustainable development) involve an improvement in the relative access to resources of excluded groups: the poor in the case of human development; future generations (and perhaps other species) in the case of sustainable development. Human development without attention to sustainability improves distribution in the present at the cost of worsening the distribution between present and future (the unborn subsidize the poor). At the same time sustainability without human development means maintaining the material levels of the over-endowed and reducing the levels of the poor, thus worsening distribution in the present (the poor subsidize the unborn and the rich).

There is a way out of this ugly contradiction: redistribution in the present. If the negative environmental impact of human activity, for which the rich of today are primarily responsible, is mitigated then any given improvement in the situation of the poor becomes more sustainable. To put the same point in another way: if negative environmental impacts are reduced then it will be more difficult to implement human development unless the rich (nations, classes and individuals) of today accept a disproportionate decline in their use of resources and production of wastes.

The conflict between the poor of today and the unborn exists to the extent that a real reduction in the negative environmental impact of the rich of today is not contemplated. Thus, human development is in danger of being unsustainable unless there is redistribution; and sustainable development is in danger of being anti-human unless it is accompanied by redistribution.

Looked at in this way, the two concepts of development and the two forms of redistribution which they imply are seen to be mutually reinforcing. Present and future justice demands that they be pursued simultaneously. They entail different (but not necessarily contradictory) kinds of changes. But they have one major common implication: to pursue both together demands a considerable reduction in the use of resources and production of pollutants by the people, classes and nations which are now rich and over-endowed. It is the same people at the same time who are wastefully using the resources needed both by today's deprived and by the unborn. If the waste continues then either human development or sustainable development or both will not be possible, or at the very least will be more difficult.

The general desire for development, about which such disillusion has been generated, should then be replaced by one not for human development nor sustainable development alone but for sustainable human development in which both kinds of redistribution are effected. Large scale redistribution of the use of resources in the world seems to be a necessary condition for sustainable human development.

The historical moment when increasing numbers of people are reaching such conclusions has, ironically, coincided with a period of triumph for the ideology of the free market which tends to produce contrary effects. The recent ascendency of free market ideologies is perversely associated with the rise of environmentalist and welfare concerns. The 'all power to the free market' faction in the old debates about the route to development has held together because they argue that the new questions really make no difference. Since for them free capitalist enterprise maximizes growth and income, and that people on the whole in a market system get what they want, questions about the persistence of deprivation or the environmental depletion and pollution are not bothersome. This convenient aspect of their doctrines is certainly not the only reason for their remarkable spread during the 1980s; but, given the disarray and confusion which the new debates produced among their former opponents, it probably made a contribution.[26]

Related to the neo-liberal counter-revolution is a growing disillusion with mechanisms of redistribution in the world. The amount of international aid, except from a few countries, and for purposes which benefit the economy of the donor, is in decline. Welfare state measures which were established, and which really redistributed income when countries were poorer then they are now, are, by some wonderland logic, threatened because, now that those countries are richer, it is said that they can no longer afford them. There has been little sign of major

---

26 Of course, even the most hard-core free market dogmatists have had to pay lip service to the problems of deprivation and the environment. But their reactions have been to strengthen and sophisticate their argument that the traditional goals, pursued by free-market means, is the best way of solving the problem. The World Bank's *World Development Report* of 1992 (*Development and the environment*), despite its increasing concern for the problems, takes the line that more actually existing development, along with market reforms is the best way of solving them. Larry Summers' (then chief economist) notorious leaked memorandum arguing (even if it was with a touch of irony) that poor countries were under-polluted and that only richer people choose less pollution was another instance of a similar argument. It should be recognized, however, that there is a difference of principle between the use of market incentives as part of a policy of environmental improvement (for instance, for pollution control) and the idea that the problems would not exist under complete laissez faire.

redistribution of income between countries. During the two decades from 1970 to 1989, according to Gini coefficients, overall world inequality either remained the same or worsened, depending on the method of conversion used.[27] According to all methods, East Asia increased its share of the world's product faster than its share of the population while Africa's share of population increased while its share of world product decreased as did its absolute level of income per head. There is evidence of a major redistribution towards the rich in a number of developed countries (in Britain the post-tax personal income of the richest 20 per cent of the population has doubled as a multiple of that of the poorest 20 per cent since 1979 (Sandford 1993 quoting HM Treasury)) as well as in some underdeveloped ones, especially in Latin America (World Bank 1993). In the absence of major political change, therefore, we must at present acknowledge that the times are not very propitious for the major redistribution necessary as a concomitant of sustainable human development.

It is, of course, very difficult to quantify the amounts by which pollution and resource depletion need to fall and so the degree of redistribution which is necessary. But in some areas research which enables us to make more reliable calculations is accumulating rapidly. The enormous data base on carbon emissions produced by the Carbon Dioxide Information Analysis Center in the United States has been widely used to spell out the dimensions of the problem. Figure 12.2 presents relatively well known figures for CO_2 emissions per head for various developed and under-developed countries. Some climatologists have argued that to stabilize CO_2 concentrations in the atmosphere it will be necessary to reduce the average level of per head emissions to about the current level of India in this graph. If such an aim is deemed to be necessary then the trans-formation in the lifestyles of rich countries (and in the way in which poor countries try to change theirs) will be profound, for many people, perhaps, unthinkably so.

Such data as these have had the effect of presenting in a very dramatic way the scale of the task and also the relative division of current responsibility for the problem. If it is the moral duty of the polluter to change then such figures as these can perform an important political role in weakening the bargaining power of the great polluters. The battle over international redistribution will be in part a battle over indicators and their interpretation (Agarwal and Narain 1991 and World Resources Institute 1992).

---

27 The value of the Gini coefficient for world distribution of GDP based on country totals changed as follows:

Basis of conversion (number of countries)	1970	1980	1989
Market exchange rate (178)	0.669	0.679	0.729
Purchasing power parity (117)	0.554	0.562	0.564
Price adjusted exchange rate (178)	0.697	0.694	0.695

Source: United Nations (1993), p 20, Table 2.

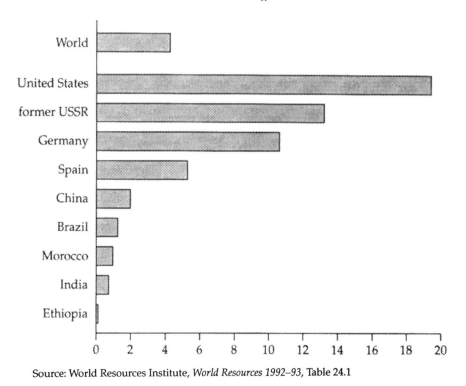

Source: World Resources Institute, *World Resources 1992–93*, Table 24.1

Figure 12.2 *Production of CO_2 from industrial sources, 1990*

Rescuing the Baby

If inequality and how to end it are questions central to the achievement of sustainable human development, we must go beyond defining concepts and attempt to give them concrete meaning. We must look to the causes of the persistence of inequalities. That surely means that we must go back to the debates about development which the new concerns have partially ousted. The rejectors of 'mutual benefit' analysed the obstacles on the route to development. Although the debates about destination have questioned their concept of development, the same or related obstacles also stand in the way on the road to sustainable human development; many of the arguments of the rejectors of mutual benefit are still valid in relation to redefined objectives.

An essential part of most rejectionist analyses of the world was that various mechanisms in the world economy produced a systematic transfer of value from poor countries to rich countries (through unequal exchange and the false invoicing of exports and imports by multinational companies, the repatriation of profits, the service of the debt and so on). In so far as this transfer of value exists (and each item has provoked controversy) it constitutes a perverse redistribution of income which can only worsen the conditions for achieving sustained human development. Regardless of one's assessment of the overall argument there is no doubt that the transfer of resources from poor to rich has on some counts risen in recent years. The two most notable items here are the enormous service of the debt since the early 1980s (Sutcliffe 1993a) and the sharp adverse movement in the terms of trade of primary products since the mid-1970s (Maizels 1992).

These events can only have had negative environmental impacts in the poorer countries. Not only do they drain resources which can in principle be used for constructive purposes, including environmental improvement, but they also tend to produce a race to acquire foreign exchange either to pay debt service or to compensate for declining export earnings. This race can lead to the development of new environmentally unsound activities such as the production of some commercial agricultural export crops or overfelling of tropical forests for timber exports; and they may discourage necessary protective investments (Cruz and Repetto 1992). They also lead to a desperate desire to reduce costs and to become more competitive which among other things may encourage a lax (cheap) environmental protection regime.[28] And they have probably led to overexploitation of some non-renewable resources resulting in the excessive rundown of reserves and lower prices which might disguise situations of shortage (Bunker and O'Hearn 1992). This is an argument against those economists who argue that price signals will control any tendency towards the excessive depletion of non-renewable resources.

Integral to some rejectionist accounts of the world has been the notion of unequal exchange through which, it is argued, rich developed countries have in the long run received imports from poor countries at prices below their values. Hardly ever has this argument taken into account the considerations now commonly raised by ecological economists that the extraction of non-renewable resources has always taken place at a cost far below its real cost since the natural stock of the material is not valued. In this sense the ecological argument vastly strengthens the argument for the existence of unequal exchange since poor countries have for centuries depleted their non-renewable resources, largely for export to the developed countries, and in so doing have literally given away a part of their patrimony (Martinez Alier 1987).

Thus ecological arguments strengthen some aspects of the rejectionist (or, if you like, dependency theory) analysis of the world; and at least important parts of this analysis remain, therefore, a necessary foundation for understanding the obstacles to sustainable human development. If development needs to be redefined, then so equally does underdevelopment. We are now witnessing a rapid accumulation of writings which in effect demonstrate how environmental and welfare deterioration have been and are in many cases the consequences of inequalities in the international distribution of wealth and power. The development of underdevelopment has also been the development of unsustainability.[29] Hence the new debate should not be

---

28 Popular organizations and journalists have reported this as a particularly severe consequence of *maquiladora* factories on the Mexican side of the Mexican border. See, for example, Tomshoe 1992.
29 Jong-il You suggests in Chapter 9 that even the most quoted example of sucessful development of the last few decades has brought a heavy environmental cost.

allowed to displace completely the old one. In the rush to reexamine dependency theory and criticize some of its undoubted limitations, the baby of rejectionism should not be thrown out with the bathwater of actual existing development.

WHERE IN THE WORLD IS DEVELOPMENT?

I have argued that the tacit accords with which development was approached have been shattered by the persistence of extreme mass privation in an ever more developed world and by growing evidence of the environmental destructiveness of actually existing development. Out of a response to these two contradictions of the process a different concept of sustainable human development is being constructed which suggests directions of change which are radically different from the directions suggested by more traditional concepts of development.

The old map of development is now difficult to use when choosing the direction in which to proceed. Some of the environmentalist critiques of actually existing development imply that it is difficult to know exactly where we are on the map, concretely how close we are to an ecological precipice. If the starting point is in part indefinable, the destination is also in many ways mysterious. But we can say that a more rational concept of development directed towards equalizing welfare and sustainablility will be radically different from every one of the five shared assumptions of the tacit accords mentioned earlier.

1. The present nature of the developed countries is not an appropriate destination. Their level of resource use and the volume of contamination which they produce are the main generators of the global environmental crisis. Despite their prodigal use of resources they are unable to meet the human needs of large sections of their populations. The globalization of the characteristics of developed countries would surely make the planet uninhabitable.

   In terms of the level of the use of resources per head a destination appropriate for the whole world must be much closer to the existing situation in most underdeveloped countries than in developed ones. As a way of illustrating this point Figure 12.3 compares the durability of various natural resources assuming that the world consumes them at the actual rate per head – of the United States, of the world and of China. The dates are not to be taken seriously since they are based on present estimates of reserves which may change for many reasons. But what is to be taken seriously is the striking difference, shown implicitly, between present levels of consumption in the US and in China (countries chosen to represent the developed and underdeveloped world respectively, and because they have comparable statistical coverage).

   Current underdeveloped country levels of consumption, if generalized, would evidently be dramatically more sustainable that those of developed countries. There are other respects, too, in which underdeveloped countries often, if by no means always, offer a better

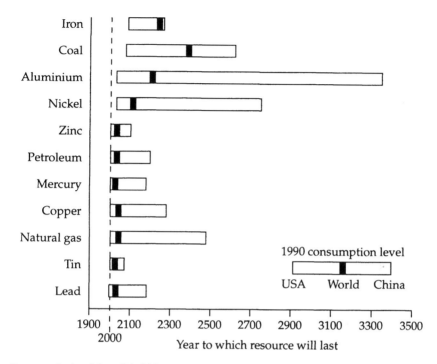

Source: calculated from World Resources Institute, *World Resources 1992–93*, Tables 10.2, 21.5

Figure 12.3 *Hypothetical life of known reserves of raw materials, 1990 based on alternative rates of consumption*

model than developed ones: for instance, the persistence in some places of more sustainable forms of agricultural production[30] and healthier vegetable-based diets which are less costly in resources; there are some examples where common rights are better maintained; and others where mechanisms of social solidarity and redistribution are more intact.

Actually existing development has been so far from sustainable human development that such a destination is likely to be at least as distant from the present location of the developed countries as from the underdeveloped ones. Development in this sense is something which has not yet occurred anywhere and which is, therefore, a valid objective in both developed and underdeveloped countries.

2. The traditional concept of development tended to assume that welfare would be a by-product. This becomes less convincing by the day. Improving human welfare on a permanent and secure basis seems to demand that it is clearly defined and is made into a primary objective of development, again in both developed and underdeveloped countries. Economic and productive change then becomes a by-product of the pursuit of welfare improvement.

---

30 World Resources Institute 1992, p 36, for a summary of various studies which reach this conclusion.

3. The new critiques of development undermine in various ways the idea that the appropriate unit of development is a country or nation. In so far as development is the fulfilment of social need it has many appropriate units: the individual, the family, the village, the city, the social group identified by ethnic origin, sex, sexuality, age and so on. While it is appropriate that the government of states assume important tasks in promoting human development, neither the power of the state nor the average material level within a country are appropriate indicators of development. Sustainability also imposes duties on national governments but it also points to other needed levels of analysis. The notion of sustainability can be applied locally, globally and anywhere in between (Jacobs 1991:96–8). Perhaps the most resolute decisions in approaching sustainability need to be taken globally; some actions of a single nation state may be pointless unless they are part of general enforceable international agreements. And the same applies to local in relation to national decisions (discussed by both Sen and Cavendish elsewhere in this volume). Sustainability, to make sense, requires action and change at all these levels together.

4. The old development debate assumed that in some way or other universal development according to the old model was possible. It now seems clear that it is not. The implication of this is that as long as the developed countries maintain their unglobalizable way of life they will in both open and hidden ways prevent development elsewhere.

5. The fifth shared assumption of the debate must therefore be abandoned along with the fourth: that equalization of development levels could occur without a major reduction in the resources used by the rich and developed. If sustainability makes it clear that such a redistribution must take place, the abandonment of the second shared assumption suggests that to reduce resource use and pollution is not necessarily to reduce the level of fulfilment of welfare, though it may involve reduced material production and reduced GDP (see the chapters by Ekins and Jacobs and Glyn).

Even in the absence of such a redistribution, it still makes sense for the people of underdeveloped countries to try to construct forms of sustainable human development. They can at least make gains in relation to welfare and local sustainability. But they can hardly be expected to make material sacrifices in order to contribute to global sustainability when this is continually undermined by the ways of life of part of the population of the rich developed countries.

WHO WANTS DEVELOPMENT? THE PROBLEM OF THE DRIVER

The extreme degrees of material inequality which exist in the world today, both between and within nations, is both a strength and weakness of the quest for sustainable human development. It is a strength because it means that there is scope for a considerable amount of redistribution of resources, as a result of which simultaneously a very small minority lose part of what they have, the deprived majority may have more of what they need, and the overall amount of resources used may be reduced, thus allowing more for the use of future generations. The weakness is that it is the very same minority which monopolizes most of the political and military power and the economic wealth which it uses to maintain its share.

There seems no sign that this minority, any more than any other in history, will voluntarily relinquish its privileges. So it seems impossible to imagine that the world can go far towards sustainable human development without destroying the power and removing the wealth of this minority. Sustainable human development is thus a task demanding radical mass political action. If we think of vehicles and routes, of maps and destinations we are in danger of reducing the problem of development to a technocratic one. While it is important to know the relationship between actuality and objective possibility, in other words to have a sense of destination, there remain the questions of the vehicle and the route (the appropriate socio-economic systems and policies) and perhaps above all the question of the driver (how a development process is managed and directed politically). These questions are closely related. The idea of human development logically requires popular participation, democracy, equity and justice both as part of the destination and part of the conditions for the journey. In other words development is not just the destination; it is also the process of reaching it.

If that is clear for the human part of sustainable human development it may also be true in a different way for the sustainable part. Part of the cause of unsustainability is the exclusion of the majority from taking a full and informed part in decisions about economic activities. The environmental knowledge of people who live and produce in very 'underdeveloped conditions' and their ability to live in a complex symbiosis with the environment is often very remarkable and contrasts with the ignorance and hostility to the environment often produced by development.

The political basis of the concept of sustainable human development which I have tried to outline in this chapter must appear to be a surrealistic alliance between those who are excluded from the benefits of actually existing development: unborn generations and the living poor and disposessed. But surreal does not necessarily mean illogical. The only hope for a radical redistribution towards the future is a radical redistribution away from the rich in the present. If greater equality in the present is one of the traditional concerns of red politics, greater equality between generations is an essential characteristic of the new green politics. But not all reds are yet green; nor do all greens look as if they will become reds. The future of sustainable human development depends on a more thorough mixing of colours.

REFERENCES

Agarwal, Anil and Narain. S (1991) *Global Warming in an Unequal World: a case study of environmental colonialism* Centre for Science and Environment, Delhi
Amin, S (1988) *La desconexión* Iepala, Madrid

Anand, S and Sen, A (1993) 'Human development index: methodology and measurement' background paper for UNDP, New York

Bahro, R (1978) *The alternative in eastern Europe* New Left Books, London

Baran, P (1962) *The political economy of growth* Monthly Review Press, New York

Bunker, S G and O'Hearn, D (1992) *Raw materials access strategies – US and Japan* draft, University of Wisconsin

Cardoso, F H and Faletto, E (1979) *Development and dependence in Latin America* University of California Press, Berkeley

Chenery, H and Srinivasan, T N (1988–9) *Handbook of development economics* North Holland, Amsterdam

Cruz, W and Repetto, R (1992) *Structural adjustment and sustainable development in the Philippines* World Resources Institute, New York

Daly, H E (1988) 'On sustainable development and national accounts' in D Collard, D Pearce and D Ulph (eds) *Economics, Growth and Sustainable Environments: essays in memory of Richard Lecomber* Macmillan, London pp 41–56

Daly, H E. (1989) 'Toward a measure of sustainable social net product index' in Y J Ahmad et al *Environmental Accounting for Sustainable Development*, The World Bank, Washington DC

Daly, H E (1991) *Steady-state economics* (2nd ed) Island Press, Washington DC

Daly, H E. and Cobb, J W (1990) *For the Common Good* Green Print, London

Elson, D (ed) (1991) *Male bias in the development process* Manchester University Press, Manchester

Emmanuel, A (1972) *Unequal Exchange: a study in the imperialism of trade* New Left Books, London

Evans, P (1979) *Dependent Development* Princeton University Press, Princeton

Fishlow, A (1991) Review of *Handbook of development economics* (ed H Chenery and T N Srinivasan), *Journal of Economic Literature*, vol XXIX (December), pp 1728–37

Frank, A G (1966) 'The development of underdevelopment' *Monthly Review*, Sept pp 17–30

Frank, A G (1992) 'Latin American development theories revisited: a participant review' *Latin American Perspectives*, issue 73, vol 19 no 2, Spring

Georgescu-Roegen, N (1971) *The entropy law and the economic process* Harvard University Press, Cambridge MA

Hardin, G (1993) *Living within limits: ecology, economics and population taboos* Oxford University Press, New York and Oxford

Hirschman, A O (1981) 'The rise and decline of development economics' in *Essays in Trespassing: economics to politics and beyond*, Cambridge University Press, Cambridge

Hobart, M (ed) (1993) *An anthropological critique of development: the growth of ignorance* Routledge, London and New York

Jacobs, M (1991) *The Green Economy* Pluto Press, London

Leys, C (1986) 'Conflict and convergence in development theory' in W J Mommsen and J Osterhammel (eds) *Imperialism and after: continuities and discontinuities*, Allen and Unwin, London

Lipton, M (1977) *Why poor people stay poor: a study of urban bias in world development* Temple Smith, London

Love, J (1980) 'Raúl Prebisch and the origins of the doctrine of unequal exchange' *Latin American Research Review*, 15, November

Maizels, A (1992) *Commodities in Crisis* Oxford University Press, Oxford

Marglin, F A and Marglin, S A (1990) *Dominating Knowledge: development, culture and resistance* WIDER Studies in Development Economics, Clarendon Press, Oxford

Martinez Alier, J (1987a) 'Economía y ecología: cuestiones fundamentales' *Pensamiento Iberoamericano*, 12, Jul-Dec, pp 41–60

Martinez Alier, J (1987b) *Ecological Economics: energy, environment and society* Basil Blackwell. Oxford

Martinez Alier, J (1992) 'Ecología y pobreza; una crítica al informe Brundtland' in I Senillosa (ed) *Pobreza, desarrollo y medio ambiente* Deriva Editorial, Barcelona pp 35–60

Meadows, D H et al (1972) *Limits to growth*, Universe Books, New York

Mikesell, R (1992) *Economic development and the environment: a comparison of sustainable development with conventional development economics* Mansell, London and New York

Mishan, E J (1969) *The costs of economic growth* Penguin Books, Harmondsworth

Pearce, D Barbier, E and Markandya, A (1990) *Sustainable development: economics and the environment in the Third World* Edward Elgar, London

Ranis, G and Schultz, T P (1989) *The state of development economics* Blackwell, Oxford

Rawls, J (1972) *A theory of justice* Oxford University Press, Oxford

Rostow, W W (1960) *The stages of economic growth* Cambridge University Press, Cambridge

Sandford, C (1993) 'How Lamont can square the circle' *Financial Times*, 11 March 1993

Schumacher, F (1979) *Small is beautiful* Blond and Briggs, London

Seers, D (1977) 'The new meaning of development' *International Development Review* (now *Development*) no 3, pp 2–7

Seers, D (1979) 'The birth, life and death of development economics' *Development and Change*, vol 10, pp 707–19

Sen, A (1990) 'Development as capability expansion' in K Griffin and J Knight (eds) *Human Development and the International Development Strategy for the 1990s*, Macmillan, Basingstoke, pp 41–58

Skitovsky, T (1992) *The joyless economy: the psychology of human satisfaction* Oxford University Press, New York and Oxford

Sklair, L (1988) 'Transcending the impasse: metatheory, theory and empirical research in the sociology of development and underdevelopment' *World Development* vol 16, no. 6, pp 697–709

Slater, D (1987) 'On development theory and the Warren thesis: arguments against the predominance of economism' *Environment and Planning D: Society and Space*, vol 5, pp 263–82

Stern, N (1989) 'The economics of development' *Economic Journal*, September

Stewart, F (1978) *Technology and development* Macmillan, London

Stewart, F (1985) *Planning to Meet Basic Needs* Macmillan, London

Streeten, P (1979) 'A basic needs approach to economic development' in K P Jameson and C K Wilbur (eds) *Directions in Economic Development*, University of Notre Dame Press, Notre Dame

Streeten, P et al (1981) *First Things First: meeting basic needs in developing countries* Oxford University Press, New York

Summers, R and Heston, A (1993) *The Penn World Table, version 5.5* National Bureau of Economic Research, Cambridge MA

Sutcliffe, B (1993a) *The burden of Third World debt* Kingston University Apex Centre, Kingston upon Thames

Sutcliffe, B (1993b) 'Desarrollo humano: una crítica del concepto y del índice' *Cuadernos de trabajo*, Hegoa, Bilbao

Thompson, E P (1969) *The making of the English working class* Penguin Books, Harmondsworth

Tomshoe, R (1992) 'Dirty work: environmental posse fights a lonely war along the Rio Grande' *Wall Street Journal*, 10 November 1992

Trainer, T (1985) *Abandon affluence* Zed, London

Trainer, T (1989) *Developed to death: rethinking Third World development* Green Print, London

Tucker, V (1992) 'The myth of development' *Occasional Paper Series* no 6, Department of Sociology, University College, Cork

United Nations Development Programme (1990-93) *Human development report* Oxford University Press, Oxford, annual

United Nations (1993) *Trends in International Distribution of Gross World Product* (Department for Economic and Social Informations and Policy Analysis, Statistical Division), United Nations, New York National Accounts Statistics, series X, no 18, special issue.

Wallerstein, I (1979) *The Capitalist World Economy* Cambridge University Press, Cambridge

Warren, B (1980) *Imperialism, pioneer of capitalism* Verso, London

World Bank (1991) *World Development Report* Oxford University Press, Oxford and New York

World Bank (1992) *World Development Report: Development and the environment* Oxford University Press, Oxford and New York

World Bank (1993) *Poverty and Income Distribution in Latin America: the story of the 1980s* World Bank Human Resources Division, Washington DC

World Commission on Environment and Development (1987) *Our Common Future* Oxford University Press, Oxford

World Resources Institute (1992) *World Resources 1992-93* Oxford University Press, New York and Oxford

Index

Printed in the United States
by Baker & Taylor Publisher Services